Easy Money

Markets and Governments in Economic History
A series edited by Price Fishback

Also in the series:

Easy Money

American Puritans and
the Invention of Modern Currency

DROR GOLDBERG

THE UNIVERSITY OF CHICAGO PRESS   CHICAGO AND LONDON

The University of Chicago Press, Chicago 60637
The University of Chicago Press, Ltd., London
© 2023 by The University of Chicago
Published 2023
Printed in the United States of America

32 31 30 29 28 27 26 25 24 23   1 2 3 4 5

ISBN-13: 978-0-226-82510-6 (cloth)
ISBN-13: 978-0-226-82511-3 (e-book)
DOI: https://doi.org/10.7208/chicago/9780226825113.001.0001

Library of Congress Cataloging-in-Publication Data

Names: Goldberg, Dror, author.
Title: Easy money : American Puritans and the invention of modern currency / Dror Goldberg.
Other titles: Markets and governments in economic history.
Description: Chicago : The University of Chicago Press, 2023. | Series: Markets and governments in economic history | Includes bibliographical references and index.
Identifiers: LCCN 2022026637 | ISBN 9780226825106 (cloth) | ISBN 9780226825113 (ebook)
Subjects: LCSH: Money—United States—History—17th century. | Legal tender—United States—History—17th century. | Monetary policy—Massachusetts—History—17th century. | Monetary policy—England—History—16th century.
Classification: LCC HG508 .G65 2023 | DDC 332.4/97309032—dc23/eng/20220623
LC record available at https://lccn.loc.gov/2022026637

♾ This paper meets the requirements of ANSI/NISO Z39.48-1992 (Permanence of Paper).

TO MY PARENTS, YAIR AND SHIRA

For we must consider that we shall be a city upon a hill. The eyes of all people are upon us.
   —John Winthrop, governor of the Massachusetts Bay Company, 1630

In this extremity they presently found out an expedient, which may serve as an example, for any people in other parts of the world, whose distresses may call for a sudden supply of money to carry them through any important expedition.
   —Cotton Mather, pastor in Boston, 1697

Contents

Preface

This book is part of an inquiry into the nature and origin of the currency of nations. Currency is the thing with which we casually buy everything, be it a good like a pizza or a service like a taxi ride. By "modern currency," I refer to the currency of the early twenty-first century: a government-issued object that has no intrinsic value (token coin, bill, or the upcoming central bank digital currency), that is not a legal claim to any intrinsically valuable commodity such as gold, and whose only legal support is being legal tender for debts and taxes in a state or a federation.

My original interest in this topic was provoked long ago, when the last thing on my mind was writing a book about colonial America. I learned in high school about Germany's hyperinflation and its presumed causal relation to World War II. I learned this in Israel, where the story was of special significance—and I learned this at a time when Israel was experiencing its own triple-digit inflation. The puzzle that intrigued me later was very basic: Why do people keep accepting the government's money when it loses value so quickly? Actually, why do they accept it *at all*, even with low inflation, when it is no longer related to gold? Approaching a businessman who had produced and sold bicycles in Israel during that high inflation, I asked: "Dad, why did you agree to accept Israeli money at all back then?" He replied that there were things he could not do in Israel with other currencies such as the ever-popular United States dollar, the chief of which was paying taxes.

The only effective anchor of the beaten shekel was its status as the only legal tender for taxes in Israel. That was enough to maintain demand for a bad asset and thus enable the government to practice inflationary money printing. What a brilliant and dangerous device! This idea already appeared, briefly, in economics' most famous book—Adam Smith's *Wealth of Nations*—but surprisingly few academic economists picked it up. Only recently the presumptuously named "modern monetary theory" publicized this mechanism, lauding its supposed ability to create heaven on Earth and downplaying its hellish potential.

After an inquiry into the *nature* of this modern currency in graduate school—with the mathematical tools economists use[1]—I turned to the *origin* of this modern currency. Finding it easily in colonial America, I published the punchline about the pathbreaking money of 1690 Massachusetts in the *Journal of Economic History* in 2009.[2] But this was just the tip of the iceberg. I spent another decade plumbing the depths of that iceberg, and the results are presented here.

Most of the work involved a thorough study of a century of American history, complementing my formal education in economics and law. This book was written with the intention that economists, historians, and legal scholars alike would be able to read it. Since these fields barely have a common denominator, the result is a book that anyone can read. No prior knowledge of any sort is necessary; I promise no equations, no statistical analyses, almost no awkward spelling of the period (it's all modernized, with an exception), and no unexplained legal terms. It is still hard-core academic research, as proven by more than a thousand notes (which contain only references).

Many people helped me on the long road I traveled. Per Krusell at the University of Rochester focused my attention on that fundamental puzzle of modern money. As my dissertation advisor, Per guided my mathematical exploration into the theory of the role of taxes, and tolerated my first errand into monetary history.[3] My transition from theory to history occurred at Texas A&M University under the careful, indispensable guidance of the economic historian John R. Hanson II, and with nontrivial encouragement from the historians Katherine Carté, Jonathan Coopersmith, and James Rosenheim. Later, the continued guidance and support of Richard Johnson, Karen Kupperman, John McCusker, Jacob Metzer, Joel Mokyr, and Richard Sylla was especially helpful. The idea for a big-picture book came from Price Fishback, editor of the series Markets and Governments in Economic History at the University of Chicago Press. The press's editors, from David Pervin to Chad Zimmerman, provided useful guidance along the way.

Many more acknowledgments are due: for a sabbatical—the Department of Economics at the Stern School of Business at New York Univer-

sity and Richard Sylla; for funding—the Melbern G. Glasscock Center
for Humanities Research at Texas A&M University, Adar Foundation
at Bar-Ilan University, the American Philosophical Society, the Open
University of Israel Research Fund, and Israeli taxpayers through the Israel Science Foundation (grant no. 252/15); libraries—Internet Archive,
HathiTrust Digital Library, Tel Aviv University, University of Texas at
Austin, and New York University; archives—Massachusetts Archives,
Massachusetts Historical Society, and United Kingdom National Archives; generations of archivists who transcribed and published enor-
mous amounts of records; generations of scholars on whose shoulders I
stand (even if I criticize some of their conclusions); participants at semi-
nars and conferences—especially meetings of the Social Science History
Association, the American Society for Legal History, and the Money,
Credit and Banking Forum of the Economic History Association of Israel; reading and commenting on selected parts of early drafts—Yoed
Anise, Roi Dor, Ron Harris, Yishay Maoz, Joel Mokyr, William Monter,
Richard Sylla, and my brothers; reading and commenting on the entire
first draft—two anonymous reviewers and Itay Cishnevsky; special lo-
gistical assistance—the Anis/Anise family, Karl Ekroth, and Sara Re-
uter; valuable conversations and useful nudging—Leonid Azarnert, Itay
Cishnevsky, Yishay Maoz, and my family; some artwork—Ronen Goldberg; future readers who will send me comments at dg@drorgoldberg
.com. Last but most—thanks to Inbal, Gilly, and Mika, for their infinite
patience.

Israel, January 2022

PART I

Introductions

CHAPTER ONE

Introduction to the Book

Monetary innovation, the development of new forms of money, has not received much systematic study from economic historians.
—Richard Sylla, "Monetary Innovation in America"

Centuries of Transformation

"There is no part of earth here to be taken up, wherein there is not some probable show of gold and silver."[1] Thus wrote an Englishman on his 1579 visit to the *West* Coast of North America. He was aboard the *Golden Hind*, the ship on which Francis Drake was sailing around the world, after plundering gold and silver in Spanish Peru. Of these dominant monetary metals, the optimism on gold would prove correct later: the place described was just north of present-day San Francisco Bay. Drake claimed the land (which he named Nova Albion) for Queen Elizabeth. He declared so in an engraved plate nailed to a post. He added to it a picture of the queen, improvised by a silver sixpence coin "of current English money" that carried her portrait. Four centuries later, in the 1970s, one such coin—perhaps that coin—was found thirty miles inland.[2]

During these four centuries, both money and English colonialism have undergone massive transformations. Two centuries after Drake, everything was upside down. English colonialism had taken hold not on the West Coast, but, reasonably enough, on the East Coast. One of its centers was New England, named after Nova Albion. Instead of claiming the land for the English Crown, the 1770s colonists disowned that Crown. The relation between coin and paper also flipped. While Drake used a coin as a substitute for a paper portrait, the colonists used paper as a substitute for coin: paper money financed their revolution against the Crown. The world took notice of this trick. The noise of the rebels' printing press was the stamp heard round the world.

Jump two more centuries ahead, to the 1970s. Although much gold had been shipped from San Francisco Bay, the United States suspended the paper's meager formal relation to gold and was back on pure paper money. Again, it led the world—this time, forcing much of the human race off gold. As in the 1570s, there was a Queen Elizabeth in England, but now both her power and the coins bearing her portrait were mere tokens.

A New Money

This book focuses on the first of these four centuries of transformation. The main part of the book begins with the very first English efforts at colonizing America, and it ends in 1692, when one colony perfected the type of currency that we all use today. The climax of the story, however, is not 1692, but December 24, 1690.

As most of the English nation gathered to celebrate Christmas Eve, the English subjects in Massachusetts were in no festive mood. For one thing, Puritans did not celebrate what they considered a pre-Christian holiday. More important, Massachusetts was broken—militarily, spiritually, morally, and financially. A large expedition sent to occupy French Quebec returned defeated. Previously confident of a divine victory against Catholics, the Puritan government declared in unprecedented despair: "Our Father spit in our face."[3] The defeat implied there was no plunder—which was supposed to pay for the expedition. In an extremely cold winter, the smallpox-infested, mutinous soldiers and sailors demanded pay. A caretaker revolutionary government had nothing to offer them. It was the day before Christmas, and in order to pacify the troops, the chief Puritan colony gave birth to its own influential baby: modern currency.

By "modern currency," I do not refer to paper currency per se, but to legal tender currency. China had paper money a thousand years ago, first backed by precious metal but later forced on sellers under penalty of death. By the time the Middle Ages ended in Europe, China had had enough of paper and its inflation, and it returned to silver. In Europe and America there had been isolated, temporary episodes of wartime pa-

per money, which was similarly forced on everyone under penalty, and/
or it was accompanied by a credible promise to convert the paper into
precious-metal coins.

In contrast, the money that was created in Massachusetts in 1690 was
not forced on anyone other than tax collectors; it was legal tender for
taxes. And yes, it was made of paper. This money was accompanied by
no credible promise of conversion into precious metal. Soldiers were
paid with this money. They were supposed to go shopping with it, and
sellers were supposed to accept it voluntarily because they could later
pay their taxes with it to the same government that issued the money. In
1692, this money was also forced on private creditors (legal tender for
debts), but not on sellers in spot transactions. Our modern legal tender
currency is of the same type. As central banks openly admit, the only legal support for their currencies concerns the discharge of preexisting obligations denominated in these currencies.[4]

The 1690 money was an invention on a global scale and a great intellectual breakthrough. It was a fundamental change in the legal foundation of money, shifting the anchor of money for the first time in history
from the intrinsically valuable goods it was made of to the circulation of
money into and out of the state's treasury. Indeed, who needs gold when
you have taxes? One Boston native, soon born into this innovative economy, famously said: "Nothing can be said to be certain, except death and
taxes." That man, Benjamin Franklin, became a lifelong promoter and
even printer of paper money.

By completely releasing the quantity of money from the supply of
metal, governments that imitated Massachusetts obtained unprecedented political and economic power. Pastor Cotton Mather, the mad genius of Boston, predicted just that in 1697 (see the epigraph to this book).
Legal tender paper money, and paper moneys inspired by it, played a key
role—for better and for worse—in some of the most important events of
modern history: the American Revolution, the French Revolution, the
German hyperinflation, the Great Depression, and the 2008 Global Financial Crisis.

Since 1971, when the United States indefinitely suspended its promise
to convert paper dollars into gold, we all use Massachusetts currency: an
object with small (or zero) intrinsic value (base metal, paper, and soon
central bank digital currency) that is produced by a central bank (or another government bureaucracy) and that nobody is obliged to convert
into gold or silver or any other commodity. Although the use of paper

and coins in purchases is declining, it is still the foundation of the entire financial system. That system consists mostly of legal promises to pay these notes and coins: bank accounts, credit cards, bonds, mortgages, student loans, insurance policies, and so on. In spite of the vocal opposition coming from gold and crypto "currencies" since 2008, legal tender money shows no signs of going away—whatever physical form it takes.

The Puzzle

In 1690, English North America was not an important place. Only 5 percent of the five-million-strong English nation lived there, including fifty thousand people in Massachusetts. They thought of themselves as ordinary English subjects who happened to live "in the ends of the Earth."[5] It is puzzling that such a momentous invention was made in a periphery of Europe, where no native colonist ever published anything about money or economics. Why didn't it happen in London, which had just started its Financial Revolution? Why not in Amsterdam, the financial capital of Western Europe? If there was something about the colonial scene to spur innovation, why didn't it happen in the older, more populous colony of Virginia, the formerly Dutch colony of New York, or the more profitable Caribbean sugar colonies?

To solve the puzzle, we must recognize the historical context. The 1690 invention did not come out of the blue. It was the climax of six decades of extraordinary monetary creativity in Massachusetts, where seashell beads, grain, cattle, beaver fur, bullets, uncoined precious metal, precious-metal coins, personal bills, and banknotes were either used or planned to be used as money. The list is remarkable not only for its variety, but also in that it largely mimics the evolution of money in the world as a whole. Why did Massachusetts do that?

As will be detailed and explained below, all colonies had a chronic coin shortage, and the typical solution was to use alternative moneys as the natural environment afforded: key agricultural products (grain, tobacco, sugar), or furs obtained in trade with Indians. Why did Massachusetts alone outdo the others and rush through the evolutionary ladder of money? The economic historian Richard Sylla singled out Massachusetts as possibly having the most severe shortage of coin because of its unique circumstances. It therefore had greater incentives than others to devise alternative solutions[6]—in other words, necessity is the mother of invention. The economic historian Nathan Rosenberg has phrased such circumstances as a focusing device.[7] The severity of the problem, compared with the reasonable state of coinage they had known in England, directed Massachusetts colonists to focus their intellectual efforts at solving that particular problem rather than other problems. However, an incentive to invent does not always lead to successful invention. The economic historian Joel Mokyr has argued that *ability* to invent is more important.[8]

In this study, I show that the mercantile and intellectual elite of Massachusetts was indeed unique in this latter aspect among colonial elites. I trace both the money shortage and the ability to solve it in Massachusetts to various effects of regulation by the English state—at home and abroad. Indirectly, the most important underlying influence was the religious–constitutional conflict in seventeenth-century England, which brought down two kings. The largely redundant evolution of money in Massachusetts was propelled at every step by ramifications of that ongoing conflict and its different phases.

Scope of the Investigation

The historical context, which is essential to understanding the 1690 Massachusetts money, needs to be specified. It goes far beyond the borders of Massachusetts, the early 1690s, and the problem of money. This book takes as broad a look as possible and as necessary with regard to area, period, and topics. It should be kept in mind that this book is not an attempt at a complete history of money in early Massachusetts; the goal here is to explain the invention of one type of money.

Area

Most colonial historians agree that investigating the history of any colony in isolation is misleading. This "Atlantic history" approach claims that the movement of people, goods, ideas, and information intimately tied together all the communities of all races on the four continents around the Atlantic Ocean. To those who are not historians, this approach is not a trivial one. We need to discard our modern notion of

FIGURE I.I. North American colonies in the seventeenth century.

water as an obstacle to transportation. Before the invention of the train,
the automobile, and the airplane, water was *the* highway. Maritime transportation was by far faster, cheaper, and safer than land transportation[9]
(it is still the cheapest). Water was an impediment only to military invasion, because landing under fire was difficult—which made water twice
as valuable as a border. This is why North American colonies formed a
narrow strip along the East Coast (with exceptions such as Albany and
Quebec, which appear along major rivers; see figure I.I), while other colonies were founded on islands. Western civilization had experienced a
similar phenomenon to the Atlantic integration when the Roman Empire focused on the perimeter of the Mediterranean Sea.

The context of Massachusetts, therefore, includes, in principle, all the
societies around the Atlantic. The working hypothesis, based on exist-

ing research, is that the most relevant context for Massachusetts can be narrowed down: it comprised Mother England, all other sister English colonies, nearby colonies of other nations, and neighboring Native nations. The English colonies included Caribbean colonies, which were intimately involved with New England. Putting these islands aside because they are not part of the later United States would be anachronistic.

A more refined working hypothesis, also based on existing research, is that Massachusetts took at first the precedent of money improvisation from earlier colonies, but then it ran ahead, looking closely mostly at developments in Mother England and elder sister Plymouth, but far less at other colonies. Therefore, regarding the period before Massachusetts became a uniquely quasi-independent colony (i.e., pre-1630), I provide a detailed analysis of all relevant colonies. From 1630 onward, the analysis is much more selective: the focus is on Massachusetts, while mention is made of inventions in other colonies that could have been inspiring for Massachusetts, such as the convertible paper moneys of English Antigua (1654) and French Canada (1685).

As pointed out by historians of colonial America, the natural colony for comparison with early Massachusetts is Virginia—the oldest and most populous English colony. In terms of society, economy, and also forms of money, Virginia led and represented the South, just as Massachusetts led and represented the North.[10] I examine Virginia from its founding until the 1650s, but after that it has little to contribute to the story.

Period

The study begins with the first English expedition that prepared colonization—1584 Roanoke. Already, in that short experiment, English eyes were opened to the possibility of conducting trade with objects other than coin. The following attempts at colonization show that Puritans did not have a monopoly on monetary innovation—almost everyone tried to adapt to the new circumstances, first regarding trade with Indians and later regarding trade within the colonies. By 1630, there was enough accumulated experience that the leaders of infant Massachusetts knew that coin shortages and money improvisations were inevitable features of colonial life. Massachusetts copied some precedents and charged ahead. The main story ends in 1692, when the money of 1690 was upgraded to full legal tender status (for taxes *and debts*) and was thus perfected as the type of currency we use today.

Topics

In terms of topics, this book is wider in scope than a typical monetary history might be, mostly because the 1690 invention involved unusual circumstances and had unusual features. The additional topics are war finance, credit, constitution, and society.

WAR FINANCE. In 1712, the Massachusetts councillor Samuel Sewall educated younger legislators: "I was at [the] making of the first bills of credit in 1690: They were not made for want of money [i.e., coin]; but for want of money in the Treasury."[11] Indeed, it was the desperate problem of paying for war that created by accident a landmark in the history of money. Therefore, public finance at war is another major issue that this book is concerned with.

CREDIT. Another valuable point in Sewall's statement is the money's name: bills of *credit*. The 1690 invention was, in a sense, the coining of credit. A big pile of debt that the colony owed the soldiers was cut into small, conveniently denominated, standardized, easily transferable, stamped pieces; when the Spanish did something *identical* to the big pile of silver they found in America, the outcome was known as coins of silver. The latter sentence, worth rereading, summarizes the profound brilliance of the Massachusetts invention.

Sure, bills of credit are not the same as coins of silver. A seller agreed to accept a coin of silver because she knew that somewhere out there, there were enough people who would want to use silver as a commodity; and yes, the treasury would also accept it in tax payments. A bill of credit had only the latter feature, but it was good enough to get the bill circulating as money. Legally, this tax acceptance was a *setoff*. A seller who accepted a bill of credit from a shopping soldier held a debt that the colony owed her. The law making this bill a legal tender for taxes meant that the seller's household could set it off against the debt the household owed the colony as a taxpayer, making coin utterly redundant in the interaction between the household and the treasury. That understanding was the lynchpin of the whole 1690 operation.

It is therefore necessary to examine the development of public and private credit in that century, as well as the various methods, such as setoff, that settled credit while minimizing or even eliminating the use of coin.

CONSTITUTION. Further away from a pure economic investigation is the colonial constitution. The extent to which the colonial legislature was accountable to the local population on the one hand and to England on the other hand had a significant effect on its willingness and ability to solve its money and war-finance problems. Pleasing one side often came at the expense of irritating the other. The 1690 money was a bold compromise between these pressures.

Another aspect of the constitution has been ignored by all historians of Massachusetts and historians of money: the 1690 money was issued not by the treasury but by a committee. The committee featured representation of the executive, the legislature, and the private sector. The goal was surely to create checks and balances in the all-important control of the money supply. The committee did not just hand the new money to the colony's creditors. It used the new money to purchase the debt instruments held by the creditors.

These two features of the committee—political checks and balances and the purchase of government debt—are familiar to modern economists as key features of the Federal Open Market Committee and its many imitators around the world. This committee, which conducts monetary policy in the United States, is among the most influential committees in the world. The modern committee itself and its traditional mode of operation date to the 1920s, starting with purchases of government war bonds. It is astonishing that in the same law that created legal tender money, 1690 Massachusetts also invented just such a committee. The explanation lies in tracking the development of committees—outside the monetary context—as a major tool of governance in Massachusetts.

SOCIETY. Finally, I describe the society itself. Books on the history of money usually do not consider the society enough, but serious monetary *theory* says that it is a must. The extent to which a society needs a currency depends critically on how the society is composed. Many colonists could actually get along without money most of the time, for varying reasons: the mythical close-knit, religiously united, small New England town could rely on neighborly credit with occasional setoffs, while most workers in tobacco and sugar colonies—servants and slaves—received no wages.

Sources

Any research on the money of an American colony starts with the best surviving records, which are the government records. As this period predates separation of powers, the same organs of government not only passed laws but also ordered executive actions and ruled in specific judicial cases. This has the incidental effect of enriching the official records, because executive and judicial actions documented actual monetary practices beyond the letter of the law. Private transactions were far less documented, and most of that documentation does not survive.

Such public bias of the records hampers a perfect investigation of money as it functioned in the everyday lives of ordinary people. But it is not a problem for this book, because this book is *not* a complete history of money in a colony. The goal here is to understand the evolution of the way in which a *government* devised alternative moneys. This culminated in a money that was based on taxes rather than commodities, and therefore—by definition—involved the government. This money could never have arisen spontaneously in the marketplace like the commodity moneys, such as grain, that had previously ruled the colonial scene.

Organization of the Book

"Part I: Introductions" continues with chapter 2, which is a math-free theoretical framework of money. It helps understanding the claims made throughout the book about the functioning of various types of money, as well as the pressures and abilities that led to inventions of new forms of money. Chapter 3 provides a basic snapshot of English society and its money and credit in the late sixteenth century. Many of these features would remain, immigrate to America, and survive there too. Chapter 4 proceeds from then until 1692. This is needed for three reasons: First, constitutional changes in England in that tumultuous century were the most important force in the evolution of Massachusetts money. Second, many ideas and practices about money, credit and banking used in America came from new advancements in England. Third, the spirit of that revolutionary century in English constitution and science may have influenced the revolutionary moment of 1690 Massachusetts.

"Part II: The Atlantic" is the main part of the book. It proceeds mostly according to chronological order, in line with the dominant force in the story—constitutional changes in England. Approximately each constitutional episode gets a chapter. It should be emphasized that my interest here is not in kings, wars, and grand events per se. In common with most historical studies today, this book is about the daily lives of the majority of people—ordinary people. The focus is on their difficulties in conducting everyday transactions: How to buy bread in the local store? How to pay a hired laborer? How to discharge a debt? How to pay a tax? The motivation here, however, is not that of the typical historical study (Marxist or otherwise), but that of mainstream economics: inflation, the recurrent scourge of a monetized economy, has always resulted from increase in the quantity of *everyday* money. It so happens—and this is the main finding in this book—that the development of the money used in such humble transactions in Massachusetts was influenced most by the constitutional–religious turmoil in England.

My focus on everyday currency is at the expense of the grand financial instruments typical of economic studies of early modern Europe— merchants' bills of exchange, government bonds, and "banknotes" of extremely high denominations. These financial assets are "money" for the financier but not for the economist. Such assets are discussed here only to the extent that they help me tell the story of currency. Bernard Bailyn's classic *The New England Merchants in the Seventeenth Century* is the American version of that European literature. He focused on the big business of merchants and their bills of exchange, touching everyday currency peripherally and only when necessary for his purposes. In most of this book I do the opposite. The two books do have a similar structure of chapters according to the constitutional–religious turmoil in England, because that turmoil affected colonial life in many ways.[12]

Most chapters include sections according to colonies whose deeds in the field of money in that subperiod are worth mentioning. My emphasis is more and more on Massachusetts as the book progresses toward 1690. Chapter 5 surveys money in colonies before the Massachusetts Bay Company relocated to America. After locally flirting with copper, Indian seashell money, and local coins, the colonial monetary standard became the main object that the colonists either raised or obtained in trade with Indians.

Chapter 6 takes us through the period when Charles I ruled without Parliament (1629–1640). This resulted in the Great Puritan Migration that founded the Massachusetts Bay Colony. The chapter is devoted to fundamental demographic, constitutional, and cultural features of this colony that were installed in that decade and stuck. These features would explain the monetary inventions that were remarkable already in that decade and even more so later, all the way to 1690.

Chapter 7 covers the same period but discusses the monetary inventions in Massachusetts and Virginia. Massachusetts adopted what it learned from Plymouth about money and tried to add Indian seashell money, uncoined metallic objects (bullets and precious-metal plate), cattle, land, and private notes to the monetary list. Virginia audaciously tried and failed to establish tobacco-based clearinghouses to reduce the physical use of that clumsy money.

Chapter 8 considers the time of constitutional chaos in England (1640–1660). The initial impact ruined the Massachusetts economy, but the colony was reborn as the hub of Anglo–American trade. Left neglected by the fighting and turmoil, Massachusetts used the opportunity to open a mint, while Virginia and Maryland tried (and failed) to make their own coins. Various types of paper money were born in Dutch Brazil and English Antigua.

Chapter 9 mostly parallels the reign of Charles II (1660–1686). Massachusetts lost its mint that violated the Crown's minting monopoly, and it also lost its constitutional autonomy. Banks of various types were attempted or discussed all across the Atlantic, but by the end of the period, none of them was in operation.

Chapter 10 demonstrates the overwhelming power of government over paper money during the few years before the Glorious Revolution (1685–1689). The dictatorial Dominion of New England, which replaced the independent Massachusetts government, sabotaged a major project of a note-issuing bank. Other schemes failed in West New Jersey and Pennsylvania because of strong unsupportive governors. It was the Canadian government only that succeeded in issuing paper money intermittently since 1685. Two of these experiments would provide partial inspiration for 1690 Massachusetts, although they differed on crucial aspects.

Chapter 11 takes a break from the chronology for a biography of Elisha Hutchinson—the chief promoter, perhaps even the inventor, of the 1690 money. This chapter is not a "great man" theory that argues Hutchinson was the indispensable hero of the story; there is not enough information on his contribution to even consider such a claim. In fact, the goal of this chapter, which follows his life until 1689, is quite the opposite: it is to illustrate the background that typical Massachusetts legis-

lators had. Hutchinson was unexceptional in having an amazing variety
of occupations and offices in an age that knew no separation of powers
and freely mixed politics with private business. His diverse background
and knowledge would have enabled him—or the legislator sitting next
to him—to understand things about money that few could understand
before.

Chapter 12 takes the story back to the chronological line, from Boston's Glorious Revolution of April 1689 to the eve of the invention of
legal tender money in December 1690. The chapter covers the immediate historical background for the invention—the restoration of representative government, charter negotiations with England, a new war,
and war finance. Chapter 12 closes part II. At this point, we will have
all the background necessary for understanding the invention of December 1690.

"Part III: A Monetary Revolution" starts with that invention. Chapter 13 describes in detail all of the money's unconventional features, and
concludes that the most peculiar constitutional and political circumstances led to it. Chapter 14 follows the money until the final upgrade
of its legal status in 1692. Along the way we gain further evidence of the
theory behind the novel currency, plus the constitutional and political
circumstances that created it. Chapter 15 briefly goes back to 1690s England to examine how its more famous Financial Revolution compared
with that of Massachusetts.

Chapter 16 provides an analysis of the entire story: the roles of supply
and demand in innovation, comparisons of Massachusetts with Virginia
and England, the critical role of regulation, the contribution of nonspecialization to innovation, other characteristics that help innovation in social institutions, and lessons from biological evolution and ecology.

Chapter 17 concludes the book. After summarizing the main points,
the story is related to general theories about colonial America, and tells
how the money clandestinely invented in a small colony gradually took
over the world. From the lessons of the past emerge dire warnings regarding two flawed phenomena that gained popular excitement during the writing of this book: purely private crypto "currencies" (which
ignore the importance of legal tender laws) and the so-called modern
monetary theory (which relies on legal tender laws way too much). Finally, with the help of witch trials and the Enlightenment, the role of legal tender money in modernity in general is examined.

CHAPTER TWO

Money and Its Inventions

Theoretical Considerations

"Money is an excellent means. One would have to invent it, if it were not already there."
—Theodor Herzl, *Old New Land*, 1902

The chapter begins with the reasons we need money. Then it discusses how the need for money can be fulfilled and how the law can help a certain money circulate. When the need is not fulfilled, argues the next part, there is need to invent a new type of money. Some people may be better than others in their ability to invent money and implement it. In economics terminology, this chapter is first about the demand for money and its supply; then, following Joel Mokyr's terminology, I turn to the demand for monetary inventions and the supply of monetary inventions.[1] The discussion is biased at times to the simpler circumstances of the seventeenth century.

Demand for Money

Money has three physical roles: a medium of exchange, a medium of unilateral payment, and a store of value. It also has a linguistic role, as a unit of account. The medium-of-exchange role is the one that makes money so important in the economy. Changes in the amount of money can cause changes in inflation, unemployment, and output. Much of this occurs through money's function as a medium of exchange.

Such a textbook introduction to money is insufficient here. To understand a new money that was invented on the backdrop of a money short-age, we need to recognize the circumstances that make money necessary to begin with. It is time to dive into the *societal foundations* of monetary economics. This is an odd niche of monetary economics, where the usual terms such as *central bank*, *interest rate*, and *inflation rate* are mostly absent.

Medium of Exchange

Money is, first and foremost, an object with which to buy goods and services. Why do we buy? Because we want to obtain goods and services produced by others. Each one of us could try to produce all the goods and services alone, but that level of autarky is inefficient. We produce best when we specialize in producing one good or service. But we are not satisfied with consuming only the one good or service we produce. We have a preference for variety, which depends on both personality and environment—for example, a family needs a larger variety of goods than a single person; while certain clothes are required by cold climate and social conventions.

Wanting to obtain goods from others does not necessarily mean that anything is given in return, as a direct quid pro quo. Actually, in most of a person's interaction with other humans, nothing is given in direct return. Such is the case within the household (typically a nuclear family), with other close relatives, and with friends, reaching an extreme form in a commune. Sharing of some resources is practiced also by members of an organization, such as a commercial company or a military unit. All get paid by the organization, and none owns the goods they provide or receive within the organization. In all the above cases, and in charity, there is no need to give anything in return. But even when something has to be given in return, it doesn't have to be money—or, at least, not imme-diately. Among some acquaintances, a gift typically implies the need for a countergift later on. Among other acquaintances, and surely among strangers, the most intuitive way to give something in return is barter.

Everything surveyed so far lies outside the realm of the monetary economy. The problem with barter is that a "double coincidence of wants," as economists call it, is unlikely. I may want the good that you offer, but you don't want the good that I offer. The more types of goods there are in the economy, the less likely it is that barter will work. It is in these situations that a *medium*, or an intermediary object, can execute the exchange: you don't really want the good that I offer, but you accept it in exchange because you believe that you can barter it later with someone else for a good that you *do* want. This is a medium of exchange.

Money is a *general* medium of exchange. It is an object that everyone in a given society recognizes as "money" or currency. You accept it because you *know* that everyone else regularly accepts this object in payment for most goods. It is used in general, rather than as an occasional improvisation. When an object is generally used as a medium of exchange, by definition it circulates in the economy. Even if it is a consumable item, most of its recipients pass it on to others rather than consume it. In the United States, the hapless $2 bill has the same legal status as the $1 bill, and it was designed as money; however, for economists, it is not without difficulty to call the $2 bill money because, as the Federal Reserve Board admits, these bills "aren't typically used for everyday transactions, so they're not circulating or passing between people very often."[2]

There is an alternative to receiving something in return on the spot: credit. Formally, credit usually works by the possibility of legal enforcement—a court can examine oral or written evidence of the debt, and rule to enforce the debt payment. Credit might function, however, even without courts. In a small, stable, cohesive community, any debtor who considers defaulting on his obligation takes into account that all future potential creditors would hear about the default and not believe his future promises. In economics terms, such a *repeated game* encourages good behavior.[3] Debtors can easily get away with defaulting in a large port town with a large transient population. But potential creditors in such a town realize this, and therefore will not grant credit to visitors. By definition, credit always involves some uncertainty about the future payment, and it might involve considerable collection costs.[4]

Today we think of credit only as postponing the final payment in money. We settle our monthly credit card bill with a money transfer between bank accounts. But credit could also postpone the completion of a barter transaction, rendering money utterly redundant: you give me bread today for a promissory note, and next month I give you a chicken in return and redeem my note. People who habitually trade with each other can periodically set off their mutual debts and cancel them, thus saving on the use of money. This can be especially useful if, as pointed by the economic historian John Hanson, physical money is such that making change is difficult.[5]

To summarize, money is needed as a medium of exchange only if all of the above fail—giving something in return is required, barter is not feasible, and credit is either not feasible or only postpones the final money payment.

Once money exists, it encourages people to specialize in production even more. A farmer who used to produce all the foods he consumes, may choose to produce only milk, sell it for money, and use that money to buy everything else he wants. Others might forgo food production altogether and produce something nonedible, such as shoes. Money is therefore a prerequisite not only for specialization but also for urbanization and therefore advanced civilization.

Medium of Unilateral Payment

The second role of money is to pay taxes, fines, damages, and other sums required by law or by courts. While such payments give nothing positive in return, the benefit one gets from making them is the avoidance of something negative, such as a prison sentence. You pay taxes, even in democracies, to avoid being kidnapped by the government and having your property confiscated and sold. Avoiding penalty is equivalent to getting a good for your money—at least, mathematically (a double negative is a positive).

A tax payment can also be viewed as a not-so-voluntary exchange. The government creates an artificial good that the taxpayer desires: a receipt acknowledging payment of the tax. When a government tax collector meets a florist-taxpayer, there is no double coincidence of wants: the tax collector wants guns for the army and can provide a receipt, while the florist-taxpayer wants the receipt and can give flowers. Money solves the problem: the government accepts the florist-taxpayer's money and later pays it to gun sellers.

Other Roles

Money can also be a store of value, helping to preserve purchasing power over time. This role was important when there was no preservation technology to keep perishable goods fresh, and when people prepared to flee to preserve their lives and wanted to take property with them. Any durable commodity could serve the role of storing value, and not any object that serves this role is money.

The role of money as a unit of account has nothing to do with the physical existence of money, but is a device that helps us list or remember prices of many goods and services. Many times in history, units of account did not correspond to actual coins in circulation.

Supply of Money

Many objects could be money. Good money is durable, hard to counterfeit, and easy to recognize, divide, transport, and store. Money could be something that people find or grow, or something that government produces. The supply of money by a government often involves not merely the provision of an object, but also support for that object to help it circulate. Throughout history, this support was more needed when the object had less intrinsic value. Kings could proclaim "this is money" or stamp "money" on the object, in the hope that people would use the object as money, but public support for money usually meant *legal* support. Laws are not mere statements; they actively impose obligations on some entities (a person, a firm, a state) or assign rights to entities. These obligations and rights are enforced by courts of law. They have real power and practical significance, so long as the state functions.

Legal support of money can take various forms. First, in the case of paper money, the law or contracts can force a treasury, central bank, or private bank to give a precious-metal coin for every note they print—that is, convert the paper into metal. This requires that the promisor obtains and maintains either a large stock of metal or reputation that the promised metal is there or will be there. Second, the law can force the government to accept the money in its sales (if it sells anything). This is weaker than convertibility, because it is not a promise of a definite amount of goods.

Third, the money can be forced on private sellers under penalty. The government needs to supervise all transactions in the marketplace to enforce such a law, which can be difficult to do both bureaucratically and ideologically. Fourth, the money can be forced on creditors under sanction of losing their case in court. Today this is called "legal tender for debts." A debtor tendering the money is discharged from the debt, whether the creditor accepts it or not. This is much weaker than it seems, because it applies only to contracts made in the domestic currency. In the United States, such a law says that a $10 debt written in a contract can be discharged with a $10 bill, but the law is inapplicable if the contract specifies payment in goods, services, or euros.

Fifth, the executive can be forced by the legislature to accept the money in tax payments. Today this is called "legal tender for taxes." On the face of it, this seems like the weakest and least relevant legal solution for a government that wants to make its money circulate in private trade—this law doesn't even relate directly to trade in goods! However, if a seller knows she can use that money to pay taxes (that is, get exemption from punishment as a tax offender) this makes the money useful for her, and so she may accept it in trade from others. Moreover, if the government refuses to accept anything else in taxes except for its own money, then this object is the *only* legal tender for taxes; sellers may accept this money in shops if they want to stay out of prison. This idea—that taxes help money circulate—has several names, the most informative one being the "tax-foundation theory of money."[6]

Demand for Monetary Inventions

A supply of money might be inadequate, potentially prompting inventions to remedy the situation. One problem is the quality of money. When money consisted of an intrinsically useful commodity, such as a coin of precious metal, its content was attacked by nature, individuals, and governments: natural wear and tear shrunk the coins; people cut pieces to steal precious metal from the coins;[7] governments reduced the intrinsic value of their coins, often to produce more coins out of a given quantity of metal, in order to finance wars.[8] With less precious metal in each coin, sellers demanded more coins in order to receive the same amount of metal as before. By definition, this meant raising prices. If the process was repeated, the result was a continual price increase—inflation.

In this book, the most relevant problem is money supply that is too low. Economists usually think this is impossible because prices should be proportional to the amount of money. Suppose, for example, that economy L uses a single type of an indivisible coin. Economy H also uses that type of coin and is otherwise identical, but has ten times more coins than economy L does. According to the quantity theory of money (one of the strongest theories in economics, when applied carefully), prices in economy H should be ten times higher than in L. There should be no difference in real economic outcomes such as output and unemployment. The amount of money in L is, indeed, lower—but it is not *too low*. It is not a problem. A good that costs ten coins in H costs one coin in L. The lower quantity of money in L does as good a job as the higher quantity of money in H does in facilitating trade.

And yet, a constant complaint in the American colonies was that the amount of coins was too low. How could this be? Why didn't prices reflect this and drop enough to make the small amount of coins sufficient for trade? The quantity theory implicitly assumes that every person in either economy has *some* coins. The quantity theory also assumes, as common in economic theory, that everything else is equal—that is, for any specific person in H there is a corresponding person in L who has ten times less coin. The shape of the distributions of money in H and L is the same; only the scale is different. But what if the amount of coins in L is very low—smaller than the number of people there? The quantity theory has nothing to say in such a situation. If most people in L don't have coins, then coins in L might not even be considered money—a *general* medium of exchange. It's not that people are necessarily poor; they may be wealthy, but they have nothing to go shopping with. They have no liquidity. The problem of economy L and the quantity theory is not exactly the small number of coins, but that the coins are not infinitely divisible. As John Hanson put it, coin is not like fudge.[9] If it were, the distributions of money in economies H and L could have been identical in shape and the quantity theory would hold.

The discussion so far refers to an economy with a stable amount of money. Decline in the quantity of money can be very harmful. Older readers will recall fears of a global ATM shutdown due to the Y2K computer bug when the calendar hit the year 2000; there were cases of currency shortage in Europe during the later euro crisis. If the decline of money leads to decline in prices (the quantity theory), businesses that promised nominal wages to workers and nominal interest payments to banks don't have enough revenues to pay and they go bust (e.g., the Great Depression). A larger decline of money can lead to a reversal of the process of specialization described above and thus to a civilization's demise (e.g., Europe after Rome's collapse). Declining prices are possible even with a constant quantity of money—for example, if the economy grows or becomes more commercialized, with more transactions requiring money, the constant quantity may become insufficient. In such a case, the value of money increases, which by definition means that prices drop.[10]

Supply of Monetary Inventions

Early modern European states took legal steps to increase the quantity of coins. Export of coins or metals could be prohibited. A state could give its coins and foreign coins higher legal values than their intrinsic values. This encouraged people to keep the domestic coins in the state and import foreign coins.[11] More metal could be sought in mines or stolen from other states. In the two latter cases, a mint is useful for turning lumps of metal or foreign coin into local coins of the right denominations. A mint can also melt local coins and remint them in smaller denominations. Without a mint, people could create small change by cutting a coin into fractions, but less than an eighth is difficult to make accurately. A mint required technical abilities and material resources that were not present in every society, but it also required that there not be a superior government prohibiting minting.

As noted by Richard Sylla, such regulations that restricted an increase in the quantity of the existing type of money were a recurrent theme in monetary history. In the context of money, Hanson claimed, "opportunities for innovative economic policy could be found in the interstices of imperial regulations." In a first-ever attempt to systematize the understanding of monetary innovation in general, Sylla showed that such innovation around regulation happened repeatedly, and explained it as an entrepreneurial, profit-maximizing activity.[12]

Such a need for more money *could* lead to inventions, but it will not necessarily do so. Given the many problems that people face in life, and the limited resources of time and wealth they have, they cannot address all problems. Nathan Rosenberg has identified "focusing devices" that attract attention to particular problems in the context of technological innovation. These are usually abrupt disappearances of components of the production process—say, striking workers, or wartime shortage in raw materials.[13] Similarly, people who are born into a world of "bad" money are less likely to focus on solving that problem compared to people who recall having "good" money and have seen a drastic decline in its quantity or quality.

Moreover, not everyone has good ideas and the *ability* to create and implement a successful invention. As argued by Joel Mokyr, history is full of losers who had the incentive to invent but failed.[14] Firms failed to invent new products, and states failed to invent new weapons. Ability makes the difference between winners and losers.

Mokyr's studies of technological innovation distinguish between four categories of people: scientists, who understand how nature works; engineers, who implement that knowledge in a physical object; technicians, who produce and maintain that object; and the users. All of them are potential inventors or improvers. Interaction and communication between these different classes are critical for coming up with improvements.

Mokyr uses this framework to explain why it was in Europe, and specifically in Britain, that the Industrial Revolution happened.[15] I apply this methodology to understand why a *monetary* revolution happened in America, and specifically in Massachusetts. Who, then, are the analogous people in the context of money? The scientists today would be economists, but in the early modern period there was no discipline of economics, so most intellectuals qualified. Those able to formulate abstract models of causality in complicated systems could lead the way; thus natural scientists were well positioned to think about money. Scholars of history and readers of Greek philosophy could also learn about money in history and theory.

There are two types of engineers in the case of money: physical experts and legal experts. This is because money is typically a physical object with legal status that supports it. Designing the production of a durable object that is difficult to counterfeit and mutilate requires specialized skills (and expensive machinery). Legal scholars and experts in commercial and banking law can be especially helpful in drafting laws on money—recognizing privately created money or creating money from scratch. The technicians of money also belong to the physical and legal realms. Mint workers and printing press workers are necessary for the production of coins and printed bills. The legal technicians are judges and lawyers in legal cases where money laws are involved. Both groups might come up with ideas of improving the money.

Finally, there are the users. Everyone uses money, by definition. But some people use money more than others: people working in the financial and business sectors, treasury employees, and tax collectors. They are prime candidates to come up with improvements. People of any profession who live or work in travel hubs are more likely to be exposed to new ideas from other places.

We shall meet people from each of these four categories and see to what extent they communicated with each other.

*   *   *

As this societal analysis of the foundations of monetary economics shows, in order to understand the use of money and its inventions in seventeenth-century America, we need to understand the societies involved. My starting point is English society—in its European context—from which most emigrants came to the English colonies in America. This task is taken in the next chapter.

CHAPTER THREE

England in the Late Sixteenth Century

Now, behold, in my trouble I have prepared for the house of the Lord an hundred thousand talents of gold, and a thousand thousand talents of silver; and of brass and iron without weight.
  —1 Chronicles 22:14, King James Version

The early modern period was a remarkable era which began when an excited Columbus stepped on the sand of a Caribbean island and ended when an excited mob stepped on the guards of the Bastille. The name of the period reflects its position between old and new: medieval dictatorship, religion, and fanaticism started giving way to modern democracy, science, and tolerance. In money, metal started giving way to law-backed paper.

In this chapter, we will meet the English people in the late sixteenth century—their social structure, constitution, religion, science, and especially their money, credit, and public finance. As late as 1692, the American colonists considered themselves English people who happened to live away from England. They were hardly distinguishable from their cousins (literally) across the pond. Very little was genuinely original in the colonists' thoughts and ideas.[1] The invention of modern money in the period from 1690 to 1692 was merely a novel application and recombination of ideas that had already existed in England long beforehand. This chapter is very selective, covering only areas relevant for the later story.

Most facts in this chapter are available in easily accessible sources on the period.[2] References are given for other specific details as needed.

Society and Constitution

England of Elizabeth and Shakespeare had four million people. The economy was based on commercial agriculture. London, the only large city, had two hundred thousand residents. The royal family led the social structure, followed by noble families, knights, gentlemen, yeomen, and other commoners. Knighthood was granted for past or expected service to the state. The gentlemen were landowners (who hired farmers), merchants, and lawyers. They formed the ruling municipal elite. Everyone from the gentleman upward was supposed to be educated and religious, and lead his local community in peace and war. The yeoman was the lowest trustworthy class, serving on juries and in minor local offices and legally recognized as a "good man" (e.g., "Goodman Smith"). He got his hands dirty with his few workers on his small plot. He was a non-affluent family man, the backbone of society. Many poor youths worked and lived as servants and maids in other households.

England had already absorbed Wales and colonized Ireland. Scotland was ruled by Elizabeth's relative James VI. The submissive Parliament was composed of the House of Lords (nobles and senior clergy) and the House of Commons, which represented the few who had enough property for the legal right to vote. Any statute required the assent of both houses and the monarch; the Magna Carta implied that this included any new tax. Traditionally, the monarch had no income from taxes but lived off the Crown's land holdings. The monarch called and dissolved Parliament at his or her will, sometimes to get tax funds. The monarch presided over the Privy Council—a government cabinet that was mostly a subset of the House of Lords.

A key feature of the English constitution was the ad hoc committee—a group of men appointed for a specific mission and then dissolved. In Parliament, each house appointed an ad hoc committee to debate and refine each bill. These were advisory committees, because each house later voted on the amended bill. The Commons also had investigative committees on electoral disputes.[3] The grand jury and trial jury were, in fact, also ad hoc investigative committees. Rarely, committees had executive authority, as in the association of merchants that was incorporated as the East India Company in 1600.[4]

Religion and Science

In this Counter-Reformation period, the Pope and Catholic kings tried to re-Catholicize the Protestant regions. One battleground was France, where Protestants were called Huguenots. Another was the Low Countries (today's Netherlands and Belgium), where a new federation—the United Provinces—rebelled against Spanish rule while becoming a growing economic power based on maritime trade. England's Reformation started with Henry VIII's divorce. After much turbulence, his daughter Elizabeth defined a middle Anglican way, adopting Catholic appearances with Protestant doctrines. Some English people were unhappy with Catholic remnants that were unknown to Jesus: cathedrals, bishops, golden altars, and originally pagan holidays such as Yule (a.k.a. Christmas). Those who wanted to purify the church from these features were called Puritans. Others wanted to establish separate churches and thus were called Separatists. As separatism was illegal, some fled to the United Provinces.

Religion played a huge role in life because reality was terrifying and unexplained, with lightning, thunder, earthquakes, comets, epidemics, and average life expectancy of thirty-five years (mostly because of infant mortality). Astronomy was mixed with astrology, chemistry with alchemy. Tycho Brahe's recent observation of a change in space (a supernova) was important because it was a clear contradiction of the leading intellectual authority, Aristotle. In science, England was a backwater. Its only two universities (Oxford and Cambridge) taught mostly religion and the associated ancient languages and history. Medicine and law were learned as practical professions in London or in European universities.[5] The royal scientist John Dee spoke with angels. The religious confusion of the era increased the belief that the devil, or Satan, employed workers on Earth (a.k.a. witches). Elizabeth outlawed witchcraft; Scotland's James VI authored the witch-hunt guidebook *Demonology*. But the future was promising. It was in England that the exiled Giordano Bruno published his support of Copernicus and his theory of an infinite universe and multiple solar systems. In 1600, when the Roman Inquisition burned Bruno, the Englishman William Gilbert published a book on magnetism, arguing that Earth was basically a big ball of iron.

Money

At first glance, sixteenth-century England seems like a pure monetary economy. There were gold and silver coins, and nearly all prices, wages, rents, debts, and taxes were denominated in units of money. The word *money* was defined as coin. When payment in coin had to be distinguished from transfer of goods of the same value, it was phrased as "in money" or "ready money."[6] The unit of account was the pound (£) and its fractions—twenty shillings, each divided into twelve pence; the farthing (quarter penny) is also worth mentioning.[7] Physical coinage was not always related to these units of account—for example, there was not yet a coin called a "pound."

The value of the pound can be roughly described according to the lowest thresholds for annual incomes of different classes: £10 (laborer), £100 (gentleman), £1,000 (noble). An average family could barely live on £10 a year.[8] Much silver came from Spanish discoveries in the Americas—Mexico and "Peru" (today in Bolivia). Spain bought everything it needed with that silver, so silver was diffused throughout Europe. Englishmen had just become aware that this created inflation, and thus started thinking in terms of the quantity theory of money.[9]

Contracts referred to "the lawful/current money of England." England was unusual in Europe in that the royal prerogative included a coinage monopoly. Royal proclamations controlled the quantities, values, and standards of coins, while Parliament restricted their exports.[10] Counterfeiting coin was high treason punishable by death, but apparently there was no consistent policy regarding the acceptance of coin in spot transactions. Usually, the monarch proclaimed that specific coins should "pass" or were "current." Only during crises, when the public rejected coins or was expected to reject them, the monarch explicitly stated that refusal to receive coin in any transaction was illegal and could be penalized, sometimes with specific penalties cited.[11] Historians therefore usually interpreted the normal legal status "current" as equivalent to the modern concept of "legal tender."[12] That is, while the monarch would have liked to see his or her coins accepted in all exchanges, it was enforced only when debtors and creditors approached courts to set-tle disputes about which coins discharged debts.[13]

The idea that coins must normally be made from precious metal was fairly ingrained in the European mind, at least regarding pay to soldiers. The word *soldier* is related to the *solidus* gold coin paid to Roman sol-diers and the gold *sol*—the French equivalent of the shilling.[14] In *Utopia* (1516), Thomas More imagined a society needing no money for internal affairs, but receiving precious metals in foreign trade only to hire foreign mercenaries.[15]

All the above might create an impression of the mythical medieval village economy, of people carrying precious-metal coins in small bags at the weekly market, to be handed over on the spot for all their shop-ping. But it was no longer so. There were exceptions: medieval bar-ter leftovers, ideas of money made from cheaper materials, and most important—credit.

To begin with barter, grain was a customary medium of payment of rent by farmers to landlords. The rent was denominated in money units but paid in grain according to a predetermined price. For example, a twenty-shilling rent at the rate of five shillings per bushel implied a pay-ment of four bushels. A new law forced the universities to receive a third of their rents only in grain ("corn"), or in coin indexed to grain prices.[16] There is no information on any other class of payments made in grain, so grain was not a general medium of exchange but rather closer to a medi-eval barter item. Contracts with young servants, called indentures, were based on barter: servants received from their masters their daily food, drink, clothes, and housing.

Henry VIII had recently shown that money could be made from cheaper materials when he debased coins so much that they had more copper than silver. Copper was so defamed that copper coinage was later avoided when possible. Small-denomination coins from gold and silver would have been tiny, so people were left with no coins for small change. Many small businesses (grocers, vintners, chandlers, and alehouse keep-ers) responded by issuing their own coins from lead, tin, latten, and leather. Presumably, the issuers implicitly promised to accept back their token coins in their own shops. The government authorized some towns to issue copper coinage.[17]

Intrinsically useless money for larger transactions was known in the-ory and history. Plato thought that money was a mere symbol. In his utopian designs, Plato objected to precious metals and preferred a domestic money that would be useless abroad. Aristotle argued that historically money had been intrinsically valued commodities (metals), later stamped for convenience, but elsewhere he explained that money (*nomisma*) was named after law (*nomo*) because actually only law determined what was money.[18]

European history has many myths and stories of money made from leather or paper.[19] Historical accuracy aside, at least some contemporaries believed such stories. In 1523, a member of Parliament, Thomas Cromwell, warned that financing a war with France might force England to "be compelled, as we once did, to coin leather."[20] In 1614, an English historian mentioned more cases: brittle, useless iron bars in Sparta; stamped leather in ancient Rome, in a medieval siege of Milan, and in the medieval English Civil Wars; and 1574 "pasteboard" money during the Spanish siege of Leiden.[21] The latter case ended when the Dutch flooded the countryside and sent the navy to save the inland town. That key moment in the Dutch war of independence perhaps publicized that paper money more than other such "siege moneys."

All of these were temporary moneys, supported—where information is available—by forcing them on all transactions under penalty and by promising redemption in coin after the war. They were seen as unwarranted under normal circumstances, perhaps due to fears of overissue and counterfeiting, impossible enforcement, or perhaps because of politically powerful mints. The only known example of permanent paper money was in Mongol-occupied China. Marco Polo's thirteenth-century book, translated into English in 1579, included a chapter on paper money, saying that Kublai Khan "makes money both small and great" from paper, with at least eight denominations, "and no man may refuse this money, for if he does he must lose his head."[22]

Credit

Credit was so prevalent that the historian Craig Muldrew has dubbed England "the contractual society."[23] Everyone participated in "complicated webs of credit and obligations." Most credit was given by merchants (wholesalers) and shopkeepers (retailers) as sales credit to their customers, and this credit was "the backbone of the economy." Much of the sales credit only postponed the timing of payment in coin. Businesses also received credit; they had debts to suppliers and workers.

The legal historian Christine Desan claims that such credit was more common than in continental Europe because in the Middle Ages, the English coins were of too-high denominations to be used in the smallest transactions; after several such transactions with the same seller, the buyer could discharge the accumulated debt with coins.[24] Muldrew argues that only in specific situations could credit not work efficiently and thus coin had to be used on the spot: between complete strangers (including travelers); between people who met infrequently; when the buyer's reputation was bad; to pay rent; and to pay taxes.

Most credit was oral, in front of witnesses, but our interest lies in credit documented in writing—account books, diaries, and separate sheets of paper. Contemporaries and historians alike have disagreed about the differences between such papers—bill, bond, note, and so on.[25] The differences concerned the level of legal formality, varying from a mere signature of the debtor on paper to a seal and delivery in front of a witness. For our purposes, it is usually sufficient and convenient to call them all "bills."

Credit sometimes allowed avoiding coin altogether. Two parties that accumulated reciprocal debts could "reckon" occasionally and make a setoff of the debts until a simple balance remained. The balance would be paid in coin or documented in a single financial instrument, allowing the parties to move on and keep accumulating new reciprocal debts. This was barter enabled by credit. The English legal system allowed such voluntary setoff, but it did not force setoff on a reluctant party. If Charles the creditor sued Deborah the debtor for a debt of £10, Deborah could not get rid of the suit by proving in court that there was a counterdebt of Charles to her in the same amount (in continental Europe's civil law, she could). She would have had to pay and then sue for the other debt. This feature came from common law, which considered one case at a time, was restricted to rigid, prewritten legal forms that described exact detailed scenarios, and never looked at the big picture. Parliament would allow general setoff only in 1729.[26]

Credit could involve third parties after the debtor–creditor relation was established. Suppose that Daniel owes a debt to Deborah, and she becomes a debtor of Charles in the same amount. Then Deborah could ask Daniel to pay Charles directly, or a court could order Daniel to do so (figure 3.1), reducing coin payments from two to one. Many laws and contracts therefore ordered that a debtor "pay or cause to be paid" to another.[27]

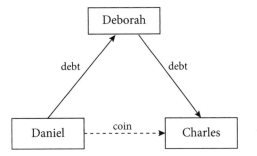

FIGURE 3.1 A simple trilateral debt settlement.

Another option was assignation of debt. It was standard in legal documents to grant specific legal rights to a person or his assignees.[28] The rights were property, so they could be sold to third parties. Therefore, laws and contracts often required that a debtor pay the creditor "or his assignee."[29] Assignation was convenient to do in writing, on the written evidence of the original debt when that was a separate paper. For example, Charles the creditor could assign Deborah's debt to Arthur the assignee, in return for goods. Then Arthur comes to Deborah, and she gives him coin. If a bill issued by Deborah is used as evidence of the debt and assignation, then this paper serves as a medium of exchange, and again the use of coin is reduced from two payments to one (figure 3.2).

The most formal bills had legal restrictions against such assignments, but many issuers found it beneficial for their reputation and business to honor their assigned bills voluntarily.[30] General assignability of bills would be recognized in law only in 1704.[31] Such multilateral settlements of debts were institutionalized in the bill of exchange that was common in international trade. In England, the elite used it to transfer funds from the countryside to London and back.[32] English financiers knew of Italian inventions—the bank, which provided safekeeping of coins and issued receipts, and the Lombard, which was a pawnshop issuing receipts for deposits of goods. Proposals to establish banks in England were not implemented.[33] When banks in Europe issued bills of exchange, the check was born.

The check would be unfamiliar to most early modern Americans. It is worth mentioning here because it is familiar to modern Americans. Showing how it works in a figure similar to figure 3.2 may help readers understand figure 3.2. Consider, then, that Deborah the debtor has deposited coin with Benjamin the banker and had received blank checks.

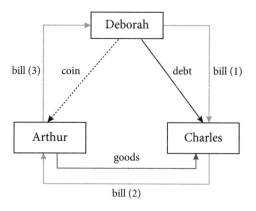

FIGURE 3.2 Trilateral debt settlement by assignment.

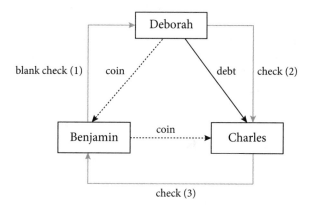

FIGURE 3.3 The check.

Later she gives a filled-out check to Charles the creditor, in fact ordering Benjamin to pay coin to Charles (figure 3.3). If Charles also has an account with Benjamin, no coin moves but the amount is transferred in the bank's books between their accounts.[34]

Toward the end of this book, the invention of 1690 Massachusetts will be explained with similar figures. Together with the abovementioned concept of setoff, we shall see that the invention could have been perfectly understood by Englishmen a century earlier.

Credit was much more than a financial device. It had profound religious, moral, and social implications.[35] The word itself—*credit*—was a new word, related to the Latin *credo* (the Christian statement of faith) and *creed*. It generally referred to the personal attribute of trustworthiness, as in court testimony. Personal trust in contracts involving credit was supposedly based on both sides being Christians. Oral credit was commonly sealed by oaths. Credit was given to those with good standing in the community, and mostly to family members. This was important enough to encourage very close relations among local merchants' oligarchies.[36] The immorality of default was one reason for imprisoning defaulting debtors, even if the imprisonment hampered their ability to earn income and repay. There were also indirect religious connotations to contracts and their obligations. Some Puritans believed they had a personal covenant with God (salvation for faith), and made explicit analogies between this covenant and their commercial contracts.[37] The legal definition of witchcraft similarly included anyone who "covenant with" evil spirits.[38]

Public Finance

The 1690 money was invented by a government that could not pay its soldiers. This had happened to countless early modern governments. While medieval kings used resources from their private domains, the Military Revolution of the sixteenth century increased the costs of European warfare too much. In the long run, this would result in a transition from the domain state to the tax state. The increasing emphasis on taxation would change the constitution, empowering the people's assembly, which controlled taxation. But this would take centuries. New sources of tax revenues had to be found, with quick, efficient, uncorrupt collection, and without provoking revolts. A vast bureaucracy had to be created.[39]

Getting the resources was only half the problem. Food and shelter had to be continuously provided for soldiers and their draft animals. One solution was to plunder anyone in sight—the enemy, your own people, even neutral parties. The first option worked only if you won. The second option could lead to revolts. The third option would gain you new enemies. It was better to pay soldiers in coin during the war so that they bought everything they needed from the local population. Enlisted civilians also needed coins after the war to compensate their families which stayed without a provider.

How to obtain coin, then? Kings such as Henry VIII produced more coins from the same amount of metal. Spain stole metal from the Americas, and English privateers preyed on that thief's ships. Other kings stole coin from the local rich. Less extreme was the forced loan; there was also the voluntary loan. Governments were the largest players in credit markets during wars, borrowing from international financiers.[40] Loans only postponed the problem of payment. Coin had to be obtained later, either by the slow collection of taxes or by plunder. Monarchs often defaulted on their loans, ruining their reputation and the financiers to avoid tax revolts and mutinies of unpaid soldiers. The latter, typically foreign mercenaries, would plunder their employers' population or defect when unpaid. This is why Spain failed to subdue the United Provinces.[41] When a state was at peace, it could lend entire units to other states at war, for huge amounts of gold and silver.

England regularly issued an awkward bond called tally—a wooden stick with notches that represented various denominations—that entitled the bearer to payment from the government.[42] Tallies were often used as assignments: a creditor of the government received a tally from the Exchequer and was sent to look for any tax collector who happened to hold tax funds; the creditor would give the tally to a collector for coin; the collector would present the tally to the Exchequer and receive a discharge from his obligation to bring tax funds (see figure 3.4, which slightly modifies figure 3.2 of private assignment).[43] The last step was a setoff of mutual debts. Setoff occurred regularly between towns and the central government: payments of taxes and fines to the government were discounted by local costs of the government's circuit judges.[44]

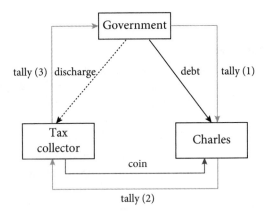

FIGURE 3.4 Public assignment.

A recurrent problem in the historiography of money and credit in England and Europe is the label *paper money* casually attached to any financial and commercial instrument: bank receipts, Lombard receipts, bills of exchange, checks, government bonds, even wooden tallies. According to such claims, paper money had continuously existed in Europe for centuries before 1690. These claims are false, confusing tradability of assets with monetary circulation. There were typically problems in trading or assigning such instruments to other people. Most instruments were named, and laws generally did not recognize their transfers of ownership. Others were "payable to X or bearer," so they could be traded to third parties. Most important, these instruments almost always had very large and/or nonround denominations, which made them utterly unfit for use as *general* media of exchange in voluntary retail transactions.[45] Their use and circulation were limited to financiers, merchants, other gentlemen, and nobles. Today's equivalents would be the millions of filled-out checks and government bonds, traded every day in financial markets, low and high. That segment of the financial system is called the "money market" because these assets can be quickly sold *for* money, but they are not money; nobody buys groceries or pays wages with such assets. Nevertheless, there was a lesson and relevance for the American future in these instruments: coin could be voluntarily set aside by law-backed paper—at least, temporarily and partially.[46]

*   *   *

In the late sixteenth century, England was hardly out of the Middle Ages. It was a backwater in Europe, having little to show in terms of constitution, science, and banking. Only its credit seemed advanced (if we disregard the tallies' material). A century later, everything would look very different.

CHAPTER FOUR

English Developments, 1584–1692

No Bishop, no King.
  —King James I, 1604

During the middle century of the early modern period, England bore twin crises. In each one, a royal turn toward Catholicism and despotism led to revolutions aided by foreign Protestant armies. These constitutional upheavals would cause in various indirect ways the development of money in Massachusetts. War finance was of supreme importance in these events. Because an economic historian might be suspected of overemphasizing this aspect, I often quote a noneconomic historian—Winston Churchill, in his Nobel-winning *A History of the English-Speaking Peoples*. Some of these financial developments would also influence Massachusetts. Revolutions in political thought and science, too, could have affected America.

Most facts in this chapter are available in easily accessible sources on the period.[1] References are given for other specific details as needed.

The Road to War

Politics

The 1588 Spanish Armada was the beginning of a war that lasted until Elizabeth died in 1603. Parliament invited the Scottish king to succeed her. He became James I of England, and he made peace with Spain. Later, James declared the divine right of kings to rule and their precedence over Parliament's laws. The clash with Parliament was expedited beginning in 1618 by the Thirty Years' War—a religious war in central Europe—as James refused to help Protestants and married his heir Charles to a French Catholic. After James died, Charles I attacked Spain and tried to help besieged Huguenots in the French port of La Rochelle.

Charles dissolved Parliament in 1629 and began eleven years without Parliament, known as the Personal Rule. One reason was the objection of Puritans in Parliament to the Church of England's drift toward Catholicism. In the 1630s, the archbishop of Canterbury purified the church from Puritan ministers, physically mutilating some of those who refused to ape the primate's liturgy.

Finance

The sailors who beat the armada were not provided with food, clothes, housing, or money upon return. Hundreds died in the streets.[2] Elizabeth was the last monarch to get away with that. In 1601, she imposed copper coins and heavily debased silver coins on rebellious Ireland. Everyone, including soldiers, was forced to accept them under penalty. The Privy Council reasserted, in a related lawsuit, that the Crown had ultimate authority over money: the monarch's will, rather than metallic content, determined what was money.[3] The persistence of private illegal lead coins led the following kings every few years to license cronies to mint copper farthings. These were counterfeited or rejected by the public, which kept minting its own tokens.[4] Money was just too useful to be left to king and cronies. Indeed, economic writers have compared money's function in the economy to blood in the body, because the economy would die without it.[5]

Charles's 1620s warfare was supposed to be financed with a forced loan, but many refused to lend. Unpaid soldiers defected, rioted in London, and chased government officials for pay. Charles resorted to billeting soldiers in private homes.[6] Parliament was called to approve war-funding taxes but instead passed the Petition of Right, which prohibited billeting and forced loans. Having dissolved Parliament, the bankrupt Charles had to leave the war, and he started collecting taxes illegally.

Financiers and merchants had long envied the United Provinces—the financial center of Western Europe. The Dutch invented the stock market (in stocks of their East India Company) and the asset bubble (in tulips). Private Amsterdam bankers perhaps invented the banknote—a transferable printed receipt (but probably in large denominations). In 1609, the public Amsterdamsche Wisselbank (Amsterdam's exchange bank, a.k.a. Bank of Amsterdam) was founded. It accepted coin from depositors and entered the intrinsic metallic value in each depositor's account. The law obliged merchants to settle debts recorded in large bills of exchange in the bank's books, transferring balances without withdrawing coin.[7] The Wisselbank became the most famous bank of the century and was imitated in other Dutch cities, but proposals for an English imitation were rejected. Instead, London goldsmiths started keeping deposits and exchanging foreign coin.[8]

Interregnum

Politics

Charles tried to change the Church of Scotland, so the Scots rebelled and in 1640 threatened to invade England. Charles summoned Parliament, quickly dissolved it; he summoned another Parliament after the Scots invaded. That Parliament enacted a constitutional revolution that eliminated many royal powers. England's weakness prompted an Irish rebellion. In 1642, the conflict in England exploded into civil war. In 1646, Charles surrendered to the Scots, who left him and English territory to Parliament in 1647. The army revolted and took power. In the Second Civil War in 1648, the army beat the coalition of Scotland, Parliament, and royalists. The army tried the king for treason and executed him in January 1649. Monarchy and the House of Lords were abolished, and the Puritan Commonwealth republic was born. The king's son was crowned in Scotland as Charles II and invaded England in the Third Civil War, but he was defeated and fled to Europe.

Parliament enacted the first Navigation Act, barring Dutch ships from the trade of England and its colonies. This resulted in the First Anglo–Dutch War (1652–1654). Parliament failed to govern, and the army's dominant general, Oliver Cromwell, became lord protector—de facto king. After he died in 1658, his son Richard lost control of the army, and one victorious general invited Charles II to return.

Finance

Charles summoned Parliament twice in 1640 only to get war funds. In the interlude, he sought loans from the City of London, Spain, France, Genoa, even the Vatican.[9] Charles then grabbed, as a forced loan, gold and silver that merchants and goldsmiths deposited in the Royal Mint for coining. The merchants' protest led him to keep only a third of it.[10] Charles ordered minting new copper coins, to be used to pay anyone but the mutiny-prone soldiers. All private monetary transactions were to be made partly in those coins. The administration failed in executing this order.[11] When the Scots invaded, the English soldiers fled because, as Churchill note, "they had had no pay."[12] The Scots plundered the countryside and agreed to a truce after Charles promised to pay the cost of their occupation. London granted Charles an emergency loan to pay the Scots and to keep his own unpaid army "from dissolving in mutiny"—on condition of calling Parliament again.[13]

Political science speaks of "the power of the purse"—the ability of the tax-legislating authority to control the other branches of government by withholding tax funds. The second Parliament of 1640 gave an awesome demonstration of that power with its constitutional revolution, but behind the metaphorical power of the purse in Westminster lay a more tangible power and purse in northern England: the soldier's decision—fight or flight—dependent on being paid.

Tradition had it that every Irish rebellion ended in transfer of rebel lands to new English and Scottish settlements. Parliament used that expectation to authorize a private army to subdue the new rebellion there, with investors paid in expected confiscated land.[14] Land, indirectly, would thus pay soldiers and suppliers.

In the First Civil War, Charles was blocked from the Royal Mint, so he founded mints elsewhere to pay his expenses.[15] Both armies repeatedly stopped marching for lack of pay, and the soldiers mutinied, deserted, and plundered the countryside.[16] The Scots left the king and northern England to Parliament only after Parliament gave them money—which it borrowed from London. Owed wages for months, the army's soldiers "were united upon the question of pay. They were resolved not to go to Ireland or be disbanded to their homes until it was settled."[17] Charles II bought uniforms on credit when invading England, promising to repay after his victory. The debt was repaid by another Prince Charles—in 2008.[18]

In the First Anglo–Dutch War, unpaid sailors mutinied, deserted, and rioted in London. The 1653 Parliament "reformed taxation in a manner which seemed to weaken the security for the soldiers' pay,"[19] so Cromwell dissolved it. Cromwell later kept sailors at sea to evade their demands for pay.[20] After he died, the army deposed his son Richard over arrears of pay.[21] In the ensuing chaos, General John Lambert, who opposed restoration of monarchy, lost because his soldiers lived off the countryside, creating "extreme disgust and scandal"[22]—and their motivation to fight was lost over the legacy of not being properly paid in the Civil Wars.[23] The resulting contacts with Charles II included a suggestion that he "promise full payment of the soldiers' arrears."[24] He was invited to return after agreeing to do so.

To summarize, throughout the period 1640–1660, parties lost control of England because they failed to pay soldiers: the king in 1640, Parliament in 1647 and 1653, and Richard Cromwell and the army in 1659.

During the First Civil War, Parliament issued paper instruments promising payment of its debts. Money lenders and suppliers received "public faith" bills, while soldiers received "debentures." Each debenture stated how much a soldier was owed. Several signatures on each debenture made it harder to counterfeit and prevented corruption in issuing it.[25] The security for paying the debts was estates confiscated from the losers—the abolished bishops and royal family, Catholics, royalists, and Irish rebels.[26] The financial instruments could be used, and were used, to buy these lands.[27]

There was extensive trade in these financial instruments. A soldier selling his debenture assigned it to another by writing the buyer's name on the debenture.[28] Most debentures were sold by poor, hungry soldiers to their richer, more patient officers. Debentures were thus traded at heavy discounts of up to 80 percent (i.e., a debenture promising £10 was sold for £2 in coin). That legacy would later doom Lambert's last effort against restoration of monarchy. In the First Anglo–Dutch War, sailors received similar "tickets," which were traded at discounts of up to 50 percent.[29]

Ian Gentles, an English Civil Wars historian, singled out Captain John Blackwell Jr. as the ace of the trade in financial instruments related to the bishops' lands. He was a young officer in Cromwell's regiment and son of a Puritan London merchant. With his father serving as a land sales administrator, Blackwell bought large plots and sold them at enormous profits. He paid for them with public-faith bills and other financial instruments he bought. His "ingenuity" and "creative entrepreneurship was very much an exception," says Gentles.[30] Blackwell later bought royal land and received Irish land for financing the Irish reconquest. In 1647, he was one of the many officers who demanded pay from Parliament. Appointed as one of two treasurers at war, he was involved in the issue and redemption of debentures. In 1649, he authorized the use of army funds to build the scaffold on which Charles was executed. Later Blackwell was a member of Parliament and one of two receiver generals of taxes—mostly receiving tax funds and paying them to the army and the navy.[31] We shall meet Blackwell again and again, in England and America, all the way to 1695.

The mint confiscation and the wars drove merchants to deposit coin with goldsmiths, who became the primary lenders, even to the government.[32] They became goldsmith-bankers. Other banks were proposed. William Potter advocated a company of merchants issuing bills, backed by their assets, to replace coin in trade. Another proposal was for a land bank: instead of theft-prone coin, or goods as in a Lombard, the deposit would be a land title, in the form of a mortgage. Depositors' accounts would be used in settling all payments above £10, freeing the existing coin to serve in everyday transactions. Historians have contested the land bank's authorship. Perhaps it was again Potter; in any case, the scheme was published by Samuel Hartlib, the most important distributor of scientific knowledge in England.[33] The private issue of token coins exploded with the abolition of royalty, reaching thirteen thousand issuers.[34]

Restoration

Politics

Charles II returned in 1660. An Act of Indemnity and Oblivion forgave nearly everyone for their 1640s deeds. John Blackwell was excepted for his role in the regicide and was barred for life from public office. He lost all his English land and barely kept his Irish land.[35] An anti-Puritan Parliament excluded all non-Anglicans from Parliament and fired all their clergy in the 1662 Act of Uniformity.

In 1665, the Second Anglo–Dutch War started and London was hit by the Great Plague, followed by the Great Fire. In 1667, the Dutch ended the war by invading the Thames and successfully attacking the main naval base at Chatham. It was the worst naval defeat in English history. Charles and his brother and heir James—inspired by their parents and by cousin Louis XIV of France—turned to despotic Catholicism, igniting the second crisis of the century.[36] James converted; Charles joined Louis in attacking the Dutch. Three consecutive Parliaments excluded the Catholic James from inheriting the throne, only to be dissolved by Charles. In 1681, a new Personal Rule began. Charles attacked royal charters which gave privileges to boroughs and cities. These charters (the most important being the City of London's) gave Charles's opponents control of parliamentary elections. Writs called "quo warranto" were issued to these corporations, demanding them to prove in court that their royal charters were valid—and royal judges judged they were not. Persecution of Puritans resumed. Charles died in 1685 and was succeeded by James II.

James tried to repeal anti-Catholic laws by packing Parliament and forming an anti-Anglican coalition with Puritans by promises of religious freedom. Fears of his Catholicism increased after cousin Louis outlawed the Huguenots. Hundreds of thousands fled France, converted, or faked conversion. In 1688, some of the English elite invited James's son-in-law and nephew to save England. He was William of Orange, the Dutch head of state.

Finance

Some historians have claimed that the banknotes issued by London's goldsmith-bankers were paper money; however, the notes had a median and mode of at least £100—a gentleman's *annual* income.[37] In contrast, a genuine paper money was issued in 1660s Sweden. A semipublic bank, Stockholms Banco, printed notes that were legal tender for taxes, payable to bearer, in round amounts, and the lowest denomination equaled a laborer's weekly wage.[38] The notes were popular partly because even high-denomination coins were made from cheap copper (and thus weighed forty pounds). The experiment ended after too many depositors wanted coins and the bank did not have enough.

In the Second Anglo–Dutch War, the treasury was run by commissioners. Commissioner Sir George Downing, back from years as ambassador to the United Provinces, planned to borrow money from the general public. His 1665 "Exchequer orders" were tradable, interest-bearing bonds. Most were issued to lenders of coin, but some were directly used by the government in purchases of war supplies. Very few had denominations of £1 (a laborer's monthly wage) and none below that. As with earlier bonds, some historians have referred to them as "paper money."[39] They were not. The orders were named; every transfer had to be registered at the Exchequer; nearly all orders had very large and nonround denominations; they were accepted in shops only at large discounts and thus workers refused them as wages; and most were immediately sold to goldsmith-bankers, who held them until maturity.[40] Others proposed "bonds," "bill money," or "paper money," payable "to bearer" to ease their transfer, as legal tender for debts and taxes. But the minimal denomination was £5—with the expectation that retailers would buy them once they had enough revenue in coin.[41] This was no money, but it came close.

During the war, sailors again mutinied and rioted in London for lack of pay, while dealers bought sailors' tickets at large discounts. The Dutch attack on Chatham was led by defecting English sailors, who yelled, "We did heretofore fight for tickets, now we fight for dollars!" (the dollar was a Dutch coin). Other sailors refused to pursue them until paid.[42] In 1672, during the Third Anglo–Dutch War, royal bankruptcy ended the Exchequer orders experiment in disgrace, ruining leading goldsmith-bankers. This, together with memories of the 1640 mint confiscation, doomed any thought of large-scale banking. Nobody in his right mind would ever again trust the Stuarts to be the stewards of a big pile of money—either in their Mint or Exchequer or under their nose in London. Also in 1672, Charles outlawed all those private token coins issued since his father's execution, and minted his own tokens.

Bank ideas developed further. In 1661, the London merchant Francis Cradock wedded the land-bank idea to the Lombard, including both land and goods in his exchange-bank proposal. Sir William Petty, a surveyor of confiscated Irish lands, promoted a land bank supported by a land registry. In 1682, London agreed to establish a Lombard, with a list of tradesmen supposedly committed to accepting its bills in trade. The abovementioned John Blackwell, now formally titled a merchant, was a partner in a 1683 bank plan that projected issuing "bank-bills of credit" backed by land and goods. None of these bank plans materialized.[43]

The Glorious Revolution

Politics

Facing Dutch invasion, in October 1688 James reversed his policies to gain popular support, including restoring London's charter. William came in November, and James escaped to France without abdicating. Parliament convened as a "Convention" because only monarchs could legally summon a Parliament. In 1689, James invaded Ireland with French forces. William and his wife/cousin, Mary, were jointly crowned after agreeing to a constitutionally limited monarchy.

William drafted England to his Dutch war against France. Churchill, who knew a thing or two about a world war or two, called it a "world war," since it also had American and Asian theaters.[44] It is known as the Nine Years' War, but it would really last a generation, while some historians mark it as the beginning of a second Hundred Years' War between England and France (ending in 1815). In 1690, William drove James from Ireland. In 1691, he went fighting on the Continent, and in 1692 England destroyed the French navy and its plan to invade England.

Finance

When James briefly controlled Ireland, he minted coins from base metal and forced them on most spot transactions under penalty, promising to exchange them for silver coins after the war. Almost all coins were used to pay James's Irish soldiers. It was just another episode of European siege money. Many refused to bring goods to market to avoid receiving these coins. James's own government preferred not to accept this money in taxes. France refused having its soldiers there paid in these coins, so they were paid in gold and silver. In 1691, the victorious William declared the coins to be no money.[45] As usual, debentures of soldiers and suppliers were backed by lands confiscated from Irish rebels.[46]

The Glorious Revolution was a unique opportunity for financial innovators because constitutional monarchy and Parliament-controlled taxation replaced the grabbing Stuarts. At last, a large-scale bank—private or public—became possible. Even better, as the new king was Dutch and brought with him financial advisors, London could become a new Amsterdam. Moreover, the expensive war made the government listen to every financial proposal.[47] An unprecedented flood of proposals was published in books and pamphlets, igniting the Financial Revolution.[48] One type of proposals was a loan to the government through a "bank" that would issue "current" receipts (bills). In January 1692, a committee of the House of Commons refused granting such legal tender status to private bills.[49] At this point, we must leave English finance—until chapter 15.

The Intellectual and Scientific Revolutions

As the First Civil War ended, England exploded with constitutional, economic, and religious ideas and experiments. This intellectual revolution included republicanism, universal male suffrage, communalism, and Quakerism.[50] Thomas Hobbes's 1651 *Leviathan* supported a despot to protect the people from anarchy, and popularized the theory of the state as a social contract. Hobbes regarded the state as an "artificial man"—equivalent to the human body and comprising all the state's residents.

Hobbes discussed "base money," which is supported only by "the stamp of the place" of issue and thus "has its effect at home only." That is, money with no intrinsic value can function only thanks to local legal support. Hobbes wrote of money in general:

> The conduits and ways by which it [money] is conveyed to the public use are of two sorts: one, that conveys it to the public coffers; the other, that issues the same out again for public payments. Of the first sort are collectors, receivers, and treasurers; of the second are the treasurers again, and the officers appointed for payment of several public or private ministers. And in this also the artificial man maintains his resemblance with the natural; whose veins, receiving the blood from the several parts of the body, carry it to the heart; where, being made vital, the heart by the arteries sends it out again, to enliven and enable for motion all the members of the same.[51]

As part of his general "artificial man" analogy, Hobbes, like previous authors, equated money with blood; he upgraded it, though, following William Harvey's recent discovery of the circulation of blood. It is remarkable that Hobbes found the equivalent to the heart in the treasury rather than in the mint that receives bullion and worn coin and emits new coin. The circulation of money is defined by everyone as both receiving money and spending it, but according to Hobbes, the state's treasury is more than that: it is the heart of the system. Money is validated in that the *treasury* accepts it and spends it, thus allowing it to flow back to the private economy and function there as money. A reader might conclude that the "base money" Hobbes mentioned earlier works that way, as long as the treasury accepts it.

After the next revolution, in 1690, the Leiden-trained Dr. Nicholas

Barbon, a member of Parliament, published *A Discourse on Trade*. His chapter "Of Money, Credit, and Interest" begins by declaring: "Money is a value made by a law." Therefore,

> it is not absolutely necessary [that] money should be made of gold or silver; for having its sole value from the law, it is not material upon what metal the stamp be set. Money has the same value, and performs the same uses, if it be made of brass, copper, tin, or anything else.[52]

A reader might conclude that legally backed paper would also qualify.

Another consequential upheaval of the century was the Scientific Revolution.[53] No explicit link can be drawn with certainty between that European-wide event and monetary innovation in America, but there is circumstantial evidence. Beginning with Plato and Aristotle, scientists and philosophers historically had been interested in the economy and specifically in money, while others like Copernicus were asked to help design their kings' monetary policies.[54] Similarly, there would be interest in monetary economics among the very few scientists in early New England. Absorbing the revolutionary developments in science may have helped them ditch old ideas about money.

Another reason to examine science is a dark shadow that hangs above the story told in this book: the shadow of nineteen people hanged in Salem for witchcraft. Some of the infamous judges of the witch trials in 1692 were among the genius legislators who created the new concept of money in 1690–1692. Understanding the confused and confusing scientific spirit of their time would explain that paradox.

The Scientific Revolution began when Johannes Kepler and Galileo Galilei proved that Copernicus was right. As Galileo famously used the telescope to observe the moon, so did the Englishman Thomas Harriot, who also discovered sunspots. The Englishman Harvey discovered the circulation of blood. James I was centuries ahead of his time in his *Counterblaste to Tobacco*, which offered reasoned objections to and policy advice on smoking.[55] A science enthusiast, James employed as chief minister the polymath Francis Bacon—the prophet of the Industrial Revolution, who called for a sustained effort to learn nature in order to use it to improve the condition of human living. Bacon promoted experiments to test theories and the inductive method that looked for empirical regularities in data.

Bacon's agenda was picked up by a group of Puritan scholars, led by the bank promoter Samuel Hartlib. According to the historian Carl Wennerlind, scientists in England envisioned and promoted unbounded economic growth, and saw an expanding quantity of money (through banks) as necessary to accompany that growth.[56] Hartlib's group was chartered after the Restoration by another science enthusiast—Charles II—as the Royal Society of London. Robert Hooke, the society's chief experimenter, popularized the microscope by observing cells and examining fossils. Robert Boyle discovered a law of chemistry. Isaac Newton invented calculus, and his book on the laws of physics, published in 1687, is the climactic, abrupt end of the Scientific Revolution.

These English achievements were part of a European-wide phenomenon of inventions and discoveries by Pascal (calculator), Torricelli (atmosphere and barometer), Leibniz (calculus), van Leeuwenhoek (germs), Pascal and von Guericke (vacuum), and Descartes (mathematics). The Scientific Revolution bridged the gap between the superstitious, backward-looking Middle Ages and the confident Enlightenment of the eighteenth century. It inspired an unprecedented, general atmosphere of learning, of daring to suggest new ideas that contradicted Aristotle and other ancient sages. The overarching theme was doubt, skepticism, criticism, and rebellion against authority. Specifically, commonsense observations were proven false: the sun did not revolve around Earth (Copernicus), Earth was not a perfect sphere (Newton), and planetary orbits were not circular (Kepler). Hobbes's and Barbon's challenge of the commonsense observation that precious-metal coins functioned as money because they were made of precious metal can be seen as part of that trend.

Paradoxically, the Scientific Revolution overlapped the worst century of witch hunting in European history. Tens of thousands of people were executed throughout Europe. The worst cases were during the social and religious stress of major wars (the First Civil War in England, the Thirty Years' War on the Continent).[57] Hobbes denounced demonology as a pagan relic, but Parliament's Act of Indemnity and Oblivion regarding the Interregnum seriously excepted "invocations, conjurations, witchcrafts, sorceries, enchantments, and charms."[58] The seeming paradox between science and witchcraft existed even at the individual level. The James VI of Scotland who authored *Demonology* was the same James I of England who wrote against smoking. Other proponents of new science against old errors strongly believed in Satan and witches.[59] One may wonder if the intense popular belief in a powerful Satan practically converted Christianity from monotheism to bitheism. Similarly, Newton researched alchemy, the laws of physics, and the laws of Moses; for him, all were equally authored by God.[60]

Some nonsense had monetary implications. During the Thirty Years' War, the English physician Robert Child wrote: "The Emperor of Germany has found a secret to turn silver into gold, by the which he pays his army."[61] Wennerlind argues that despair of alchemy led English scientists to support banking as a method of increasing the money supply.[62] (Although the alchemical path to gold proved to be a ridiculous dead end, we know that, indeed, one element could be turned into another for military purposes. Ask Hiroshima.)

*   *   *

If in 1584 England was hardly out of the Middle Ages, by 1692 it was on the verge of the modern age, emerging as a leader on several fronts: constitution, banking, public finance, and science. The balance of power shifted decisively toward Parliament. Goldsmiths' banknotes and checks were routinely used by the elite, and dozens of proposals for better public finance were floated after the Glorious Revolution. The theory of land banks was developed. A mass issue of government war bonds had been attempted.

The English knew far more about the natural world than their grandparents. In exact sciences, humanities, and social sciences, the old and traditional was giving way to new and innovative. When some of the very foundations of society—the king, his church, and Aristotle—were questioned (even beheaded), what was there to keep gold and silver in the definition of money?

England experienced a chaotic century. Its constitutional shocks created large waves that rocked the distant American boat repeatedly, and as an unexpected side effect propelled the evolution of money in one colony.

PART II

The Atlantic

B ernard Bailyn of Harvard University was one of the greatest scholars of colonial America. In 2012, at age ninety, he published a history of English America before 1680, titled *The Barbarous Years*.[1] The term *barbarous*, the contemporary variant of *barbaric*, was reserved at the time mostly to describe Indians, and referred to both their physical conditions and behavior at war. Bailyn's point was that the European colonists were barbaric in similar ways. Relative to European standards, they lived in deplorable physical conditions, and their behavior at war was not exemplary.

Indeed, Spaniards, Portuguese, French, Dutch, English, Scots, even Swedes, Finns, Baltic Germans, and Arabs violently competed for the vast material and human resources in that humongous "Wild West" known to historians as the Atlantic World.[2] Much of the violence concerned not wealth in general but currency specifically. To produce the silver coins needed to pay for their endless European wars, the Spaniards stole Indians' metal and labor in forced mining. Silver from Spanish America could be stolen by English pirates or Dutch privateers in the Caribbean, brought to a nearby friendly colony, only to be sacked by French pirates, who would ship the coin again toward Europe, eventually to be stolen in the Eastern Atlantic by pirates from Algiers. Welcome to the jungle.

Bailyn's broad characterization of barbarity also affected colonial currency. The colonists found their new physical conditions intolerable, and so they tried to buy every possible manufactured good they could from Europe, even if that meant sending all their coin there in return, on top of commodities they exported. With no coin left, they improvised other, more crude forms of money for local use, thereby exacerbating

their barbaric physical conditions. Not only did they have no feather pil-
lows and glass windows, but they had to buy local goods and labor services with bushels of wheat and pounds of pork. The currency problem
hit again, given the constant threat of violence from colonists, pirates,
and privateers of other nations, and from Indians. War finance was thus
a recurrent problem. How would soldiers get paid quickly when there is
no coin for taxpayers to pay the treasury?

However, the distance from Europe gave the colonists considerable
freedom to try new solutions for both their money and war-finance problems. Some of them used that freedom to the fullest.

CHAPTER FIVE

Before 1630

Harvesters of Money

Get thee out of thy country, and from thy kindred, and from thy father's house, unto a land that I will shew thee: And I will make of thee a great nation, and I will bless thee, and make thy name great.
—Genesis 12:1–2, King James Version

The 1690 invention of modern money in Massachusetts was the climax of a six-decade-long monetary innovation in the leading Puritan colony. This did not come out of the blue, nor did the Puritans have a monopoly on monetary innovation. English monetary improvisation began in the first colony: 1580s Roanoke. Between that and the emigration of the Massachusetts Bay Company to America in 1630, there were dozens of colonization attempts. Almost all of them failed. The smaller the colony and the shorter its life, the less is known about its monetary practices; but such colonies probably had no money at all, as will be explained below. Only colonies that provide relevant information are reviewed here.[1]

This chapter establishes the regularity of coin shortage and its causes, and the adoption of local products as alternative commodity moneys in all English colonies, and a few others too.

King Copper

The main theme in standard histories of money in English America—
from Jamestown to Independence—is lack of metal. It is surprising to
find that the colonists' first money, or near money, was metal. The dramatic rise and fall of copper money is told here for the first time.

Roanoke

In 1584, an English expeditionary force reached present-day North Carolina. It was sent by the courtier Walter Raleigh, who sought gold and
silver, either by looting Spanish Florida or by mining.[2] Raleigh's men
bartered with Indians during their short stay. Among the objects the
English offered, there was only one that Indians had already used: copper, the elite's jewelry.[3] In 1585, Raleigh sent colonists to settle Roanoke
Island and who subsequently confirmed copper's importance.[4]

Roanoke's governor, Ralph Lane, observed that copper was used to
"buy" within Indian society.[5] His choice of word implies that he saw copper as money. Most anthropologists, followed by sociologists and some
historians, see all exchange in traditional societies as gift exchange between acquaintances rather than monetary exchange, and so do not recognize that copper was money.[6] This apparently small academic dis-
agreement with economists and others is actually a cornerstone in the
biggest debate in social sciences—whether capitalism or communism is
more consistent with human nature. I can skip over this minefield because this book is not about Indian exchange; it is about the invention of
modern money by colonists, for use among colonists. Indian money matters here only to the extent that it influenced colonists' view and usage
of money. Colonists' view of Indian exchange, even if distorted, is the
one that matters here. Incidentally, it is the same as economists' view of
money.

The colonists regularly used copper to obtain all their food (mostly
maize) from Indians. They forced a copper-for-maize trade during a
failed expedition to find copper mines. Governor Lane described what
was objectively barter in this way: Indians "sell" and colonists "buy"—
implying again, but now in an intersocietal context, that copper was
money.[7] And why not? As he had done in shops in England, he gave
metal and received food. Copper was perhaps not exactly money, be-

cause it did not circulate between the societies; it flowed from the English to the Indians on a one-way ticket. In the only documented offer of payment from Indians to English (ransom), no copper was used.[8]

There is no information about usage of money within the colony, and probably there was none. The few colonists were all Raleigh's employees. They worked together, using his resources and eating from the pool of food they "bought." Like NASA astronauts on the moon, they did not establish economically independent households.

Fearing more coerced trade, in 1586 the Roanoke Island chief hired other tribes with his new copper to attack the colony.[9] This was no different from the contemporary use of gold and silver between kings in European wars. The colonists fled to England and recommended settling northward, in Chesapeake Bay. New colonists heading there stopped by in Roanoke in 1587 and disappeared. The armada and its aftermath then halted colonization.

Raleigh kept searching for the lost colonists. The scientist he had sent there in 1585, the future astronomer Thomas Harriot, helped him in 1602 by listing items to be taken on board, including hundreds of square or round pieces of copper in a variety of specific sizes.[10] Perhaps he specified a full range of denominations of copper money. This list was composed just after Elizabeth sent new copper coins to colonized Ireland.

Jamestown

James I's peace with Spain renewed colonization. In 1606, he granted a charter to two groups of investors—from London and England's western ports—to settle in America to find "gold, silver, and copper." The charter allowed each colony to "establish and cause to be made a coin, to pass current there between the people of those several colonies, for the more ease of traffic and bargaining between and amongst them and the natives there." James ordered an initial cooperative period, with all produce collected and equally distributed, making money initially quite redundant within the colony.[11] The charter perhaps implicitly allowed exporting coin to the colony (as "necessary" or "needful" items), but a 1609 charter explicitly allowed exporting coin. That charter turned the London group into a large corporation (henceforth the Virginia Company). The export right and the coinage right remained intact in an extended 1612 charter.[12]

The London group targeted Chesapeake Bay and founded Jamestown in 1607. The area was populated by Indians similar to Roanoke's. Copper was their key form of wealth, status, and jewelry.[13] White beads, cut from seashells with stone tools, were another object of decoration and wealth.[14] These *rawrenock* beads were commonly called *roanoke* by the English—after the lost colony.[15] Seashell beads were among the most common forms of jewelry in human history because every society had the requisite technology to process them, while only few learned later to process metals.

Much like metals, seashell jewelry doubled as money all over the world (according to economists rather than anthropologists), and it was probably the most common form of money in history.[16] A Jamestown official telling of an Indian transaction wrote that "they use [beads] and pass one to another, as we do money." The colonist John Smith provided a general description: "Their manner of trading is for copper, beads, and such like; for which they give such commodities as they have."[17] This is the definition of a general medium of exchange.

Indeed, colonists documented copper and beads as dominating intra-Indian transactions: pay for labor, for service in war and heroism in war, for taxes, for tributes to king and gods, and for brides (the latter with the terms *buy, sold, pay,* and *price*).[18] Usually, copper served transactions of high economic value, while beads were for traditional and symbolic transactions. Most important, the payment of these objects as alimony and in charity indicates that they were expected to buy all of life's necessities.[19] Copper and beads also dominated pseudomonetary contexts: Indians were "covetous" of them, bet on them, hid them in the ground, took them for travel, stole them from travelers, and were executed for stealing them. These objects caused wars like Europe's gold and silver, wrote Smith.[20]

The colony's leaders were one degree of separation from Roanoke's scientist Thomas Harriot,[21] and it was probably he who advised them to bring copper. They also brought glass beads, other "toys" such as bells, and iron tools such as hatchets.[22] The colony obtained food from Indians, and hired guides, canoes, and rowers.[23] Colonists' terminology was mostly of barter ("commodities" given in "trade for corn"), but there was some use of monetary terms—again, the colonists "buy" while Indians "sell."[24] Noticing Indians' estimation of copper, John Smith gave the local leader, Powhatan, a copper gift, and later crowned him as a vassal of James I with a copper crown.[25] For two years, colonists generally gave copper in exchange for goods, services, and men (English captives) and used copper as a medium of unilateral payments. They said that two Indian guides "would have betrayed both their king and kindred for a piece of copper," reminding of how Jesus was betrayed "for thirty pieces of silver."[26] Copper was also the unit of account, and Smith apparently followed Harriot in suggesting standardized copper pieces for payments ("an inch square").[27] Again, there is no evidence of copper circulating back to the English. In many transactions, the colonists offered "beads," of either glass or seashell. The latter were produced in Jamestown by hired Indians.[28]

Flooded with copper, in 1608 the Indians raised maize prices and in 1609 rejected copper altogether, leading Smith to forced trade.[29] He later extorted "contribution" as protection money, which was probably paid in maize.[30] In 1610, the colony was briefly abandoned and restarted as a military garrison. The devalued copper—far less common after 1610, per archeological findings—still served as a unit of account, but was eclipsed in monetary contexts by beads and hatchets.[31] Copper was still king only faraway, on the Potomac River. In 1613, colonial traders there paid copper to ransom an Englishman, and the chief who betrayed Pocahontas to the English was rewarded mostly "with a small copper kettle."[32] Thus the daughter of Powhatan, King Copper, was sold for copper.

The new monetary king was glass beads shipped from England. In 1621, the company referred to glass beads as "the money you trade with the natives," and sent Italian experts in a vain effort to produce beads locally.[33] In 1622, a surprise Indian attack killed a third of the colonists—and the Virginia Company, because King James revoked the charter and his heir, Charles, turned Virginia into a royal colony. With the company gone, no more evidence was left of the monetary use of beads, copper, and hatchets.[34]

Another Indian-related money was fur. In the very beginning, colonists illegally traded the colony's tools and arms to Indians in exchange for furs, then traded the furs for food and alcohol clandestinely provided by individual sailors of supply ships.[35] Fur functioned as money in the limited sense that colonists regularly accepted it from Indians only for purchasing European goods. The later martial law outlawed all trade with any outsiders.[36]

As a cooperative, Jamestown at first supposedly did not need an internal medium of exchange, but archeologists have found many coins there. Colonists expected this and brought coin weights to measure the coins' intrinsic worth.[37] The later martial law outlawed internal trade in

Virginia Company–owned goods and services.[38] Payments from the colony to individuals were rare but sometimes necessary, as for soldiers in dangerous expeditions to obtain maize. These and others were rewarded with maize, which was often ruined by rain, rats, and worms.[39]

Copper as a Dead End

In both Raleigh's Roanoke and the cooperative-turned-garrison of Jamestown, there was hardly any role for money in the colony. The main action was the use of copper in the essential trade with Indians. The English discovery of copper in America had diametrically different results from the Spanish discovery of silver in America. The latter discovery flooded Europe with silver and resulted in inflation. Copper, on the other hand, would not affect money in Europe and would not even be money in America among colonists. On the contrary, realizing the demand for it in America, the colonists imported copper from Europe, came close to minting it, overused it in exchange, caused inflation, and ruined its traditional exchange use among Indians.

Roanoke and Jamestown could influence the monetary thinking of prospective colonists. Discovering copper and seashell money among Indians perhaps reinforced their Old World view that jewelry material was proper money. But it also opened their eyes to materials other than precious metal and to forms other than coins. This was one small aspect of Europe's exposure to Native American ideas and practices.[40] Most important, it showed that an object which English people found to be intrinsically useless could function as money—if only with non-English people.

King Tobacco

After harvesting virtually nothing but sorrow, beginning in 1615 Virginians raised tobacco for export.[41] Tobacco transformed not only Virginia but the entire English colonization of warm areas, where it quickly became both the only export good and the leading money. Virginia's colonists traded tobacco directly with European ships for European goods. Some used monetary terminology (colonists "buy," company ships "sell").[42] It was prone to look like a monetary transaction, since each planter gave one object and received in return a large variety of commodities. But our interest lies in monetary trade within the colony. The transition to tobacco was simultaneous with a transition from a cooperative garrison to a privatized democracy. When plots were privatized, the rent was paid in the "best Indian wheat" (maize). The "best" was required because naturally planters would prefer to pay the worst. Everyone also had to contribute a period of work for the colony. Instead of salaries in coin, officials were given half the produce made by company servants on company land. Land was used to reward anyone paying for the importation of new colonists.[43]

The privatized economy had more potential for internal trade, but the standard description of Virginia (among contemporaries and historians alike) left little need for money. First, supposedly "every man" grew only tobacco for export, not even raising enough grain for their own consumption.[44] What, then, could they trade with each other? Second, most colonists were young single men. They lacked the demand for the wide variety of goods and services that families, and thus normal societies, require. This should have made barter more feasible. Third, and more important, these men were indentured servants. Picked from the streets and prisons of England, these tired, poor, huddled masses were treated little better than livestock by tobacco planters. Their barter contracts required no money, giving them minimal food, drink, clothes, and housing to stay alive.[45] The few stolen Africans had the same status at that stage. Each plantation was a household with no internal payments: master, family, and servants. Fourth, because tobacco quickly exhausted the land, planters dispersed in isolated plantations. Trade required a boat, and time. Planters did not need to go to Jamestown to export their tobacco, because Virginia's numerous rivers are very deep; European ships came to each plantation and bartered there for tobacco.[46] Richard Sylla has concluded that Virginia "possibly had less internal commerce" than normal, diversified contemporary societies.[47]

While Sylla is certainly correct, the "buying and selling" or leasing of servants, and legal maximum wages for nine professions, indicate there was a role for a medium of exchange, while the presence of resident merchants shows more-sophisticated commerce than usually imagined.[48] Credit was difficult because the isolated plantations did not constitute a genuine community, and because about 50 percent of colonists died every year from disease and war. In the role of money, coin and maize were soon defeated by tobacco. In 1618, the proprietors in England of one plantation gave "ten shillings," probably in coin, to every man they sent.[49] The company demanded rent in shillings and pence, but the colonists' first assembly in 1619 petitioned not "to exact money of us (whereof we have none at all, as we have no mint), but the true value of the rent in commodity" (i.e., tobacco).[50] Why did they have no mint? The local council could establish one, according to the charters, but the colony was dirt poor, with neither tools nor professionals. It did not even have a single working plough.[51] However, the absence of a mint cannot be the only reason for having no coin "at all." Almost all counties in England did not have mints, and yet they usually had enough London-issued coins. I will return to this at the end of the chapter.

The 1619 assembly used monetary units (i.e., pounds, shillings, pence) in most laws, but its tax was denominated in tobacco.[52] By 1624, tobacco was referred to by colonists as "our money," while Smith wrote, "Tobacco . . . passes there as current silver."[53] It did take over all the functions of money—it paid for goods and services, and it paid wages, debts, taxes, fees, and fines. The colony's budget was listed entirely in pounds of tobacco. Laws required that only "merchantable" tobacco be paid. The term was defined in the sister colony of Bermuda as tobacco which was "sufficient and worthy to pass currently among merchants."[54] Nobody wanted to receive tobacco that, down the line of payments and transactions, would be refused by merchants shipping tobacco to Europe. The government probably accepted the reality of tobacco money as it emerged in the private economy rather than initiate it. However, once the government accommodated to that situation and endorsed it in laws specifying taxes, fines, fees, and maximum prices and wages, it reinforced and cemented tobacco's use in the private economy.

But tobacco was a bad money—perishable, bulky, seasonal, and heterogeneous in quality.[55] The local government complained:

> We find that nothing has hindered the proceedings of arts [i.e., artisans' work], manual trades and staple commodities, more than the want of money amongst us, which makes all men to apply themselves to tobacco, because there is not tobacco (which is our money) all the year, to pay workmen, and the recovery of debts, as the crop is not without trouble, and the condition of what they shall receive uncertain.[56]

Because Virginia specialized in tobacco, it emerged as money. People had no incentive to specialize in anything else, as they would in a normal monetary economy, because there was no good money to be paid for the job, and so their best resort was to grow tobacco like everyone else. Virginia was trapped in a tobacco addiction.

Such a bad money made credit more appealing. One governor's will ordered selling all his property, prominently including "debts," for tobacco.[57] These debts were probably bills that others issued to him. It implies that bills, presumably denominated in tobacco, were tradable. Trilateral settlements of debt saved on transport costs: as in England, creditors of the colony were sent to nearby tax collectors to receive the tobacco owed them by the colony, instead of having everything sent to and from Jamestown.[58]

Privatization created a new problem for war finance. Those leaving their private plantations and serving as soldiers required compensation from the rest. Maize looted from Indians was the official medium of payment to soldiers, so expeditions were scheduled to the season in which ripe maize was on the ground. As in Europe, payments to soldiers could dictate the most important military decisions. There was also a tobacco tax to fund a garrison.[59]

The Islands

After a Virginia Company fleet crashed unto uninhabited Bermuda, it was included in the 1612 Virginia charter, but in 1615 a charter was given to a new, offshoot company. The economy was similar to Virginia's and had the same transition from monetary units, coin, and grain to tobacco. More colonies were founded by courtiers and merchants in Caribbean islands: Saint Christopher (today Saint Kitts), Barbados, and Nevis. They also grew tobacco and used it as a medium of paying rents and taxes.[60] Further north, Newfoundland was the great crossroads of Atlantic fishermen. A succession of courtiers left a paper trail of colonization (including a 1610 coinage privilege) but few results on the ground.[61] One governor was instructed to buy from fishermen the staple goods—dried fish and oil. Fines were later collected from fishermen in these same goods, even though local laws specified fines in monetary units.[62]

Bermuda is important as the first English colony with a special coin. Already in 1612 the governor was promised "coin sent unto you" to pay wages, and in the meanwhile he was to register all debts for wages and workers' debts to the company's store. The governor and minister barely kept the population working for the company with promises of impending pay.[63] The Bermuda charter gave a coinage privilege to the General Court of shareholders in London.[64] In 1616, the governor received from the new company

> a base coin . . . whereby you may give to such men their weekly wages . . . with which coin it shall be lawful and free for them to buy any provisions out of the store or any fish, corn, tools or any other thing in the islands where they can get the same. And to that end you shall proclaim the said coin to be current to pass freely from man to man.[65]

The Bermuda Company thought that a little, isolated faraway community did not need precious metal. The company's commitment that its "store"—the only regular supplier of European goods—would accept this intrinsically useless coin was a critical feature. Thus, the first English coin of the New World relied not on intrinsic value but on a closed circuit, centered in a monopoly that both issued the money and accepted it in its store.

There is scant evidence that the coins circulated. John Smith wrote about company workers' compensation in 1616: "Besides meat, drink, and clothes, they had for a time a certain kind of brass money with a hog on the one side, in memory of the abundance of hogs [that] was found at their first landing." Smith or someone else added that this coin "was, in a scoff, termed by the people hog money."[66] (Less than a hundred such coins, in fact made from bronze, have survived. Denominations are two-, three-, six-, and twelvepence.[67])

Why did the coins fail in the long run? First, the scheme was optional, as the default arrangement was for workers to receive tobacco dividends rather than fixed wages in coin. Second, tobacco crowded out all alternatives as in Virginia—aided by the company that sometimes demanded to be paid in tobacco.[68] Third, token copper farthings had failed in England a few years earlier.

As tobacco became the main money, those with monopolistic power— the alcohol seller, the ferryman, the minister—still demanded precious-metal coins.[69] The government paid such coins only to finders of the only exceptional natural resource—stinky, expensive ambergris.[70] Export of coin and gold was restricted because paying for imported alcohol in coin resulted in the utter ransack of these islands of the small store of coin they formerly had and the overthrow of commerce and trade amongst us the inhabitants through want thereof, as we feel by daily and woeful experience.[71]

While Virginia was a disastrous battleground with Indians and tropical diseases, the more peaceful Bermuda proved that many features of English credit could be replicated in a colony: bills, assignations, setoffs, trilateral debt settlements, and debtors' prison.[72] There may even have been public-finance inventions when the governor issued personal bills to public workers (a later tax gave him tobacco to redeem his bills), and taxpayers were allowed to issue bills to the treasury if they were short of tobacco.[73]

The Separatists of Plymouth

English Separatist exiles in Leiden partnered with English merchants to fund their relocation to America. They established Plymouth in 1620 as a partial commune, but privatized agriculture in 1623.[74] Privatization created opportunities for internal trade, while the dominance of families could have implied high demand for money, except that the Separatists had humble material demands.[75] Maize was first treated as a commodity, but soon became the unit of account and medium of paying taxes, peaking as money in 1624. Governor William Bradford noted:

> They began now highly to prize corn as more precious than silver, and those that had some to spare began to trade one with another for small things, by the quart, pottle, and peck, etc.; for money they had none, and if any had, corn was preferred before it.[76]

Soon monetary units of account made a comeback and dominated, while maize continued dominating as physical money. There were occasional transactions in which the medium of payment also served as the unit of account—coin, maize, cattle, beaver fur, or Virginian tobacco.[77]

The monetary legacy of Plymouth's Separatists was separating the unit of account from physical money. In England, that was common only in agricultural rents, and that was the Separatists' background. Their agricultural economy generalized the separation and took it to a new level.

The separation of the spoken word from the physical item was natural to all English people, who often said "pound" without there being a coin called pound, or said "shilling" while giving a bill instead of a coin.

The few Separatists could establish long-term credit with their literate church "brethren," in writing or otherwise. It was not necessarily a problem that most Plymouth colonists were non-Separatist employees of the English merchants, because law enforcement and the cold calculation of reputation could work just as well, especially in a tiny, isolated, stable community. Credit was made more feasible when starvation ended, and there was indeed credit at least at the community's storehouse.[78]

No great thoughts on money could be expected from farmers who generalized the most primitive form of payment in English society. Only their leader, William Brewster, was a gentleman. But in retrospect, we could expect more from them. They had lived in Leiden, where paper money had been printed in the famous 1574 siege. Could their printer Edward Winslow and soldier Miles Standish not hear about it while living there? How about the nearby Bank of Amsterdam? They did adopt Dutch institutions they liked.[79] Perhaps the convertible siege money and merchants' bank in a world of gold and silver coins seemed too different from their circumstances to imitate.

The elite developed expertise in trade in order to survive, and so, by 1628, Bradford, Brewster, Winslow, and Standish designated themselves "merchants."[80] The staple product they shipped to Europe was beaver fur for the hat industry. They obtained it from Indians in northern areas, in exchange for nearby wampum—the Long Island version of Virginia's roanoke seashell beads.[81] There is no record of wampum being used within the colony during that decade. Plymouth learned about wampum's utility from its Dutch neighbors.

Seashells in New Netherland

The United Provinces granted New Netherland to its West India Company. From 1623, the company colonized the Hudson River with trading posts in New Amsterdam on Manhattan Island and Fort Orange (today's Albany) upstream close to beaver sources. As with roanoke, colonists thought wampum had already functioned as intra-Indian money. New Netherland's chief merchant Isaack de Rasieres provided the first detailed report, in the 1620s: Indians "consider it as valuable as we do money since one can buy with it everything they have."[82]

The colonists bought land, fur, and food from Indians. Manhattan was "purchased . . . for the value of 60 guilders," but it is unknown what objects were given in return. In other transactions, the Dutch gave cloth, metal tools, glass beads—and wampum. How did the Dutch obtain that wampum? In some cases, they traded tools for it.[83] Wampum thus circulated back and forth from Indians to Dutch and back. Northern tribes near Fort Orange were given wampum for furs, and de Rasieres taught Plymouth to do the same in northern New England.[84]

Inside the colony, the fur traders were fed by local farmers. The latter were also allowed to sell food surpluses to company workers. There is no information on how transactions were made within the colony, but the presence of regular money ("geld") was noted.[85] Wampum probably did not yet circulate within the colony (de Rasieres would have reported it).

Beavers in Canada

New France was a similar collection of trading posts of beaver furs, but it relied on food shipments from France. It was organized in two jurisdictions: Canada on the Saint Lawrence River, and Acadia (today's Nova Scotia, New Brunswick, and Maine). Even though only one distant tribe was known to have used fur as money, fur became full-fledged money in Indian–French relations. Indians gave fur for manufactures, food, and political support, and in unilateral payments. It was the unit of account in the fur trade and other transactions. It circulated back to Indians when the French obtained from them food and made unilateral payments (presents) to Indians.[86]

With less than a hundred inhabitants, Canada needed an internal medium of exchange only because the inhabitants belonged to different groups: old and new chartered companies, two missionary orders, a royally appointed government, and private colonists. Fur was the money among them all, and with European ships, generally used to buy manufactures, food, and travel to France. Although the company had there a stock of coin, only one coin transaction was documented—and the unit of account was fur.[87] Even the Scotsman David Kirke, who occupied Canada in 1629 as part of the Thirty Years' War, treated fur as money.

He gave the colonists food for the journey to France in exchange for fur, which all recognized as the most important local property.[88]

A Theoretical Reappraisal: Follow the Money

There was considerable variation among the colonies surveyed: English, Dutch, or French; owned by kings, courtiers, or companies; with or without an assembly; starting communally or not; situated from the frozen to the tropics; with populations of dozens to thousands; with or without a coinage privilege. All this variation did not matter for money. Where information is available, a colony's main harvest became its internal physical money and usually also its unit of account: beaver fur in Canada, fish in Newfoundland, maize in Plymouth, tobacco in Virginia and the southern islands. Monetary items that were considered valuable only to Indians—copper and seashell beads—did not (yet) circulate within colonies as far as we know.

Every colony started with little coin, because individual colonists did not bring much coin. There was nobody around to buy from (except Indians, who preferred other objects), and most colonists worked for the same company or cooperative. The many servants were too poor to bring any coin. But why did the problem remain? The great variety of different types of commodity money in America has long been noticed by economic historians. Following the colonists' complaints, scholars have attributed this practice to a chronic shortage of coins. That shortage was caused, so it is argued, by a deficit in the balance of trade: the colonies exported too little and imported too much.[89] The colonists found themselves in a Stone Age environment, and were utterly desperate in their demand for basic manufactured European goods—especially clothes and iron tools—and sometimes food. Their export of products such as tobacco and fur was not enough to pay for imported goods, so they settled the deficit with coin. Then there was no coin left for internal trade within each colony.

The economic historian Farley Grubb recently explained why coin was used so much in buying imports. Think of the individual colonist's dilemma, of what to do with a coin he has. He can buy with it either a local good or an imported good. Grubb shows that it could be optimal to use the coin for an imported good because a local good could be obtained through barter, especially "efficient barter" of a store's book credit.[90] While a random visiting European ship might never be seen again and so would demand finalizing a transaction on the spot with coin, a neighbor would be there for the long run, happy with a later setoff.

But if the colonists were the ones who chose to send the coins away, why did they complain about it? When one colonist decided to use coin to buy from a ship, he took into account only how this would affect himself. But in taking that coin out of the local economy, he took it out, in fact, from an indefinite amount of consecutive transactions that this coin could have facilitated in the local economy. In economics, this is called an *externality*—one person's action influences others' well-being without it being priced and traded in the market. A modern example would be a driver's contribution to a traffic jam he complains about.

The colonists found themselves in the situation analyzed in chapter 2: so little coin that, at any moment, many didn't have any at all. Could prices have gone down and solved the problem? The data do *not* show prices and wages clustered at the lowest denominations of fractions of a penny. Far from it. Why didn't prices decline to that level? One possible reason, following chapter 2, is the indivisibility of coin, which distorts the quantity theory of money. A colonial mint, reminting European coins into the smallest denominations, might have solved the problem. But the pre-1620 colonies that got a coinage license were physically and financially unable to pull it off. Only the relatively peaceful Bermuda had such coins, and those were probably sent from England. Most charters granted after 1620, when the Crown started losing control at home, were no longer generous with this part of the royal prerogative.[91] Without a mint, colonists could have broken every coin available into fractions, as happened in Virginia. But it was impossible with simple tools to go below one-eighth of a coin.

Another reason is that the quantity theory of money—connecting prices to the amount of money—is not an automatic mechanism. It works through the presence of shoppers and their money in shops. If the amount of money is low, fewer shoppers show up and/or each shopper brings less money, and this forces prices down. Colonists could have stayed home, frustrated without coins, waiting for prices to decline (probably in vain, because of coins' indivisibility).[92] But they outsmarted the quantity theory. Not content with the amount of coin and its indivisibility, they brought to the shops alternatives: commodity money or barter, with or without credit. However inconvenient physically, that kept the demand in shops high and, as Grubb put it, created "a price floor" that prevented prices from declining.[93] The quantity theory of money probably did not fail in America, if we count not only coins but alternatives too.[94] The colonists' ingenious response to indivisibility of coins, though, locked them into a monetary equilibrium of awkward moneys.

CHAPTER SIX

The Puritan Exodus, 1629–1640

General Features

Then the Lord said unto Moses, go in unto Pharaoh, and tell him, Thus saith the Lord God
of the Hebrews, Let my people go, that they may serve me.
  —Exodus 9:1, King James Version

Within a decade, a new group of colonies emerged in New England,
led by Massachusetts. On average, the new colonists were more
affluent, educated, and religious than previous ones. The basic constitutional and demographic structure of Massachusetts was established
in this decade.[1] This included an awkward corporate structure, a fragile
state of near independence from England, a lay leadership knowledge-
able in law and commerce, an intellectual religious elite engaged in economic policy, an accountable and partially representative legislature,
executive committees with checks and balances, and an open mind for
adaptation to the new circumstances. These features are covered here
and would be relevant for the monetary invention of 1690. (The search
for a convenient money began in this decade; this topic, along with methods of war finance, is deferred until the next chapter.)

Corporate America

The constitutional and religious troubles of late 1620s England, together
with Plymouth's success, led some Puritans to consider moving to New
England. The western ports' investors of the 1606 Virginia charter had

been rechartered as the Council for New England just before the Separatists squatted on their land. Later, Robert Rich, the Earl of Warwick, the chief pro-Puritan noble, served as president of that council. He somehow got these Puritans a council grant and then a royal charter in 1629.[2] Within days, Charles dissolved Parliament and began his Personal Rule, putting Warwick's achievement at risk. "The Governor and Company of the Massachusetts Bay in New England" would spend enormous amounts of time, energy, money, and legal skill, for decades to come, in order to preserve the charter.

The company had a General Court of shareholders to make laws, appoint officers, and annually elect the Court of Assistants, which ran the company. That latter court included the governor, the deputy governor, and eighteen assistants. The company was granted most of the usual rights of colonial charters, including making laws "not contrary or repugnant to the laws and statutes" of England, and exporting to the colony everything "necessary" for the colonists' "use" and "for trade with the people there" (perhaps including coin).[3] Like other late charters, it lacked a coinage privilege.

Soon the company, led by London merchants, made an unprecedented decision in the history of English colonization: transfer the government and charter to America. Most grantees and shareholders stayed in England. In 1630, Governor John Winthrop and Deputy Governor Thomas Dudley led a few assistants and seven hundred emigrants to Massachusetts Bay. More than ten thousand people followed them that decade.

Demographics

Civil Leadership

The Court of Assistants that moved to America was unimpressive, having neither nobles nor important merchants. The only knight, Sir Richard Saltonstall, unknightly fled back after the first winter. The court was composed of gentlemen experienced in law, business, and administration. Winthrop, a barrister's son, was a Cambridge dropout who later studied law. He was lord of a manor and justice of the peace of his community. Winthrop was an attorney at a special royal court in London, and wrote bills for parliamentary committees. For the following two decades he would dominate the Massachusetts government. Dudley was a clerk to a judge and later the steward of a deeply indebted earl. The assistants had similar education and experience, and one had been a member of Parliament.[4] These serious men organized colonization better than in most colonies, and had only one year of hardship; they were not Plymouth's amateurs. Their main advantage over London merchants who controlled earlier colonial companies was their presence on the ground and their noncommercial mission. They went to build their own durable home, not to make a quick profit.

There was a promising young generation of assistants. John Winthrop Jr. was a brilliant polymath. He studied at Trinity College, Dublin, studied law in London, served in the La Rochelle expedition, and was an amateur chemist, alchemist, and engineer.[5] Dudley's son-in-law, Simon Bradstreet, studied at Cambridge. Winthrop and Dudley became relatives after their children's marriage, initiating a custom of elite inbreeding. Little social mobility at the top joined with the customary English deference, and the nonmigration of the nobility, to enable a few gentlemen dynasties to play the role of nobility.[6] Toward 1690, we will meet two of John Winthrop Jr.'s sons, another grandson of John Winthrop Sr.; Dudley's son; and the elderly Simon Bradstreet himself, all playing key roles.

Religious Leadership

The emigrating ministers had mostly studied at Cambridge, and some had taught there.[7] New England Puritans differed from most Puritans in that the pillar of their theology, polity, church structure, and even militia was the contract. The covenant of grace postulated a contract between God and every person, promising success in life and the afterlife in return for faith. Pastors regularly used contractual legal terminology: *covenant, agreement, compact, engagement, treaty, indentures, contractor, bonds, mutual obligations, surety, suit, written and sealed.* God's debt was likened to a monetary debt that must be repaid. From this theology they derived a political contract between government and people ruled by their own consent (at the colony level and town level), and a contract between members of each church. Such a Congregational church, which elected its officers, was a completely autonomous unit. This structure also inspired a covenanted militia in which soldiers nominated their officers.[8] Perhaps this contractual foundation of emigration and settlement gave an extra moral value to contracted debts. It may be relevant for the invention of a money that relied only on public debts.

The leading ministers were formidable intellectuals. Though barred from civil government, lay leaders regularly consulted them on key matters such as constitution and war, because the only goal of the colony was to serve as a religious refuge.[9] Ministers were also engaged in economic issues. For example, excessive prices and wages bothered them as "great dishonor of God, the scandal of the gospel," so a committee of twenty-nine legislators and ministers considered the problem. John Cotton, the clergy's star, instructed merchants how to price goods and loans ethically.[10] A lawyer's son, he drafted a legal code for the court. After presenting the form of government, his document has four economic chapters before the criminal chapter with those biblical death penalties that Puritans cherished.[11] Some ministers understood investments and financial instruments.[12] Hugh Peter, stepfather-in-law of John Winthrop Jr., exceeded them all: before and after his appointment as Salem's pastor, he promoted fisheries, shipbuilding, and home production of goods during winter, and he was involved in international trade.[13]

The presence of dozens of university graduates and ministers on a religious mission resulted in the ambitious plan to establish a college to educate the next generation of ministers and lay elite, "not only in divinity but in other arts and sciences and in law also, for that would be very material for the welfare of our commonwealth."[14] The quick founding of the college, with a library and a printing press, put Massachusetts decades ahead of other English colonies. The press's first products were the freeman's oath, an almanac for farmers and mariners, and a religious book.[15]

Cotton's code punished witchcraft—"fellowship by covenant with a familiar spirit"—by death. He and Winthrop suspected female religious opponents of having connections to witchcraft, and attributed their "monstrous" newborns to their "monstrous errors" in religion.[16] Winthrop was curious and superstitious about other unusual natural phenomena—he believed in cruentation and documented others' reports of strange lights in the sky.[17]

Land of the Free

Massachusetts's colonists were the first to have a majority of middle-class families—headed by gentlemen, yeomen, and affluent artisans.

FIGURE 6.1 New England in 1640.

They were literate and numerate. Extended families and networks of friends arrived together, often following their ministers. The immigrants spread out across Massachusetts Bay and later across New England, creating tiny colonies such as Connecticut and Rhode Island. In New Hampshire and Maine there were also Anglican colonists sent by proprietors of the Council for New England (figure 6.1). The dominant form of settlement was a Plymouth-like village centered around the meeting house, which was used for both religious and civil gatherings. Strong community spirit was maintained by regulating town size, visitors, and real estate sales to outsiders.[18]

The middle-class immigrants liquidated their England estates and used the proceeds to pay for their initial expenses in America. Once these resources were gone, they had to find a way to buy English goods.

Their customary lifestyle implied high demand for high-quality domestic manufactures and food, but they had neither an easy staple product like tobacco nor as much beaver as other colonies. Ships bringing the first immigrants left Massachusetts empty.[19]

The colonists found three solutions: First, they built houses, cleared fields, raised grain and livestock, and sold them to newcomers who arrived gradually. The most desired English goods were therefore agricultural equipment, consisting of items from spades to windmills.[20] Most farmwork was done by family members. Servants (including very few Africans) were only a third of the workforce.[21] Second, Massachusetts became a trade center, connected to all other English people in the Atlantic—in Ireland, Virginia, Bermuda, the Caribbean colonies, privateer ships, even the new Catholic refuge of Maryland. Ships began returning from Massachusetts to Europe with products of other colonies.[22] Third, new fishing towns harvested the Newfoundland waters, and Massachusetts sent the processed fish to Iberia, where Catholic dietary restrictions assured permanent high demand. The merchants received in return wine or fine wool, which they sold in England, and used the proceeds to buy manufactures.[23]

Constitution

The immigrants' tasks included preserving their charter from a hostile king, and modifying the corporate structure into an accountable, effective government. A key tool for the latter task was the committee.

Home of the Brave

Unlike earlier colonies, Massachusetts was completely independent in church and nearly independent in state. Physically separated by three thousand miles from the Church of England, the colonists converted in a practical sense from Puritans to Separatists. They neither saw nor would obey a bishop ever again. Unlike Plymouth, Massachusetts thought that religious independence required constitutional independence. As the king's father put it: "No bishop, no king" (chapter 4's epigraph). The only thing Massachusetts wanted from the king was to be left alone. To maintain independence, the charter was followed when not too inconvenient, in letter if not in spirit.[24]

The Council for New England deposed its president, the Earl of War-wick, and cried foul about the charter. A subcommittee of the Privy Council, chaired by the terrorizing archbishop of Canterbury, was authorized to revoke charters and appoint colonial governors. Massachusetts responded with military preparations to defend itself against an armed English invasion. Instead came a torrent of legal threats, orders, and commissions. The lawyerly elite found technical reasons in their defense, and practically ignored everything, even a message that the charter was revoked. Massachusetts bought time until the Scottish rebellion distracted England.[25]

Accountability

With almost all shareholders staying in England, the General Court became identical to the Court of Assistants—governor, deputy governor, and assistants. These men held all the executive, legislative, and judicial powers. They became known as magistrates, since each one was also given judicial authority in his community. Though up for election every year, they practically became an aristocracy. Inspired by the English constitutional tradition of checks and balances between Lords and Commons, the absent shareholders in the General Court were replaced by two deputies from each town.[26] (For most purposes of this book, it does not matter whether something was ordered by the General Court or the Court of Assistants [a.k.a. council], so references will be made to "the court.")

Magistrates and deputies were elected by residents who were made freemen of the colony. The novelty was that only male members of churches could become freemen. One was admitted a church member only if he or she proved to the congregation to have had a genuine transformative experience of faith and lived a "saintly" life.[27] There was no priority in church membership for rich merchants over poor laborers.[28] The freemen were a minority; by 1640, when there were nine thousand residents, the freemen list had a thousand names, including many who died or left.[29] However, most of the nine thousand residents were women, children, and servants—who could vote neither there nor in any other contemporary English jurisdiction. Therefore, the freemen were a very significant percentage of the free men, meaning that Massachusetts was more democratic than most places. On economic issues, court members were far more accountable to the population than in England's wealth-based representative system.[30]

Another key feature of the Massachusetts constitution was the town meeting, held in the meetinghouse, which mostly served as a church. There was no mayor, but each town was managed by annually elected selectmen. Complaints and ideas about any issue could have been raised at the town meeting—by anyone—and the message conveyed by the deputies to the court. Nobody was banished, silenced, or punished over economic ideas, as they were for religious and political dissent.

As soon as the freemen sent deputies to the General Court in 1634, legislation became more attuned to the needs of the lower free classes (e.g., a property tax rather than a head tax), and some orders started with "whereas complaint has been made" to show attention to popular will and to justify legislation to constituents.[31] The deputies pushed for a code of laws to preserve people's rights against magisterial whims. One attempt to write it started from below, with each town's freemen submitting proposals. The court sent a draft code back to all freemen for consideration.[32] This was unthinkable in other contemporary English jurisdictions. Overall, the elected leadership was highly accountable to a significant part of the population, and was expected to solve their problems.

Committees

One critical tool of the Massachusetts government that historians have completely overlooked is the committee—surely the least exciting of topics. To remind, and to motivate the reader, this topic is relevant because the 1690 money would be issued by a committee with political checks and balances. Moreover, this feature is present today, as the quantity of money is determined by the world-famous Federal Open Market Committee and its many imitators around the world.

Like other commercial companies, the Massachusetts Bay Company appointed committees while in England, because the Court of Assistants was either too large or not representative enough for some purposes.[33] In America, the transformation of the company into a self-governing colony required a permanent administrative apparatus that was missing from the charter.[34] The solution was found in the routine creation of ad hoc committees for many issues.[35] Such committees were also employed by towns, judicial courts, and churches.[36]

Court-appointed committees had several basic, lasting features. First, they can be categorized to four types. Most were executive committees, having a specific, important operational task to perform, such as preparing for an expected English invasion. An administrative committee was similar, but the job was less important and required far less discretion (e.g., paying creditors from an estate). There were also advisory committees and investigative committees as in England (p. 27).[37]

Second, committees were prominent in military emergencies, because then the nakedness of the central government was fully revealed. As a typical early modern state, the central government normally did very little, relegating most affairs to town, church, and the private economy. The war committee preparing for invasion was aided by other committees that fortified and armed the colony.[38]

Third, committee members could be either magistrates, deputies, or other freemen. The typical committee was "mixed," to use a later term that would describe the General Court—that is, the typical committee included members from at least two of these groups. Deputies, however, dominated committees.[39] Compared with magistrates, they were numerous and were off duty when court was not in session. Perhaps they used their power in court to force their appointments to most committees, balancing the magistrates' legislative power with their own involvement in executive issues. Magistrates dominated committees only on critical issues such as war and the college. Compared with unelected freemen, deputies were considered more capable, they were known in person to the magistrates with whom they sat at the unicameral court, and they usually had executive experience in their towns.[40] The frequent use of *former* deputies in committees is consistent with this explanation.[41]

Fourth, half of the unelected committee members would soon be elected deputies.[42] They were political startups, and committee membership became an ordinary early step in a political career. There they got a first chance to show their skills to their superiors, who in turn acted as mentors, through the intimacy of committee work. Fifth, executive and administrative committees often acted by majority rule. This allowed a committee to function when there was no consensus or when not all members were present. Several signatures on legal documents issued by a committee could prevent counterfeiting and corruption.[43] Sixth, members were typically listed in the commission according to rank, similar to attendance lists of court meetings: governor, deputy governor, treasurer (these three with their titles), other assistants, deputies, and other freemen.[44]

*   *   *

In early 1640, Massachusetts was a successful, booming, full-fledged colony. Its nineteen villages and towns included a Cambridge with a college, a printing press, and a library. It was already an exceptional colony.[45] Massachusetts's offshoots were in the miniature, Plymouth-like phase. The Puritans were bold adapters and improvisers who used trial and error to figure out a way forward in the strange, new land. The changes to the General Court and the reliance on committees were prime examples, but it is surprising that people who made the drastic step of leaving their homeland only to have their religious rituals just right were content with improvised lay preaching when ministers were missing.[46] Less adventurous was their imitation of older, experienced Plymouth, as in the form of independent churches and the ineligibility of ministers to serve in civil government.[47] Massachusetts's contact with other colonies was far less influential.

Learning from Indians was more difficult than elsewhere due to the arrogance of the gentlemen and ministers who doubted the humanity of these "beastlike men"[48] to the extent that they questioned the applicability of adultery and marriage to Anglo–Indian relations.[49] Their missionary company seal depicted an Indian saying, "Come over and help us" (based on Acts 16:9)—not "Come over and we will help you."[50] The colonists Anglicized almost every Indian name of place and chief, while the charter's awkward "Massachusetts" was usually substituted with "New England."[51] Winthrop was especially prejudiced against Indian ways. In his journal, the use of Indian things usually foreshadowed calamities, perhaps because his son Henry drowned while trying to catch a canoe.[52] However, necessity forced colonists to adopt Indian methods and objects: the canoe, the wigwam, small raiding parties at war,[53] and especially "Indian corn" (maize).

CHAPTER SEVEN

Massachusetts Takes the Monetary Lead, 1630–1640

And Abraham weighed to Ephron the silver, which he had named in the audience of the sons of Heth, four hundred shekels of silver, current money with the merchant.
　—Genesis 23:16, King James Version

The many trials and errors of 1630s Massachusetts included currency, credit, and public finance. The educated, experienced immigrants, equipped with political independence and serving in an accountable legislature, put Massachusetts beyond the primitive improvisations of earlier colonies. Virginia also tried to solve its currency problem in various ways, all of which failed.

Massachusetts: Juggling Moneys

Before departure from England, the emigrants' leadership surely knew about monetary improvisation in the colonies. They could read John Smith's books on Virginia and Bermuda—and talk to him (he was one degree of separation from them).[1] A former tobacco planter from Barbados sailed with Winthrop's fleet: his son Henry.[2] By the time they reached America, the emigrants could learn more from meetings with shipmasters coming from Virginia and going to Scottish-occupied Canada.[3]

The colonists' lifestyle implied high demand for goods and services, and their families required a large variety of goods and services. On the supply side, there was higher ability of producing such variety than in other colonies: more than two dozen professions are cited in Boston, the only town for full-time artisans.[4] All this implied a low likelihood of a double coincidence of wants, which in turn implied that barter on the spot was difficult. This gave a critical role to money and credit. Money was needed most in Boston. It became New England's hub; many non-residents passed through on their way to and from England and other colonies. Special courts were established to handle the commercial disputes these strangers were involved in.[5] They could not rely on credit, and so more coin was used there than elsewhere.

The colony's near independence allowed its leaders to solve the money problem as they saw fit, without asking permission from anyone in England—except for issuing coin. Issuing coin would have been repugnant to the laws of England and thus a charter violation. The colony had an advantage over earlier corporate colonies in that the leaders were in place to experience the money problem themselves. Even if Winthrop could buy everything on his personal credit, the court included humble deputies who could not. Simple farmers and artisans could complain to their neighbors—towns' deputies—about the difficulties of shopping that they encountered, or that their disenfranchised wives and servants encountered.[6] Massachusetts was influenced by Plymouth's combination of monetary units of account with grain as the key physical currency. But Massachusetts employed a much larger variety of alternatives.

Unit of Account

The court denominated almost all payments in monetary units (with exceptions mostly in 1630[7]). No law stated this general principle, but the court may have inspired it through monetary interaction with the private economy: taxes; fines; sales and rents of public land; salaries and fees of officials; debts and other payments made to the government or by it; bonds to appear in court, for good behavior, or for paying fines; rewards for killing wolves and foxes and for capturing stray cattle; maximum wages and prices; compensations and other payments ruled in civil and criminal cases; and valuations of property.

The court went out of its way to keep monetary units. Taxes and fines imposed on trade of beaver, wampum, and maize were surely paid in these objects, but monetary units were specified.[8] Winthrop's journal and court records reported monetary units regarding their transactions in tobacco colonies and with Indians, even though these were surely conversions from the units of tobacco, beaver, and wampum actually used in such transactions.[9] The motivation was probably to not succumb to what the proud Puritans perceived as barbarism. Towns denominated in grain only the salaries of the most inferior public workers, cow keepers.[10] Monetary units also dominated the private economy, in sales of real estate, cattle, and other commodities, in wages and lawyers' fees, and in bills, bonds, mortgages, other debts, accounts, and wills.[11]

Coin

The colonists thought the charter's implicit license to export coin to the colony was sufficient. In the beginning, bringing coin was useless, as there were neither shops nor goods to buy.[12] Emigrants mostly brought goods for their use and for sale. Winthrop—always careful when writing to England—thrice instructed John Jr. to bring coin for the family's use, but only as a residual after packing goods.[13]

In the second half of the decade, as shops opened and perhaps customs enforcement proved to be ineffectual, emigrants brought coin to buy everything they needed.[14] Veteran colonists used this coin to buy English goods from merchants, who sent it to England to buy more manufactures. Coin did not stay for long, and perhaps some pieces went back and forth on the same ship. Another permanent source of coin was founded by a privateer who spent in the colony the standard coin of the Atlantic—the Spanish silver "piece of eight."[15]

Coin had supreme legal status: the court allowed discharging all debts in grain, but not if "money" was "expressly named" in the contract; deputies were paid in coin rather than grain to cover their expenses; and exporting coin to England and to Indian society was restricted.[16] But the amount of coin was not enough. Coin was little used in public payments—mostly in officials' salaries in 1630. Only once did the colony ask for pay "in money," and even that was optional (the alternative was a pig). Boston made coin optional in its land sales.[17] In the private sector, coin was present and used, and was expected to be available.[18] Many other references to "money," rather than "in money," loosely meant "funds" or "wealth."

Commodity Moneys

The immigrants were practical adapters, so the shortage of coin prompted them to find imperfect alternatives. Just as they allowed lay

preaching as substitute to formal preachers when needed, they allowed
humbler forms of money as substitute to formal money (coin). In contrast with tobacco colonies, there was no trivial choice, so a large variety
of experiments was made.

GRAIN. As in earlier colonies, the initial subsistence economy raised
grain to the monetary forefront. As in Plymouth, grain remained dominant as a physical medium in the long run. In 1631, the first legal tender
law stated: "Corn shall pass for payment of all debts at the usual rate it is
sold for, except money or beaver be expressly named."[19] The "debts" certainly included taxes, but the "usual rate" [i.e., price] was so volatile as
to cause significant losses to one party or another.[20] This probably motivated a more detailed legal tender law for taxes, enacted shortly after
deputies were added to the court: it became "lawful for any man to pay
his rate [i.e., tax] to the Treasurer in merchantable corn of the country
at 5 shillings the bushel."[21] Every year a new tax was enacted and re-
set these official prices for grain, presumably somewhat related to market conditions, but still great losses were incurred.[22] A 1640 law started
a customary distinction between types of "corn" (maize, wheat, rye).[23]
Such laws would become the most permanent monetary feature in court
records—until paper money replaced grain in 1691. As the historian
Curtis Nettels remarked long ago, these laws were important for establishing a link between money and taxes: "There was always a local demand for commodity money commensurate with the fiscal needs of the
colonial government; hence a person could receive a designated product
with the assurance of disposing it again in payment of taxes."[24]

A perennial problem was who would bear the costs of transportation
and storage of grain, and this impacted the timing of tax payments.[25]
Grain quality differed vastly across time and place.[26] The standard of
"merchantable corn" in taxes, known from earlier colonies, was enforced by tax-collecting town constables. This threshold probably influenced the minimal quality that sellers agreed to receive in private
transactions. What the treasury accepted could therefore matter for the
private economy.

The decisive evidence on the private monetary use of grain comes
from Winthrop's complaint during a 1640 crisis that suddenly "corn
would buy nothing" and "it would not pass for any commodity: if one offered a shop keeper corn for any thing, his answer would be, he knew not

what to do with it. So for laborers and artificers."[27] Winthrop thus implicitly stated that grain was a general medium of exchange in the 1630s.

BEAVER FUR. Beaver was supposed to be the staple good as in all northern colonies.[28] It was prominent in interaction with Indians throughout the decade.[29] It naturally became an early commodity money, and the court ordered that "merchantable beaver shall pass at 10 shillings the pound."[30] Three orders mentioned above regarding coin—exception to the law making grain legal tender for debts, deputies' pay, and export restrictions—actually used the term *money or beaver*, giving this pair the same supreme monetary status.

The only strong evidence of beaver's actual monetary function is Winthrop's complaint during the 1640 crisis that "men could not pay their debts, for no money nor beaver were to be had."[31] The only contemporary evidence is that constables held small fur stocks, presumably collected in taxes.[32] Furs were apparently indivisible in the sense that merchants exporting them to Europe would reject their bits and pieces. They were therefore more fit to discharge obligations than to be used in daily shopping or paying daily wages.

CATTLE. Other than coin, cattle was the most important type of movable property. Bovines particularly were the perfect machines, turning useless grass into beef, milk, hide, manure, and ploughing energy. Their economic importance was overwhelming, and cattle defined the categories of rich, middle class, and poor.[33] Cattle holdings were too indivisible to be everyday money—that is, two halves of a cow are not of the same value as a living cow. Therefore, when estates were liquidated, cattle were sold like other assets.[34] But cattle do appear as large payments, sometime as an explicit alternative to coin: an annual salary, payment of an accumulated debt of the colony to Winthrop, land sales, wills, and a merchant's bill.[35] In 1640, six types of cattle were made eligible for tax payments, but each animal had to be appraised in its town by a committee.[36]

LAND. The normal way for individuals to obtain land was through a grant by their town.[37] The court regularly granted land to most magistrates (or their family members) and to many ministers and deputies.[38] Unlike land attached to offices in Virginia and Bermuda, these were personal grants of permanent ownership, because Massachusetts public servants were there to stay. No explanation was given in court records for most grants, it being obvious that nonsalaried court members deserved compensation for their work and that ministers (paid salaries by towns) deserved extra encouragement. Therefore, grants were given even to prospective assistants for future service.[39] Land was thus a special medium of exchange used by the government to buy public service. Grants usually had a definite size in acres, but the location was often left open, making their value highly uncertain.

UNCOINED METAL. Some uncoined gold and silver was present.[40] Probably thanks to a privateer who brought "plate" in 1639, the following annual tax law stated that "in payment silver plate should pass at 5 shillings the ounce."[41] It is important to realize that "payment" then mostly meant "discharge [of] a debt," not a spot transaction.[42] The court would have minted that plate into coin, making it a more convenient money, if permitted by English law.

In 1635, this appeared in the court records:

> It is ordered, that hereafter farthings shall not pass for current pay.
>
> It is likewise ordered, that musket bullets, of a full bore, shall pass currently for a farthing a piece, provided that no man be compelled to take above 12 pence at a time in them.

Winthrop's journal reported these odd orders but, uncharacteristically, did not explain them.[43] Why? The answer, as will become usual here, relates to England. The preceding year, the public in England rejected farthing token coins of the king's crony more than ever before, because of counterfeiters and speculators.[44] Massachusetts therefore rejected the coins too. However, afraid to mint its own substitute tokens as many businesses in England had long done illegally, the court found an alternative.

Bullets were easy to make by molding lead into balls of standardized size to fit muskets. Molds were probably common in the colony. The transformation of lead lumps into bullets and back was so easy that they were universally considered equivalent.[45] Lead had sufficient supply and demand regardless of its monetary use. Supply from England was matched by Massachusetts's demand as an armed society. Every man legally had to own a gun and twenty bullets;[46] this also helped recognition of that currency. Everyone knew what a proper bullet looked like, and nobody would accept a bad one that could lead to disaster. Therefore an official stamp authenticating the metal, as in a coin, was redundant.

The caution shown by both the colony (in not minting lead like the English public) and Winthrop (in not explaining these orders) was prudent enough for any time. It was even more justified by the timing— preparations for English invasion. There was no need to make England any more hostile. That emergency itself made bullets more important and accessible.[47] However, nothing was ever heard of the farthing tokens and the monetized bullets after that, perhaps because the traditional use of bullets soon helped Massachusetts obtain a better form of small change: wampum.

WAMPUM. Massachusetts was exposed to wampum in interaction with Indians and learned from Plymouth to use it to buy fur.[48] In 1634, a former Massachusetts colonist referred to Indians of Long Island Sound: "The northern, eastern, and western Indians fetch all their coin from these southern mint-masters."[49] In 1636, wampum suddenly appeared in several contexts: John Winthrop Jr. started sending wampum from Saybrook—a colony he ran in Long Island Sound—to business partners in Massachusetts; the court considered licensing the wampum-for-beaver trade with local Indians; and wampum was listed in the inventory of the wealthy widow Sarah Dillingham between stocks of coin.[50]

For this book, wampum is the most important of the types of money that emerged in the 1630s. The Puritans, like earlier colonists, could also learn from contact with a different culture that, contrary to conventional wisdom, money did not have to be made from metal.[51] The nineteenth-century historian Berthold Fernow called wampum "the first fiat money in the New World" because these beads were "intrinsically worthless representatives of money, not secured by valuable deposits." The historian Mark Peterson has similarly called it "fiduciary money."[52] From the colonists' subjective point of view, it was indeed as intrinsically useless as a piece of paper. To Indians, it was commodity money because they had alternative uses for it as jewelry, similar to how colonists viewed their own silver coins. But as Fernow noted, Massachusetts fur traders could not demand the wampum-issuing southern Indians to redeem wampum in fur; those Indians did not necessarily have furs, and they had no legal obligation to do so.

But Fernow was not entirely correct, since *northern* Indians did voluntarily redeem wampum with furs. That was enough for fur traders to value wampum. Since it also had good physical qualities as currency, and coins were missing in Massachusetts, wampum apparently began to be used between colonists. For Widow Dillingham, the expectation that some entity outside the colonists' market (i.e., northern Indian society) would always voluntarily convert wampum into beaver was good enough to accept it as money, even if it was intrinsically useless to her and everyone else she knew.[53] This was an advancement in monetary practice, created by accident through the interaction of societies that had different esthetical preferences. Nobody in England could learn such a lesson. The closest thing in England would be goldsmith-bankers' banknotes, but they did not yet exist (and would have huge denominations).

Murders of colonial fur traders by Indians in Long Island Sound escalated into a short war. In 1637, near the present-day romantic village of Mystic, Connecticut, forces torched a town of the Pequot tribe, killing hundreds of men, women, and children. The rest of the tribe was hunted down with the help of Massachusetts soldiers. The latter returned home with plundered wampum and wampum tributes given by intimidated tribes.[54] As Peterson observed, "it was no accident" that on the same year, Massachusetts made wampum an official, limited money, which "should pass at 6 a penny for any sum under 12 pence."[55] To be accurate, this happened three months after the soldiers returned, presumably because supply became sufficient. This law was perhaps in imitation of New Netherland and Plymouth, which may have had such laws earlier.[56] After the war, Massachusetts settled occupied Pequot land, perhaps partly for access to wampum shores.

After becoming an official money, wampum could teach the colonists another lesson. Some tax obligations, fines, and other debts to the colony were not in round shillings.[57] According to the wampum law, if debtors chose to make such payments partly in wampum, the treasury had to accept it. Then wampum could have been accepted in trade among colonists not only because of Indians but also because the treasury had to accept it at whatever value the legislature determined. The lesson: a subjectively intrinsically useless object, which nobody legally promises to redeem in metal, could circulate if accepted for taxes or other payments to the government. This lesson also could not be learned in England, and from 1690, Massachusetts would teach it to the rest of the world.

Credit and Its Settlement

The middle-class colonists had been accustomed to using all forms of credit on a regular basis in England, and they kept doing so in America, far more than in other colonies. The early records of the private economy are full of bills, bonds, book credit, and mortgages of land, houses, and cattle.[58] Merchants emerged as the lending class.[59] The legendary Puritan village was a cohesive community. It was a small, homogenous, stable, selective community, where the bulk of residents were landowning families and had higher life expectancy than those in southern colonies due to peace and nontropical climate.[60] In the best of times, community spirit was so strong as to approach what McCusker and Menard call "utopian communalism."[61] This was ideal for neighborly credit to function. The frontier environment did not diminish most formalities of English contract law: the elite, trained in law and commerce, kept doing what it knew, and contacts with England regarding estates and trade required continuous conformity with English law. This included the normal authentication procedures: contracts were indented, signed, sealed, and delivered in front of witnesses.[62]

Regarding public credit, the treasurer was considered, in his person, the colony's debtor for the tax proceeds he received and the colony's creditor for the expenses he made by court order. The town constable was in a similar position relative to the treasurer. The treasurer often spent his private funds for public purposes in anticipation of taxes, as did the rest of the elite.[63] There were so many public debts and credits that all debtors and creditors were referred to an accounting committee.[64] Some public debts, such as the cannoneer's salary, were unpaid for up to two years.[65] The court ordered towns to sell weapons to poor residents on credit.[66] In general, the "Governor and Company" used its legal right as a corporation to sign contracts, with all the formality of private contracts and more.[67]

Three devices of credit are particularly relevant in this book: setoff, trilateral settlement, and assigned bills. Setoffs were common practice in the colony's dealings with towns and individuals, saving transfers of money back and forth. The colony was owed taxes, fines, and other debts, and it set these off against various debts that it legally owed (including salaries and overtaxation), or that it gave by benevolence, to the same people or towns.[68]

The elite was familiar with bills of exchange, which were essential in removing their estates to America and for trade with England.[69] This perhaps contributed to the use of trilateral settlements of private debts within the colony.[70] More relevant are cases involving the treasury, especially when it stood between creditor and debtor: the debtor was ordered to deliver the funds directly to the creditor and leave the treasury out. This included directing tax funds straight from the collecting constable to a nearby creditor of the colony, as in England and Virginia.[71]

The English idea that any asset and legal right could be assigned to another—including a debt—was the background for Massachusetts's first monetary invention, in 1631: "Any bill assigned to another shall be good debt to the party to whom it is assigned."[72] In one line, centuries of cumbersome English legislation about formalities and assignation of different types of paper instruments were thrown out the window. *Any* bill could be used as private paper money. (England, you may remember, would not have such a law until 1704.) The order went further: "Such debts due upon bill shall be paid before any other."[73] This not only encouraged creditors to accept bills, but also allowed easy setoff of bills because they were all at the highest legal status (setoff is problematic with debts of different priority[74]). It was also ordered: "The party that gives such bills shall renew them upon demand & delivery in of the old bill."[75] The court, merely a year after coming to America, already understood the potential of transferable paper to replace coin, with each piece potentially circulating so much and for so long as to be worn out and in need of replacement.

If reputable men made bills in small, round amounts, these could function as private paper money, but there is no evidence of that happening. The very few known bills averaged above £25, and the smallest was £5. (For comparison, the maximum annual wage of laborers was £22.5.) These were mercantile and real estate transactions—which is why their existence was documented. Most amounts were not round. Some bills mentioned the creditor's "assignees," but there is no evidence of any bill being assigned.[76] It would be tedious and costly for the issuer to split any amount that happened to be agreed upon in a contract into small, round amounts. A printing press issuing small, preprinted forms, or bills, would be helpful for that; the first product of the Cambridge press—the freeman's oath—was exactly that (p. 72). But there is no evidence that small, private bills were printed. And why should have anyone thought of that? There was nothing like it in 1630s England.

Other Alternatives to Payment

The easiest way to avoid the money problem was autarky, and indeed initial food shortages and abundance of land turned nearly everyone into a farmer, at least part time. That unpaid cannoneer probably survived on that, which is consistent with his very low salary (£20 for three years).

Barter was common. Pay in salted fish, apples, pigs, planks, posts and rails, wine, labor, land (between private parties), and coats (to Indians) were documented too rarely to qualify as money.[77] As in earlier colonies, employers on farms often provided food and drink on the spot to hired labor, which was deducted from wages denominated in monetary units.[78]

Similar to barter was the public sector's levying of taxes in labor services to build officials' houses and town fortifications.[79] This reduced the amount of tax funds sent to the treasurer, who would have hired workers with those funds; but this medieval method (common in earlier colonies) blindly and inefficiently lumped together people of different skills and circumstances.

Summary: Early Massachusetts Money

In the context of religion in New England and Bermuda, the historian Charles Andrews wrote of "the influence of distance and the frontier environment" in generating "freedom from the restraints of a highly organized ritualistic body."[80] Such freedom was observed also in the constitutional structure of Massachusetts and in its monetary legislation. Beaver and grain were joined—in either law or practice—by bills, bullets, Indian jewelry, uncoined precious metal, and in a limited way also cattle and land. The emigrants who were most inspired by Genesis 17 on the covenant of grace found themselves in the monetary world of the Old Testament, where grain, jewelry, uncoined precious metal, and cattle had functioned as money.[81]

To make the vast monetary experiment of the 1630s comprehensible, the discussion here has separated the various currencies and alternatives as much as possible. In reality these were confusingly intertwined in this decade of trial and error. In 1630, the colony offered its officials not only salaries in monetary units but also housing, grain, cattle, or fish. The 1640 tax law distinguished between types of grain and added silver plate and cattle. Boston sold land for "corn, cattle, or moneys." An estate's debts could be paid in labor or pigs.[82]

Another step forward was the multifaceted exploitation of credit—with setoffs, multilateral settlements, and especially assigned bills. New England colonists had the best understanding of the relation between what the government took and what it spent, because they were not owned by anyone in England—king, proprietor, or company. Everything that was collected in the colony was spent there. The treasury's humbling intermediary position was obvious more than elsewhere, and this would have consequences.

Most important here are the transformation of debt in a bill into potential currency, and use of the consumption value that wampum had to Indians. These objects, with no intrinsic value to the colonists, could circulate indefinitely and teach the colonists that money could be made of any object that was convenient to carry and store. This lesson could not yet be learned in England, and it paved the road to the future: in 1690, this would enable the creation of legal tender paper money.

Public Finance in War

Plans for some fortifications, a warship, and an expedition against French Acadia to help Plymouth did not materialize because of costs. Winthrop apologized: "We had then no money in the treasury."[83] The currency problem increased the costs of tax collection and contributed to this problem. The main fiscal challenge was the Pequot War.

EXPENSES AND INCOMES. The first expedition in the war was supposed to cost only £200 because the soldiers were "all volunteers, and had only their victuals provided, but demanded no pay," Winthrop claimed. But later the soldiers did have demands, some "not able to bear the loss of so much time, and some others seem not willing to bestow their service freely." The loss of time—traveling back and forth and fighting—translated into loss of income for three weeks. The court appointed a committee to "allow them such recompense as they shall think equal."[84] For the second expedition, payments were promised to soldiers and owners of drafted carriages and horses. Decades later, the court complained to the king about the "great charge" of that war, listing it before casualties.[85]

Income sources were taxes and plunder. Taxes soon rose to new levels (figure 7.1). They were not explicitly linked to the war, but the 1636–1638 spike cannot be explained otherwise. Right after the first expedition, and for the next few years, there was unprecedented mentioning of the

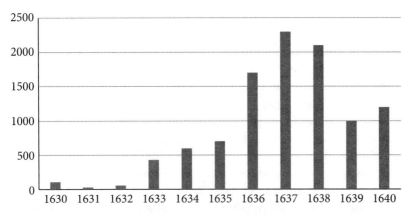

FIGURE 7.1 Taxes in Massachusetts (in pounds), 1630–1640. Source: MAGC I.

colony's debts in the records (in part to justify the higher taxes), and tax collection was expedited.[86]

The first expedition soldiers, who "demanded no pay," surely enlisted for a share in the plunder. The court ordered taking possession of the land and capturing the women and children to sell them as slaves (all men were to be executed). This was performed only in the second expedition. Other plunder included maize and wampum.[87]

The occupied Pequot land was not given to the soldiers; it was to be sold or leased, and that income was to be used to pay the war's expenses.[88] When a treasurer-led committee was appointed to grant land to "men that want land, and have deserved it," military service was *not* a criterion. Decades later, aging veterans who petitioned the court for land (anywhere) as reward for their service did get it.[89] The elite were treated differently: military officers and the accompanying minister were granted land in Pequot or elsewhere. Land grants were hard to execute, however—for example, that minister got his land only twenty-three years after the war.[90]

SETTLING THE DEBTS. The committee appointed to compensate the first expedition soldiers had a typical membership: three assistants and four deputies. The assistants included a recent treasurer and the next treasurer, while the deputies included a merchant and a member of the public debts committee.[91] They were only to write "upon a note under the hands of the said commissioners, or the greater part of them, of any sum allowed to any such person; the Treasurer shall make payment thereof accordingly." These warrants to the treasurer, each signed by at least four men, were issued to the soldiers who were to carry the warrants to the treasurer and receive pay. These financial instruments could be legally assigned to third parties, according to the 1631 law on assignation of all bills. In England, such instruments would become famous as debentures—a decade later.

Before the second expedition, owners of impressed carriages and horses were to be given "bills to the Governor & Council," who in turn would give "warrant" to the treasurer to pay.[92] In a general trilateral settlement at the time, not explicitly related to the war, all creditors of the colony were to "make demand of their debts . . . of the constable of the town" and leave the treasurer out.[93] Similarly, a maimed soldier was compensated with some fines ruled in court.[94] Setoff was used when the expedition's leader was exempted from taxes for a year, and when a soldier's fine was "to be discounted out of his wages."[95]

The soldiers and suppliers were almost certainly paid in grain, since contemporary tax laws did not mention other options. Also, the court noted the "loss fallen upon many by the receiving of corn at five shillings per bushel from the country." A committee of five current and former deputies, "or any three of them," was ordered to fix the problem "according to equity."[96]

The 1690 episode would have some identical features: there would be ex ante reliance on plunder; payments to soldiers would be facilitated by tradable financial instruments; and those instruments would be issued by a mixed, majority-rule committee. Those instruments would be modified in 1690—with small, round denominations, and notions of trilateral settlements and setoff—to become a revolutionary money. And yet, the 1690 invention could not happen in 1637. The theory and practice of money, credit, and banking were not there yet.

Virginia: Failed Monetary Reforms

In the 1630s, Virginia tried escaping its monetary tobacco addiction. There were three fronts in the battle: the unit of account, special coins, and the settlement of debts. The key figure was the overbearing Sir John Harvey, who arrived as royal governor by 1630. He was deposed by his council in 1635 and sent to England. The king reappointed him just to make a point, he returned in 1637, and was replaced in 1640.[97]

Monetary Units of Account

In 1632, the assembly revived monetary units of account, and in 1633 the unit of account in all public and private transactions and documents was ordered to be "in lawful money of England only . . . according to the custom . . . in the Kingdom of England," because tobacco units "bred many inconveniencies in the trade, and occasioned many troubles."[98] Historians have explained this reversion by the glutted international tobacco market, which crashed tobacco's value and made it a bad unit of account.[99] However, the mention of formal conformity with England—the last thing Virginians cared about—suggests that the royal governor was perhaps involved. The same assembly only partly obeyed its own rule: many items in that year's budget were in pounds of tobacco.[100] No budgets survived from the rest of the decade.

Debased Coin

In 1632, the assembly petitioned the Privy Council "that a current coin debased to 25 percent, may be sent unto us" because "nothing will be more useful."[101] This old European device induced people not to export coin because it would be worth less elsewhere. The petition was ignored. In 1636, when Harvey was in England, he complained about coin shortage and the resulting problem of paying wages before harvest. He asked the king that farthing tokens—recently rejected by the people in both England and Massachusetts—be sent to Virginia.[102] In 1638, as Harvey was back in Virginia, the king suggested that the assembly make these coins "current to pass in payment between man and man in their commerce and trade within the colony." The assembly refused, notwithstanding fury of the governor and council. It argued that the coins would be universally rejected because they were heavily debased and thus subject to extreme, arbitrary revaluations or devaluations by the Crown. The assembly again asked in vain for slightly debased silver coin, arguing this was necessary for a diversified economy.[103]

Settlement of Tobacco Debts

Virginia was a smugglers' paradise. Those deep rivers that enabled European ships to travel between plantations to pick up tobacco in exchange for European goods, also allowed evasions of customs and quality control.[104] Harvey's personal income was based on customs.[105] Probably at his insistence, an elaborate 1633 law aimed at regulating the international trade of tobacco for manufactures. The law established "five stores . . . unto which the planters shall be obliged to bring in all their tobaccos . . . and in the same stores to be repacked, viewed and tried by sworn men." The "good and merchantable" tobacco was to be entered in the "accounts of those that were the planters thereof."

The relevant part of the law is this:

> No person or persons do or shall pay or receive, or cause to be paid or received, any tobaccos before it have been viewed, tried and entered into the stores aforesaid. And all payments of debts shall be made and done at the said stores, with the privity and in the presence of the store keepers; and all tobaccos shall there remain, until such time as the same be laden away aboard some ship or ships to be transported out of this colony.[106]

Historians have considered this law as merely a system of quality control.[107] But there is profound monetary significance here. This cited paragraph is remarkably similar to operations at the Bank of Amsterdam, in which all large bills of exchange debts were paid by book transfers between merchants' deposits of coin (p. 40).

The similarity was not a coincidence. The Bank of Amsterdam was famous, and its imitation in England was urged. Much of Virginia's tobacco (perhaps most of it) was bought by Dutch ships sent by Dutch merchants, since the United Provinces dominated international trade and tobacco processing. The Dutch were all over the area—based in New Netherland, investing in English Caribbean tobacco colonies, and buying tobacco in Bermuda. One English-speaking Dutch shipmaster came from New Netherland a month after the law was enacted and documented his friendly and informative discussions with Harvey and the elite.[108] One personal connection was Edward Bennett, a former London merchant who lived as a Separatist in Amsterdam. As a merchant he probably had to be a customer of the Bank of Amsterdam. He lived in Virginia in the 1620s and was one of the largest planters. At the end of the decade, he returned to London, leaving management of his plantation to his nephew Richard Bennett. By 1633, Richard had served as member of the assembly and a judge.[109]

The circumstances, however, were different between the two. Unlike the Bank of Amsterdam's coins, Virginia's tobacco did not stay where it was deposited but was quickly shipped to Europe. It should therefore more properly be called a clearinghouse system rather than a bank system. This system, regulating all private debts in the colony, has another implication: just as the Bank of Amsterdam was founded on the background of usage of bills of exchange, so is it likely that debts in tobacco were already prevalent in the colony, and the new system meant only to regulate them—not to bring them into existence. If true, this implies that by 1633 colonists did *not* go shopping in other plantations or in Jamestown with barrels of tobacco, but only with pen and paper to write bills. This should not be surprising. As a physical medium of exchange, tobacco was a travesty, and the sharp decline in its value made its transport very costly.[110]

The law was also flawed. The tobacco was to be shipped out of the colony from each regional storehouse, but another section of the law had all European goods landed and all contracts made in the Jamestown storehouse alone.[111] A generous interpretation would have goods landed in Jamestown and contracts made there for the delivery of tobacco from the regional storehouses. Planters would carry all imported goods from Jamestown to their plantations in their boats, and shipmasters would trust planters that tobacco would await them at the regional storehouses, free of all debts to fellow colonists. This was a lot to ask in the circumstances of 1633 Virginia.

The awkwardness of the law resulted from a compromise between two considerations. The colony's dispersion could not allow a single clearinghouse in Jamestown, analogous to the single building of the Bank of Amsterdam. But Harvey wanted effective customs collection, and this required centralization. Half a year later, the law was reenacted with some changes. Most relevant, the number of storehouses increased to seven, but the exchange of imported goods for tobacco was to be physically made in Jamestown only.[112] Apparently, after clearing local debts in local storehouses, planters would carry their tobacco to Jamestown and trade it for imports in the central storehouse.

As usual in Virginia, laws and reality were far apart. By 1638, the system was still not in existence. Harvey kept fighting for it and for his personal profit from it.[113] He got the king on his side, who suggested that the assembly implement the system. The same 1638 assembly that rejected token coins refused this royal suggestion too, with these arguments:

storehouse construction would be too costly; they had no boats for transportation to storehouses; and tobacco would be at risk from water while
transported and from fire while stored.[114]

*   *   *

By 1640, Massachusetts abounded with ideas and experiments in money
and alternatives to money. In monetary innovation it took the lead
(partly with lead bullets) over the once-innovative Virginia, which failed
in all its painful attempts of tobacco withdrawal.

Elsewhere in the Atlantic, Maryland was founded by the proprietor
Cecil Calvert, Lord Baltimore. His feudal charter granted him the rights
of the semiautonomous County Palatine of Durham in England, which
perhaps still had a minting privilege.[115] Imitating neighboring Virginia,
however, Maryland adopted tobacco as its main product and money.[116]
In the Caribbean, the English colonized Antigua and Montserrat with
tobacco. Soon the older islands started shifting to cotton as both staple
good and money.[117]

Tobacco and cotton were also used in Providence Island off the Central American coast. It was chartered in 1630 to Puritan nobles and gentlemen, who were influential enough to get a coinage privilege. The
historian Karen Kupperman has used Providence as a unique natural
experiment on the role of Puritanism in colonization. That colony was
nothing like its Puritan sister colonies in New England and every bit like
the other island colonies. What made New England different was its autonomy and property rights. These features drew civil and religious leaders of high quality who faced the consequences of their independent
decisions. Kupperman's general conclusion also holds for monetary innovation: while Massachusetts exploded with ideas, there was nothing
special about money in Providence.[118]

CHAPTER EIGHT

A New Hope, 1640–1660

In those days there was no king in Israel, but every man did that which was right in his own eyes.
—Judges 17:6, King James Version

During the chaotic Interregnum, the flows of immigrants, manu-factures, and currency from England were disrupted, but so was the flow of governmental orders. Therefore, although immediate conse-quences of the period were bad, in the long run the colonists could try even bolder ideas about money. Massachusetts scored high while Vir-ginia failed again, and other southern colonies entered the scene with paper-money contributions.

Massachusetts: Minting Success

The following discussion of general issues—empire, government, and population—will inform monetary developments that are discussed later.

Imperial Relations

The colony founded by the constitutional–religious strife in England had considerable interest in the Civil Wars. The official records, not know-ing who would win, are very cautious.[1] Massachusetts did not seek reuni-fication with Puritan-led England, but used the opportunity to increase its independence, becoming a de facto state. As a corporation, Massa-chusetts could not legally reproduce and create other corporations. But right after monarchy was abolished, Massachusetts granted a charter to the college.[2]

Massachusetts became a regional empire, expanding aggressively in all directions, with a creative interpretation of the charter and other rights derived from conquest in "just war." It annexed New Hampshire and Maine, claimed Hudson River land, and kept Springfield on the Connecticut River and part of Pequot land from Connecticut.[3] The Pequot War led to a military alliance with Plymouth and Connecticut (and New Haven, which would be absorbed into the latter).[4] Massachusetts heavily dominated these United Colonies of New England. In Acadia, Massachusetts took sides in intra-French intrigue.[5] During the First Anglo–Dutch War, a Massachusetts force commissioned by Oliver Cromwell occupied Acadia. Colonel Thomas Temple of England obtained Acadia's governorship with monopoly on beaver trade and relocated to Boston.[6]

Massachusetts's biggest problem was that the return of Parliament in 1640 stopped emigration to New England at once. Winthrop complained that Puritans had an "expectation of a new world" in England, so they forgot about the New World.[7] Since the Massachusetts economy was dependent on continuing immigration, the economy crashed. Massachusetts reinvented its economy, selling fish, livestock, and grain to southern colonies. The Puritans found themselves trading all over the Atlantic, with people of every creed, and had to welcome all types of visitors.

Government

Deputies' accountability increased as the General Court split, in imitation of Parliament, into an upper Council and a lower House of Deputies. Any action required consent of both Houses. To the magistrates in the council, the split cemented their status as "aristocracy."[8] The deputies could now freely speak and vote their minds. They reminded the magistrates that they merely delivered the freemen's wishes to the court.[9] The deputies were probably those who initiated referenda, including on the semiconstitutional collection of laws—the 1641 Body of Liberties composed by the minister Nathaniel Ward. The freemen were not shy to reject some proposals.[10]

The Body of Liberties allowed nonfreemen to attend all public meetings, and there question, complain, and petition, and access nearly all public records.[11] They served in local offices and juries and voted in local

elections.[12] Charles Andrews has concluded that the limited franchise at
the colony level did not seriously harm the nonfreemen.[13] Anyone could
have complained about the money problem and offer solutions. In response to "frequent complaints" of "inhabitants" (not freemen) of having no orderly way to know the laws, the court composed a legal code
and noted that England never had such a collection.[14] The court had
each annual budget audited and published throughout the colony for the
inhabitants' "satisfaction."[15] No contemporary English government was
more accountable.

At the splitting of the General Court, the church elders clarified
that executive, legislative, and judicial powers belonged to the General
Court. When it was not in session (nine or ten months per year), executive authority belonged to the Court of Assistants, with one exception: ad hoc committees that had been appointed by the General Court.
The elders confirmed that committees could include freemen unelected
to the court.[16] Even beforehand, some commissions explicitly noted or
hinted that the committees were mixed.[17]

Population

Some colonists went back to fight in England; others returned to England or left elsewhere because of the economic crisis. An Atlantic Winthrop network emerged as three of the governor's sons left: Stephen, a
former deputy, returned to fight; Samuel became a planter and merchant
in the Caribbean; John Jr. founded New London in Pequot and later became governor of Connecticut. Their cousin George Downing, a graduate of the college's first class (1642), toured the Caribbean, served as a
chaplain in Cromwell's army, later led the army's intelligence unit, and
finally became ambassador to the United Provinces. The entrepreneurial minister Hugh Peter, related to the Winthrops by marriage, was sent
as an agent of the colony to Parliament, and stayed to become the army's leading preacher.[18] Peter was also part of an Atlantic network of
ministers—Massachusetts regularly exported college graduates to Puritan communities across the Atlantic, and received Puritan ministers ex-
pelled by Anglican colonial governments.[19] Both networks were a source
of information on the Atlantic.

Boston and the rest of the Bay enhanced their riches and their dominance as the colony's economy reoriented toward Atlantic trade. The
Bay towns had half the wealth and population of the colony.[20] The "great

concourse of people and increase of trade there" led the court to appoint juries of merchants and mariners for commercial lawsuits, then to establish a special merchants' court in Boston, and finally to study mercantile law.[21] Winthrop repeatedly mentioned in his journal the "merchants of Boston" only after 1640 and always in the context of overseas trade.[22] These merchants began to hold significant political power.[23] It was their commercial interest that drew the colony into violent French Acadian politics.[24] The only other town often mentioned in the context of international trade (and always with Boston) was Charlestown, just across the Charles River.[25] Some of the elites' residences far from the Bay became a problem for governance, especially in winter, so Bay residents took over. They dominated appointments to executive committees and were consulted by the governor upon emergencies.[26]

At the college, students entered with basic Latin and learned Greek, Hebrew, grammar, logic, rhetoric, arithmetic, geometry, astronomy, metaphysics, ethics, science, and medicine. The bachelor's degree, granted to a few men every year, was a liberal arts degree. Only graduate school was specifically for training ministers, and only half the graduates became ministers. The court noted the "necessity and singular use" of a college education "in managing the things of greatest concernment in this commonwealth"—specifically, training magistrates, officers, judges, and physicians.[27] The innovative spirit was manifested not only in constitution and money, but also when the court granted monopolies to an "experiment" or "invention" in heating, an "engine" to cut grass, and John Winthrop Jr.'s "new way" of producing salt.[28]

Not innovative, relative to England, was the routine blaming of the devil for any serious dispute or error. A public education law was thus motivated: "It being one chief project of that old deluder, Satan, to keep men from the knowledge of the Scriptures." A witch panic in war-torn England was promptly exported to New England.[29]

A Crash Course in Monetary Economics

Remarkably, Winthrop's first comment on the stop of emigration was about monetary economics: "There came over great store of provisions . . . but few passengers (and those brought very little money)." Therefore,

> now all our money was drained from us, and cattle and all commodities grew
> very cheap. . . . The scarcity of money made a great change in all commerce.

Merchants would sell no wares but for ready money, men could not pay their
debts though they had enough, prices of lands and cattle fell soon to the one
half and less, yea to a third, and after one fourth part.

Winthrop and others diagnosed the causality running from less money
to lower prices—the quantity theory of money.[30]

The court concurred and discovered what economists now call down-
ward wage rigidity: wages did not decline as they should, given the decline in prices.[31] One reason is long-term contracts; another is that workers naturally demand wage increases when prices rise but refuse wage
decreases when prices fall. As servants stopped coming from England,
those in the colony demanded higher wages when their contracts expired, and there was no coin for that. The elitist Winthrop was terrified
of social upheaval:

> The master, being forced to sell a pair of his oxen to pay his servant his wages,
> told his servant he could keep him no longer, not knowing how to pay him
> the next year. The servant answered, he would serve him for more of his cat-
> tle. But how shall I do (said the master) when all my cattle are gone? The ser-
> vant replied, you shall then serve me, and so you may have your cattle again.[32]

As colonists started leaving, they sold off their property and exacerbated
the deflation, bringing prices to 20 percent of their precrisis level. They
also took with them coin and plate. Grain collapsed as money, rejected
by shopkeepers, laborers, and artisans.[33] Monetary units of account were
temporarily abandoned.[34]

A decade of intense monetary experimentation made the court qualified to deal with such a dramatic monetary calamity, and it responded
with unusual steps. First, it reduced the prices of grain in tax payments
to match the drop in market prices. Second, all workers were threatened
with trial for price gouging if they refused to accept lower wages at whatever form of payment was available. Third, all obligations could be discharged not only "in money" but with "corn, cattle, fish, or other commodities." The "corn" was extended to include barley, while the "other"
specifically included peas, hemp, and flaxseed; but all commodities were
legal tender for all monetary obligations (including taxes and public
debts).[35] Such commodities used to pay obligations were named "country pay" or "current/lawful pay of New England."[36]

With no coins, how would the colonists buy European manufactures?[37] The court, like most contemporary governments, tried to increase the amount of coins with the policy of mercantilism—encouraging exports and discouraging nonessential imports, with positive and negative incentives. The exports would be more successful. Inspired by the Iberian trade triangle that involved fish, another triangle formed: merchants exported livestock and food, which had been made for prospective immigrants, to the Caribbean colonies, which used their small space mostly for producing tobacco, cotton, and the new sugar. Massachusetts merchants accepted these crops as payment, sold them in England, and used the proceeds to buy manufactures desired in New England (figure 8.1). This triangular exchange, relying on the heartless exploitation of slaves on the islands, was—from an economic perspective—a perfect exploitation of the comparative advantages of each of the three locations. Off season, when Caribbean crops were not ready, the livestock and food were sold there for bills of exchange drawn on merchants in England, with the same final use of the funds obtained in England.[38] Massachusetts merchants did not just upload cargoes in Boston harbor; their own ships and crews came to dominate the trade triangles. As the

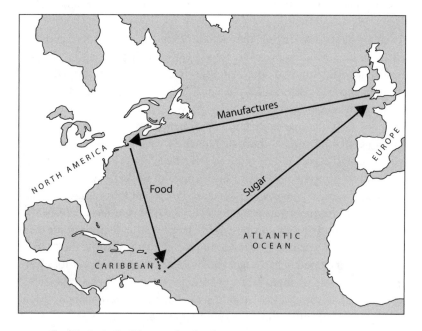

FIGURE 8.1 The basic Caribbean trade triangle.

economic historians John McCusker and Russell Menard put it, "The New Englanders became the Dutch of England's empire."[39]

These changes had direct monetary effects. First, as Mark Peterson has noted, in trade triangles no coin was needed to be exported for English goods. I disagree with Peterson's other claim, that the new form of exchange between local farmers and merchants required a well-functioning currency.[40] On the contrary, currency was needed less than before in this context. In the 1630s, farmers sold supplies to unfamiliar newcomers, so they had to insist on payment in coins, and then they used these coins to buy manufactures from merchants. Now these intermediary newcomers were out of the picture, and all that remained were direct long-term business relationships between farmers and merchants. They could work for years with barter enabled by credit: farmers provided merchants with food to export in a new triangular venture and received in return manufactures (including agricultural tools) imported in the previous venture.[41] Therefore, a second direct monetary effect of the changed economy was a reduction in the internal demand for coin. Money remained necessary only for transactions that did not have such lasting relationships, a prime example of which is purchases by visitors in the Bay. As the number of creditless visitors increased, a third effect was an increase in the amount of coin in the Bay. A fourth direct effect took place when Caribbean activity led to trade of food for coin with privateers and pirates.[42]

As the court ruled on intercolonial mercantile lawsuits, it became familiar with the various moneys of the Atlantic, even ordering payments in sugar.[43] The merchant class—powerful in court and holding the treasurer's office—was more exposed to such monetary practices. Moreover, a Boston merchant sending his ship to Barbados and then to England might have realized that sugar served as a medium of exchange for him. He regularly accepted sugar not to consume it but to pass it on to someone else, as one does with coin.[44] Winthrop understood this point: he referred to beaver as potential "returns" (the normal term for international barter) to be traded for "English commodities"; however, regarding the trade triangle he used monetary terminology: "The commodities we had *in exchange* there for our cattle and provisions, as sugar, cotton, tobacco, and indigo, were a good help to *discharge our engagements* in England" (my emphases).[45]

More generally, specialization in long-distance marine trade has proven useful for financial innovation in medieval Italian city-states that invented the bank, the bill of exchange, and the check, and in the contemporary United Provinces. By becoming "the Dutch of England's empire," Massachusetts merchants were on a path to a groundbreaking invention of their own.

Atlantic exposure made Massachusetts the first English colony to adopt the European method of circulating foreign coin and encouraging its importation by legally valuing it above its intrinsic value. In 1642, the court ordered the Spanish piece of eight and the Dutch dollar to "pass" and be "current . . . in all payments." The piece of eight, intrinsically worth four and a half shillings, was to pass at five shillings.[46]

Mercantilism implied attempts at local production of import substitutes, which diversified the local economy and potentially increased the demand for money (by making barter less likely). The leading venture—and the one most consequential to monetary developments—was John Winthrop Jr.'s ironworks.[47]

After the Storm

From 1646, Massachusetts's new economic structure as the chief Atlantic trade hub was in place, and monetary units bounced back to complete domination. Coin appears more often than in the first decade, but the problem was not solved. Most public payments were not in coin. When the ironworks wanted to sell iron locally only for coin, the deputies complained: "Some men have here Spanish money sometimes, but little comes to our smiths' hands, especially those of inland towns," the reason being that "our ingate exceeds our outgate"—that is, imports were larger than exports, and so "the balance must needs be made" in coin.[48]

Most of the commodity moneys of the 1630s continued, at least in law. Grain remained dominant in public payments, but the court did not dare force agents of English merchants to accept it in settlement of debts.[49] The "good & merchantable" standard of grain was applied to all goods.[50] Massachusetts's imperialism was partly motivated by access to beaver—in Springfield, the northeast, even the Delaware River—and beaver does become more common in records after 1640.[51] Land was used to pay monetary obligations (public and private) and even to buy such obligations.[52] The value of land titles was strengthened by a land registry, a requirement to make all sales in writing, and a blanket confirmation of all past sales.[53]

Wampum rose and fell. At first, its legal value was raised and it was allowed in taxes and for larger debts than before.[54] Wampum's low value made it popular on the Charles River ferry, the profits of which belonged to the college. The college sold wampum to fur traders, but complained that "the Indians abused the English with much false, bad and unfinished" wampum, which eventually made it to the college and the fur traders. Then fur-selling Indians refused the bad wampum, so the traders kept it in the colonial economy: they "leave their refuse to pass to and fro in the colonies." The court withdrew its support for an object that nobody valued and whose quantity was not under the court's control. The court lowered wampum's official value as legal tender for debts, and considered it "passable or payable" or "current in payment of debts" only if "entire, without breaches or deforming spots." Later, the court declared that wampum could not be used for taxes.[55] To help the college as well as the court-licensed ferrymen, the court allowed ferrymen in 1648 to "refuse any wampum, not stringed or unmerchantable."[56] After the 1640s, wampum appeared in records almost only in Indian contexts.[57] A rare exception was a highly unusual 1657 ferry law which declared that "it shall not be lawful for any passenger to refuse to receive" good wampum as small change.[58]

Atlantization made wine so common that it became money. Many workers were "forced" to take it as pay, and either got drunk or passed it on to buy goods or pay debts. The court outlawed passing it along because selling alcohol was licensed for social reasons.[59] Merchants and others in the alcohol industry were allowed to pay alcohol customs and other debts with alcohol.[60] Officially sanctioned barter transactions included coal for ironworks stocks and iron for cannons.[61] Students provided the college with any goods—including butter, eggs, honey, wax, and a sword—in exchange for instruction and housing.[62]

The Mint

In a mint, a piece of metal is standardized in quantity and quality, and a sign is stamped on it as assurance of its intrinsic value. Living in a world of several commodity moneys taught colonists that *metallic* coin was only a special case. Other objects—grain, animals, wampum—could also be standardized and/or stamped, in one way or another, to approximate coin.

From 1647, one of the selectmen of each town was also a "sealer of weights and measures." He made sure that the weights and measures used in all shops, such as a bushel and a yard, were identical to the colony's official set.[63] These officers indicated their approval with seals. Adam Smith would argue that similar offices in Britain were "exactly of the same nature" as that of a mint master: control of the quality of a measure that is necessary for trade.[64] The sealer of weights and measures in an economy where grain was a dominant money was close to being a de facto mint master. Grain could not be sealed, but the measure of its volume could.

Cattle have been a problematic money for millennia, because as money they are neither easily divisible nor standardized. In Massachusetts, cattle were often gruesomely divided nevertheless, to be packed and shipped in casks. From 1651, towns appointed gaugers for these casks to assure standardization. The job description used language applicable to mint masters playing with various metals: gaugers were to make sure, regarding beef and pork, "that the best be not left out," while fish had to be "packed all of one kind and that all cask[s] so packed be full." The sealed end products were, in some sense, large coins of meat or fish. This perhaps prompted the court to allow discharge of one debt with "merchantable beef, pork."[65] The analogy went further when "lean cattle"—the equivalent of a worn coin—was refused in taxes.[66]

In October 1648, the court came as close as technologically possible to minting wampum. It enacted the use of only "suitably strung" standardized "parcels" with quality supervision and differentiation of quantity and quality that formed eight denominations, from a penny to ten shillings. The historian William Weeden has described this law correctly as "a process more like coinage than any thing . . . found among the Indians" and reminding "of the mint." More accurately, this new wampum was analogous to standardized lumps of metal used in the Old World before coinage. This order was "for trial until the next Court," and was not renewed.[67]

Perhaps the experiment failed, but perhaps it was not renewed because when the court reconvened in May 1649, there was no longer a royal coinage monopoly. King and monarchy had been beheaded, and a new hope emerged regarding the sorry monetary situation that had tormented the colonists for two decades. Minting coins became an option, and perhaps discussions about it started. But, unlike thousands of businesses in England, which immediately began minting their own coins, Massachusetts enacted a mint law only three years later. Perhaps the court waited for the Third Civil War to end.

An urgent motivation for a mint was the damage caused by the Spanish coin brought by privateers and pirates, which was "light, base" and "counterfeit," due to a major debasement fraud at the Peru mint. It was reported that "many people were cozened," "merchants and others sustained" "great injuries," and the result was "a stoppage of trade."[68] The court toyed with the idea of merely restamping foreign coins according to their intrinsic value.[69] Eventually, though, it opened a mint. Decades later the mint would be justified in England as "little more than" that "customary" private coinage in England, occurring "when there was no King in England, but the government out of course."[70]

The 1652 mint law ordered building a mint in Boston. Anyone could bring there "all bullion, plate, or Spanish coin" to be melted and coined into three-, six-, and twelvepence. Each coin was to have one-sixth less silver than analogous English coins. The coins received supreme legal status as "the current money of this commonwealth, and no other, unless English (except the receivers consent thereunto)." They were to "pass from man to man in all payments accordingly." John Hull, a goldsmith, was appointed mint master. The court described the mint order in unprecedented terms as "being of so great concernment," and thus justified the appointment of five Bostonian court members as a committee to execute this law.[71]

The text on the coins was simple: "Massachusetts in New England," the year 1652 (even in later coins), the denomination, and a tree. As the historian Jonathan Barth notes, there was no mention of England.[72] Soon the court clarified that no contractual creditor could be forced to take goods instead of coin.[73] But there is little evidence of locally made coin circulating by 1660, and even the court kept working mostly with country pay.[74] The coin was exported to other colonies, and the court prohibited exportation with its worst economic penalty ever—confiscation of *all* the offender's land and goods.[75]

Credit and Its Settlement

The court complained often of inability to pay the colony's debts because there was no "money/stock in the Treasury."[76] While individuals were arrested for debts as in England, the colony could incur only divine penalty for nonpayment: when a gunpowder depot blew up, Winthrop knew it happened because the colony never paid for it.[77] It was also morally wrong; the court once apologized to creditors "who have *trusted* the country" to receive "their *just* due" but might get less "of what in *justice* they might expect" (my emphases). That particular loss was caused by a discrepancy between the market price of maize and its price in tax payments. The court made a compromise between its creditors and debtors by resetting the latter price, going two-thirds of the way toward the price that would have left the creditors unharmed. Other public obligations also featured what I shall call a "compromise of thirds," with public creditors losing one- or two-thirds of the debt.[78] This was an old English tradition, manifested, for example, in the aftermath of the 1640 Royal Mint's confiscation.

Best practices of public-debt settlement were institutionalized in new laws. The fundamental tax law of 1647 ordered that tax revenues be sent to Boston only if they could not be used locally to pay the colony's expenses there.[79] An auditor general was instructed to conduct a setoff whenever he found a creditor of the colony who was also a debtor of the colony.[80] Applying methods of private finance, the treasury paid to one's "order," appointee, or "assignees," while debtors of the colony were ordered "to pay, or cause to be paid."[81] The treasurer himself issued a "note" of nine pounds to buy ammunition.[82]

As with all documentation, there is more evidence of private bills in this period, but no small bills survive.[83] A large transaction was usually paid in installments, and sometimes this promise was recorded on a single bill. In rare cases, the debt was split into several bills (of £20 minimum) to increase their liquidity—the ease with which they could be exchanged for cash.[84] The 1631 law of assigning bills was clarified in the 1647 legal code, including the form of assignation.[85] All surviving bills mentioned both sides' "assignees," and some were actually assigned.[86] Some bills were payable "to bearer," or "to order" like checks.[87] The creative colonists even assigned judgments issued by courts to parties who won private lawsuits. The court later outlawed that—but still later, it did the same.[88] The court accepted private bills as payments of fines and other obligations, and as security to make such payments, and assigned private bills to its creditors.[89] New Haven accepted private bills for church taxes.[90]

The innkeeper in Lynn, where the ironworks were mostly based, promised to pay Bostonians with bills issued by the ironworks or their manager. As the largest business in the colony, the ironworks were known enough to get their bills circulating, and to be accumulated by merchants—until their bankruptcy.[91] In 1684, the court justified its mint with this recollection of the 1640s: "For some years paper-bills passed for payment of debts, which are very subject to be lost, rent, or counterfeited, and other inconveniences." Bills apparently paid debts, probably accumulated over time, but were not used in daily purchases. The counterfeiting perhaps prompted a 1646 law against forgery of "bond, bill" and other documents.[92]

Also in 1652, a committee was appointed as a "council of trade." It included the chief financial officers (treasurer and auditor general), three merchants, and the agent of the largest English investor—all Bay residents. They mentioned to the court the idea of "raising a bank," but no specific details survived.[93]

Virginia: Giving Up

Harvey's legacy was eliminated after he was replaced in 1640. The budget was again entirely in tobacco units.[94] In 1641, keepers were appointed to a few regional storehouses, but this is the only evidence for some implementation of the 1633 storehouse law.[95] The following year, this law was repealed by the assembly together with the 1632 unit of account law and many other Harvey-era laws.[96]

More surprising is that the 1642 backlash even included an official refusal to enforce contracts stipulating payment in coin:

It shall not bee lawful . . . to make any money debt . . . , and if any refractory person shall, notwithstanding, pass or take money bills or bonds or make such debt, they shall not be recoverable in any court of justice under this government.[97]

Why didn't the king's colony recognize the king's coin? Presumably there was not enough coin, and then courts would need to choose between imprisoning debtors and overriding clauses in contracts.

A new royal governor, Sir William Berkeley, was also against tobacco, and so a special 1644 tax to fund his salary listed fifteen other items for tax payments, including grain, butter, cheese, "good hens," beef, pork, and "pigs to roast."[98] During a visit to England to solicit the king's help in a new war with Indians, Berkeley, a recent courtier, fought alongside the king.[99] By November 1645, he was back in Virginia and joined in passing a coinage law. An unusual preamble emphasized the importance of the act, as 1652 Massachusetts would do:

> having maturely weighed and considered how advantageous a coin current would be to this colony, and the great wants and miseries which do daily happen unto it by the sole dependency upon tobacco.[100]

The law made the piece of eight pass at six shillings—a probable imitation of Massachusetts, as there was pervasive trade between these colonies.[101] A coin legally worth six shillings and intrinsically worth four and a half shillings was exactly what the assembly had petitioned for in 1632: a coin debased by 25 percent. The law also ordered minting copper tokens of two-, three-, six-, and ninepence—debased by 92.5 percent. Whereas in 1638 the assembly rejected the debased coin of the king's crony, now it was going to keep the minting profit. Captain John Upton was appointed mint master, "we reposing much confidence in his care, ability and trust."[102] This copper coin was to be "current" with Spanish coin, while using tobacco as money would become illegal.

Why did Virginia violate the king's minting prerogative? The historian William Ripley thought the First Civil War made Virginia practically independent.[103] Indeed, Virginia is referred to in this law, for the first time, as a "state" and "republic," and the law does not mention the king. This is not consistent with Berkeley's relationship with the king. If he got the king's personal approval to mint coin while he was in England, why wasn't the approval or the king mentioned in the act? Perhaps, as in the storehouse law, the awkwardness resulted from a political compromise between governor and assembly. Either way, once again, Virginia failed. In the following session, in March 1646, another act mentioned "the hopeful expectation of a current coin, to be made in the colony, which cannot be so readily effected as was then expected."[104] The Virginia mint and coin were never mentioned again, and probably they never existed.

This marks the end of an intense experimental period, after which there was largely acquiescence to the rule of King Tobacco. Only the revaluation of foreign coin became standard monetary legislation for decades.[105] In 1658, Virginia deteriorated to forcing money under penalty: "Pieces of eight that are good and of silver shall pass for five shillings current money upon penalty of twenty shillings to be paid by the

refusers of them."[106] This law was an absurd travesty: during an Anglo–
Spanish War, an English colony forced the *enemy's* money on English
subjects.

In 1645, Virginia finally had a success: it invented the rule of setoff
in English law. Anyone sued for a debt could present a counterdebt—
"bill, bond or account"—and have the court "balance accounts." The official goal was to avoid lawsuits, but this novelty saved costs of sending
tobacco back and forth to discharge debts. Common law, dealing only
with one case at a time, could not do that. Parliament would follow Virginia only in 1729. But when Virginia confirmed the law the following
year, it added an old English feature of sealed bills, which was a fatal
blow to bills' monetary potential: that "no bills or accounts whatsoever
be passed or assigned over without the knowledge of both parties."[107]

New Holland

In 1630, the Dutch West India Company occupied the Portuguese colony in Pernambuco, Brazil, and renamed it New Holland. It was a typical southern colony—growing sugar and using it as money. There was
almost constant warfare with Portugal, Spain (which owned Portugal),
other Iberian colonies, and local rebellious colonists.[108] In 1637, Count
Johan Maurits of the ruling Dutch family of Nassau was appointed governor. He brought military experience, cosmopolitan humanistic education, and interest in science.[109]

Maurits ran out of small-denomination coins to pay his soldiers and
complained that the result was disobedience, including plunder of occupied Portuguese planters. He paid every four or five soldiers a single
high-denomination gold coin for their combined monthly wages, letting
them sort out what to do with it.[110] In 1640 and 1643, he paid soldiers
with "ordonnantien," payment orders similar to debentures, and forced
everyone to accept them in all transactions.[111] This was the first paper
money in America, and no specimen of it has survived. But with its
forced acceptance, it was essentially the Old World device well known
long beforehand. Maurits was perhaps inspired by the famous Leiden
episode; his family had already led the republic back then, and Maurits's scientists were from Leiden or studied there.[112] He merely planted
the old Holland paper money in New Holland. Not surprisingly, Maurits
printed too much paper money, and it quickly lost value.[113]

The paper-money story could have reached New England—English mercenaries were the largest group in Maurits's army.[114] New England had prolific contacts with Dutch merchants and shipmasters who operated throughout the Atlantic.[115] A 1654 Portuguese reconquest eliminated New Holland, and many of its Dutch colonists dispersed across the Atlantic. Some of them moved to another colony of the company, New Netherland.[116]

Antigua

The first public system of paper money in any English jurisdiction was born in Antigua. The only information on it comes from a law reviving the system in 1669. The preamble says:

> By several acts formerly passed, an exact way for bringing tobacco of the growth of this island into public storehouses has been much endeavored, but more especially by an act of the 26th day of April 1654, in which an effectual progress in to the same (to the great ease and accommodation, both of merchant and planter) was not only begun but constantly continued until the late war with France that it was impeded and interrupted, and whereas to the same grounds & reasons for making such an act do still continue & not so only but more forcibly than ever require it for the propagation of trade, ease of the merchants and ready payment of the planter, who having his storehouse notes can pass them in all places of the island like ready money, as well to buy what he wants, as [well as] discharge his just debts and engagements.[117]

Apparently, such a system had operated at least from 1654 until a brief French occupation in 1666. While Virginia's storehouses were to settle private bills in their books, the Antiguan storehouses issued their own bills. These bills were banknotes, except that the deposits were eventually shipped overseas. As the rest of this 1669 law is strictly about the revived system, and it cannot be known how much of this law was novel, the rest of the story of the 1669 law is deferred to the next chapter, which is about the period 1660–1686.

Why was such a novel system invented in Antigua, an island of 108 square miles? Constantly attacked by Indians from other islands and having no more than 1,200 men for defense, the residents were so poor that their Leeward Islands government exempted them from taxes.[118] A

1655 list of tobacco-denominated debts from Antiguans to Dutch traders includes dozens of private bills.[119] The bills are in no more round or
small denominations than the other debts. But two of them are from
Samuel Winthrop, and he is one clue as to why Antigua.

Samuel, John's son, was born in England in 1627 and lived in Massachusetts from 1631 to 1645. He spent his childhood in the greatest monetary laboratory of the era. After dropping out of college, he sought a
mercantile career in London, Barbados, Saint Christopher, the Canar-
ies, and the Azores. After marrying a Dutch woman in Rotterdam, he
became a planter in Antigua in 1649, and left to neighboring Saint Christopher in 1654.[120] Perhaps he carried to Antigua his unique heritage of
monetary experimentation, and Dutch knowledge too.

Also relevant is Governor Christopher Keynell, recently a captain in
the English Civil Wars.[121] He surely had personal experience with debentures, and perhaps he was familiar with the emerging goldsmith-
bankers and the new banking ideas. The island's tiny size and isolation
may have helped the government oversee that monetary experiment.
Venice, a leading financial innovator for centuries, was also basically a
small island.

The Meaning of Monetary Laws

The 1650s saw for the first time two colonial laws of explicit forced acceptance of money: wampum in the Massachusetts ferry and pieces of
eight in Virginia.[122] I argue that these were the exceptions that proved
the rule, and that, in general, there was no forced acceptance of money
in the English colonies. All other monetary laws mentioned neither ille-
gality nor penalty. They merely stated that these objects were to "pass"
or be "current" or to "pass current," sometimes referring specifically
to "payments" (then mostly meaning discharge of debts), "debts," or
"rates" (taxes).

Although the phrase *pass current* sounds like a spot transaction, earlier (pp. 29–30) I cited with agreement the prevailing view among historians that in England's monetary proclamations, the meaning of *pass
current* was, in practice if not in theory, equivalent to the modern notion
of legal tender. That is, the state enforced the circulation of the monarch's money only when preexisting obligations (mostly debts and taxes)
reached courts. It was illegal to reject money in ordinary exchange only

if the proclamation explicitly stated that—a device reserved for crises in which there was actual or predicted wide refusal of money.

The case is much clearer, in favor of a legal tender interpretation, in Massachusetts and probably in other colonies. The Massachusetts General Court loved controlling and punishing—but under the rule of law. The first section in the legal code allowed the government to harm people only under "some express law . . . sufficiently published."[123] The court persistently worked hard to inform judges, officers, inhabitants, and visitors of its penal laws and other laws that had to be known to "every man."[124] It sometimes forgave offenders because of their ignorance of laws.[125] And yet, none of the monetary laws of Massachusetts mentioned any penalty for rejecting any moneys, or even stated that such an act was illegal (except the wampum-ferry law). Records of judicial courts in Massachusetts (and early Virginia and Bermuda) have no trials over money rejections. Most telling is that Governor Winthrop told of several cases in which individuals—*even entire groups or most colonists*—rejected in spot transactions types of money that had been ordered to pass current. According to him, they were punished (if at all) only by God, in having a financial disaster afterward.[126]

When the court really wanted to promote some money in law, it stated the criminality of refusal (the wampum-ferry law) or specified the penalties (laws against export of coin).[127] Forcing someone to accept a type of money he does not want amounts to forcing a transaction. The court forced transactions in other contexts only in very rare cases, and the law was always explicit about it.[128] The ferry law was not even really about a forced transaction, because it imposed a tiny, small-change obligation only on people who had chosen to ride the ferry and failed to bring the correct amount of money.

The absence of any evidence of forcing money in spot transactions is especially revealing in Massachusetts, which was *not* a textbook example of free markets. The government was heavily involved in the economy from the beginning.[129] The Puritan spirit of supervision and discipline appointed what the economic historian Jonathan Hughes has called a "small army" of "viewers, searchers, wardens, constables, informers, . . . , sealers of weights, measures, and casks, clerks of the market."[130] Their authorities were carefully specified in law. Monetary supervision of daily transactions could have been included, or special officers could have been appointed for the purpose. But none of that happened. Laws limiting wages and prices could have easily said something about mandatory media of payment, but that happened only once, during the 1640–1641 crisis.

I agree with historians of money in England and America that the typical colonial monetary laws merely gave "legal tender" status rather than forced transactions.[131] Where contract law is the legal foundation of the economy, the legislature must determine which objects discharge contractual liability if the parties did not do so specifically enough. Otherwise, there would be no way to end some lawsuits, and no state can allow that.

*   *   *

In December 1659, Barbados petitioned Parliament to have a "mint house" as that of "New England."[132] At the same time, Lord Baltimore sent from London specially made silver coins to Maryland to "pass current" "for all payments upon contracts or causes." Probably because of the constitutional chaos playing out in London, Baltimore was undaunted when the Council of State summoned him for this "offense." A bigger problem was a local revolution in Maryland in March 1660 that sabotaged his plan.[133]

By 1660, then, the three most populous continental colonies—Virginia, Massachusetts, and Maryland—had tried to have special colonial coinage within the previous fifteen years. All attempts probably related to the constitutional vacuum in England. Of the islands, Bermuda had tried long beforehand. As of 1660, only Massachusetts succeeded, while Virginia practically gave up. But as the House of Stuart crawled back to power, the future of currency was signaled by the tropical colonies, which introduced government-issued paper money to America—backed by either a commodity or a penalty.

CHAPTER NINE

The Empire Strikes Back, 1660–1686

My father hath chastised you with whips, but I will chastise you with scorpions.
  —1 Kings 12:11, King James Version

This chapter brings the story from the Stuart Restoration to the end of the Massachusetts court, a period that overlaps the heyday of goldsmith-bankers in London and, as we shall see, the spread of banking ideas throughout the Atlantic.

Massachusetts: Paradise Lost

Imperial Relations

Charles II confirmed the Massachusetts charter but demanded that Interregnum laws that were "contrary and derogatory to our authority" be repealed. This implicitly included the mint law, which violated the royal prerogative. From the beginning of Charles II's rule, Massachusetts's enemies in England marked the continuing minting of coin as a great offense against the Crown. Massachusetts did not repeal the mint law, and it obeyed other royal demands, such as on suffrage, literally rather than in substance. In 1664, the king sent commissioners to inspect New England. They proposed specific changes to Massachusetts laws to reflect the king's authority, including repeal of the mint law, which, they pointed out, was treason. The court ignored them, and soon the king was wholly distracted for a decade by Anglo–Dutch Wars, the Great Plague, and the Great Fire. The mint issue was rarely mentioned again in England before 1676.[1]

King Philip's War started in 1675 and ravaged central and southern New England for a year. As the United Colonies defeated the Indians (and another war just started in the northeast), the attack from England resumed. Edward Randolph, a royal messenger, was followed by England's Privy Council and top legal officers in bombarding the court with accusations and demands for the following seven years.[2] The court and its agents repeatedly asked for pardon for all past "errors." The hottest symbolic issue was the minting—unauthorized and without the king's name or portrait. Randolph, the king's chief scorpion, repeatedly emphasized it as the worst offense and the epitome of treason.[3]

A secondary offense, less noticed by historians, was "power assumed . . . to make money current," i.e., making that coin legal tender.[4] Virginia's royal governor explained the practical problem this caused, in his report to the Privy Council:

> The mint . . . is extremely prejudicial to all his Majesty's subjects, in all other places whatsoever, that deal with them, for they call the piece they coin 1 shilling, and it goes current in all small payments, & great ones too, without special contract . . . equal with the English shilling.[5]

The problem was that the Massachusetts shilling had less silver in it, and Massachusetts judicial courts enforced payments in those lighter coins on other colonists who expected English coins, unless they had "special contract" which explicitly specified otherwise. Making a coin current implied setting an official value to it, and that was also part of the royal prerogative.[6] Making coins legal tender was a separate offense from making coins.

Massachusetts had no chance to keep its charter, because in the new constitutional–religious battle in England, all the charters held by Puritans were targeted, including London and Bermuda. Charles II vacated the charter in 1684. His successor, James II, imposed on Massachusetts a royal government that took over in May 1686.[7] Thus ended fifty-six years of the General Court in America.

Massachusetts also lost influence of its neighborhood. The king gave New Hampshire and Maine to heirs of proprietorships granted in the 1630s by the Council for New England (Massachusetts bought back Maine). New Netherland was occupied by England and became New York—the private colony of James, Duke of York and heir to the throne. The grant from his brother included Pemaquid, north of Maine. Under

Governor Edmund Andros, New York aggressively encroached on the borders of neighboring colonies.[8]

A European treaty returned Acadia to France, but economically, Acadia remained just another small New England colony, sending its furs to Thomas Temple in Boston in return for food and European manufactures. Temple's nephew and heir John Nelson was the chief merchant and lender to Acadia in the early 1680s, owning a storehouse next to the governor's house. He served as a diplomat and as an attorney for both English and French. Intercolonial relations were amicable enough for French officials, including Canada's intendant Jacques de Meulles, to plan to send their children to Boston in the early 1680s to learn English.[9] Other French connections emerged with direct trade to France, as well as when Huguenots from La Rochelle found refuge in New England.[10]

Law of the Land

In that agricultural age, land was of critical importance. As today, it was the main security that people could offer their creditors;[11] and land banks issuing paper money were the hottest financial idea in the English Empire. The court took land law very seriously, because insecure land ownership would eliminate people's incentive to turn woods into farms. Court rulings on land ownership were strictly executed.[12] Land was almost always secure from arbitrary confiscation.[13] The court was flexible for the economy's sake, finalizing transactions halted by the death of the seller, and preferring squatters to absentee owners.[14]

During the battle of the charter, actual and expected changes in jurisdictions made land law a hot political issue. In 1664, the king's commissioners claimed a part of Pequot land and ordered the Massachusetts colonists to leave.[15] The colonists and the court were outraged: the land was conquered in a just war, "improved" at great cost, and "long possessed"; evicting Englishmen without legal process was against local law and Magna Carta; and all land titles would be undermined if some were annulled at the arbitrary whim of commissioners.[16] The rest of Pequot had been granted to Connecticut in a charter, and even there Massachusetts colonists complained of being "injured in their possessions and rights" by Connecticut.[17] After Massachusetts bought Maine, it confirmed land titles there.[18]

The court suspected that land within Massachusetts was also endangered, and reminded the king that they purchased the land "of the natives" and incurred large expenses on settlement.[19] Randolph claimed that by violating the charter the colonists lost not only the right of government but also the land; however, he recommended that the king promise confirmation of land titles as necessary for a peaceful transition to a new regime.[20] The colonists begged for "security in the peaceable enjoyment of their houses and lands, of which they . . . had uninterrupted possession for more than 50 years."[21] When legal proceedings began against the charter in 1683, the king did "declare" that all "properties . . . shall be continued and preserved." Randolph kept working toward such "assurance" and "confirmation" becoming part of the new regime.[22] His partner in that effort was the assistant Joseph Dudley. Son of the late governor Thomas, he had been an agent of the court in London in the battle of the charter. There he betrayed the court and helped designing a postcharter regime.

Similar promises on land failed to deliver in the new royal government of New Hampshire,[23] so upon rumors of the charter's death in 1685, the court prepared for trouble: all former land grants made by the court or towns were confirmed with all conceivable formalities (including the corporation's seal), and towns and individuals obtained Indian backup deeds. The last committee appointed by the court, in 1686, secured "such papers . . . as refer to our title of our land, by purchase of Indians or otherwise."[24]

Paradoxically, this danger to land titles was simultaneous with a huge increase in the supply of land and some new demand for land. Most Indians of the region fled or died in King Philip's War. The Massachusetts elite led a land rush on these areas. The predictable end of the charter stimulated them to grab for free as much land as possible as long as they could. Leading the charge were those who expected to have good relations with the expected royalist regime: Joseph Dudley; his business partner, the assistant William Stoughton; and the Anglican merchant Richard Wharton.[25]

The constitutional–religious crisis of 1680s England led some Puritans to consider emigrating to New England. One of them was our old acquaintance, sixty-one-year-old John Blackwell (chapter 4), who settled in Boston. As the most senior veteran of Cromwell's regime ever to have settled in Massachusetts, he joined the elite and was almost elected an assistant. He was granted land for a new town with potential emigrants.[26] Expecting the regime change, the Cromwellian veteran partnered in the largest land purchases with the leading royalists.[27]

Elites

Economic prosperity drew many merchants—mostly Puritans fleeing Restoration England, but even some Anglicans.[28] As most merchants lived in the Bay, that area dominated economic and financial committees, especially those auditing the treasurer and obtaining loans for the diplomatic effort.[29] Within the Bay, it was probably an intentional check on Boston's power that since the 1640s the treasurer was almost always a Charlestown merchant.

John Winthrop Jr. came to London as governor of Connecticut to obtain a charter for that colony. He was already a member of the "Republic of Letters"—a European-wide network of scientists who communicated with each other by letters and publications and were the main institution behind the Scientific Revolution.[30] In London, Winthrop became the only American member of the newly established Royal Society. His expected contributions were not only American curiosities and "inventions," but also his own chemical-commercial inventions. He was requested "to season and possess the youth of New England" with "this real experimental way of acquiring knowledge" in the spirit of the Scientific Revolution. Back in Connecticut, he achieved little, but he passed the torch to the college in Massachusetts. It was a long torch—English America's only telescope. It was used by the college president, Increase Mather, a pastor who was John Cotton's son-in-law, and by his own son Cotton. They mostly watched comets. In 1683, Increase Mather founded in Boston the Philosophical Society, the first colonial imitation of London's Royal Society.[31]

In line with the consensus among England's scientific community, science mixed with nonsense. John Jr. succeeded in stopping a witch-hunt craze in Connecticut with his combined prestige as a physician and an alchemist. Increase Mather published a collection of local miracles and witchcraft cases. As an amateur astronomer, Mather preached and published that comets were portents of disasters. The court agreed.[32]

Money

Also during the period of 1660–1686, Massachusetts got rid of its Indian-produced commodity moneys. Wampum lost its legal tender status in 1661 due to "much inconvenience," while beaver became irrelevant when it became largely extinct in Massachusetts. These moneys survived only outside the colony's bounds, mostly with Indians, even if beaver furs from faraway were still shipped to and from the Bay.[33]

For two decades, the mint was not disturbed by the Restoration. It took time for the mint to make an impact. More payments in coin appear in court records from 1674.[34] Many public and private payments, such as the college president's salary, were partly in coin and partly in commodity money.[35] Complaints of coin shortage continued,[36] to some extent because illegal coin export continued.[37] Most English colonies gave Massachusetts coin official status as a prime foreign coin, and Montserrat even fined people "refusing" these coins.[38]

From 1673, it became the rule to abate a quarter of a taxpayer's tax if he paid it in coin. During the war, this fraction increased and peaked at a half in 1679, after which another mechanism dominated: following a Plymouth precedent, the court forced some fraction of each tax to be paid in coin. In 1683–1684, *most* taxes were to be paid in coin (figure 9.1).[39] The treasurer kept separate accounts in coin and in country pay.[40] The change was officially attributed to the battle of the charter in London, where supposedly only coin was accepted.[41] It was impossible to continually bribe officials for access and favors with bills of exchange.

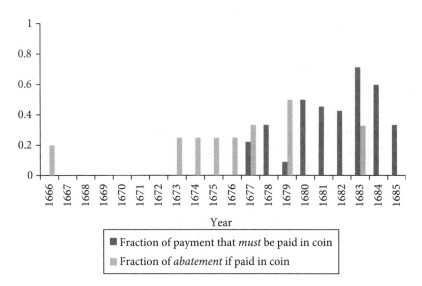

FIGURE 9.1 Court preferences for coin in taxes (as fraction), 1666–1685. Source: See note 39.

This policy required that constables convert commodity money they collected into coin, which could generally be done only in the Bay.[42]

These changes can perhaps be attributed in part to the personal interest of the mint master John Hull, who advanced from deputy to treasurer (1676) to assistant (1680). As treasurer, he asked the court to increase the pro-coin abatement even more.[43] Hull may have realized that demanding or incentivizing tax payments to be made with some object artificially increases demand for that object; such policy can induce the object's wider acceptance in the private economy. But it was surely not only Hull's interest, since the mandatory coin payments continued after both the mint and Hull had died.

Because each Massachusetts coin contained less silver than an English coin of the same name, a new unit of account was born, paralleling the terminology of money in England: *New England money/silver* or *lawful/current money of this colony/country/New England*. Not all payments so phrased were actually made in coin. These terms became the default in real estate deeds, in which there was probably not enough coin to execute the transactions.[44]

The battle of the charter killed the mint, probably in 1682, when the last contract with Hull expired.[45] The court reverted to the 1640s practice of legalizing Spanish coin with neither reminting nor restamping.[46] The supply of such coin was augmented by pirates who were allegedly protected by the colony.[47]

Banking and Finance

While London banking started with goldsmiths, even the most prominent Bostonian goldsmith (John Hull) left no evidence of banking activity—that is, of lending other people's money or issuing standardized banknotes and checks.[48] Boston did gain experience with large-scale private finance, but it originated elsewhere.

THE FUND. A pamphlet titled *Severals relating to the Fund* was published anonymously in 1682 by Boston's printing press.[49] The author told of his attempts, over more than three decades, to solve the money problem of New England through a bank. It began with discussions in London in 1649 with the financial projector William Potter (p. 43). The author attempted his own plan from 1664 after moving to New England. He operated the Fund in 1671, until "putting a stop to it" in 1672, "when bills were just to be issued forth." In 1681, he restarted the project in Boston and began "to pass forth bills, to make an experiment," and soon he published the pamphlet.[50]

The project's name, "Fund," meant a "deposit in land: Real, durable, and of secure value."[51] The plan was flexible—a public or private bank, based on deposits of land titles or "merchandise," with several methods of transferring purchasing power: "book entries," "bills of exchange for great payments," and "change bills" of less than five pounds as "running cash" or "pocket expense" instead of coin.[52] Massachusetts records document seven mortgages of land, mostly in Boston, made to the Fund from 1681 to 1683. The Boston mortgages were made by artisans, a merchant, and a mariner, and ranged from £14 to £100. They were all made to trustees of the Fund—three Boston merchants, one of whom was Adam Winthrop, a grandson of John and the first Winthrop to graduate from the college.[53]

Who was the Fund's author and leader? Only one "Director" is known from the mortgage records, the merchant Daniel Henchman; but the author identified himself as a minister rather than a merchant.[54] James Hammond Trumbull, the nineteenth-century Connecticut historian who discovered the pamphlet, conjectured the author to be John Woodbridge, a Massachusetts minister who returned to England in 1647 and back to Massachusetts in 1663. Trumbull's conjecture is circumstantial: Woodbridge lived in England in 1649 (the Potter meeting); he was connected to the elite through marriages; and his son would launch paper money in 1704 Barbados.[55]

Trumbull's conjecture has remained undisputed and widely cited to this day.[56] As I show in detail elsewhere, however, a careful reading of the pamphlet reveals that the author was *not* someone who migrated back and forth.[57] Moreover, Woodbridge's elite contacts disqualify him since the author described two degrees of separation from the magistrates.[58] The only nonmerchant prominent in the mortgage records was the shipwright Timothy Thornton. He did most errands for the Fund: getting clients, witnessing their deeds, accepting Fund bills, and liquidating clients' debts. It's interesting that his father, Thomas, was a minister who came from England in 1663. Is it possible that Thomas was the author?

Thomas Thornton moved to Yarmouth in Plymouth, rather than Massachusetts. Although historians have assumed that all the Fund's history occurred in Massachusetts, nothing in the pamphlet disqualifies Plym-

outh as the place where the Fund was under consideration for two decades before being implemented in Boston. Timothy may have been the
real manager, though, since his seventy-four-year-old father lived in Yarmouth.[59] Timothy may have been what the author described as that combination of "spirit, purse, and hand" that relaunched the Fund in 1681
Boston.[60]

No mortgages were given after February 1683, and the only later records are of redeeming mortgages in 1684–1685. The Fund perhaps
ended because of the uncertainty of all land titles due to the battle of the
charter. In November 1683 the colony learned that the king started legal
proceedings to vacate the charter.[61] It was no time to base a new credit-
and-payments system on land titles. But we will meet Timothy Thornton
and the trustee Adam Winthrop again in 1690.

If the Fund's bills were printed, they were surely printed at Boston's
press, which printed the Fund's pamphlet. That press was managed by
Samuel Sewall, a graduate of the college and a friend and relative of the
Fund's director, Daniel Henchman. Both were protégés of the merchant
John Hull, whose only surviving child was Sewall's wife. Sewall was appointed to the press by the court after the press's owner died, "at the instance of some friends" (perhaps the assistant John Hull).[62] As the basic mechanism of printing on paper was similar in principle to that of
stamping coin,[63] perhaps Sewall was appointed because he had acquired
managerial or technical skill from mint master Hull. Although the press
was probably imported from England, goldsmith Hull was best suited
to produce metallic movable type when necessary.[64] When Hull died in
1683, Sewall inherited his closed mint and his mercantile empire.[65] The
following year, he became an assistant and left the press.[66] Sewall became the only colonist with either the experience, knowledge, or equipment for producing both coin and paper money.

THE GOSPEL COMPANY. The Company for Propagation of the Gospel in
New England was a chartered English company, headed by the scientist Robert Boyle, that financed the Christian conversion of Indians. The
corporation's funds were sent to the commissioners of the United Colonies, and they appointed a treasurer in Boston. That office was filled in
the 1670s by John Richards, who was already treasurer of Boston and of
the college. In the 1680s, the treasurer was the assistant William Stoughton.[67] A single 1685 list shows fifty-three outstanding loans, ranging from

£5 to £416, and totaling £3,435. The borrowers ranged from illiterate widows and artisans to merchants and assistants. Almost all these loans were secured by bonds and/or mortgages, depending on the borrower's wealth and the loan's size.[68] It was not a bank, because there were no depositors to whom interest was paid; in modern terminology, that treasurer in Boston was the chief financial officer of an English corporation.

Public Finance in War

The existential war of 1675–1676 took the problem of public finance to a whole new level. The same basic principles were used as in the Pequot War, but the scale was a significant complication.

EXPENSES AND INCOMES. Massachusetts spent more than £46,000, including £10,000 in soldiers' wages.[69] Soldiers were promised "a gratuity in land besides their wages" before a critical battle—or so claimed a 1731 petition by old veterans and heirs of others who asked for land. Plymouth did make such a promise, as well as a promise that all lands and other plunder be "security for the soldiers' pay."[70]

Most expenses were paid by taxes, measured in a unit called a "rate" that had been set as the expected tax in normal years: twenty pence per man and 1/240 of one's property.[71] Figure 9.2 shows the amounts of rates enacted per year from 1646 until the end of the charter government.

The government became far more active during the war, suddenly needing to feed, clothe, and arm thousands of soldiers. Taxes were enacted more frequently and collected more urgently. One tax was to be paid within a month "for the payment of soldiers." Most tax exemptions and loopholes were suspended. Towns were not exempt even from paying the taxes of emigrants and of the dead.[72] But the effects lingered long afterward, because taxpayers could not discharge all the government debts at once, and the war debts combined with new costs from a northeastern war and the battle of the charter. The tax burden in the final decade of the charter era was twice as that of the three preceding decades combined. Many could not pay taxes in time, and this led to increased social and political tensions.[73]

Military fines were a minor source of income. Fines were threatened against frontier civilians "deserting" their homes, after the court threatened to confiscate their lands to pay garrison costs.[74] The main movable

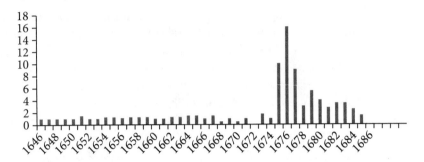

FIGURE 9.2 Taxes in Massachusetts (in rates), 1646–1685. Sources: MAGC II, IV-I, IV-II, V, *passim*.

plunder item was "188 prisoners at war, sold,"[75] but the most valuable plunder was "the conquest lands," sold off by a joint United Colonies committee.[76]

DEBTS AND SETTLEMENTS. During the war, the treasury was "exhausted," so the court asked "gentlemen in Boston" and merchants for loans of funds and war supplies, and ordered ministers to "exhort" the people to lend. The urgency brought unprecedented promises: the treasurer would give lenders receipts under his hand and seal; lenders were promised repayment at a specific time or in coin, or that "for further security" the colony would reserve "all public and common lands within this jurisdiction, and all the interest . . . in any conquered lands."[77] Commissioners for the war were to "pass . . . debenture" to each soldier based on his officer's report. These were the Pequot War notes, renamed after the Civil Wars' debentures. Debentures and other war accounts were audited by a merchants' committee and sent by the thousands to the treasurer John Hull. He was aided by his relative, the future Fund director Daniel Henchman.[78]

Creditors "for wages, horses, provisions, etc." could ask that their claims be sent to constables for trilateral debt settlements, and, indeed, constables paid "bills drawn upon us from the Treasurer."[79] Setoff was generally applied only when the value of clothes provided to soldiers was "deducted" from debentures upon payment.[80] The court ordered setoff with petitioners, including having taxes "discounted" from their claims.[81]

Most expenses were probably made in commodity money. Few payments in land were explicitly related to the war.[82] The large war expenses in Connecticut River towns, and the transportation costs there, resulted in a compromise of thirds: the treasurer was "ordered to pay them two-thirds of what is their just due."[83] The court was silent about the last third.

Atlantic Banking

Barbados

In 1661, the London merchant and bank entrepreneur Francis Cradock (p. 45) partnered with a royal official in a petition to the king for an "experiment" in Barbados—a bank based on land and goods. Thus the sandy island was to serve as what is known today as a "sandbox" (for experiments in software and financial regulation). England ordered the Barbados government to assist the project, which was to be controlled by Cradock as well as royal and local interests. While the bank could receive sugar—the main crop—the bank's bills and transfers between accounts were supposed to exclude physical sugar as legal tender for debts.[84] The bank was never heard of, probably because both the emigrating Cradock and the royal representative in the bank's management, Sir John Colleton, were on bad terms with the local government for unrelated reasons.[85]

Connecticut

The polymath entrepreneur John Winthrop Jr. had a project of which few details are known. It was "a way of trade and bank without money" or "bank of lands and commodities," but at some point he was skeptical about land. In 1661, Winthrop communicated about it with the influential science and banking promoter Samuel Hartlib (chapter 4). In 1663, Winthrop presented the plan to the Royal Society, to which he belonged, hoping it would achieve "the great advance of trade" as achieved elsewhere by "banks of ready money." He hoped the society, given its "acquaintance and interest . . . in the gentry, merchants, and citizens," and "the sufficient insight that many of them have into matters of trade and exchange," would promote the idea or make "a trial . . . among gentlemen and merchants." Although "understanding men" were expected to consider the plan after Winthrop left, it was never heard of again.[86]

Perhaps the plan was similar to Antigua's tobacco banknotes—a "bank without money" and without land. It had existed at least since

1654. John's half-brother, Samuel, left Antigua that year but returned from neighboring Saint Christopher in the early 1660s. Samuel treated John Jr., twenty-one years older than him, as a father figure, calling him "the chief pillar of our family" after their father died. He wrote to John Jr. regularly—more than to anyone else, as far as we know. Their correspondence revolved around family issues (Samuel sent some of his children to live in New England), their business relations, and religion.[87] There is no trace of the Antiguan banks in their surviving correspondence, but information could have been transmitted verbally through bearers of letters who usually gave additional information.[88]

Antigua

The tobacco-backed banking system, destroyed in a 1666 French occupation, was revived in 1669, perhaps with some modifications. The law ordered bringing all tobacco to a regional "public storehouse." After quality inspections,

> the said storehouse keeper shall give to each party a receipt or storehouse note under his hand, containing the weight of the tobacco he received from him and the day of the month when brought in, which said note is to be at the only dispose and for the proper use of the owner of the said tobacco, his heirs and assignees.[89]

It was ordered that "no payment into tobacco shall be otherwise made from the planter to the merchant or from one planter to another than by the said storehouse notes." Complaints about keepers' frauds, in which "merchants and others" who presented notes for redemption received a third less than the amount promised in the notes, led to elimination of the system in 1675.[90]

That revived system was perhaps known in New England, even more than in the 1650s. Samuel Winthrop is again the leading candidate for transmitting such information. Around 1670, he reached the top of Antigua's political and economic elite. He kept doing business with New Englanders, including half-brother John Jr. and the Boston merchant Richard Wharton. Always desiring to move back home, he kept some of his sons in Boston to "learn to write and cipher and gain some knowledge in accounts."[91]

West New Jersey

In 1681, the Englishman Mark Newbie arrived from Dublin to the new
Quaker colony of West New Jersey. He brought thousands of special
copper coins of unknown origin. In 1682, he was elected councillor, and
West New Jersey passed this law:

> For the more convenient payment of small sums . . . Mark Newbie's half-
> pence, called Patrick's half-pence, shall . . . pass for half-pence current pay
> of this Province, provided he the said Mark, give sufficient security . . . that
> he . . . will change the said half-pence for pay equivalent, upon demand; . . . no
> person . . . obliged to take more than five shillings in one payment.

The extent to which Newbie's coins circulated is not clear, because by
1684 he was dead, with thousands of coins in his possession.[92] The importance is that base coin was given the status of legal tender for small
debts, and that it functioned like a banknote: Newbie had to redeem
these token coins in goods or proper coin upon demand. The security he
deposited was, not surprisingly, a land title.[93]

Other Projects

In 1691, a claim would be made in Boston regarding private bills passing
elsewhere for some years, perhaps including the early 1680s:

> One gentleman's bills at Port Royal for diverse years, and that among for-
> eigners; or another gentleman's bills in the western parts for as many or more
> years . . . gain so much credit as to be current pay, among the traders in those
> places; yea, that the bill (as I have heard) of any one magistrate in the western
> English plantation shall buy any commodities of any of the planters.[94]

Regarding Port Royal, Acadia's capital, there is only one candidate: the
Boston merchant John Nelson (p. 118). This is implied by his biography and confirmed by his biographer Richard Johnson.[95] The "western
parts" and the "western English plantation" meant—for contemporary
Bostonians—the Hudson River area.[96] These note-issuing gentlemen
had "a good bottom for their credit in their warehouses," meaning they

were merchants whose goods could be legally seized if they failed to redeem bills.

In Maryland, after Lord Baltimore's rule was restored, his government asked him for a local mint. The only legal status supporting the money—as debased as in Massachusetts—was to be its acceptance in all payments to the proprietor, with the usual term *current* mentioned only regarding other coins.[97] Although payments to Baltimore were formally rents rather than taxes, the mechanism was similar: only the government issuing the money had to receive it, and this commitment seemed necessary and sufficient to get a debased money to circulate. Eventually Maryland had special "current" coin of an unknown mint. Later there were complaints about this coin in England, but apparently Baltimore was permitted to continue minting.[98]

*   *   *

It took Restoration England twenty-six years to kill the charter government. The delay had consequences. First, Massachusetts minting survived long enough to come to fruition and make an impact. It presumably increased people's dependence on money, encouraging more occupational specialization. Second, by the time the mint died, the practice and theory of banking in the English Empire had advanced so much that Massachusetts had alternatives. Actual or projected land banks, goods banks, and goldsmith-bankers—in England, Massachusetts, Connecticut, Antigua, Barbados, and West New Jersey—made paper money a far more realistic option than in 1660 at the Restoration. Land, already the basis of traditional credit, was especially relevant for America because of its relative abundance. After land's use extended to soldiers' compensation and lenders' security during the great war, it was used as the basis for the Fund in Boston—but its legal status was severely threatened by England.

In the end, the mint's violation of the royal prerogative made no political difference in the battle of the charter. The charter would have been killed anyway, because Charles II targeted all his enemies' charters. However, the coinage offense and the battle of the charter would still have an impact. First, a legal paper trail was created in England on the coinage offense, and would be used again. Second, the delay allowed the court to receive thorough training in law and diplomacy, which would soon become useful.

CHAPTER TEN

Governments and Paper Money Projects, 1685–1689

Then saith he unto them, Render therefore unto Caesar the things which are Caesar's.
—Matthew 22:21, King James Version

The 1690 Massachusetts money, legally supported only by its acceptance for paying taxes, could be created only by a government. Government's power over paper money—with different legal support—was demonstrated several times in the few years preceding that invention, in Massachusetts and its nonimmediate neighborhood. Where governments refused to cooperate with paper money projects or projectors, paper money had no chance. Where a government created paper money, it succeeded.

The Massachusetts episode will also bring the story to the eve of the Glorious Revolution. The effects of that episode would be consequential even after the Revolution.

The Dominion of New England

Imperial Relations

To ease Massachusetts's transition to a royal colony, England appointed a temporary local president. The useful idiot was the former assistant Joseph Dudley. He presided over a council, appointed by England, that controlled the Dominion of New England—Massachusetts, New Hampshire, Maine, and part of Pequot. Dudley appointed as deputy president his business partner, the former assistant William Stoughton. Councillors included Wait and Fitz-John Winthrop, sons of the late John Winthrop Jr. The president and the council bore the mark of the new king, James II: absolute authority on all legislative, executive, and judicial matters.[1]

Why did Dudley and the Winthrops betray the heritage of their legendary Founding Fathers in leading a dictatorship? The historian Theodore Lewis blames the land rush, in which they were involved. To keep their land, they needed to be in power.[2] Other councillors were enemies of the charter regime, such as Edward Randolph and Richard Wharton. As Dudley's council took power in May 1686, it appointed committees as a partial substitute to the missing assembly, most notably in a thirty-two-member "grand and standing committee" of merchants to advise on trade and economic matters.[3]

Soon the former governor of New York, Sir Edmund Andros, was appointed governor of the dominion. He arrived in December 1686 to take over Plymouth, Connecticut, and Rhode Island too. Dudley was still called president, and he and Stoughton were judges of the Superior Court. Councillors would later complain that Andros actually ruled without them; colonists referred to Andros's government as French, alluding to Louis XIV, and "as arbitrary as the Great Turk" (the Ottoman Sultan).[4] Andros usually consulted the New York cronies he imported: the deputy secretary John West, attorney generals George Farewell and James Graham, and the Superior Court judge John Palmer. Sheriff James Sherlock had arrived from serving another dictator in New Hampshire. The Puritans complained bitterly about these "strangers."[5] In 1688, Andros received a new commission that added New York, East New Jersey, and West New Jersey to the dominion.

As soon as the Massachusetts charter died, there was renewed interest in England and among royalists in reviving the mint under royal authority. Dudley's council, Randolph, and Andros tried to convince England that "our trade for want of money is much perplexed and decayed." They failed, due to the Royal Mint's objection to any coin lighter than its own.[6] Other evidence is not decisive regarding coin shortage; the most remarkable one, though, is the town of Hingham's delivery of empty milk pails as tax payment.[7]

Law of the Land

The biggest story of the dominion period was Andros's land policy. He was instructed by the king to examine the largest land projects and report home, and to "dispose of" land "for which our royal confirmation may be wanting."[8] Andros used the latter instruction to launch a total attack on all Massachusetts lands—one befitting a foreign occupation, as the colonists had feared all along.

Andros disappointed the large land investors of his council by blocking their legal efforts and recommending that England reject their claims. After appointing crony John West as land registrar, Andros told people that *all* titles to settled land were fatally defective according to English law, for several reasons. First, although the Crown granted the land to the company, the land reverted to the Crown once the charter was revoked. Second, the court did not seal its grants in real time as requested by the charter, and the frantic ex post sealing of grants in 1685 was invalid because the company was legally dead. Third, as a corporation, the company could not create other corporations, so the towns were unincorporated. Thus all the towns' grants to individuals were void. Fourth, Andros told colonists that Indian deeds were worthless. The Charlestown merchant Joseph Lynde testified:

> After showing [Andros] an Indian deed for land, he said that their hand [i.e., signature] was no more worth than a scratch with a bear's paw, undervaluing all my titles, though everyway legal under our former charter government.[9]

All this concerns mortgageable lands—the foundation of credit; but all other lands and other types of property were also specifically targeted: town commons, Puritan churches, the college, Gospel Company funds, and wrecks of both ships and whales. The colonists believed Andros would use "tricks, juggles, and designs" to seize all their "money, ships, goods, merchandizes, . . . houses and lands."[10]

Andros implemented his "defective land title" policy gradually to avoid a revolution. He told some people that they had to ask for warrants to survey the land they claimed and later apply for confirmation that the land was theirs. His cronies led by example and also applied for personal ownership of town commons.[11] The main policy lines came to the forefront by July 1687. The value of any mortgageable land was seriously reduced: unconfirmed land could have been grabbed by anyone, while confirmation would result in very high legal fees and, later, rents to the king. The fees, of course, were the whole point—generating income for Andros's cronies.

The colonists argued that possession and improvement of the land for half a century were more important than the technical defects Andros cited, and that purchases from Indians were valid. They asked for a blanket royal confirmation of their land holdings, as had been done regarding civil marriages in Andros's commission.[12] They organized legal action at town meetings and took cases to court, so Andros outlawed such meetings, and leaders of legal action were threatened with increased legal fees and prosecution.[13] In 1687, leading colonists sailed to England to lobby against Andros's policy: councillor Richard Wharton, who was the largest land investor; two former assistants; and college president Increase Mather. Most colonists procrastinated with title confirmations, hoping for the lobbyists' success.

On July 5, 1688, Andros received the new royal commission that extended his territory and said nothing of his land policy despite the colonists' lobbying.[14] A week later, the emboldened governor launched a legal attack with writs of intrusion, that accused the recipients of illegally possessing the king's land.[15] Writs were issued to two Boston merchants and two Charlestown merchants—the councillor Samuel Shrimpton, former assistant Samuel Sewall, former treasurer James Russell, and former deputy Joseph Lynde—all of whom had had specific land disputes with Andros. Attorney General James Graham said that all the rich would be targeted for all their lands.[16] The writs sent a clear message: all land titles were worthless.

The colonists were stupefied. One wrote, "Some in power have said that it is not for the King's interest that this people should enjoy it [i.e., the land], and if another people had it would be more for the King's interest than now."[17] Sewall, Russell, and Lynde petitioned for surveys of their lands, as did others, lest they be targeted too.[18] Sewall also wrote to the lobbyists in London, sent them money, and then joined them in person. In London, he wrote to a member of Parliament:

> The title we have to our lands has been greatly defamed and undervalued: Which has been greatly prejudicial to the inhabitants, because their lands, which were formerly the best part of their estate, became of very little value, and consequently the owners of very little credit.[19]

Undermining land titles was ruinous to credit.

Banking

John Blackwell arrived in Boston in 1685 with the idea of the bank of credit project he participated in two years earlier in London (p. 45).[20] In a prospectus, he proposed issuing "bank-bills of credit, signed by several persons of good repute" with a minimal value of £1.[21] This was considerably below the value proposed in bank schemes in England. The bank's partners and others "of all trades, callings, ranks and conditions" were supposed to publicly commit to accepting the bills in trade "as ready moneys." The bank offered loans in its bills in return for mortgaged assets (mostly lands rather than goods). Defaulting borrowers would lose these assets, and proceeds of the assets' sale would be available for banknote redemption.

Blackwell's bank scheme won exceptional progress in 1686. In July, Blackwell proposed it to the new council, which referred the proposal to the standing trade committee. The committee was in favor, and in September the council approved the committee's report and promised to act for the bank—"a public and useful invention"—so that it could solve the coin shortage. The council even made the prospective banknotes "current moneys in all receipts and payments," including taxes paid to "the Treasurer and the receivers thereof."[22]

It is highly unusual in monetary history, before and after 1686, to give the status of legal tender to private financial instruments. Why were the bank and its bills so favored by the trade committee and the council? Merits of the bank aside, Blackwell headed the trade committee. Two other senior members of the committee would soon become senior bank officers, while the bank directors would be Blackwell and three councillors—Joseph Dudley, William Stoughton, and Wait Winthrop.[23] It is unknown when these men joined Blackwell's project, but such symbiotic relations between the absolutist government, the advising trade committee, and the private bank were typical of the era; no large-scale private business could succeed without giving the ruling elite its personal share.[24] Blackwell's chief partners were large land investors, and the bank would have allowed them to convert land into money.

Enter Andros, scorpion-in-chief. His land policy was a fatal problem for the bank. Dudley apparently tried to make Andros a bank partner.[25] While Andros's policy was low key, the bank plan still progressed, as late as January 1688.[26] The writs of intrusion of July 12, 1688, killed the bank. Four days later, on the day when petitions of frightened colonists to survey their lands peaked, Blackwell aborted the bank. His letter indicates that trials had been made with printing bills but that his partners had already showed signs of backing off. The writs sealed the deal for Blackwell, and formal liquidation occurred a month later.[27] A Restoration victim, Blackwell knew the consequences of a constitutional change on property: game over for a bank relying mostly on lands with "unquestionable good title," as his prospectus stated.[28] As Sewall put it, no land could be used as a source of credit. Bank directors Dudley, Stoughton and Winthrop could do nothing while Andros "resolved and practiced to make all men's titles quite null and void," as the latter two would testify.[29] Andros probably did not kill the bank on purpose, but simply had better uses for the land. Like the land investors, he also wanted to convert land to money—but for him, it was in the form of fees.[30]

Quaker Banking

The new Quaker colonies, being led by merchants, moved toward banking almost immediately.[31] The merchant Thomas Budd was councillor and treasurer of West New Jersey. As land commissioner, he received the mortgage that the coin importer Mark Newbie gave as security for redeeming his token coins (p. 129).[32] In 1685, Budd published a book on the economic potential of the Quaker colonies—Pennsylvania and the New Jerseys. He plagiarized two proposals from a 1677 book published in England by Andrew Yarranton: (1) registering all bills and making them transferable by assignment, and (2) a land registry to support a land bank.[33]

According to the historian Katie Moore, Budd's bank could not be established in West New Jersey because of a power struggle between Edward Byllynge, an absentee governor in England, and the local assembly, which elected its own governor. With no "land security and political stability," says Moore, a land bank had no chance.[34] The dispute was apparently resolved in Byllynge's favor by Quaker arbitrators in London during the same year Budd's book was published. Unfortunately, Budd was one of the leaders of the opposition to Byllynge.[35] Immediately after losing the fight, he relocated to Pennsylvania. There, Budd found five partners for a bank project, wisely including two councillors. In February 1689, they petitioned, "setting forth their design in setting up a bank for money, requesting encouragement from the Governor & Council for their proceeding therein."[36] The governor was . . . John Blackwell.

On the same day that Andros issued the writs of intrusion that killed Blackwell's bank, Pennsylvania's proprietor William Penn (living in England) appointed Blackwell governor of Pennsylvania. Penn heard of Blackwell's wisdom, ability, and integrity, and thought this financial expert would turn the colony from charging bills of exchange to the proprietor to paying him rents. In December 1688, Blackwell moved from Boston to Philadelphia.[37]

Blackwell's response to the bank proposal was not enthusiastic. He acknowledged local coin shortage, but before leaving Boston he had proposed something similar to Penn, and he was awaiting a reply. He told the partners instead to "give their personal bills to such as would take them as money to pass, as merchants usually did bills of exchange."[38] Blackwell essentially threw the partners out the window—back to the beginning of the century. His procrastination (perhaps because he was not made a partner) was soon followed by the confusions of the Glorious Revolution, and the matter died.

Canada's Card Money: Old Idea, New World

Since we left Canada in 1630, it had become a royal colony of a few thousand people, still dependent on furs. Its governor general handled military and external affairs. The real autocrat was the intendant—a bureaucrat educated in law, who was in charge of local civil affairs, including treasury, legislation, and police. He chaired the Sovereign Council, which validated all ordinances by registering them. Communication with France was usually made once a year, due to the winter freezing of the Saint Lawrence River. French ships arrived in the summer with manufactures, royal orders, new settlers, soldiers if needed, and new coin. In the fall, the ships returned to France with furs and officials' reports.[39]

Canada conformed to the monetary methods of other colonies, with an authoritarian twist. Official currencies included fur and wheat. French coin was overvalued to keep it in the colony. A debased French colonial coin was barely present. Foreign coin was overvalued and forced on all transactions under penalty.[40] In 1682, a new, absolutist intendant arrived, Jacques de Meulles. He ordered a merchant to sell guns to all men for grain and pork. Since the forced foreign coins were light and worn, they did not circulate; De Meulles opened a mint that restamped these coins to authenticate their true weight.[41]

Just Another Siege Money

In 1683–1684, hundreds of soldiers were sent from France to Canada due to tense relations with Indians. Instead of sending clothes, food, or coins to pay the soldiers, France sent goods, such as guns and lead, and bills of exchange drawn on local merchants. The bills were very hard to sell or redeem for coin. De Meulles complained in November 1684: for "subsisting the troops, one must have one thing only—ready money." In February 1685, he started paying soldiers from his own resources, taking out personal loans to do so. In March, he prohibited the use of coin in buying fur from Indians. In April, he let soldiers work for wages with locals, but many could not find jobs. Local credit dried, and the ships from France—the only supply of coin—were late. De Meulles was desperate.[42]

He obtained playing cards, cut each into four pieces, wrote on them three denominations, signed them, and gave them to the soldiers. In June, he issued an ordinance that was registered by the Sovereign Council and promised redemption in coin: "They shall be paid from the first funds, which His Majesty will surely send us." For enhanced credibility, de Meulles added a personal guarantee on the ordinance's margin: "We are answerable for them in our personal and private name." The ordinance continued, "We forbid all persons of whatsoever quality and condition to refuse any of them, or to sell their supplies for them dearer than customary, under penalty."[43]

In September, the ships arrived with the expected coin. De Meulles gave all cardholders eight days to redeem the cards for coin. He reported the whole affair to France, claiming that the cards did circulate, were redeemed as promised, and were then destroyed. In February 1686, while de Meulles was away, his deputy issued another batch and called it *monnoye de cartes* ("card money"). In September 1686, ships arrived from France with the king's disapproval of the 1685 episode due to fear of counterfeiting. However, the deputy's promise was honored, and all cards were redeemed with newly arrived coin.[44]

Why cards? Scholars speculated about lack of writing paper and a printing press, and an abundance of playing cards made of durable paper, with printed pictures that could help the many illiterates identify denominations and prevent counterfeiting.[45] Cards were abundant because, though officially frowned upon, they served a critical pastime during the long idle winters.[46] Cut in four, cards had the right size and were really just rectangular paper coins. Furthermore, they had blank back sides that could be used to write denominations and signatures.

Inventions and discoveries are known to take place when the inventor thinks about the problem while physically handling what turns out to be the solution—Archimedes's Eureka moment, Edison's light bulb.[47] Perhaps, during a card game, de Meulles noticed that the cards, just like coins, were durable hand-to-hand objects with royal portraits. There was a technical similarity between stamping playing cards and stamping coins.[48] Moreover, the most probable origin of playing cards—in China—is as paper money;[49] paper money simply came full circle in Canada.

De Meulles claimed it was his original idea. He might have copied it, consciously or not, from an earlier episode, such as the one reported by Marco Polo; a 1480s Spanish siege money, forced on the population, had been reported in a French political book that was very popular at the beginning of the seventeenth century. Maybe de Meulles found it among the books of his father—a royal councillor and treasurer general of war supplies.[50]

The card money story has been attacked by many historians in the United States and Britain who have tried to crown the 1690 Massachusetts money as the first paper money in America. One legal scholar has argued that it was not money because it was imposed by a dictator, the redemption mechanism was not written on the cards, and France disavowed it ex post.[51] Such legalistic arguments would disqualify most moneys in history and are irrelevant for the economic definition used here. Another scholar has argued that card money was only a "promissory note,"[52] but it was more: unlike debentures, it was designed with three denominations in order to function as money, and it did function as money. John Kenneth Galbraith relegated the card money to a footnote in his discussion of the 1690 Massachusetts money, stating inaccurately that this card money was merely a contemporary "experiment."[53] These scholars mention only the 1685 episode, and not the decades of card money that followed, making it look like an anecdotal curiosity. Other scholars have implicitly ignored the card money when claiming that Massachusetts issued the first paper money in America.[54]

Card money's goofy appearance begs for mockery,[55] but improvising an invention from an existing product is common in the history of technology. James Watt improvised a piston and a cylinder with a syringe, while the Wright brothers—bicycle repairmen in trade—practically used bicycle parts in their clumsy flyer.[56] It is the *function* of the final product that is of significance, not the appearance.

How Did Massachusetts Know?

The greatest scholar of Massachusetts money, Andrew McFarland Davis, took it for granted that by 1690 Massachusetts knew about Canada's card money, but he argued it was "of little consequence" for Massachusetts's paper money. Only Blackwell's planned banknotes, he argued, affected 1690.[57] The circumstances suggest otherwise. Canada issued paper money for the same reason that Massachusetts would—to pay soldiers during a military emergency. This was far different from land-backed paper money issued to borrowing farmers in peacetime. Canada's contribution was bringing the old idea of emergency paper money for soldiers from distant or ancient episodes to the neighborhood of Massachusetts. It was a key ingredient in the 1690 Massachusetts invention, which had nevertheless entirely different legal support and economic theory behind it.

We shall see later that, beyond a reasonable doubt, the Massachusetts court indeed knew about Canada's card money in 1690. How could it know? De Meulles was only two degrees of separation from the very top of the Massachusetts elite after visiting Acadia in the 1685–1686 winter. He got stuck for five months, "bored to death," at the house of the recent Acadian governor Michel la Vallière—who told him about John Nelson.[58] That Bostonian merchant, the "gentleman" whose bills circulated in Acadia, would have been interested to hear about card money. Nelson and other merchants did keep contact with Acadia and France, despite the dominion's better enforcement of Parliament's new Navigation Acts.[59] Nelson was member of Boston's elite social-military club, the Artillery Company; his wife was the niece of Deputy President William Stoughton.[60]

Another important potential route involves the Huguenots. As de Meulles was heading to Acadia and his letter was heading to France, Louis XIV outlawed Protestantism. Hundreds of thousands of Huguenots fled during the following years, including to America. Many refugees were merchants from the main Huguenot city of La Rochelle—the conduit for most of the communication with Canada. Some formed new trade routes with relatives in France who converted or pretended to convert.[61] In the dominion, both Puritans and Anglicans welcomed these fellow Protestants, even raising money for them. A French church was established in Boston, and Cotton Mather had a professional association with its minister. Large landholders, including Dudley, Stoughton, Blackwell, and Wharton, settled Huguenots on their lands. The settling refugees interacted with both locals and government.[62] Perhaps some refugees knew about card money.

A third potential route went through the Indian-populated forests between the French and English colonies. It was inhabited by French traders who sold fur to the English. The traders often spent all their money in Canadian towns before returning to the woods. These men would have been a continuous source of Canadian information to the English. The forests also saw Canadian Huguenots, including soldiers (perhaps firsthand recipients of card money), fleeing to the English colonies.[63] All this interaction was mostly with Albany, but Massachusetts and New York were always in contact, and in 1688 both were members of the dominion.

*   *   *

Money is power. But often, power is money. Governments could determine what would and what would not be money, especially when it was intrinsically useless and thus in crucial need of some legal support. All the cases reviewed here involved Old World–style dictators, but this precept would remain true even for the upcoming, relatively democratic government of Massachusetts. Moreover, two of the episodes just reviewed would inspire crucial components of the 1690 money.

CHAPTER ELEVEN

The Massachusetts Legislator

The Case of Elisha Hutchinson

Then Elisha said, Hear ye the word of the Lord; Thus saith the Lord, To morrow about this time shall a measure of fine flour be sold for a shekel, and two measures of barley for a shekel, in the gate of Samaria.
—2 Kings 7:1, King James Version

The preceding chapters describe all the knowledge necessary for 1690 Massachusetts to construct its novel legal tender law. But there was no computer to receive all the relevant information as input and eject a new monetary law as output. Laws are written by humans. Before proceeding chronologically to the Glorious Revolution in America and its consequences, it is time for a closer look at the background of the Massachusetts legislators who would enact the 1690 money. Here we focus on a biography of one assistant who would have a special importance in 1690, and whose qualifications were representative of his class.[1]

A Dynasty of Troublemakers

In the beginning, there was William the Conqueror, who solidified his rule in England with mass murder (the Harrying of the North). His fourth-generation descendant was the bad king John, who was forced to grant the Magna Carta. John's grandson, Edward I, dedicated his life to giving the Middle Ages a bad name. Unusually tall for the period—

six feet, two inches—he was nicknamed Longshanks. He united the island by occupying the Welsh and Scots and butchering their leaders
alive: the last Prince of Wales (whose title he stole) and William Wallace. They were hanged, drawn, and quartered, under the new crime of
"treason"—against a king who was not theirs. Edward united the English people with violent antisemitism, aptly summarized by the historian
Alan Ereira: "The Third Reich would adopt his entire program." Edward deported all the Jews he did not murder.[2]

Before becoming king, the pious barbarian and his wife went to the
Holy Land to save the collapsing crusader kingdom, which defended its
last acres in the town of Acre. Edward's daughter Joan was born there.
As an adult, she outraged him by marrying a nobody of her own choos-
ing. As her descendants deteriorated in social status, just before Elizabeth's reign we find the last knight among them. That knight's grand-
daughter married the minister Francis Marbury, who was repeatedly
imprisoned for Puritanism. With such a combined troubling heritage, the
Marburys' daughter, Anne, was also a troublemaker—but in America.[3]

The extended Hutchinson family settled in Boston during the 1630s'
Great Puritan Migration. Historians refer to Anne Hutchinson's husband, William, as a merchant.[4] He had been one in England, but in
America he was referred to as a "gentleman," living off the work of his
servants and tenants on the lands he bought or received from the colony
and Boston for his social status and public service.[5] Anne soon provoked
the most severe and traumatic crisis of 1630s Massachusetts. She briefly
carried most of Boston (and Boston's merchants) behind her with proto-
Quaker views on the redundancy of ministers, churches, and God's ordinances. For the latter heresy, she and her followers were called antino-
mians ("against law" in Greek). In 1637, John Winthrop crushed them.
Anne was banished for "traducing the ministers and their ministry" and
for prophesizing "the Court ruined, with their posterity." Seventy-five
men, mostly Bostonians, were disarmed to prevent civil war.[6] Many of
them—including leading men in commerce, religion, and military—were
banished or left.

That first American feminist, with family and followers, founded
Rhode Island, near Roger Williams's Providence. Her son Edward, born
1613, soon returned to Boston. In legal documents, he was then titled
"Sergeant," "gentleman," or "mercer."[7] He married Catharine, a lawyer's daughter. Bernard Bailyn gives the Hutchinsons (implicitly Ed-

ward) as an example of those merchants who depended critically on merchant relatives in England for supply and credit. These relatives were two Richard Hutchinsons, citizens of London.[8]

Young Elisha

The fall of 1641 was uneasy for both colony and Edward Hutchinson. Massachusetts verged on economic collapse, England was heading toward civil war, and a brother of Edward was "banished, upon pain of death" "for calling the church of Boston a whore."[9] Edward was probably walking on eggshells, scattered on top of thin ice, when around November 15, 1641, his third child was born. The baby enters history with his November 28 baptism in church records as "Elisha of Edward Hutchinson."[10]

Elisha was named after a biblical prophet and miracle worker. The name combines two Hebrew words: *Eli* means "my God" and *Yesha*—an etymological relation of *Jesus*—means "salvation." *Elisha*, or "my God's salvation," was an increasingly popular name among Puritans and Separatists in that spiritually challenging era.[11] Perhaps he was thus named because in 1641 both Edward and Massachusetts needed God's help.

Elisha never knew his exiled grandparents. After William died in 1642, Anne moved near Dutch Manhattan. In 1643, Winthrop reported that during a Dutch–Indian war, Indians "came to Mrs. Hutchinson's in way of friendly neighborhood, as they had been accustomed, and taking their opportunity, killed her . . . and all her family."[12] When Elisha was between eight and ten years old, his mother died.[13]

Elisha's mercantile career was probably foretold. As a future gentleman, he probably studied in grammar school—a secondary school that taught classics in Latin and Greek as preparation for college.[14] College was useless for a merchant, but Latin was useful for legal and financial documents, and for communication across the Atlantic World, both in its own right and as an introduction to French, Spanish, and Portuguese.[15]

As a young man, Elisha was a poster boy for New England's healthy environment and good nutrition, which enabled his genetic height potential to materialize. A visiting Londoner would remark that Elisha was "the tallest man that I ever beheld"; Elisha's grandson Thomas described him as "a very stout man, 6 feet 2 inches high, and large bones"—exactly like his scary ancestor Edward "Longshanks" I. He was also tough: he "would lie down and sleep in the open air in the field or upon the deck of a ship."[16]

In the 1660s, Elisha entered private and public records as an adult. At age nineteen, he was recruited by his father to the Atherton land company. That association of twenty men, led by Major Humphrey Atherton, bought Indians' land with wampum. It then paid a wampum fine that the United Colonies imposed on belligerent tribes, in return for a mortgage on the tribes' lands. The mortgage was foreclosed. The company included Connecticut Governor John Winthrop Jr. and Massachusetts Assistant Simon Bradstreet, but the manager was Edward Hutchinson.[17] The jurisdiction of the area would be disputed between Connecticut and Rhode Island for decades, and the Atherton land company sided with the former.[18] Edward's considerable land holdings perhaps prompted Elisha to learn the profession of land surveyor. At age twenty-five, he laid out land at the request of the court. (A later job description of surveyors included drawing a map of the land, measuring its size "by protractor, scale, & compass, according to art," and determining its quality.)[19]

Elisha was authorized by Boston "to sell strong liquor by retail."[20] He entered his father's mercantile business by sending livestock and provisions to cousin Peleg Sanford, a Rhode Island councillor, who shipped it to his own brothers in Barbados.[21] Horses sent to Barbados operated mills that squeezed sugarcane, extracting the sweet juice and leaving out the slaves' blood, sweat, and tears. Sanford referred to the twenty-five-year-old Elisha as "merchant." The New England merchants routinely dealt with bills of exchange, and assigned and offset debts, because of their transactions all over the Atlantic. Merchants were the ones most exposed to the different moneys of the Atlantic and to banking ideas. They turned sugar from a Caribbean money into an Atlantic one by buying manufactures in England with it. As a merchant, Elisha had credit and credibility. He signed as a surety on a bond posted for releasing a bankrupt merchant from prison. He signed as a witness, together with the council's secretary and a former deputy, on a contract of the colony relating to customs collection. Soon, however, he was accused of evading customs.[22]

Around 1665, Elisha married Hannah, daughter of the late Captain Thomas Hawkins—a shipwright turned merchant and a Boston deputy. Soon Elisha started trading in real estate he received from his family.[23] In 1666, Elisha became a freeman of the colony. Three decades after his grandma's turmoil, he joined his father in protest over persecution of Baptists.[24] Elisha signed as a witness on Boston land deeds of people close to him—his brother-in-law, a widow of a vintner with whom he perhaps had business, and one of his Richard Hutchinson relatives.[25] (The two Richard Hutchinsons are difficult to distinguish. One or the other had been: treasurer of the Navy in England throughout the 1650s, regularly receiving tax funds from the receiver general and future Boston banker John Blackwell; a senior member of the Gospel Company; and represented in Boston by his merchant son Eliakim, who was either Edward's cousin or Elisha's cousin.[26])

The early 1670s marked a generational change of guards. Edward, occasionally a deputy, retired from public responsibilities, while Elisha advanced on all fronts. As a land surveyor, he worked with the elite in land committees appointed by the court and Boston. He bought land from the deputy governor. Boston appointed him to collect all the gunpowder in town, store it safely, and inquire about violations. The court appointed him a lieutenant in a Boston militia company. He was admitted to the Artillery Company, of which most members were merchants.[27] By 1675, Elisha was a successful man, and his future seemed bright.

Annus Horribilis, 1675–1676

In 1675, as King Philip's War began, Edward Hutchinson was sent by the court on an important mission to secure peace with Indians in central Massachusetts. He was sent due to his recent diplomatic success with the powerful Narragansett tribe and, according to one report, because the chiefs wanted to talk to him only. It was a trap. The delegation was ambushed, and Edward was gravely wounded. The survivors were besieged in Brookfield, and during evacuation to Boston, Edward died in Marlborough.[28] In line with Puritan tradition, the Boston pastor Increase Mather knew why he died:

It seems to be an observable providence that so many of that family die by the hands of the uncircumcised. His mother (long ago) & sister. And now himself. His own rashness brought his death on him. The last Sabbath he was in Boston he went out of the meeting house in a discontent, because the [blank] admonished a [blank] that had been diverse times drunk. Some say he refused to join, that he would hold communication with the [blank] no more at the Lord's table.[29]

As a captain, Edward was the highest-ranked fatality of the war, and his grave was the first in Marlborough, at the center of today's Spring Hill Cemetery (figure 11.1). The original tombstone was replaced, but the original spelling remains:

Captin Edward Hvtchinson aged 62 yeares was shot by treacherovs Indians Avgvst 2 1675 dyed 19 Avgvst 1675.[30]

The text was probably composed by his heir as patriarch of the Hutchinsons, Elisha.

Wills and estates of the deceased were handled not by professional lawyers but by ordinary capable people. Relatives had a priority, followed by merchants, and so Elisha was naturally the executor of his father's will and took care of the estate's debts and credits. He submitted Edward's final accounts with the colony in a chilling, formal document: "The Country is debitor to Capt. Edward Hutchinson for his service at several times & expenses." This includes: "To a journey to Quabauge where he received his death's wounds, being 3 weeks before he died." At the wage of £2 a week for diplomats, his painful endurance was worth £6. Together with "his expenses and charges there & at Marlborough," and similarly for earlier diplomatic missions, the colony owed the estate more than £20 (figure 11.2).[31]

Elisha also had legal problems that year. He had lost a lawsuit for not paying a shipwright. He owned 25 percent of the ship, as did his Barbadian cousin Elisha Sanford. There were three other partners. Splitting ownership among owners of ships was a standard method of diversifying investments; each merchant bought shares in a few ships instead of owning one entire ship, to avoid putting all eggs in one floating basket. In the lawsuit, Hutchinson served as attorney for the faraway Sanford, which was normal among merchants and especially among relatives. The defendants were ordered to pay damages, partly "in money" and partly "in goods at merchants' price." In a world of commodity money, merchants' pricing of commodities determined the size of payments. Hutchinson "undertook" to pay Sanford's part, and surely entered it into their accounts to be offset later.[32]

A different legal problem—more of a commitment—was Elisha's appointment as one of three administrators to the estate of his fellow Boston merchant Free Grace Bendall, who drowned with his wife and left eight orphans. Another administrator was the Boston merchant William

FIGURE 11.1 Edward Hutchinson's grave in 2012. Source: Author's photograph.

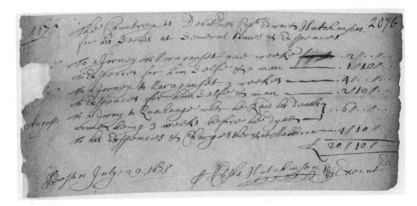

FIGURE 11.2 Edward Hutchinson's final account with the colony, written by son Elisha. Source: Massachusetts Archives Collection, vol. 69, p. 207b, "Payment to Capt. Edward Hutchinson, July 29, 1678." SCI/series 45X. Massachusetts Archives, Boston.

Tailer—John Nelson's partner in the Acadian trade (Nelson would marry his only daughter). Hutchinson and Tailer worked as Bendall's administrators for six years, until Tailer committed suicide.[33]

Thirteen months after his father died, Elisha lost his wife. In September 1676, like so many other women, she died of her seventh childbirth within a decade. The baby died soon too.

The Multitasking Elite, 1675–1686

The death of his father and wife left Elisha, at age thirty-five, alone in charge of the family and its businesses. Because someone had to take care of the kids, Elisha quickly remarried. His second wife, Elizabeth, was also daughter of a former Boston deputy—Captain Thomas Clarke, one of the wealthiest Boston merchants. Elizabeth had recently been widowed when her husband, the merchant John Freake, was killed in a freak accident: a Virginian ship exploded in Boston harbor.

Elisha was part of an inbreeding network of Boston merchants. His aunt Faith was married to the Boston merchant Thomas Savage, whose son married into the Tyng family of Boston merchants. Sister Elizabeth was married to Edward Winslow, a nephew of the Plymouth founder and brother of John, a Boston merchant. Sister Catharine was married to Henry Bartholomew, a merchant's son. The merchant cousin Eliakim Hutchinson married into the Shrimpton mercantile family. Sisters of his wives were married to the Boston merchants John Richards, Thomas Kellond, and Humphrey Warren. As Bailyn put it, Boston's merchants were "a single interrelated family."[34]

Elisha inherited land from his father. Elisha was one of the Atherton land company partners who petitioned the court during King Philip's War to defend their titles from intruding Rhode Islanders. In 1678, the partners advertised a call for settlers, signed by a committee that included the assistant Simon Bradstreet (soon to be governor) and Elisha.[35]

The elite signaled Elisha to take his father's place in public life. Within a month of his father's death, Elisha was appointed for the first time as foreman in a trial jury at the Court of Assistants; on the following elections of the Artillery Company, he was elected its top officer, captain.[36] Elisha started his public career in earnest in Boston, where, as in all towns, all officers were elected annually. In 1678–1679, he was elected to four municipal offices for the first time: one of seven selectmen (town councillors), an office he would hold almost continuously for a decade; one of seven judges in Boston's merchants' court, a position he would hold for six years in a row; the sealer of weights and measures (an office reminiscent of mint master), an office he would hold for five years; and, after fire consumed most of the town, Elisha was appointed one of sixteen fire officers. Also in 1679, the court promoted him to captain of a Boston militia company.[37] All these offices constituted public service with no direct income.

For his next political advance, Elisha had the king to thank. During the battle of the charter, the king insisted that there be eighteen assistants in the council, as the charter ordered, rather than ten as usual. This demand kicked Deputy John Richards up to the council, together with his natural replacements as Boston deputies—Elisha's uncle Thomas Savage and the mint master John Hull. Their advance made room for Elisha, who was elected in 1680 as one of Boston's two deputies. He also replaced Richards in the trustworthy office of commissioner to receive and deliver Boston's votes for assistants and county treasurer.[38]

Court records from that period almost never indicated what a certain person said, so most of the information on members comes from their committee memberships. Elisha's first committee, as soon as he entered the court, was appointed to consider revisions of laws according to England's objections. In his second session, he represented the deputies in a committee that selected laws of that session for printing.[39] These appointments indicate that he had acquired a reputation as a competent legislator at the town level. The former committee gave him his first taste of imperial diplomacy, and apparently he did a good job, because later he was appointed to unusually large diplomatic committees with the governor and deputy governor. The committees prepared documents sent to the agents in England, corresponded with the agents, and financed them.[40]

Edward Randolph—the king's chief man on the ground—soon identified Hutchinson as a leader of the party objecting to a constitutional compromise with England. Writing to the bishop of London, Randolph listed Hutchinson as one of three deputies who were "great opposers" and who, with three like-minded assistants, should "be sent for to appear before his Majesty."[41] The two almost had a duel during a heated exchange at the Exchange. That place in Boston, imitating London's Royal Exchange, was the place for merchants' meetings under the townhouse. Randolph complained to Hutchinson and another Boston select-man that they levied a town tax on him. Hutchinson called Randolph "a knave," and Randolph said, "Though you are longer [i.e., taller] you may find them that are wiser." Randolph hinted his wish to use his sword against Hutchinson, to which Hutchinson replied, "Try now," though being armed only with a staff. Randolph retreated and walked away. The incident was important enough for Hutchinson to submit an affida-vit about it and for later historians to print this as the only evidence of a near-physical encounter between a local man and public enemy no. 1 during the battle of the charter.[42]

The king's first legal attack on the colony came in a 1683 quo war-ranto writ.[43] It required thirty men (listed by Randolph) to explain in a court in England by what right they exercised power of government in Massachusetts. Elisha was the twenty-second person on the list, with Boston's two other deputies (Boston had become important enough to be the only town with three deputies). Although there were several mer-chants on the list, Hutchinson was the only one titled "mercator" ("mer-chant" in Latin). Randolph hated merchants more than others because they sabotaged his enforcement of customs laws.[44] Elisha would have found no consolation knowing that it was his ruthless ancestor Edward I who had invented that writ (for stripping the nobility of their powers).

Back to court committees, Elisha became a leading deputy on pub-lic finance. Annual committees auditing the treasurer's accounts were dominated by merchants (for expertise), by deputies (for control of tax funds), and by Bostonians (for proximity to the treasurer). Elisha was all three, so he was the only deputy serving on all five committees ap-pointed during his deputyship.[45] His other committees handled bread regulations, pacified a dysfunctional town, and repaired Boston's prison and castle. The repairs committees were authorized to give orders to the treasurer what money to spend on wages and materials.[46] Elisha was never chosen as the deputies' speaker, yet he signed for the depu-ties on legislative bills more than twenty times. The bills were mostly about militia and public finance—another indication of his expertise and interest.[47]

Elisha was also the court's land expert. In 1682, the court ordered that its land grants henceforth be surveyed only by eight "known, able, and approved" (i.e., licensed) surveyors. Elisha, the only deputy on the list, was listed first. He served on a committee that organized records of lands granted outside towns (for tax purposes), and on a committee to solve a private land dispute. He received from towns accounts of their "waste lands" for tax purposes.[48]

Unpaid as a deputy, Elisha kept his mercantile business, worked as a private land surveyor, and kept trading in land.[49] He was one of the representatives of the Atherton company before a royal committee packed in their favor.[50] When Elisha's father-in-law died, Elisha inherited land in Pemaquid—the area north of Maine claimed by New York. Inhabitants there complained to New York that they were "disturbed by people that come here to claim lands by former and pretended rights," namely "old mortgages that were made before the wars." They singled out Hutchinson for his "severe threatenings that he will come and take away our land." They asked the New York government for "assurance of our lands."[51] Elisha knew well the largest producer of local money in Maine, that private province of Massachusetts: cousin Eliakim owned the most important sawmill, which apparently made a tenth of all boards, and boards were the main Maine money.[52]

Proving to be a useful deputy, in 1683 Elisha was nominated by many voters to be on the ballot for assistants, and the following year he was elected an assistant. It was part of an unusually large changing of the guard: Joseph Dudley and other assistants who favored a compromise with England were replaced by Hutchinson and other hard-liners.[53] The son finally surpassed his father. Elisha would be reelected again in 1685, when the court no longer legally existed, and in 1686, just before Dudley took over. His committee work went on—in finance, commerce, land, and logistics—but by any measure, he was a junior assistant. Of Hutchinson's municipal offices he kept only that of selectman, winning most votes in 1686.[54]

Elisha took his offices very seriously. The Boston Athenaeum holds a book that belonged to him, a collection of the colony's laws that he used as a judge and legislator. It is full of notes that he added to make his work more accurate and efficient. Bound with the laws is a handwritten copy of the 1641 Body of Liberties—the only surviving copy of the first English code of laws in America.[55]

Still unpaid as an assistant, Elisha kept working as a merchant. He got in trouble with the royal customs surveyor but was acquitted and compensated by a friendly local court.[56] The Gospel Company accounts reveal that Elisha owed it £100 on loan in 1685. Of course, he was not required to mortgage property.[57] In March 1686, he headed for the first time an Atherton land company committee that warned Rhode Islanders not to intrude those disputed lands. A new fellow committee member was Richard Wharton, who was a partner on account of marrying a Winthrop.[58]

Dominion and Diplomacy, 1686–1689

In May 1686, Joseph Dudley arrived with the commission to rule the Dominion of New England. The third-term assistant Elisha Hutchinson was one of those approving the court's unanimous reply to Dudley and his council. The absence of an assembly to pass laws and lay taxes was a red flag. The court's parting response was uniquely English— understated but shockingly bold. In the spirit of 1640s England, the deposed court warned the new council and prophesized: "We think it highly concerns you to consider whether such a commission be safe, either for you or us." Hoping for a miracle, the court "adjourned" to October, with "many tears shed," reported Sewall.[59]

The council was dominated by local merchants and especially by Wharton, Hutchinson's land partner.[60] It renewed appointments of militia companies' captains, and only Hutchinson refused. The council removed him from his old office of securing gunpowder in Boston, but appointed him with Sewall "to receive and distribute" donations solicited in churches for arriving Huguenot refugees. He was later ordered to give the funds to the Atherton company committee (of which he was a member), because there the refugees were to settle.[61]

The Atherton land company committee, now led by the councillor Wharton, published an "Advertisement" to prospective settlers there. The council recognized the committee's records as the official Book of Records for the area. A special court assembled there, with President Dudley and the councillors Fitz-John Winthrop, Randolph, and Wharton. Apparently, Hutchinson and Blackwell were made justices of the peace there. The committee members petitioned the king against Rhode Islanders and asked the king to refer the dispute to the dominion's upcoming "General Governor" and council.[62]

Hutchinson was not so lucky in Pemaquid. New York Governor Thomas Dongan sent officials to resolve land disputes there. John Palmer was to negotiate with "inhabitants for taking out patents," while John West assisted him as deputy secretary. Palmer simply granted

Hutchinson's land to West, and West evacuated Hutchinson's tenant. Hutchinson informed a London co-owner: "The pretensions are that we did not hold [title] under the king, and therefore our Indian deeds, possessions and improvements are nothing worth." Even Elisha's nemesis, Randolph, agreed:

> They placed and displaced at pleasure, and were as arbitrary as the great Turk; some of the first settlers of that eastern country were denied grants of their own lands, while these men have given the improved lands amongst themselves, of which I suppose Mr. Hutchinson has complained.[63]

And then came Andros. In February 1687, Governor Edmund Andros held a hearing on Atherton company lands. The company's committee appeared, unwisely including Hutchinson. Andros noted the former assistant's presence and ruled against their claims. An appeal did not help. Wharton petitioned separately to confirm some of that land to himself, and succeeded. Hutchinson followed suit, but Andros ignored him.[64] He petitioned again, in more submissive terms: he was "sensible what need he has of obtaining his Majesty's gracious confirmation." He made the usual (but doubtful) claim that the land was "settled on" at his "great charge," emphasizing that the plot neighbored Wharton's confirmed plot. Andros ignored him again.[65]

By June, Hutchinson joined Blackwell's Bank of Credit as partner, listed as one of four "deputy managers" together with former Fund trustee Adam Winthrop.[66] But Hutchinson was dismayed to see the thief John West moving from New York to Boston to serve as deputy secretary and land registrar, beginning to implement the same land policy in the dominion. With that policy becoming clear, Wharton left for England to lobby against Andros. Hutchinson followed, in what was perhaps his first visit to England. As common then, Elisha obtained a letter from his pastor, recommending him to whatever Puritan church he would wish to attend in England:

> our beloved brother Mr. Elisha Hutchinson has been an approved member of the first gathered church in Boston these many years and one in reputation with us for his gifts and graces wherewith the Lord has adorned him, as also for his Gospel-becoming conversation, I doubt not of your readiness to receive such as becomes saints [i.e., Puritans].[67]

This first departure of a former assistant, in November 1687, was significant enough for the Winthrop councillors to correspond about it, and for Sewall to report it to his diary and to a cousin in England. Sewall described Elisha as "a worthy gentleman of this town."[68]

Elisha arrived in London early in 1688 and joined Wharton's business initiatives. Wharton was pessimistic about the Atherton company, but he, Hutchinson, Stoughton, and others of the elite had already conceived a new project: extracting newly discovered ores and resins. Wharton envisioned a monopolist corporation presided over by Wait Winthrop. He was about to petition with London's mayor and other investors for a charter,

> when Capt. Hutchinson arrived, who gave new life to my undertakings by the samples he brought and report he made; and although my progress varied much from his instructions, and the projections in New England, yet he being satisfied those were impracticable, and these methods would at least equally conduce to a public good, he cheerfully joined with me in the petition, and accompanied me therewith to the King and Council, where it was well received.

But while Hutchinson was flexible and open-minded, he was still a pedantic judge and legislator at heart:

> Soon after considering the heads of a charter, Capt. Hutchinson, being exceeding and as apprehended unseasonably tender and careful of some little privileges, estranged himself from me.

This "misunderstanding" almost derailed the entire venture, but in the end, the two partners were "firmly united" and agreed "to yield in little matters for obtaining greater." In June, they presented a draft of a charter to the Committee for Trade and Plantations of the Privy Council, and in August, the attorney general was ordered to prepare a new draft.[69]

Hutchinson also had public responsibilities. The college president, Increase Mather, and the former assistant Samuel Nowell left Boston right after he did. Mather, as agent of the college and churches, met the king in the spring and petitioned him mostly on religious freedom. However, his joint petitions in the summer with Nowell and Hutchinson had different emphases. They asked the king first that the colonists

may be quieted in the possession of all property, both in houses and lands, as
they enjoyed them before the government was changed . . . and that the ancient records there settled for title of lands may be confirmed.

Only then did they ask for religious freedom, an assembly, town meetings, and control of the college. They also petitioned the Committee for
Trade and Plantations to make the dominion council more representative, internally democratic, and transparent.[70]

Hutchinson planned to return home the following winter,[71] but events
took a dramatic turn with the expected Dutch invasion. Right after the
panicked James restored London's charter, he met Mather, Hutchinson, and Wharton. Wharton reported home that James "assured us our
properties shall be continued and confirmed," adding that they would
be happy to stay and lobby if given financial support.[72] In the winter of
1688–1689, Elisha was privileged to see the Glorious Revolution—the
defining event of that generation.

The Social Life

Assistant Samuel Sewall, the former printing press manager and mint
owner, wrote the most informative diary of the period that began in
1685. Bailyn presented Sewall as the prototypical Puritan merchant of
the period, and named Hutchinson as the first among "like-minded individuals with similar attitudes and styles of life."[73] Bailyn's conclusion
is based on many entries in Sewall's diary that document their friend-
ship. They were first elected assistants together, and they were relatives
through marriage: Hutchinson's cousin Ephraim Savage was referred to
as "cousin" by Sewall as well, because their wives (of the Quincy family)
were cousins. Sewall's diary provides random snippets of Hutchinson's
social life from 1685 until Hutchinson's departure in 1687, and it reveals
their social circles.

Most recorded events were funerals and deathbed visits, because such
was life before the Industrial Revolution, even for the affluent elite of a
peaceful society in a healthy climate. The deceased were mostly ministers and Hutchinson's peers—a former assistant, a merchant, and a militia officer. Hutchinson and Sewall went to funerals of each other's ba-
bies twelve days apart.[74] By 1689, Elisha had married twice and fathered

twelve children, of whom he buried one wife and seven children.[75] This was terribly normal.

There were also dinner parties, dominated by present and former captains of Boston's militia, who were also Artillery Company members: "cousin" Ephraim Savage; John Walley, a recent Bostonian merchant and Fund trustee who became a Plymouth assistant and then a dominion councillor; and John Phillips of Charlestown, a former deputy and merchant who had recently refused the colony's treasurership. Other attendees show that Hutchinson was in touch with lower classes: a shipwright, a shopkeeper, a blacksmith, and a cooper who was brother-in-law of the late Fund director Daniel Henchman. Hutchinson attended the wedding of Phillips's daughter with Cotton Mather, son of pastor Increase.[76]

Boston merchants could pay for recording their appearances in portraits. Surviving portraits from the 1670s and 1680s include those of John Freake and family (including Elisha's future second wife), Adam Winthrop, Samuel Shrimpton, and uncle Thomas Savage. One portrait at the Harvard Art Museums is similar in style to Savage's 1679 portrait and shares Artillery Company insignia (figure 11.3). The art historian Jonathan Fairbanks saw Elisha Hutchinson as the "best" candidate to be the man in the portrait, given his age in 1679.[77] The periwig, however, seems out of place, because Sewall and ministers still utterly despised it as the epitome of Anglican decadence.[78] Perhaps the portrait was made a few years after 1679.

*   *   *

Elisha Hutchinson had, by modern standards, a dizzying diversity of occupations and offices. By 1689, when he was forty-eight years old, he had considerable experience at the highest level in intercontinental trade, land (measurement, appraisal, and development), politics, diplomacy, executive office, legislation, justice, finance, and military. When the great economist Joseph Schumpeter looked for an exemplar of similar nonspecialization in leadership, he resorted to the prehistoric "chieftain."[79] But Hutchinson's story was entirely typical of the colonial elite. Sewall's career components have significant overlap with Hutchinson's, while Elisha's father and grandfather were not much more specialized.[80]

All English colonies inherited the English stratified social order, except that the nobility did not emigrate. In New England, their traditional

FIGURE 11.3 "An Unknown Gentleman," perhaps Elisha Hutchinson. Source: Harvard University Portrait Collection, gift of Robert Winthrop, class of 1926, to Harvard College, 1946, photo © President and Fellows of Harvard College, object no. H527.

offices in government and military were left to the gentlemen; that class was dominated by merchants and so the merchants did almost everything at the top level of town government, colony government, and the private sector. Massachusetts became a small merchant republic, like medieval Venice and the contemporary United Provinces. In Barbados, the same happened with the sugar planters.[81]

Such a drastic lack of specialization must seem inefficient to economists. (This problem will be taken up later.) Other readers may be concerned about separation of powers, since Hutchinson filled most of these offices simultaneously. However, Montesquieu, the champion of separation of powers, was only born in 1689. Moreover, the Massachusetts constitution was originally not of a state but of a commercial corporation, where none should expect such a degree of separation.

Another anachronistic concern is the relation between government and private business. Hutchinson got at best a refund for expenses in most of his public offices. These offices took much of his time and thus hurt his income. On the other hand, these offices gave him the ability to influence legislation and policy in ways that benefited his private business. It was not viewed as corruption, but as the nature of the elite—they had special obligations to society, and they had their privileges too. As Blackwell knew, one such privilege was partnering with entrepreneurs or else sabotaging their projects.

Through his offices, trade relations, family relations, social relations, and intercolonial property holdings, Elisha Hutchinson was exposed to most of the Atlantic's moneys and alternatives to money: all the Massachusetts experience; board money in Maine; sugar money in Barbados; bills of exchange on England; and the Fund and the Bank of Credit in Boston. He may have been exposed to Canada's card money through his social connections with Nelson or through his charity and land connections to Huguenot refugees.

Having learned about Hutchinson, and through him about the typical Massachusetts legislator, we can now return to the chronological storyline and examine how events unfolded in the wake of the Glorious Revolution in England and America.

CHAPTER TWELVE

The Return of the General Court, 1689–1690

Thus saith the Lord God unto these bones; Behold, I will cause breath to enter into you, and ye shall live.
   —Ezekiel 37:5–6, King James Version

The Glorious Revolution rocked not only Europe but America too. The people of Massachusetts revolted, dismantled the dominion, and revived the General Court.[1] Skirmishes with northeastern Indians escalated and merged with the great Anglo–French war across the Atlantic. In the winter of 1689–1690, joint French and Indian forces massacred populations of frontier towns in New York and New England. The English colonies decided to uproot the French colonies. In May 1690, a Massachusetts expedition forced Acadia to surrender. In August, a larger fleet from Massachusetts and Plymouth sailed to Quebec, while New York and Connecticut tried to attack Montreal by land. Both expeditions failed. The Massachusetts forces, escaping the freezing of the Saint Lawrence River, straggled back home, most of them arriving in November. Throughout 1690 in Boston, and in the fleet to Quebec, a smallpox epidemic killed hundreds of people.[2] In December, morale was exceptionally low.

This chapter first examines the revival of the Massachusetts General Court, and especially the constitutional constraints at home and from England on its actions and words. Then war finance is discussed. The intersection of war finance and the constitutional problem would result in the monetary invention of December 1690, which is the topic of the next chapter.

The Glorious Revolution in America

In April 1689, news of the Glorious Revolution arrived in Boston and prompted a popular uprising. The militia seized senior government officials. An ultimatum for Governor Edmund Andros to surrender was signed by fifteen men, led by the councillor Wait Winthrop. Another Winthrop on the list was cousin Adam, a militia captain. The ultimate New Englanders—the Winthrops—were restored to power. Pastor Cotton Mather authored *The Declaration of the Gentlemen, Merchants, and Inhabitants of Boston, and the Country Adjacent* to justify the revolution;[3] Mather wrote it because ministers had long been constitutional advisors, and at age twenty-five he was already one of the most eloquent of New England's writers. The revolution, wrote Mather, was "in compliance with" the "Glorious Action" taken by "the nobility, gentry and commonality" in England. They were equivalent to the "gentlemen, merchants, and inhabitants" in the declaration's title. The declaration mentioned the outrage over land titles: "We were every day told, that no man was owner of a foot of land in all the colony."[4]

As Andros surrendered, the signatories of the ultimatum declared themselves a provisional Council for the Safety of the People and Conservation of the Peace. Its president was Simon Bradstreet—the last charter-era governor and the last Founding Father. They invited more men to join the council, and then asked towns to send deputies.[5] At the deputies' request, the magistrates of the last General Court of 1686 were restored until upcoming elections in May 1690.[6] Adam Winthrop was demoted to Boston deputy.[7] The court generally reinstated the laws that were valid in 1686, and by the end of 1689 resumed the main functions of government.[8] The court reestablished its government in Maine, while besieged New Hampshire rejoined Massachusetts as a county.[9]

Back in England, regime change implied that lobbying for the charter started from scratch. As Nowell and Wharton had died since the summer, only Mather and Hutchinson remained, but then Samuel Sewall arrived and helped the lobbying effort. In their spare time, Elisha and Sewall visited the Royal Mint. Sewall, the owner of the closed Boston mint, noted with disappointment: "none to see the milling"—the latest anticounterfeiting method.[10] Both men surely saw goldsmiths' notes and checks. They returned to Boston in December 1689 and resumed their assistant positions. Hutchinson was promoted to major, leading the Boston regiment.[11] He attended nearly all court and council meetings.[12]

Ahead of the May 1690 elections, two prospective assistants were made freemen: Wait Winthrop and Sir William Phips. The latter, the only local knight, was a thirty-nine-year-old Maine man recently knighted and enriched for salvaging a sunken Spanish treasure ship.[13] The prestigious Election Day sermon was delivered by Cotton Mather, soon elected fellow of the college.[14] Simon Bradstreet was reelected governor. After serving in court more than five decades, he was the living embodiment of the five thick volumes of General Court records. It is impossible to tell how much he remembered, at age eighty-six, of all the monetary and constitutional events he took part in, but he seems to have functioned reasonably well.[15]

Boston's increasing importance made it eligible to send four deputies. Adam Winthrop lost his deputy seat. In Boston he continued as a selectman, but apparently refused reappointment as a judge.[16] Another Boston deputy, Speaker Penn Townsend, is of special interest; he was a thirty-nine-year-old alcohol merchant who rose quickly in society because of family connections. He was an Artillery Company member, a militia captain, and a Bank of Credit officer. During the revolution, he was a fresh Boston selectman and was invited to the extended Council for Safety. Soon he was elected deputy. In March 1690, he was appointed commander in chief of the Acadia expedition, but quickly gave it up to Phips. He was soon elected speaker, a Boston judge, and Boston's elections commissioner.[17] This multiple trust positioned him right under the level of Boston assistants such as Hutchinson and Sewall. The latter two were recognized for their recent diplomatic experience: Sewall was appointed one of the commissioners to the revived United Colonies of New England, while Hutchinson was appointed one of the commissioners in reserve.[18]

The nature and pace of the constitutional steps mentioned above were determined by external and internal constraints. The future of the court lay in England, as Increase Mather tried to revive the charter, so the colony had to display its best behavior toward England. But there were also many in the colony who opposed the old-new regime and questioned its legitimacy. The court had to deal with both pressures.

The Constitutional Problem with England

The most important task of the regime was to get England's approval. Arresting a royal governor and dismantling a royal regime were no trivial matters. Even if William remained in power, he might have resented such defiance of royal authority. The worst offense would have been a unilateral restoration of the charter, which was legally possible only for the Crown or Parliament to enact. The council therefore sent its revolution's declaration to the monarchs, emphasizing they merely "imitate" with "conformity" the revolution in England. They hoped for "our share in that universal restoration of charters" that they presumed was taking place in England.[19]

The restored 1686 magistrates stated on record that they ruled only "according to the rules of the charter," without claiming resurrection of the charter itself, until England directed "an orderly settlement of government." They declared to both population and Crown "that they do not intend an assumption of charter government; nor would be so understood."[20] The hairsplitting rhetoric—de facto restoration but not de jure—was the difference between a necessary caretaking government and treason. For the same reason, any charter-era terminology was initially avoided (table 12.1).

The use of the term *convention* was an imitation of the revolutionary English parliament of 1689, which called itself a convention since it was not called by a monarch.

Progress on the exercise of government powers was slow and hesitant until Hutchinson and Sewall returned in December 1689 with William's approval of the temporary government. William expressed

TABLE 12.1 **Change of Terminology**

Old name	New name
Council, Court of Assistants	Council for the Safety of the People and Conservation of the Peace
Governor	President
Deputy Governor	None
	(Thomas Danforth listed after the president in meetings)
Treasurer	Stewards for the Public Affairs
Secretary	Clerk
Deputies	Representatives
House of Deputies	Convention of the Representatives
General Court	Convention, General Convention

Source: MS 53–55, 59, 66, 88, 102, 135.

"approbation" and "acceptance" of both the revolution and the provisional government "until we shall have taken such resolutions, and
given such direction for the more orderly settlement of the said government." Only then did the Court of Assistants really resume its judicial
function, and a hesitant reversion to charter-era terminology was soon
completed.[21]

The court sent new agents to join Mather. They were instructed to
mention "the despair" when "those in the late government sought to
turn them out of their lands and possessions." The court wrote the king
that the court's domestic opposition also opposed the revolution in England. From the queen the court asked for "help for the confirming to us
what God has given to us to possess, both as to the good things of Earth,
and Heaven."[22]

Hutchinson and Sewall had helped Mather's meetings with the new
English government.[23] They learned how damaging the mint was to the
colony's reputation. The mint, (and by association the making of the
coins legal tender) was resented even by the new regime in England because the new regime was informed about the charter revocation by the
same hostile professional jurists of the early 1680s.[24] When the court reinstated the old laws, it excepted "any that are repugnant to the laws of
England,"[25] in a rare quote from the charter. This exception implicitly
voided the 1652 mint law, which had never been formally repealed. But
the court wanted to resume coinage, so it ordered the new agents "to solicit that the liberty of coinage may be allowed us." It was the only specific privilege the court sought that was not in the charter. It was the
only matter to be lobbied for, which was not related to the revolution or
the war. As a bill for restoring all charters was pending in Parliament,
a pamphlet war ensued in England, in which the coinage offense was
again listed at the top by the court's enemies. From Boston's jail, Randolph argued that it was a major reason for the revolution:

> Their liberty of coining money is taken away, which encouraged pirates to
> bring their plate here, because it could be coined and conveyed in great par-
> cels undiscovered to be such. Mr. Sewall, another of the agents attending in
> England, was Master of the Mint, and a loser by putting that down.[26]

At the king's demand, the dominion leadership was sent from jail to
a trial in England. In preparation for the trial, former dominion councillors prepared, at the court's request, a document with incriminating in-

side information.[27] This show of consensus was meant to strengthen the court's position in England, where things did not proceed as planned. The bill for restoring all charters did not pass in Parliament, and rumors about Massachusetts's future included a royal governor.[28]

The Constitutional Problem at Home

The revolutionaries wanted political consensus to avoid civil war. The Council for Safety therefore displayed perfect political balance: five dominion councillors, five charter-era magistrates who were not dominion councillors, and five men who never held office at the colonial level. Decades of politically balanced committees led to such perfection. The latter group was composed entirely of Boston merchants, including John Nelson, who led the militia at a crucial moment of the revolution.[29] The consensus was widened by enlarging the council and summoning deputies twice until enough of them showed up.[30] The court delayed the imposition of taxes until November, due to questionable legality and despite mounting war expenses. When the court did impose new taxes, the record states that the deputies resolved it unanimously.[31]

Many of the colony's inhabitants were nonfreemen and wanted a more democratic regime. These included the non-Puritans, who were more powerful than they were in the 1630s and 1660s when freemen rules were set. At that time they were mostly servants, but by 1689 they included merchants and large landowners. The court handled the opposition with the carrot-and-stick approach, but the stick came first: it harshly suppressed opposition that materialized as open disobedience or speech thereof, then tried to placate resentment with popular measures.

The fountainhead of the opposition was the dominion leadership in jail. Joseph Dudley, Sir Edmund Andros, Edward Randolph, John West, John Palmer, James Graham, George Farewell, and James Sherlock were listed by the deputies as unbailable.[32] All but Dudley were the "strangers" involved in the land titles fiasco, while Dudley was listed first for treason. As Randolph was spewing letters to England, the deputies demanded tightening security in jail, isolating the prisoners, and disarming the opposition. The royal warship in Boston was grounded. Its crew was suspected of "mutinous" speech and sabotage, leading to investigations and arrests.[33] The opposition included important locals: a deputy and a charter-era deputy were dismissed from all offices and fined, and a merchant was arrested.[34] Some "gentlemen, merchants, and other inhabitants of Boston" petitioned the king for a dominion with an assembly. The signatories were led by the nonfreeman Nelson, who was again without political rights.[35] The government responded by publishing the king's approval of the government as a broadside throughout the colony to encourage "obedience."[36]

Obedience was hard to obtain during the war, as inhabitants and soldiers deserted the frontier.[37] The government was in full wartime emergency mode and curtailed individual liberties with no qualms. It was worse than in the 1675–1676 war, because of the new diplomatic front and home opposition. Frontier inhabitants were ordered back to their homes or—threatened the deputies—they would lose their land titles; movement of Indians was severely restricted; Sabbath loiterers were stopped and questioned; letters to England were perhaps opened; trade with French and Indians was outlawed; export of arms and ammunition was licensed; judicial courts were postponed; an embargo was imposed on all shipping to Europe; and Shrove Tuesday's "tumultuous gathering" was prohibited.[38]

The shipping of the prisoners to England marked a shift from stick to carrot: popular pressure, which included veiled threats, led to a massive extension of the suffrage ahead of the May 1690 elections. The property requirement was slashed by 60 percent, and the local minister's approval of candidates for freeman status was replaced by selectmen's approval. More than seven hundred men, perhaps a thousand, were made freemen in 1690.[39] In the charter era, it had taken at least a decade to enfranchise so many people.[40] Disobedience reports indeed became rare.[41]

The preparations for the Quebec invasion renewed wartime measures: committees searched and seized gunpowder and pressed ships, departures of ships were licensed, cannons were pressed, and letters were opened. While the fleet was away, the first English newspaper in America—*Publick Occurrences*—was terminated by the furious court after one issue.[42]

Committees

The institution of ad hoc committees was immediately revived, and was widely applied to the war effort. More than thirty committees were appointed during the eighteen months from the resurrection of the court to the invention of legal tender money. Old features remained: a majority of executive committees, an explicit mix of both legislative houses, numer-

ical dominance of deputies over magistrates, all-magistrates committees on critical executive issues, and inclusion of men who were not court
members.[43] The latter group was more conspicuous relative to peacetime
charter-era committees because of the war's workload. Almost a third of
the committees was composed only of such men, and they dominated a
third of the other committees.[44]

Almost half of the executive committees handled war logistics—
pressing men and equipment and sending both to the front. Merchants
knew best how to move people and goods and how to finance that, so
they were conspicuous in war committees. As usual, merchants (especially Bostonians) dominated financial and commercial committees.[45]
Nelson, who resumed Acadian trade (if he ever suspended it), was a
member of the committee that planned the Acadia expedition, and he
was asked by the court how to conquer Acadia.[46]

Hutchinson served on most of the all-magistrates committees, handling diplomacy, fortifying Boston, and negotiating taxes with alcohol
sellers.[47] In the latter committee, he appeared for the first time in the
most esteemed company of present and former treasurers—John Phillips, James Russell, and John Richards (of course, all Bay merchants).
Hutchinson emerged as the leading man on war finance and logistics. He
served on the three executive committees that prepared the Acadia and
Quebec expeditions; the only other man on all three committees was Sir
William Phips, who led the expeditions. In October 1690, Hutchinson
served on an investigative committee, headed by Russell, "to examine
the state of the country with respect to their debts, by the treasurer's
accounts, which may give light how to grant sums for defraying of the
same." In November, he headed an unusually large executive committee "to procure the sum of three or four thousand pounds in money upon
loan for the present paying of seamen and soldiers at their return from
Canada, and for other emergencies upon the public credit." By December 1690, Hutchinson was the *only* man who had served on all the war-
related fiscal committees of that year.[48]

War Finance

In 1689, the Council for Safety appointed two members, the Boston merchants John Foster and Adam Winthrop, as co-treasurers and chief logistics officers.[49] Adam was not only Wait's cousin but also the stepson

of the councillor John Richards. As that council was replaced, Foster and Winthrop were replaced by a treasurer, fifty-six-year-old John Phillips,[50] whose political power stemmed at least partly from his relation to Increase Mather.

Expenses and Incomes

The court sent at first dozens of soldiers to the northeastern frontier, then hundreds, then hundreds more to Acadia, and finally thousands to Canada. Soldiers were promised wages, initially with extra pay per scalp or captive; later they were also promised plunder (including Indian women and children). Some soldiers reportedly doubted the government's ability to pay.[51]

To pay for these expenses, taxes skyrocketed: six rates in November 1689, one and a half in December (for the agents), ten in March 1690, two and a half in July (for the land frontier), and finally twenty rates in November just before the defeat in Canada became known.[52] Recalling that a "rate" included 1/240 of one's property, these forty rates meant that every taxpayer had to pay an entire sixth of his or her property, besides the poll tax part of the rate. These taxes dwarfed the taxes of the previous war, just as that war had dwarfed the taxes of the preceding peace (figure 12.1).

Back taxes from Andros's time were also ordered to be collected.[53] This enormous increase, together with the government's questionable legitimacy, threatened the regime's popularity among taxpayers. Delays in payments were significant, as towns argued for poverty or frontier status. The court perhaps mistrusted towns' property valuations, made extra efforts to justify taxes to taxpayers, and threatened to fine delinquent tax officers. Dr. Benjamin Bullivant, a dominion official arrested by the revolutionary government, wrote in February–March 1690 that many refused to pay taxes; objective evidence of some refusal is available for that November.[54]

Another expected source of income was plunder. Phips violated the terms of Acadia's surrender by sacking Port Royal and personally stealing the property of Governor Louis-Alexandre des Friches de Meneval. The private share of Acadia's plunder was given to soldiers by committees headed by Boston's treasurer, the merchant Richard Middlecot.[55] Regarding the greater armada to Canada, Hutchinson wrote about expectations of "plunder enough taken to defray all the charges." Others

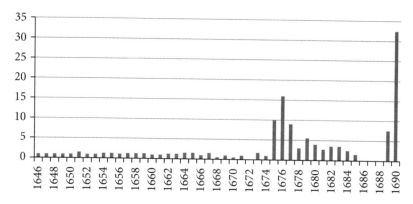

FIGURE 12.1 Taxes in Massachusetts (in rates), 1646–1685, 1689–1690. Sources: MAGC, II, IV-I, IV-II, V, *passim*, MS, *passim*.

agreed, and the court promised a share in the plunder to soldiers and lenders.[56] There was probably a religious aspect to placing such confidence in plunder: God was supposed to help finance an anti-Catholic mission carried out for him.[57] Elected for the first time as Boston's tax commissioner in August, Hutchinson soon had to reckon with the failure of these expectations.[58]

Settling the Debts

As usual, in 1689 the treasurer was personally the lender of first resort.[59] The court asked the populace and especially "gentlemen" and "merchants" to lend resources in money, goods, or food, with a promise of payment from the next taxes, upon the "public faith," "public credit," or "trust."[60] The treasurer was ordered to "draw his notes" on lenders, as with bills of exchange—that is, he paid suppliers with bills promising that other private people would redeem them in money or goods. Deputy Penn Townsend was requested to pay such a bill and was promised repayment from future income of alcohol taxes.[61] He was probably chosen because he was an alcohol merchant; some of that repayment could have been replaced by setoff.

In December 1689, a committee was appointed "to pass" debentures to soldiers, and later to all war-related creditors. The committee, receiving audience at the Boston townhouse, included four Boston merchants, headed by Eliakim Hutchinson (Elisha's relative). A fifth member was Thomas Brattle Jr., a scientist whose late father was a merchant and Boston's treasurer. Authority to issue was given to these five men "or any three of them."[62] A soldier's debenture looked as follows:[63]

Boston in New England. [date]

Mr. Treasurer.

There is due unto _____ for serving their Majesties against the French and Indian enemy as a _____ under the command of _____ the sum of _____ .

[signature]
[signature]
[signature]

The hostile Bullivant wrote in March 1690:

> The soldiery about this time that were returned from the eastward were in a high disgust for their pay . . . and spoke very insolently to their new masters [i.e., government] publicly in the streets. . . . In the mean time to stop the soldiers' clamors, they had debentures on the constables, but could not be paid unless they would abate for present pay some 25, some 50 per cent, according as their necessities were.[64]

Translation: instead of letting soldiers wait for tax receipts to reach the treasury, the constables redeemed debentures. But constables did not give the tax funds they had and promise more later; rather, constables personally bought debentures at large discounts. That was legal in a culture that lacked separation between the person and his public office. This claim, made about "the constables of Charlestown & Boston," is consistent with the infamous secondary market of debentures in the Civil Wars. It is also consistent with the court's usual policy of occasionally ordering constables and customs collectors to pay public funds they held directly to specific local creditors of the colony.[65]

Following the English practice of distinguishing between soldiers' debentures and sailors' tickets, another committee was appointed after the Acadia expedition to pass tickets to sailors. This three-man committee was led by Major Thomas Savage Jr., Elisha's cousin.[66] That both debentures and tickets committees were led by Hutchinson's relatives is another indication of his growing influence in fiscal matters. This committee was never heard of again, and only the debentures committee handled the later Quebec expedition.

Between expeditions, Cotton Mather's Election Day sermon had an unusual reference to credit. Speaking to the revived court, Mather preached on Nehemiah, who led the revival of Judea. Mather brutally forced on the biblical text a notion of a General Court and a governor who "[seemed] to erect a bank of credit" with "credit so passable."[67] Mather, the treasurer's son-in-law, probably reflected contemporary discussions about public credit and about establishing a public bank. The audience probably included the recent "bank of credit" entrepreneur John Blackwell. Tired of the Friends' unfriendliness, he had resigned as governor of Pennsylvania and returned to Boston.[68] Soon people lent funds for the Quebec expedition. They were mostly merchants, who gave "much of it in ready silver." If no plunder was taken, they were "to be paid by the country when able."[69]

In December 1689, it was ordered that soldiers awaiting pay of wages from the dominion era should "reserve" part of their recent taxes, implying a tentative setoff, "until further order."[70] In the huge tax of November 1690, this setoff idea was generalized: "All persons that have credit with the country to pay by discount."[71] Finally, setoff became a legal right rather than the treasurer's discretion. It was a deviation from common law, seen before perhaps only in Virginia. The implication for returning soldiers was that they could present debentures to constables and significantly reduce—perhaps even eliminate—their large tax obligations.[72]

The court resumed pro-coin discrimination in tax collection: some taxes had to be fully or partially paid in coin, while in other taxes the amount was abated one-third for those paying in coin.[73] Initial optimism that soldiers could be paid in coin was later replaced by the use of country pay, as in the previous war.[74] The court paid coins mostly where country pay would have been too expensive to transport: expenses in England, expenses in the frontier, and payments to men traveling on the court's behalf.[75] The lists of prices for taxes included (as usual by then) wheat, barley, barley malt, rye, maize, peas, and oats.[76] In October 1690, beef and pork—the favorite foods of soldiers—made their first appearance on such a list, following a recent Plymouth precedent and their listing as preferred items for loans to the colony. They had to be "merchantable" and "sealed by a sworn packer"[77] (i.e., sort of coined).

Discovering Canada's Card Money

Perhaps Canada's card money of 1685–1686 had become known in Massachusetts by 1689, as detailed above. If not, there were new routes in 1690. Acadian prisoners of war were brought to Boston and were disposed to local families, to work for their livelihood until shipped to French dominions. One "Lavalier"—perhaps the former Acadian governor who had spent a winter with de Meulles—was delivered to Deputy Joseph Lynde.[78] Governor Meneval was released to Nelson's house. Other French soldiers were captured or deserted in the land frontier and disclosed considerable information.[79]

Some historians have argued that the expedition to Quebec could have directly and physically exposed Massachusetts soldiers to Canadian money.[80] The armada captured French ships on its way to Quebec and back. The Puritans raided houses below Quebec and fought French soldiers there. Prisoners were taken and interrogated. The retreat involved a general prisoner exchange, returning to Massachusetts about twenty people captured in the land frontier. They had spent months in Quebec in relative freedom and were well informed of the situation in the town, which was then using its third generation of card money.[81]

On the Brink

The only history of the war written by a contemporary was composed by Cotton Mather. In 1697, he described the state of the colony in the fall of 1690:

> Of the disaster which now befell poor New England, in particular, every one will easily conclude, none of the least consequences to have been the extreme debts, which that country was now plunged into; there being forty thousand pounds, more or less, now to be paid, and not a penny in the Treasury to pay it withal.[82]

Enemies of the government estimated the debt at up to £55,000 and equated it to the cost of "Spain's 88"—that is, the Spanish Armada.[83] The problem was not just that the treasury was empty, and not even that there was probably not enough coin around to pay such high taxes.

More important, the required taxes were probably more than the population could spare from its current income and illiquid property. Mather wrote about "the sailors and soldiers, now upon the point of mutiny," and quoted a Roman historian about the danger to the regime: "The one who refuses what is just, gives up everything to an enemy in arms." Contemporaries cited "much murmuring" and "clamors" of soldiers and sailors, and fears of civil war.[84] Could Boston see a reenactment of England's 1667 Chatham disaster (pp. 43, 45)?

Debentures, which promised payment from the hapless treasurer, could be used for tax payments. Soldiers could also offer debentures to shopkeepers when trying to buy goods; but debentures had large denominations, because each single debenture was given for the three months' expedition. For example, one Edward Budd (of whom nothing else is known, so he was surely a simple soldier) had a debenture for two pounds, nineteen shillings, and two pence. At the prices of the latest tax law, it was worth thirteen bushels of wheat, which is what a family of five would eat over three months.[85] Senior soldiers and officers had even larger debentures. Did the typical soldier want to spend such a big amount in one shop at one time? Did any shopkeeper agree to accept such a large, nonround sum? Did the shopkeeper's ability to pay his own taxes with a soldier's assigned debenture induce him to accept it as payment for goods? The soldiers' noisy complaints testify that the answers are negative.[86]

The first meeting of a governmental body after the soldiers returned was a council meeting on November 29. Having received no letter from either the agents or the king that year, the despairing council wrote the agents about "the awful frown of God" and that "our Father spit in our face."[87] Another matter in that meeting was the complaint of the plundered Acadian governor Meneval against his plunderer—Assistant Phips. Meneval was represented by John Nelson.[88] With the fiscal abyss on everyone's minds, Nelson could have used the opportunity to inform the desperate council about the Canadian monetary solution to the problem they faced.

Following almost daily funerals in the smallpox-infested colony, the last entry in Sewall's diary before the court's next session is from December 8. He dined at a Boston tavern, the Royal Exchange, with eleven men. Their combined backgrounds of past and present offices is remarkable. In the political realm there were three assistants, two deputies, two members of the Council for Safety, and three Boston selectmen. Judges included the assistants and three municipal judges. Military men included a general, three captains, and an ensign. Three were intellectuals—that is, graduates of the college: a leading pastor married into an important mercantile family, a scientist who was a merchant's son, and a merchant who had managed a printing press and owned the closed mint. Fiscal men included a county treasurer, a Boston treasurer, a tax commissioner, and three constables. Half of the men were merchants. Four supervised the Boston market as sealer of weights and measures, culler of staves, wheat-price setter, and clerk of market. One was member of the Acadian plunder committees. Most intriguing is that *four* were members of the five-man debentures committee that was just then issuing debentures to the returning troops.[89] Solving the financial mess was an obvious topic of conversation, and this group was typical of the multitasking, inbreeding elite, which represented the interests, perspectives, and knowledge of soldiers, officers, tax collectors, legislators, magistrates, judges, intellectuals, merchants—and issuers of public-debt instruments.

Summary of Part II

Before proceeding to the December 1690 court session, it is time for a longer view, summarizing the main relevant points that came up since 1630.

Much of part II is a biography of the General Court of the Massachusetts Bay Colony. Born in London in 1629, it relocated at age one to America, where it grew and became wise and experienced. At age fifty-seven, it entered a three-year coma, and as of December 1690 it had been back to life for a year and a half. Governor Simon Bradstreet alone embodied the court's history. The colony had fifty thousand inhabitants living in more than fifty towns and villages, with one-seventh of these people living in Boston—English America's biggest town.[1] Like English towns, and especially trade hubs, it was dominated by merchants.

The court was sophisticated in its relations to England, fully committed to maintaining its near independence as much as possible, for the one and only sacred goal of preserving the integrity of the largest Puritan refuge on Earth. The court was a formidable political and legal player. It used everything in its arsenal—legal arguments, friends in England, bribes, tributes, procrastination, pretensions, subterfuges, hairsplitting rhetoric, half-truths, distance from England, and consequences of key events in England—to secure its autonomy during Charles I's Personal Rule, again for a generation after the Restoration, and then to regain that autonomy after the Glorious Revolution.[2]

The court was attentive to the needs of the population. In spite of the rule of the minority—the freemen—the court was accountable at least on anything not directly related to the religious mission. Had it ignored justified complaints about the economy, the economy would have been hit and people would have left. Suffrage was expended when the court was pressured to it by English events: the Restoration and the Glorious Revolution.

A standard tool of government was the ad hoc committee. Executive, administrative, investigative, and advisory committees were regularly appointed, especially in war. As the constitutional extension of the court between its sessions, the committees routinely included magistrates, deputies, former deputies, and political upstarts (usually listed by rank). On commercial issues, the overwhelming dominance of the Bay and particularly Boston, with Charlestown at a distant second, was reflected in committees. Merchants from these places were the key workforce, especially on economic matters, because committee work often required being at the central location, where any colonist could access the committee and the committee could access the governor, treasurer, court records, and other merchants who could lend money or goods to the colony. While the institution of the ad hoc committee was used instead of an orderly government bureaucracy as in England, the community of Bay merchants became more than a pool for economic and financial committees. It sometimes seemed like a pseudo treasury department: every few months, some of its members were called up for some committee work.

Massachusetts had the only college in English America. Although there was hardly any scientific basis for some of the materials taught there—whether medicine or religion—the college did encourage some smart people to think abstractly and not spend their entire time on the farm, in the workshop, or at the countinghouse. Those who became ministers were expected to be involved in key constitutional and economic issues. There was little to no scientific or technological advancement in Massachusetts, but there was much creative thinking and boldness in monetary innovation. The variety and sophistication of commodity moneys was unique. Coinage, broadly conceived, was attempted or approximated not only with metal pieces but even with wampum, cattle, fish, and grain. Tradable financial instruments—simple promissory notes, notes of land banks, or debentures—had been on the court's mind since 1631. Credit was very common and well developed, with setoffs and trilateral debt settlements often used in the public and private sectors. These efficient methods were most needed in time of war, when there were no spare resources of time, equipment, and funds to transport grain as money over large distances.

The smallness of each colony and town, and the small role of governments in the economy, helped people understand the court's repeated dictum that the treasury was a mere intermediary. The treasury's debt to a soldier had to be paid by a tax imposed on the soldier's neighbor. If the neighbor paid taxes in bad money, the soldier would have difficulty buying food with that money.

The Atlantic World abounded with ideas of using paper (in account books or as bills) or cheap metal instead of precious-metal coin. Legal support came in the form of compulsion, convertibility into coin, backing by land, or legal tender status. Boston, Connecticut, Quebec, Pennsylvania, West New Jersey, Antigua, Barbados, Bermuda, Virginia, Dutch Brazil, Ireland, London, and probably Plymouth were all involved in that advance in monetary theory and practice. New England merchants were well positioned to know about all these ideas, through a great variety of information channels.

All the components of the 1690 invention have just been reviewed here. Let Hutchinson and company connect the dots for us.

PART III

A Monetary Revolution

Having traveled the long road from 1584 Roanoke, we can now finally understand the revolutionary Massachusetts law of December 24, 1690. Reading, let alone writing, an entire book to understand just one document is an effort befitting a constitution. Indeed, this 1690 document is the constitution of our modern currency.

The main task is to examine the law itself—based on all the insights of part II. We will understand every aspect of this law, and, equally important, understand what was supposed to be in it but was *not*. I will suggest a political explanation regarding such puzzling omissions. Within a year and a half, the 1690 money would gradually converge in legal status toward our modern legal tender currency. It would need three more centuries to take over the world—for better and for worse.

CHAPTER THIRTEEN

The Legal Tender Law, 1690

War is the father of us all.
  —Heraclitus

The Session

On Wednesday, December 10, the General Court reconvened. As usual that year, only half the magistrates showed up, including the governor, the deputy governor, the treasurer John Phillips, Samuel Sewall, and Elisha Hutchinson. Hutchinson hardly missed a meeting of the council or General Court since the elections. Sir William Phips, as usual, stayed home. Wait Winthrop was home injured, but was later visited by Sewall. Only half the towns bothered sending deputies—mostly Bay towns and northern towns, which were most exposed to an expected Canadian attack. Ice and smallpox prevented others from showing up during the two-week session. It was probably smallpox, however, that arranged an odd meeting, halfway through the session, between Hutchinson, the council's secretary, the speaker, the former assistant John Richards, and the Boston treasurer Richard Middlecot. They could have a lively financial discussion while carrying the coffin of the Boston deputy Dr. John Clark.[1]

The court handled many issues, including a first letter to the king since the French entered the war. They wrote of the Acadia success and the Quebec failure. Warning that "some may seek to misrepresent us," the court asked as usual for "confirmation of the charter government." The desperate court made its first-ever request for military aid from England.[2] December 23 was a busy day at court, Sewall reporting "being detained at the townhouse all day." The council passed an order for printing "bills" and the exact form of these bills. Both were approved by the deputies, but the following day, December 24, the council added a limitation on the quantity of bills. The court expedited the granting of debentures and adjourned until March 1691.[3]

The Preamble

Important laws in England and the colonies had preambles, the length of which depended on the importance of the matter and the justification required. The preamble to the paper money law was unusually long:

> Whereas (for the maintaining and defending of their Majesties' interests against the hostile invasions of their French and Indian enemies who have begun and are combined in the prosecution of a bloody war upon the English of their Majesties' colonies and plantations of New England) this colony has necessarily contracted sundry considerable debts, which this Court taking into consideration and being desirous to approve themselves just and honest in the discharge of the same and that every person who has credit with the country for the use of any of his estate, disbursements, or service done for the public, may in convenient time receive due and equal satisfaction; withal considering the present poverty and calamities of the country and (through scarcity of money) the want of an adequate measure of commerce, whereby they are disadvantaged in making present payment as desired; yet being willing to settle and adjust the accounts of the said debts, and to make payment thereof, with what speed they can.

There are important points here. First, knowing that its laws could become known in England, the court emphasized that the expedition was sent for the monarchs' interests, as it claimed in the contemporary letter to the king. Second, the debts were "contracted," so discharging them with "due and equal satisfaction" was "just and honest," but at the moment the court could only "settle and adjust the accounts of the said debts" rather than discharge them. Third, there were three types of creditors, giving either "estate" (e.g., ships hired), "disbursements" (e.g., food), or military "service." Finally, as Sewall would write years later, the bills were born not for lack of money in the colony per se, but for lack of money in the treasury.[4] That happened partly because there was no convenient money for paying taxes. As a contemporary Englishman in Ireland noted, money was both "the sinews of war [and] life blood of trade."[5]

The Law

After the preamble comes the law itself:

> It is ordered by this Court that Major Elisha Hutchinson, Major John Phillips, Captain Penn Townsend, Mr. Adam Winthrop and Mr. Timothy Thornton or any three of them, be and are hereby appointed and empowered a Committee for the granting forth of printed bills in such forms as is agreed upon by this Court (none under five shillings nor exceeding five pounds in one bill) unto all such persons who shall desire the same, to whom the colony is indebted, for such sum or sums of money as they shall have debentures from the Committee, or Committees that are or shall be appointed to give out the same. Every of which bills according to the sums therein expressed shall be of equal value with money, and the Treasurer and all the receivers subordinate to him shall accept, and receive the same accordingly in all public payments. No more of said bills, to be printed or granted forth than for the sum of seven thousand pounds. And the colony is hereby engaged to satisfy the value of said bills as the Treasury shall be enabled. And any person having of said bills in his hands, may accordingly return the same to the Treasurer, and shall receive the full sum thereof in money, or other public stock at the money price as stated for that time. And if any of said bills be worn in any person's hands, so as they desire to renew them, returning them to the Committee, they shall have new ones of the same numbers and sums given out.

The order, with the preamble, was the only document of that session published as a broadside (figure 13.1).

The form of the bills was enacted:

> This indented bill of twenty shillings due from the Massachusetts Colony to the possessor shall be in value equal to money and shall be accordingly accepted by the Treasurer, and receivers subordinate to him in all public payments, and for any stock at any time in the Treasury.
>
> Boston in New England, December 10th 1690. By Order of the General Court.

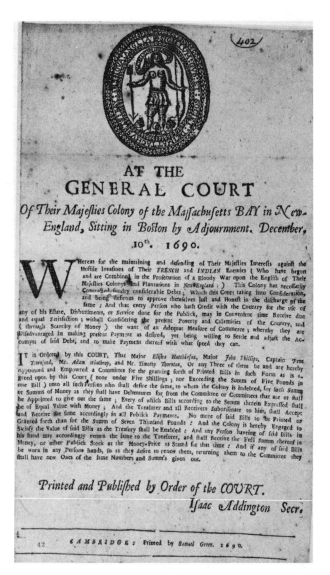

FIGURE 13.1 The order for paper money. Source: Massachusetts General Court, *At the General Court of their Majesties Colony of the Massachusetts Bay in New-England, sitting in Boston by adjournment, December 10th, An order for the granting forth of printed bills for seven thousand pounds Cambridge: Printed by Samuel Greene*, Cambridge, Massachusetts, 1690, https://www.loc.gov/item/rbpe.03302500/.

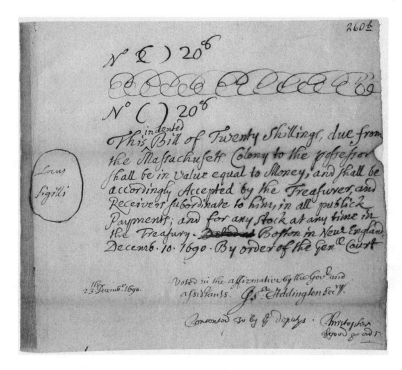

FIGURE 13.2 The draft of a bill. Source: Massachusetts Archives Collection, vol. 36, p. 260b, "Bill of Twenty Shillings, December 23, 1690," SCI/series 45X, Massachusetts Archives, Boston.

The date does not imply that the draft of the bill was written on December 10. It was merely the first day of the session, and court sessions were always dated in official records that way, no matter how long they lasted.[6] The draft was written by Sewall, who had the clearest handwriting among magistrates (figure 13.2).[7]

It is time to dissect the law and look in detail at each and every component of it, except for the committee which will be discussed later.

Issuing Bills

PHYSICAL FORM. These were "printed bills," unlike the handwritten playing cards of Canada. With thousands of soldiers, sailors, and suppliers to be paid, the technological ability to print small forms was a prerequisite. Cotton Mather wrote that the bills were "printed from copper plates,"[8] as the Bank of Credit bills were supposed to be. Decades after copper starred in Roanoke and Jamestown, it was used to print the first English paper money on the mainland.

The bill was indented and carried the company's seal (figure 13.2). Indentures and seals were routinely used to prevent forgery in legal documents. The message was that each bill was a binding legal document. A charter-era law mandated the use of company seal on all commissions and "writings of public concernment" or "public instruments" issued by court or council. The seal had been used on a debt instrument only once before, regarding £1,000 borrowed by agents in England in 1666. The treasurer also had a seal.[9]

It was obvious that debentures did not carry company or treasurer seals because they were issued not by court, council, or treasurer, but by a committee. Debentures were addressed to "Mr. Treasurer." An exception was made for the 1690 paper money—probably the first instrument issued by a committee that carried the company seal. Indeed, while debentures began with "There is due" and not specifying from whom, the bills specified "due from the Massachusetts colony." The bills were given the strongest possible formality (if we ignore the fact that the company was legally dead).

The law ended with the provision that "worn" bills in "any person's hands" could be renewed. The bills were expected to be used till worn, and the replacement would not necessarily be to the original recipients of the bills but to "any person" holding them. These bills were designed as money.[10]

DENOMINATIONS. No bill was to be worth less than five shillings or more than £5. The highest denomination was far lower than the £100 of London goldsmiths' notes; the lower bound was five times higher than the largest coins locally minted, but it was close to the value of the piece of eight, so it was certainly money. At the prices of the latest tax law, the amount of five shillings was worth slightly more than a bushel of wheat, which could feed a family of five for a week.[11] The bills were of the right denomination for a soldier, typically a young family man, returning home after three months and needing to buy food. The bills were not meant to buy beer at an inn or ride the ferry (a few pennies' cost), but they were certainly not restricted to mercantile and land transactions only. As John Hanson has argued, too-low denominations during war could slow the production and issuance of bills too much, especially when each bill required three handwritten signatures.[12] That debenture of almost £3 cited above was just above the average of the lowest and highest denominations. Its recipient could trade his single debenture for twelve bills of five shillings each, and give coins or country pay as change.

The whole point was that bills replaced debentures of high, nonround denominations. Both financial instruments had the same intrinsic value (zero) and the same basic legal status (they could be used to pay taxes). Debentures were de facto reminted into smaller pieces, more convenient for the market. This is what the local mint had done when reminting pieces of eight (about five shillings) into coins of a shilling or less. Similarly, the minting of pieces of eight by Spaniards turned silver mines into smaller, standardized, convenient sums.

The scholars Drew Boyd and Jacob Goldenberg call this method of innovation "preserving division":

> You can frequently make groundbreaking innovations simply by dividing a product into "chunks" to create many smaller versions of it. These smaller versions still function like the original product, but their reduced size delivers benefits that users wouldn't get with the larger, "parent" product.

Their examples include multitrack recording, memory sticks, packaged foods, and radiation therapy.[13] Debentures were divided in a way that allowed the smaller chunks to function as money in shops, and did not take away from the soldiers any legal right or economic ability they had when holding debentures.

The wide range of possible denominations that the court gave the committee—from five to a hundred shillings—granted the committee considerable discretion and responsibility. If the chosen denominations were too small, effectively converting all debentures into the most convenient money, it could take too much time and prices might jump. If the chosen denominations were too large, the bills would not function as money and soldiers might mutiny.

QUANTITY AND TIMING. After the law passed both Houses, the magistrates amended it with an upper bound of £7,000. Deleted text in the draft indicates that the original intention was probably to issue bills for all the colony's debts. In the spirit of experiments—which characterized both the court's history and the Scientific Revolution—the cautious magistrates had second thoughts and decided to try first with £7,000, leaving out the rest of the £40,000 debt. The committee could issue fewer bills if it wanted, which was another important part of the discretion given to it. The committee could stretch the operation for months, experimenting with denominations and the rate of emitting the bills.

OPEN MARKET PURCHASES. The bills were not forced on any creditor of the colony; they were to be given to debenture holders "who shall desire the same." This operation was *not* redemption of debentures, because debentures, just like bills, promised pay in conventional money. It was merely a *swap* of financial instruments—bills for debentures. There already was active trade in debentures that year, and the committee entered that secondary market, agreeing to purchase all debentures at face value. Since that market was open to anyone, modern jargon calls it "open market" and calls that procedure "open market purchases."

The Legal Status of the Bills

One difference from debenture was that the bill was an evidence of debt to "the possessor" rather than a named person. Debentures were tradable but had to be assigned in writing from one possessor to another. The bills, in contrast, were designed to pass easily from hand to hand, just like coins. The order decreed two uses for the bills: bill holders could ask the treasury to redeem them in coin or goods, and any payment to the colony could be discharged with these bills. Let us examine these uses in turn.

CONVERTIBILITY. Although the 1690 money is typically presented by historians as an inconvertible currency—and indeed, it was *not* converted by that government into coin or goods—the letter of the law did promise convertibility. The promise was to convert bills to either coin or "other public stock" held by the treasurer. These were the goods that had a "money price . . . stated" in tax laws (country pay).[14] What was the credibility of this promise? Legally, it meant almost nothing because it held only "as the Treasury shall be enabled."

And if it was not "enabled"? Initially the treasury was empty, which was the reason for issuing bills. In the immediate future, until the huge taxes were paid (presumably with agricultural produce) during a difficult winter by a sickly population, there was no hope of obtaining coin or goods to redeem bills. Other sources of funds were not available: the loss in Quebec proved that expected plunder was unreliable, and the war was on hold for the winter; financial aid from England was unprecedented and unthinkable; the colony never earned revenue from producing and selling goods; it no longer produced coins; potential lenders were "out of cash," claimed an antigovernment merchant;[15] and proceeds from land sales were unreliable, as will be explained below. For the first few months, at least, the convertibility promise was a dead letter, and everyone knew it.[16]

LEGAL TENDER FOR TAXES. The court decreed in a somewhat alchemical spirit that bills "shall be of equal value with money." But only the treasurer and his receivers were obliged to accept bills according to this pompous declaration. The mentioning of the treasurer and his receivers in such a context was almost an exact quote from the Dudley council's approval of the Bank of Credit (p. 135). The "receivers subordinate to him" were tax-collecting constables, marshals who collected fines, and customs officers. Other payments to the treasurer could have been made from people who owed money to the colony for other reasons and from purchasers of land. But these, just like fines, were uncertain. Effectively, only taxes could be relied upon. With the convertibility being a dead letter, all the burden was on taxes as the legal support for the bills. You may recall, the usual commodities could also be used to pay taxes, so bills did not have a monopoly, even in tax payments.

The colonists may have viewed tax acceptance as necessary—if the issuing government itself would not accept its own bills, why should anyone else accept them? It was the one necessary legal requirement. It was important especially given the absence of any other legal backing. It is time to examine the economic mechanism of this tax acceptance.

The Economic Mechanism

Figures 13.3 to 13.5 show the economic working of the legal tender money as designed. Figure 13.3 shows the problem: the government owed a debt to soldiers, while taxpayers' debt to the government was not yet paid. The taxpayers were mostly private sellers of goods and services. All debts were supposed to be paid in coin or country pay.

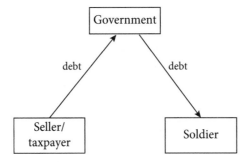

FIGURE 13.3 The problem.

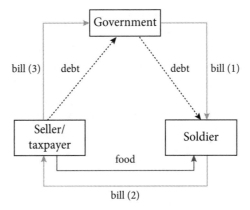

FIGURE 13.4 The solution.

Figure 13.4 shows the solution. The soldiers get bills, with which they buy food, and then the sellers, who are also taxpayers, pay taxes with these bills. The bills complete a full circle and the problem is solved. There are no payments in coin or goods of either original debt, and the bills are not redeemed by the treasury in coin or goods.

The larger significance is displayed in figure 13.5: not all sellers necessarily pay taxes with all the bills they get from soldiers. Sellers can circulate bills between themselves—the baker uses bills he gets from soldiers to buy shoes from the shoemaker, who uses bills to buy tools from the blacksmith, and so on; occasionally, after a bill circulates and passes many hands, one seller uses the bill to pay a tax. In the figure, it is the nth time that the bill has changed hands. This is how a medium of pay-

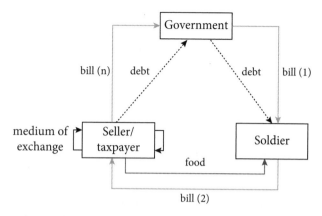

FIGURE 13.5 A general medium of exchange.

ing taxes, if conveniently denominated and easily transferable, becomes a general medium of exchange—a true currency.

Bills of Credit

It was indeed a *credit* operation, and the difference from known practices should be clarified. A trilateral settlement of debts as in figure 3.1 could work if there had been a single taxpayer and a single soldier, with the former's tax obligation equal to the latter's credit, and if the taxpayer had enough coin or grain. But reality was much more complicated. In using bills, the solution of figure 13.4 is similar to figure 3.2 (trilateral debt settlement by assignment) and figure 3.4 (assignment of public debt). The difference is that in those cases the use of coin was reduced from twice to once, but it was still there. In figure 3.2, the bill is eventually redeemed in coin, while in figure 3.4 the tally is traded for coin. But in figure 13.4, there is no coin at all. It is a coin-free settlement of public debts between three groups on a massive scale.

The mechanism can also be seen as voluntary exchange followed by setoff. Consider first a constable visiting a soldier who is also a taxpayer. The constable tells the soldier-taxpayer that he owes one pound in taxes and asks for coin or grain. The soldier-taxpayer shows a bill of £1 and claims, "But you owe *me* coin or grain at the value of one pound—so let's have a setoff." Paper for paper, claim for claim. No physical goods involved. To the unsophisticated eye, it would seem like payment of taxes in paper money. Next, consider a shopkeeper who voluntarily accepts a bill from a soldier. That action transfers the colony's debt from the soldier to the shopkeeper—who is also a taxpayer. Now the colony owes coin or grain to the shopkeeper-taxpayer, and his payment of the tax with a bill is a setoff.

Learning the Tax-Foundation Theory

How did the court realize this could work? For decades, Massachusetts taxpayers paid taxes in coin and goods—as long as the goods had "merchantable" quality. Sellers could learn the minimal quality of goods that the treasury accepted for taxes. For example, in 1690 a bushel of barley discharged four shillings of tax liability. A shopkeeper offered by a farmer fifteen bushels of barley of sufficiently good quality as payment for goods knew that this barley could at the very least be used to discharge sixty shillings of his tax liability. The tax law's prices put a lower bound on the value of these commodity moneys. Sellers probably accepted some payments in grain only because they knew it had a sure value in tax payments. This guarantee should have increased the demand for grain, including grain of marginal quality.

Producers of other types of money apparently understood the importance of this mechanism for increasing the demand for, and the value of, their money. John Hull, the mint master and treasurer, probably influenced the statutory discount for taxes paid in his coins and the forcing of taxpayers to use his coins as part of their payments. Similarly, Blackwell used political connections to obtain for his Bank of Credit's notes the status of legal tender for debts and taxes.

Hull's son-in-law and heir (Sewall) and Bank of Credit officers who were legislators in 1690 knew the power of this mechanism: if an object was acceptable for tax payments, it was more likely to function as money. Indeed, empirically, objects acceptable for taxes also functioned as money in the private economy. Theoretically, taxpayers could make good use of this object, so they might agree to accept it in return for goods and services they provide to others. Shopkeepers would accept it for shop payments and workers would accept it as wages. If it was the only acceptable object for taxes, then it would be *necessary* for them to accept it. But what if some Richard had enough of that money to pay taxes with in the foreseeable future? Given a high enough tax burden, Richard should still be willing to accept it, because the next seller he meets (Katherine) might not already have all of that object to pay *her* taxes, so Katherine would accept it. And so on. This is why the court dared supporting its novel money with this mechanism alone.

Compared to grain, local coins, and Bank of Credit notes, the 1690 money—being intrinsically useless and unbacked—merely took this mechanism to its limit. It promised that paper would discharge tax liabilities according to its face value. Every seller was supposed to understand that regardless of the acceptability of bills in the market, they were still useful for tax payments. The guarantee that £1 in paper discharged a £1 tax liability was supposed to put a lower bound on the bills' value. The intrinsic uselessness of the bills was not supposed to matter to sellers any more than they had cared about the quality of grain as commodity money so long as it was at least at the treasury's threshold of acceptability.

The court perhaps thought that in the long run it was on safe ground with such a combination of legal tender for taxes and an empty promise of convertibility. It seemed like a win-win plan: if all bills were rejected in shops, then sellers would pay taxes in coin and goods as usual, and then there would be "money, or other public stock" in the treasury with which to redeem bills; if all bills were accepted in shops, then seller-taxpayers would probably prefer to get rid of paper rather than coin and goods when tax collectors show up; then the government would have no "stock . . . in the Treasury" with which to redeem bills—but it would end up holding all the bills, so nobody would ask to redeem them.[17] A perfect plan. Easy money.

The Missing Parts

The 1690 money has been usually portrayed as a natural, almost trivial development from recent paper moneys, such as Canada's and Blackwell's.[18] It clearly differed in that the convertibility promise was a nonbinding dead letter. But other key features of those recent moneys were not even written into the 1690 law: monetary terminology, forced acceptance, legal tender for debts, and backing by land. These differences from past practices have sometimes been noticed by scholars but never explained. We need to be reminded how odd the absence of these features is, and then I will propose a single factor that may explain the absence of them all.

Monetary Terminology

The bills were called simply "bills." There was no justification to call them "money" because that meant coin, but "paper money" and "bill money" had long been proposed in England, Canada had "card money" and the Fund used "change bills." Clear monetary terminology could have helped the population realize what they were expected to do with the bills. It might have induced sellers to accept them. Why was there no monetary terminology?

Forced Acceptance

At least some of the previous governments that issued paper money in a military emergency, such as that of 1690 Massachusetts, forced everyone to accept the new money in trade under threat of penalty. This definitely happened in China, Spain, Dutch Brazil, and, most important, in contemporary, neighboring Canada. With a harsh legislative record in general and draconian wartime measures in 1690 in particular, the Puritan colony should be expected to do the same. But the court did not force everyone to accept paper money. In fact, it forced nobody but itself. Why?

Legal Tender for Debts

The normal status of coins in England and the colonies was "pass current." Any monetary obligation could be discharged with such coins, including all debts and taxes. If a contract denominated in pounds had been created without specifying the medium of payment, these "pass current" objects were good enough to discharge the debt at face value, and the creditor would lose if he sued for nonpayment. That was the case for most of Massachusetts's previous moneys, including local coins and Bank of Credit notes. But the 1690 money was legal tender only for taxes and other payments to the treasurer. It wasn't even legal tender for payments from the treasurer to others—soldiers and suppliers. Why was the 1690 money an exception?

Backing by Land

From time immemorial, land was used in payments of debt, or at least as security for such payments. Such use had critical importance in wars.

Wars were expensive and created large debts; wars were often about land disputes, and the victor often gained land. Therefore, it was routine to pay land for war debts or to make land security for paying war debts. As shown above, this happened in the Civil Wars, in Ireland, in the Pequot War, and King Philip's War. This financial use of land led to proposals of land banks. The idea of backing paper money with land was the foundation of both the Fund and the Bank of Credit in the 1670s and 1680s. It was the hottest financial idea of the period in the English-speaking world.

There were personal connections between that money-land tradition and the 1690 money. Governor Simon Bradstreet and Deputy Governor Thomas Danforth were among the assistants who pledged land as security for the colony's debts during King Philip's War.[19] Sewall printed the Fund pamphlet (and its printed notes, if there were any) in 1681–1683. Bank of Credit officers included Wait Winthrop, James Russell, Isaac Addington, Elisha Hutchinson, and Penn Townsend, who would be legislators in 1690. John Blackwell himself was almost certainly in Boston in December 1690 (see below). As the foremost financial expert in America, he was surely consulted.

Given the success and prevalence of this financial use of land in the previous wars (in which new lands were won) and the numerous personal connections to land-backed financial institutions, it is remarkable that the financial use of land is *completely absent* from the records in 1689–1690. Before and after each of this period's expeditions, the forces were promised a share of the "plunder," while loans were secured by future tax revenues or "plunder." That word never included land before and did not include land in this war either. Land in foreign occupied lands was too important and consequential to be included implicitly with movables like furs and guns. Land was not explicitly promised before any expedition, nor explicitly given after it. The bills were neither convertible into land nor backed by it. Even an empty promise was not made regarding land backing, as was made about redeeming the bills with coin or goods. It's as if all the financial legacy of land in Massachusetts was suddenly completely wiped out. *Terra incognita.*

A Political Explanation

It should be clear now that the 1690 paper money was nothing like its predecessors, and was *not* a trivial development from recent paper moneys. It was a money lacking monetary terminology; it was an emergency money with no forced acceptance; it was a money designed to pay a debt, but was not legal tender for debts and was forced only on its issuer; it was a money not supported by the most obvious device for that time and place—land; it was a money that promised convertibility into everything the government did not physically have (coin or goods), but did not promise convertibility into the only thing the government did physically have (land). What can explain such an odd, paradoxical, even absurd type of money? The answer is: England.

THE PLAUSIBLE DENIABILITY OF MONEY. Massachusetts had not received the right to mint coins in its charter. When the court was caught doing that, it paid a diplomatic price. Recent assistants John Richards and William Stoughton were among the agents who had begged Charles II to pardon the mint offense, and could have informed the court in case anyone forgot. More important, the court kept paying that price. The minting accusations resurfaced in Increase Mather's face in 1689, as Hutchinson and Sewall surely told the court. The court knew that the new battle of the charter was tough, and it did not want to give ammunition to its enemies. Minting coins in 1690 would have been a colossal mistake. Issuing paper money might have been just as bad; it would have opened a debate on whether the ancient royal prerogative included a monopoly on issuing coins or on issuing any objects specifically designed to function as money.

What to do when soldiers need money but England presumably does not allow money? The solution was to eliminate all nonessential monetary features. First, consider monetary terminology. Hairsplitting rhetoric was second nature to the court when dealing with England. Just as the restored court operated "according to the rules" of the old revoked charter without formally reviving the charter itself, and the court's terminology was replaced entirely (table 12.1); so were the "bills" designed to function *according to the rules* of money without being formally money and without monetary terminology. It was called "bills" rather than "money" for this reason.[20] Moreover, as the historian Jonathan Barth has noted, the bills were "of equal value with money"—and so formally distinct from money.[21]

Second, the legacy of accusations against Massachusetts coinage included not only the fact of minting but also the making of the coins "current" for debts. This monetary feature was not essential for the tax-foundation economic mechanism. In theory, taxes alone should have made it work. Moreover, legal tender for debts is a weak mechanism, forced only on creditors not careful to specify otherwise in contracts. Making bills legal tender for all debts would imply that soldiers had to accept them. It was a feature that could not have been hidden in those circumstances of 1690.

Third, if making an object legal tender for debts was too much of an explicit monetary feature, forced acceptance in spot transactions was so much worse. Therefore, even though it was a military emergency, this paper money, unlike most or all of its predecessors, was not forced on anyone in regular trade.

Additional considerations required extra care. First, while England repeatedly objected to the Massachusetts coins, which were, according to the Royal Mint, debased by 22.5 percent, the paper money issue amounted to opening a mint with 100 percent debasement. Second, while the colonists got away with minting for decades under Charles II, they might not have been so lucky with the new king, who came from the world's financial center. Third, the revolutionary constitutional settlement made William one of the weakest kings in English history. Formally he ruled only with wife Mary, and Parliament took from him significant powers to assure that the Stuart tyranny never resumed. Such a king might have been more reluctant than previous ones to give up the royal coinage prerogative—one of his few remaining powers. His great-grandfather James I stopped granting coinage authority to colonizing companies when Parliament challenged his general authority.

In conclusion, of all the types of transactions and payments in the Massachusetts economy, the court could force the bills on nobody but itself. The sensitive situation of charter lobbying in England did not allow anything more than that. What Massachusetts created was formally not money. It looked like a simple credit instrument and was named as such. It was a bill, or a promissory note, which happened to be issued by a colonial government rather than an individual. There was nothing illegal or sovereign-like about that, as any person was allowed to issue bills.[22] The court had already compared once its legal rights to those of an individual, in another context.[23]

A typical bill issued by English people had four standard features:

first, it was redeemable in coin or goods; second, it had an indenture, and perhaps a seal too; third, it was not forced on anyone; fourth, it was not called "money." The 1690 "bills" formally fulfilled all these criteria. The paper money was thus disguised from the king as a simple promissory note. How about acceptance of the bill for tax payments? Is that not a sovereign act? Not at all. Any issuer of a bill was expected—by commercial custom and common sense (though not by common law)—to accept it to offset debts owed to himself. By accepting its own bills in tax payments, the court was on safe grounds because it was just a setoff. If anything, tax acceptance made the bills seem even more like simple promissory notes.

ANDROS'S SHADOW OVER LAND. The financial legacy of land was not forgotten. It was suspended, pending England's repeal of Andros's land policy, which invalidated all land titles and decreed that the land belonged to the Crown. Some private plots had been confirmed by Andros, but all public lands—those which could be granted to soldiers or could back paper money—still belonged to the Crown according to Andros's interpretation. Though the royal governor was deposed along with his boss, a decision made by him was perhaps valid until repealed by a new royal governor or by the king. The court probably learned by December that the king exonerated Andros of all allegations.[24] This implied that there was nothing obviously wrong with his land policy. William was too busy fighting to make any further policy decisions about Massachusetts.

Therefore, as of December 1690, it was doubtful whether either the colony or most colonists legally owned *any* land. Some 1690 legislators were personally affected by Andros's policy. He ignored Hutchinson's land claims, and he served writs of intrusion against Sewall, Russell, and Deputy Joseph Lynde. The best indication of the uncertainty and its importance is that in November 1690, the agents in London asked the king for a new charter and "to confirm to them the enjoyment of their lands and properties." It was their only specific request at the time.[25] Further evidence from 1691–1692 is related below.

So, as of December 1690, the king could have confirmed Andros's policy and could have been angry at the court for giving away *his* land, or for promising *his* land as backing for the colony's money. Avoiding any reference to land seemed like the safest course of action while the colony's fate was under discussion in London.

Summing It Up

Four standard, traditional ingredients are missing from the 1690 law: monetary terminology, forced acceptance, legal tender for debts, and land backing. The political explanation—trying to keep on good terms with England while the fate of the charter hung in the balance—can explain all four anomalies. The first three relate to the coinage offense, while the last relates to the land problem. Diplomacy required complete silence on both issues: the colony did not produce something that was formally money or looked too much like money, and it made no movement on the doubtful land ownership. The claim that a single cause can explain multiple puzzles, is, at the very least, desirable according to the logical criterion known as Occam's razor. The four dogs that didn't bark in 1690 were silent because they were terrified of the single lion in the room—the lion on King William's coat of arms.

The court's caution is consistent with the general behavior of colonial elites. Rhode Island, Connecticut, and Plymouth were friendly to the Crown while trying to obtain a charter in the 1660s.[26] Most New England governments were careful in 1689–1690 regarding their constitutional status, fearing royal disapproval. They did not revive their old charters after unilaterally dissolving the dominion, even though the dominion had been established, and the charters revoked or suspended, by the new king's enemies.[27] Before the king approved the revolutionary Massachusetts government, the latter was extremely cautious when exercising authority over taxation and justice.

The Monetary Committee

The Members

We have already met the committee members. Elisha Hutchinson, the top expert on public finance in 1690, received a full chapter. This grandson of "anti-law" Anne headed the creation of a purely law-based money. John Phillips was the treasurer. Penn Townsend was speaker of the House of Deputies. Adam Winthrop had been a trustee of the Fund, deputy manager of the Bank of Credit, co-treasurer after the revolution, and a deputy. Timothy Thornton, however, is a puzzle worth examining.

Thornton did not have the status of his colleagues. By 1686, he advanced from "shipwright" to "merchant" in legal documents. In 1689, he was one of Boston's price setters of grain. In 1690, he was elected in Boston as a judge, and, surprisingly, also as a "scavenger" who cared for cleanliness of roads. The court appointed him an ensign in a Boston company, and he worked for the court on minor ad hoc committees—to search and seize gunpowder and to take names of refugees who fled the frontier.[28] He was on the same path to deputyship that Hutchinson took in the 1670s and Townsend in the 1680s. He was a typical political upstart, and would indeed become a deputy. In retrospect, with two assistants and current, former, and future deputies, this committee was entirely typical.

But this was no regular committee. Thornton's signature was to appear not on a committee report seen only by the court, but on many bills distributed throughout the colony in its most consequential, risky financial operation ever. This was no time for mentoring an inexperienced man. His status was far lower than the others who had the reputation of office or heritage—the treasurer, an assistant, the speaker, and a Winthrop who was a recent co-treasurer. His only proximity to power at the colonial level in December 1690 was literally standing near Sewall and Hutchinson at a soldier's funeral.[29] Thornton seems to have been way out of his league on that committee.

The simplest solution to his membership in the paper money committee is to accept the hypothesis that he was the manager or deputy manager of the Fund from 1681 to 1685. For the first issue of paper money by the colony, it would be obvious to appoint the *only* man around who actually succeeded in circulating bills issued by an organization (the director, Henchman, had died by this point).

Another oddity is the treasurer's low profile. One would expect the most important financial committee in the colony's history to be led by the treasurer; however, Phillips was listed second, and his office was not even mentioned. Listings of committee members was almost always according to rank. Probably Hutchinson headed the list because he sponsored the bill, as modern parlance would have it. He may have invented it, or he may have supported and promoted it when others doubted. Perhaps he was listed first because he dominated the fiscal-military committees of that year and especially in the fall of 1690.

Members' Characteristics

Cotton Mather described the committee as an "able and faithful committee of gentlemen."[30] The adjective *able* regularly appeared in orders

to draft soldiers and hire ministers, and indicated the necessary qualifi-
cation required to perform a job.[31] For that daring *credit* operation, the
people chosen indeed had to be "faithful" (literally "credible"). Similarly, the Bank of Credit's prospectus promised the "bank-bills of credit"
would be "signed by several persons of good repute."[32]

All committee members were merchants. Historians have sometimes
overidentified merchants, ascribing that status without evidence to any
important, rich man.[33] If any important man was a merchant, then an all-
merchant committee was as trivial as an all-male committee. But since
there were also rich men who lived off lands they leased, an all-merchant
committee was not a trivial fact. At the same time, by now the court's
choice of such a committee should be obvious. The merchants were the
financial experts who have long held the offices of treasurers of the colony, counties, towns, the college, and the Gospel Company, and dominated all commercial and financial committees, including the committees of auditing, accounting, and granting debentures. Nobody was more
qualified than them to issue financial instruments.

In this specific case, an all-merchant committee had more advantages. First, no one could better estimate what would be the appropriate denominations, timing, and total amount of the bills to be issued;
the consequences of bad choices could be serious. Second, expected
doubts among the population regarding a new type of financial instrument with little legal support could be countered only by the prestige of
merchants—who were the economic and financial backbone of the community. Third, the quality of commodity money had long been defined
everywhere by the merchants' standard: "merchantable." Who could
better vouchsafe for the value of a new money? Fourth, merchants' qualifications made them natural officers in banks. Except for the treasurer,
all committee members had experience in 1680s banking: Thornton
was part of the Fund, as was Adam Winthrop. Adam, Hutchinson, and
Townsend were part of the Bank of Credit. Finally, the appointment of
merchants guaranteed there would not be high inflation. Not only were
the merchants always the main creditors in the economy, but they were
the ones who lent money for the Quebec expedition, and inflation would
have hurt them. The only known list of lenders to the colony around that
time includes eleven merchants, most of whom were partners, friends, or
relatives of the committee members.[34]

Except for the treasurer, who was from Charlestown, they were all
from Boston. Bay affiliation had long been typical in financial commit-

tees, and was especially appropriate in this case. The Bay is where most soldiers and sailors disembarked, and where some of them stayed or returned to demand their pay. The committee was expected to sit in an accessible place for weeks, if not months, in the dead of winter. It had to be in the Bay, and thus the men had to be Bay residents.

Hutchinson, Phillips, and Townsend were titled by their military rank. Perhaps it was a signal that this was a time of war, which required radical emergency measures. It could also be a signal to soldiers that this proposed solution to their problem was managed mostly by some of their own officers and not only by detached civilians.

Checks and Balances

Why were there five members? Regardless of the workload of signing thousands of bills, almost nothing of importance was done in the colony by a single man. Committees were the norm. In particular, committees issuing financial instruments had at least three members that signed each paper. This helped prevent corruption among the issuers and counterfeiting by anyone else. Cotton Mather confirmed it when writing that "besides" designing bills in such a way "as to make it impossible to counterfeit[,] . . . they were all signed by the hands of three, belonging to that committee."[35]

Why five members rather than three? One trivial answer is the workload, as in the debentures committee (but unlike the tickets committee). But there was probably another reason, which was not present in the debentures and tickets committees: with five members, there could be political checks and balances. The debentures and tickets committees were *administrative* committees. They required very little discretion. They required reliability, credibility, and financial knowledge, but nothing else. None of their members was a court member. The paper money committee, in contrast, required considerable discretion regarding the denominations, timing, and quantity of bills. It was an *executive* committee that had to make political decisions.

Indeed, the affiliation of the committee members is the most interesting part. They were two assistants, a deputy, and two private men (one a former councillor and deputy). As any three members of the committee could act on its behalf, no group had a majority. Not a single bill could be issued unless some coalition, let alone a consensus, could be reached.

One such minimal coalition could be the three court members; after all, they had been elected to handle such situations. This was also a coalition of senior military officers. Another minimal coalition could be one from each group. Yet another minimal coalition could be all the nonassistants. They could block any attempt by the executive branch to inflate the debt away (that is, print it all as paper money and let the ensuing inflation erode the debt). Every bill given for military service had at least one signature of a senior military officer. The committee was a masterpiece of checks and balances, building on a long tradition of mixed committees.

Legal Tender for Debts After All?

While the legal tender law has captured all the attention of economic historians, there is another relevant law from that session. Already, on December 12, the deputies had passed this:

> Ordered that all country pay with one third abated shall pass as current money to pay all country debts, at the same prices set by this Court, except what has been borrowed in money, which shall be paid in money.[36]

The magistrates approved this law only on December 24, the same day they finalized the legal tender law.

This law was about paying the colony's debts in country pay, excluding only debts borrowed in coin—given by merchants and other gentlemen as the court had solicited. The abatement of a third was in line with a long history. When a loss had to be borne by one or two sides, a compromise of thirds was often the solution. The soldiers were expected to take a loss of one-third of their pay.

However, this penalty applied only if the soldiers wanted to be paid in country pay. There was no abatement for those agreeing to swap their debentures for bills, because accepting bills was no redemption. Consider a soldier who is owed sixty shillings, when barley is priced according to the tax law at four shillings per bushel, and assume this is also its market price. Normally the soldier would be paid fifteen bushels. With this new law, he would be paid only ten bushels. Together with the legal tender law, the choice he faced was between sixty shillings in bills for certain or ten bushels that might be in the treasury in the future.

With sixty shillings in bills, he could hope to get fifteen bushels of barley in shops. Better to get fifteen bushels than ten. This was discrimination against soldiers demanding country pay from the treasury.

To understand what this really meant, take this idea to the limit. What if the options were fifteen bushels in the market (in exchange for bills) versus *zero* bushels at the treasury? Then the bills would be, practically, legal tender for the colony's debts: any soldier refusing them would lose his claim entirely. Because the pay in the treasury was reduced from fifteen bushels to ten rather than to zero, we could say that the bills were one-third of the way to becoming legal tender for debts. With some linguistic freedom, they were not *fully* legal tender for the colony's debts, but only one-third legal tender for the colony's debts.

This "country pay" law was part and parcel of the whole legal tender package. It indirectly boosted the legal status of bills. Although the bills were only one-third legal tender, and only for the colony's debts, the £40,000 colony debt was a large one in the Massachusetts economy. The bills were legal tender for a significant part of outstanding debts. The one-third abatement mirrored the customary one-third abatement for tax payments in coin. Instead of benefiting those paying coin to the government, the court benefited those receiving bills from the government. Both cases were discriminations against the use of grain.

The "country pay" law, which should have induced soldiers to accept bills, has gone unnoticed by historians.[37] It was separate from the legal tender law, and the two laws did not even mention each other. This separation perhaps resulted from the bicameral structure of the legislature: the magistrates initiated the legal tender law, while the deputies initiated the country pay law. But the separation might have been done on purpose. If England had noticed this country pay law and realized its meaning, the whole ploy might have been considered another violation of the prerogative.

*   *   *

What led Massachusetts to break with monetary tradition (including its own) and dare support a new paper money with such an extremely flimsy law at such a critical time? The unique political situation in 1690 is the answer. Massachusetts was ruled by a provisional government while its agents in London were lobbying for restoration of the colony's charter. The illiquid colony had to issue money to soldiers to avoid a mutiny, but some of its traditional methods of supporting currencies—legal tender for debts and land backing—could have upset the king, who was then considering charter restoration. Under those regulatory circumstances, the colony had no legal right to use these methods. The solution was to disguise the new money as private-like promissory notes that were not backed by land. The new money was seemingly not forced on anyone other than the government itself and happened to be convenient for use as money. Stuck between a rock and a hard place, Massachusetts invented a new currency, which was de facto inconvertible legal tender. Easy money.

The invention did not come out of the blue. Paying soldiers in paper was known from China to Canada. The exact legal way to pull it off in 1690 was a recombination of legal features, long known in England: bill, debenture, assignation, setoff, trilateral debt settlement, and legal tender for debts and taxes. This is similar to the history of technology, where many inventions involved a recombination of components from existing machines.[38] In 1690 Massachusetts, constraints from England resulted in a specific recombination of these methods rather than others. Decades of monetary experiments gave the court the confidence that this unprecedented recombination would work. The fact that it was merely a recombination does not diminish the intellectual achievement. Curtis Nettels overstated how the invention "grew naturally out of the use of private credit" and "came as the culmination of financial practices long in vogue." He failed to explain why something so "natural" was not invented before 1690 or elsewhere.[39]

Most important, this recombination was not one more variation on the legal status of money. Most pre-1690 currencies had intrinsic value, and the rest had been supported by committing public or private parties to convert them into intrinsically valuable objects. The 1690 money was a conceptual shift in the foundation of the monetary system from tangible assets (coin, goods, land) to monetary obligations involving the state (taxes and the government's debts). It was a monetary revolution. That this happened during war is no coincidence but reflects one of the most important developments of the early modern period—the rise of the fiscal-military state. It was a landmark in monetary and fiscal history, and its consequences will stay with us long after government-issued, legal tender paper currency is replaced by government-issued, legal tender digital currency.

CHAPTER FOURTEEN

Aftermath, 1691–1692

A new mint raised here of paper money.
  —One of "several gentlemen & merchants from Boston" writing to London, 1691

W e now know how, and why, American Puritans invented the money of 1690. But it wasn't exactly like our money; it would become nearly identical to our money only in 1692. Therefore, we must continue the story a bit more. This brief period offers more evidence on the importance of imperial politics to the design of the new money, and unique explicit evidence on the monetary thought behind the experiment.

Market Crash

Five days after the court adjourned, Samuel Sewall wrote to Increase Mather in England and carefully stuck to official terminology: "Here is a project on foot of passing bills."[1] James Lloyd, an opposition Boston merchant, wrote to England on January 8, 1691. Mocking the stupidity of appointing Phips to lead the expedition just for his knighthood (granted for a diving operation), Lloyd wrote of a "pumpkin fleet . . . commanded by a person [who] never did exploit above water." He added:

> The present way of raising money (the subscribers [i.e., potential lenders] being out of cash) is by a bank: Papers from the Treasurer to pass as money, which may be undervalued—debentures being already sold at half price.[2]

His skepticism on the value of the bills is derived from the contemporary price of debentures in the market for government debt. The 50 percent discount is consistent with Benjamin Bullivant's testimony and even the Civil Wars. Lloyd's testimony is consistent with the interpretation that the injection of bills into the economy occurred through open market purchases of government debt.

The first bills were soon issued. On January 20, Sewall sold wood for a war widow's "bill of ten shillings, no. 21." Leading by example, this assistant added "money-bills" with "cash" (coin) in his accounting—at face value. He kept the incriminating monetary terminology ("money-bills") to his private business papers.[3] The only surviving bill of the original issue is shown in figure 14.1.

Soldiers turned in their debentures voluntarily and accepted the bills, but they had difficulties buying goods with bills. The opposition happily reported this to London; one member stated that a man "may buy £20 [in bills] for £13 in money." The trade of debentures for coin was thus expanded to a trade of bills for coin. One of "several gentlemen & merchants from Boston" wrote of the new money: "There are not many that take it, and they that have it scarce know now what to do with it." Another argued: bills "will not pass in trade between man and man, nor can these poor soldiers and seamen get any thing for them to above half their value, they being only used to pay rates [i.e., taxes] with."[4] Friends of the government agreed, scorning their fellow colonists. One complained: people "cheat the needy persons to whom the bills were first given, of half the worth of them," elsewhere describing the market discount as 30 percent or 25 percent. Another wrote: "It is strange that . . . bills should not pass between man and man." He mentioned "refusers to receive" bills, and soldiers "selling them at under-rates."[5]

Contemporary Monetary Theory

It often happens in history and archeology that disasters lead to documentation and evidence that would not otherwise be available (e.g., Pompeii). Happily for historians, the bills' troubles indirectly revealed some of the theory behind the bills. The crisis prompted the second original publication in New England on monetary issues (after the Fund's 1682 pamphlet). It is a pamphlet that includes two open letters written

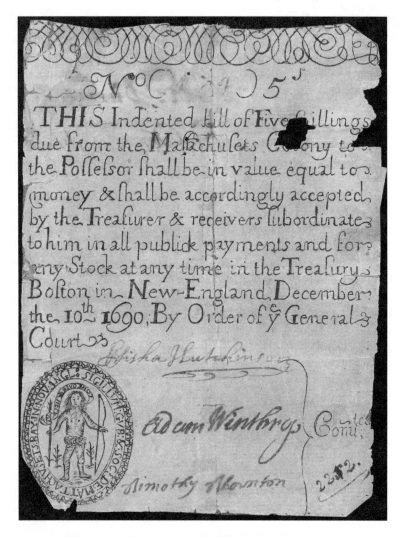

FIGURE 14.1 The only surviving legal tender bill of 1690. Source: Currency Collection, 1690–1910 (MSS 831), Phillips Library at the Peabody Essex Museum, Salem, Massachusetts.

anonymously—as usual in political works of the time. Scholars have used typography, biographical hints in the text, and similarity in content to texts of known authorship, to identify the authors as court friends Cotton Mather and John Blackwell.[6]

Both men were almost certainly heard during the deliberations of

December 1690. Blackwell's presence in Boston was recorded in March and July 1690, and in April 1691 he was referred to in England as "lately come from New England."[7] It would have been irresponsible not to consult a former phenomenal trader of wartime financial instruments, treasurer of war, member of Parliament, receiver general of taxes, merchant, bank entrepreneur, and governor. The court had reasons to hear Pastor Mather as well. First, a minister's role in political life was to advise on constitutional issues, and the new money had profound constitutional implications. Second, paying debts was a moral issue and thus within the interest of ministers. Third, there was a tradition of ministers advising on the economy, starting with Mather's grandfather John Cotton. Fourth, Mather expressed interest in public credit, as seen in that year's Election Day sermon, as well as in abstract monetary theory (see below). Just as European kings employed gifted experts such as engineers in their wars and hired brilliant scientists as general advisers,[8] so was it natural for the court to hear the prodigy Mather on monetary issues. He enjoyed easy access to the court: the treasurer Phillips was Mather's father-in-law, and Mather was invited for that session's fast day. Mather was also an extremely prolific writer, notorious for expressing his opinion even when not asked.

Since we have no protocol of the December session, the Mather–Blackwell pamphlet serves as a unique window into the opinions expressed in court. Of course, not everything said within closed doors was fit to be published, and not every popular argument was fit to be seriously considered by the legislature.

Cotton Mather

The first letter was titled

> *Some Considerations on the Bills of Credit now passing in New England, Addressed unto the Worshipful John Philips, Esq.; Published for the Information of the inhabitants.*

Writing to his father-in-law, Mather reminded him that "you and I have had some former discourse about the nature of money," in which they expressed the Platonic view that money was a mere "counter." Sufficient knowledge of "writing and arithmetic" made metal redundant, argued Mather.[9] He therefore condemned the great indiscretion of our countrymen who refuse to accept that, which they call paper-money, as pay of equal value with the best Spanish silver.

Mather continued:

> What? Is the word "paper" a scandal to them? Is a bond or bill of exchange for £1000 other than paper? And yet is it not as valuable as so much silver or gold, supposing the security of payment be sufficient? Now [in] what is the security of your paper-money less than the credit of the whole country? If the country's debts must be paid (as I believe they must, and I am sure in justice they ought), whatever change of government shall come, then the country must make good the credit, or more taxes must be still raised, till the public debts be answered.[10]

The only problem, claimed Mather, was constitutional uncertainty—people fearing "that we have no magistrates, no government, and by consequence that we have no security for any thing which we call our own." Otherwise, "there would not be the least scruple in accepting your bills as current pay."[11] Mather knew that a new regime might repudiate the bills or abolish the taxes, especially if James were to win.

The treasury was a mere intermediary, but its monetary dealings with both soldiers and taxpayers should have inspired use of bills among individuals:

> It is strange that in the meanwhile between the government's paying the people, and the people's paying the government, the government's (or rather the country's) bills should not pass between man and man.[12]

He could have cited Hobbes's *Leviathan* on the treasury as the heart of the monetary system, and he did cite *Leviathan* there in another context.[13] Mather understood a key part of the economic mechanism when he asked: "Is not discount in accounts current good pay?"[14] Translation: running accounts can be settled by setoff.

Mather compared the colony's bills to an individual's bills. After mentioning the private bills in Acadia and "the western parts" (p. 129), he admonished his people who

> deny credit to the government, when it is of their own choosing. Had the . . . gentlemen (above named) a good bottom for their credit in their warehouses,

and are not the whole estates of the Massachusetts as good? Is the security
of one plantation-magistrate better than that of all the Massachusetts Representatives? Can that one magistrate give force to the contracts, and cannot all
our government do the same?[15]

Using a Latin phrase meaning "it is right to be taught even by an enemy," Mather concluded:

> The French (I hear) at Canada pass such paper money without the least
> scruple; whereby the government is greatly fortified, since they can at all
> times make what they need. Now if we account ourselves to transcend the
> French in courage it is a shame for us to come so far short of them in wit and
> understanding.[16]

Mather had legislative recommendations. First, to increase taxes for
those "debasing the credit of your bills either by purchasing them with
little money or selling commodities for them at excessive dearer rates."
This was in essence a fine. Second, those refusing to receive bills should
have "their taxes demanded in silver," as opposed to country pay, which
was still a legal option. Third, to make the bills legal tender for all private debts until the public debt was discharged:

> Declare by a law, that if any man tender these bills for payment of his debts . . .
> if any private person will not receive them so, that then the government will
> not concern themselves for the recovery of those debts.[17]

John Blackwell

The second letter was titled by the publisher

> Some Additional Considerations Addressed unto the Worshipful Elisha
> Hutchinson, Esq. By a Gentleman that had not seen the foregoing Letter.

At the end of the letter, this anonymous author testified: "Many proposals have been made unto the government, for establishing the
credit of our bills." Addressing the head of the monetary committee,
he cited "your desire of seeing some thoughts upon the subject."[18] Elisha Hutchinson, the dominant fiscal-military man of the 1690 court,
had nobody to turn to for public advice—except for the elderly finan-

cial sage from England who had employed him in a projected bank, John Blackwell.

Blackwell wrote about "the BILLS of CREDIT now passing (or that should be so) among us" (original emphasis).[19] This was the first documented use of the phrase *bills of credit* for the government bills, named after the bills in Blackwell's 1680s London and Boston banking ventures. He pounded on the credit aspect again and again. He agreed with Mather that the concept of setoff was relevant: "No man that deals but for ten pounds, will refuse to grant, that discount in accounts current is good payment." But he superseded Mather in getting the crux of the economic mechanism: "All these bills enable people to discount with the Treasurer at last." His conclusion from this, surprisingly, did not revolve around seller-taxpayer incentives to accept the bills but around Puritan morality: "Therefore it is but fair and just [the bills] should have a general circulation."[20]

Similar to Mather, Blackwell suggested that dishonest traders have their taxes increased to compensate the soldiers[21]—strange words from the ace of such trading in England decades earlier. Perhaps he recognized that activities such as his helped ruining the military effort to halt the Restoration a decade later—efforts led by his father-in-law, General John Lambert. Having witnessed the Protectorate collapse, he now warned, far more than Cotton Mather, that not paying taxes and rejecting bills, would be "moral madness" that would destroy the regime, society, and all property in face of a French invasion.[22] Chatham could repeat even in New England.

Blackwell gave the nearest example available for "such" bills: "When Canada shall be better known to us, we shall find, it is a common thing for the government at Quebec to pay their men in such ways."[23] He proceeded to the mercantile world in general:

> Yea, there are no men of business through the world, who do not use as well as know the way of dealing by bills of credit. How many credible merchants are there, whose bills do pass as ready money, with hundreds of people with whom they have had no immediate concernment? And shall not the government of this colony, have much credit with a people that choose all, and make part of it?[24]

As the leading financial expert in English America, he could tell stories about his recent specialty—banking:

The more sensible part of mankind have thought banks of credit on many accounts preferable to silver in their pockets; it is so in Venice, Paris, Leghorn [Livorno] & Amsterdam, and other such trading places. We shall find men who have had store of money, have carried it into banks, from whence they have taken only bills of credit, with which they have managed all their businesses, bills being less troublesome & cumbersome, than silver would be, and more safe.[25]

He claimed that in Venice bills were worth more than coins, and hoped for the same in Massachusetts: "If we as well understood our interest, these bills would in a little time be so valuable, that men would cheerfully give silver, to purchase them at their full credit." Such men would "thereby save a shilling in a pound,"[26] meaning that market forces would make bills worth 5 percent more than coins.

Blackwell acknowledged that the new bills, unlike Europe's, were based on taxes rather than coins:

It is true ours are founded on the acknowledgement which the country has made of their being so much in debt, and their resolution of raising what is owing. Now suppose, that fund, be never so tottering, it is a sufficient bottom for those few bills which there have yet been order for.[27]

Land-banker Blackwell understood that bills could be backed by anything of value—coin, land, or taxes. He therefore condemned "the foolish flout" of calling the bills "paper-money."[28] To absorb all these tax-based bills within a year, he argued, taxes should be "vigorously raised."[29]

Blackwell testified that merchants had lent thousands of pounds to the colony, much of it in coin, without interest, and were repaid entirely in bills. As a bank entrepreneur in 1683 London, he probably knew that in 1682 the City of London agreed to establish a Lombard based on a list of tradesmen who committed to accepting the Lombard's bills of credit in trade. Blackwell thus had another suggestion, expecting Boston's merchants to step up again and collectively save the day:

If but a competent number of men, who deal much, would now give yourselves the trouble of meeting, to debate, agree, conclude, and engage upon giving a just reputation to our bills, the whole country must and will join with them in it. And if they will further give themselves the trouble of publish-

ing to the country, what may rectify some common mistakes, and how willing they themselves are to pay and also to take bills at a due price, doubtless it
would much promove the cure of this distemper among us.[30]

Evaluating the Letters

Mather and Blackwell were important government supporters, addressing the assistants on the monetary committee. Both authors hung on
past and present practices, indulged in name-dropping of this or that episode of credit and/or paper money, arguing that it was all the same: forget about the details, it's credit on paper, and that has worked so far.
Most of their examples are misleading, because they skipped the differences and the features that made the 1690 bills unique in monetary history. For example, the Canadian money, which both cited, was backed by
criminal penalties to its refusers and by a credible promise of convertibility. However, the examples they gave were indeed components in the
state of monetary thought that led to the 1690 breakthrough. The commercial hub of English America had enough merchants in power who
knew and understood all current practices and implemented what they
could in 1690.

The authors also appealed to logic and explained the workings of the
tax-foundation mechanism: accept it for your own good, dear seller, because then you pay your taxes by setoff. Like good lawyers, they tried to
play both cards: First, they tried to convince the people that there was
nothing new and remarkable about the new money. To paraphrase the title of a 2009 influential book, this time was *not* different. They tried to
harness the momentum of history to their cause. But if people did not
buy that, then the authors were set on an alternative course: teaching the
public why the government thought it should work nevertheless.[31]

In policy, it is the differences between Mather and Blackwell that are
most marked: Mather, for whom (divine) ordinances were supreme, recommended solving the problem by law; Blackwell, the former financial
trader and merchant, preferred a market-oriented solution.

With both of them mentioning Canada's card money, we conclude
the issue of whether the court knew about this financial tool in December 1690. If Mather or Blackwell had the information by December, they
surely shared it with the court. But when did they write their letters?
Their pamphlet was dated 1691, but no month was specified. On April
21, Blackwell was referred to in England as being "lately come from New

England."[32] With a minimal sailing time of three weeks,[33] he left before April. From December to March, there was no further contact between the French colonies and the English, courtesy of a horrible winter. While there is no positive proof that the court or anyone in the colony knew in December about Canada's card money, it seems that this was the case — beyond a reasonable doubt.

Upgrade and Normalization

The awkward bills, designed for a single, exceptional purpose, gradually became normal paper money during 1691, converging through various upgrades toward the modern currency we know. It started when Bradstreet summoned the court, ahead of schedule, to February 3, 1691. One major reason was that the amount of £7,000 in bills was "far short of what is absolutely necessary." It was also an opportunity to improve the bills, subject to known constraints. The legal tender law was amended.[34] First, the official name changed to Blackwell's "bills of credit." Second, the committee was ordered to "proceed" issuing bills without limit. Third, bills were to be given not only for debentures but also to specific debtors as directed by court or council.[35] Fourth, the range of denominations expanded in both directions, from two shillings to £10, giving the committee more flexibility. This brought the lower-denomination bills much closer to the coins formerly minted in Boston, and the committee indeed started issuing bills of less than five shillings.[36] (The higher authorized denominations were probably meant for the merchants who lent the expedition.) Fifth, the bills were made better than coin for tax purposes:

> every of which bills of the sum of twenty shillings shall be accepted in all public payments by the Treasurer, and all constables, or other receivers subordinate to the Treasurer, in lieu of money at twenty one shillings, and so proportionally for all bills of greater or lesser sums.

A taxpayer who owed 105 shillings could discharge them in 105 shillings in coin, or 105 shillings' worth of goods, or 100 shillings in bills. The idea apparently originated with Blackwell. His bank prospectus encouraged the use of bills in a similar way: those redeeming their mortgage in coin rather than bills had to pay 2 percent more.[37] This feature was combined with the hope in Blackwell's letter that the bills would be worth 5 percent more than coin on the market. Bills issued from then on bore the date "February the third 1690" because back then the new year began on March 25.

Another Blackwell advice was followed as the court enacted new taxes of £32,000 over four years to strengthen the bills' only solid support.[38] Legislating sums of money to be collected in taxes had *not* been the norm since the 1640s, but there was a problem in legislating taxes by the number of "rates" as usual. Such taxation was not transparent. When the court voted twenty rates in November 1690, how much was that in pounds? Nobody outside the court knew. It was common knowledge, however, that the size of the debt was tens of thousands of pounds; the new taxes were therefore written in pounds rather than rates. In May, the court declared: £40,000 is "what the country is indebted and will probably be called in again by the rates already granted."[39] So, the £32,000 enacted in February were meant to complete a £40,000 tax package—just enough to pay the debts. There would be enough taxes to get all the bills into the treasury. The bills would be 100 percent backed by taxes. The new taxes were to be paid "either in bills of credit," or the customary objects.

In May, commodity money suffered another blow:

> Ordered, that the money prices of grain and provisions for the payment of the rates now appointed to be gathered, shall be one third abated of the prices ordered for the last rates.[40]

A taxpayer owing sixty shillings could previously pay it with twenty bushels of maize. Now maize's price in taxes was cut from three to two shillings, meaning that thirty bushels were needed to pay the tax. This 50 percent increase in tax burden on those paying in commodity money was actually a fine on those refusing to accept bills. It was the last explicit reference to country pay in the context of taxes—after six decades. Farewell, Middle Ages.

The court capped the total printing at £40,000 because this was the size of both the debt and the taxes. Another committee was appointed to then take the plates for printing and dispose of all the bills that reached the treasury, "as there may be no danger of their coming forth again into any private hands."[41] That committee burned more than £10,000 in bills collected in taxes, and did not mention any bills obtained from conversion of bills into coin or goods.[42] But the resolve to destroy all bills was soon cracked. First, the government used bills as collateral for a loan of coins it took.[43] Then the court ordered the treasurer, rather than the monetary committee, to give bills to some creditors, using the explicit word *pay* rather than the original word *adjust*.[44]

The bills simply proved to be too useful to be discarded. Unlike the old local coins—which surely deteriorated over time and could not be re-minted, and thus each one of them had a different intrinsic value—wear and tear did not affect the bills' uniform value. Their zero intrinsic value made them immune to export—a problem that had troubled the colony for six decades, with English coins first and local coins later. The bills thus became normal money, circulating into the treasury and out of it in "pay," while both coin and country pay were discriminated against in public payments.

It's All Politics: A Savage Manipulation by Randolph

The political game played by the court was not over in December 1690. The court's enemies justified its fears of getting caught issuing money. Letters cited above regarding the money's performance were written to people in England. One stated: "Now to cheat the men we have paper money."[45] The phrase *paper money* was mockery in Boston, irritating Mather and Blackwell, but in London it was an accusation. "Money," normally meaning coin, was something the court was not allowed to produce. One of several "gentlemen & merchants from Boston" was more explicit:

> We have found a way to stop the mouths & assuage the passion of the soldiers & seamen by a new mint raised here of paper money, the other good kinds being almost quite exhausted, our Treasury being quite empty.[46]

Another letter referred to the bills as "ps of paper,"[47] short for "pieces of paper." It was an allusion to "pieces of eight" coins, often written as "ps of eight."[48] The same author later wrote about "bills of credit, vulgarly called paper money, for we love to be fingering the royal prerogative."[49]

The only real-time London publication that referred to the bills was printed in April 1691. Its title is:

> *An account of the late action of the New-Englanders, Under the command of Sir William Phips, Against the French at Canada. Sent in a Letter from Major*

Thomas Savage of Boston in New-England, (who was present at the Action)
to his brother Mr. Perez Savage in London. Together with the Articles of War
composed and agreed upon for that purpose.

On page 12, the pamphlet refers to the performance of the "bills":

> But they will not pass in trade between man and man, nor can these poor sol-
> diers and seamen get any thing for them to above half their value, they being
> only used to pay rates with.

The description combines the worst of all previous accounts: 50 percent
discount or rejection. This is surprising because Major Thomas Savage
(Jr.) was a man of unquestionable loyalty to the court. He was Elisha
Hutchinson's cousin, head of the tickets committee, and the first officer
to storm the beach near Quebec.[50] Why would he write that and have it
published in London?

He wouldn't. It was a fraud. It was perpetrated by Edward Randolph
to discredit the bills of credit. Randolph had a new job, working on the
London docks in search of smuggled merchandise,[51] when Savage's February letter arrived.[52] It was sent to brother Perez, who had tried to re-
locate to London but was captured by Arab pirates and died in Africa.
Randolph took the letter and published it without permission.

Why would Randolph publish a letter of someone loyal to the court?
He used Savage's letter as a host to the content of opposition letters. It
was standard practice to lump into pamphlets and books material by different authors, as in the Mather–Blackwell pamphlet.[53] Not all parts were
always listed in the title page. The title page of this pamphlet indeed de-
clares that after Savage's account, one could find the articles of war. But
there was another item not listed: a summary of opposition letters.

An outright forgery would have been too risky. Justly considered by
the colonists to be a grand liar, forger, and manipulator,[54] Randolph
committed a "small print" fraud. The last item in the pamphlet starts
on page 11: "By other letters from New England are these further par-
ticulars." Page 12 reports the bills' performance. Page 13 has a facsimile
of a bill, which seems authentic: ten shillings, no. 2161, dated December
10, signed by Penn Townsend, Adam Winthrop, and Timothy Thornton.

Strictly speaking, there is no forgery. Page 11 admits that the following is taken from "other letters." A careful reader would know that everything on pages 11–12 is not by Savage. However, Randolph's longtime

boss in the English government, William Blathwayt, could stand in front of the Privy Council with the pamphlet and declare with a straight face: "I hold here a letter from Major Thomas Savage. It says that the bills are either rejected or received at a 50% discount."

This is not a conspiracy theory. Massachusetts's agents and/or friends caught Randolph in the act, wrote to Bradstreet about it, and accused Randolph of being "of late grown very eminent for his new inventions in the arts of forging letters and false news."[55] Only future generations were misled. Historians have attributed that specific incriminating line about the bills to Thomas Savage personally, or, without qualifications, to "Savage (1691)," as this publication has been cataloged by librarians.[56]

Meanwhile, memoranda on the charter revocation were prepared at the royal court. As usual, some of them recalled the mint offense, often at the top of the list.[57] In spite of this, Randolph's efforts—and more defaming letters coming from the opposition in Boston[58]—there is no evidence that anyone in government compared the new money to the old illegal coins or cared about the Massachusetts bills. The court's trick worked; it got away with issuing money. Easy money.

It's All Politics: The Land Uncertainty

I argued above that land was still a major problem in December 1690, citing the agents' request in November for a blanket confirmation of all land titles in a draft of a new charter. They did it again in January 1691. This request entered one draft but was erased by royal officials from later drafts, before Increase Mather had it restored at the last moment.[59] On October 14, 1691, the court wrote the king for the first time since issuing the bills, asking "that they may be continued, and fully confirmed in the enjoyment of their charter rights, and their religious, and civil liberties, and their properties."[60] The last word shows the lingering uncertainty about land titles.

In fact, a new charter for the Province of the Massachusetts Bay was just being finalized. Mather informed the colony about it, opening thus:

> The charter for the Massachusetts colony passed the great seal on the 16 instant [i.e., October 16]. The king reserves power to himself to appoint the Governor, Deputy Governor, and Secretary. But all men's properties are confirmed as before the judgment against the old charter.[61]

Only then did he mention other huge achievements: (1) an elected assembly and limits on the appointed governor's powers, and (2) the annexation of Plymouth, Maine, and Acadia. The latter was not just a bonus; according to the historian Mark Peterson, it amounted to ratification of decades of contested economic and territorial expansion.[62] The fact that Mather started the good news with "properties" (which for Mather meant land[63]) shows how critical the issue was to the colonists, and attests its uncertainty until October 1691. In February 1692, the court received a copy of the charter. As many colonists were unhappy with it, Cotton Mather wrote *Political Fables* to market his father's achievements, and there he emphasized that all landowners owed gratitude to his father for the confirmation of their titles.[64]

Legal Tender for Debts

In May 1692, the new governor, Sir William Phips, arrived with the new charter. The charter provided political insurance by a new mechanism: all new acts had to be sent to England for approval.[65] The new charter would not be revoked like its predecessor just because the king disapproved of certain acts. With the risk of revocation removed, the colonists immediately restored their monetary tradition. In July, in the very first legislative session under the new charter, the bills were upgraded:

> All bills of public credit . . . shall pass current within this Province in all payments equivalent to money, for the sum in each bill respectively mentioned (excepting all specialties and contracts made before publication hereof), and in all public payments at five per cent advance.[66]

The legal status of bills was expressed in the same terms as in pre-1690 monetary laws: *pass, current, all payments*. There was no penalty for refusal in spot transactions. The law therefore applied only to obligations such as debts and taxes. The legal historian Arthur Nussbaum has referred to this measure as "the legal tender feature."[67] The first-ever use of *legal tender* in the English language is, to the best of my knowledge, in discussions on a 1712 Massachusetts paper money law, and it, too, implies the equivalence of "current" and "legal tender."[68]

To conclude, in 1692, Massachusetts formally made the bills of credit legal tender for both debts and taxes. They became nearly identical to the currency of the early twenty-first century. The remaining difference was the 5 percent premium in tax payments.

Regarding England, in the worst case, this act would have been vetoed by the king, without endangering the charter. Since the colony had formally made all earlier currencies full legal tender and made this change only after the new charter was secured, it indicates that political considerations were the only impediment to a formal full legal tender status in 1690.

Retrospective: Cotton Mather in 1697

Phips died in 1695, and in 1697 Cotton Mather published his biography. It included an account of the paper money affair, merging the laws and events from November 1690 to May 1691. He argued that the tax-foundation mechanism had been perfectly understood then:

> The people knowing that the tax act would, in the space of two years at least, fetch into the Treasury as much as all the bills of credit thence emitted would amount unto, were willing to be furnished with bills, wherein it was their advantage to pay their taxes rather than in any other specie [i.e., type of money], and so the sailors and soldiers put off their bills, instead of money, to those with whom they had any dealings, and they circulated through all the hands in the colony pretty comfortably.[69]

But it was not that smooth, and even in 1697 Mather insisted that the only short-term problem was the constitutional uncertainty coming from England (resolved by 1692):

> Had the government been so settled, that there had not been any doubt of any obstruction or diversion to be given to the prosecution of the tax act, by a total change of their affairs, then depending at Whitehall [i.e., the royal palace], it is very certain that the bills of credit had been better than so much ready silver; yea, the invention had been of more use to the New Englanders than if all their copper mines had been opened, or the mountains of Peru had been removed into these parts of America. . . . But many people being afraid that the government would in half a year be so overturned as to convert their

bills of credit altogether into waste paper, the credit of them was thereby very much impaired; and they, who first receive them, could make them yield little more than fourteen or sixteen shillings in the pound.[70]

Mather the historian tells of organized private action in the markets:

That which helped these bills unto much of their credit was the generous offer of many worthy men in Boston to run the risk of selling their goods reasonably for them. And of these, I think, I may say, that General Phips was in some sort the leader; who at the very beginning, merely to recommend the credit of the bills unto other persons, cheerfully laid down a considerable quantity of ready money for an equivalent parcel of them. And thus in a little time, the country waded through the terrible debts which it was fallen into.[71]

The reference to a single "offer" (rather than "offers") made by "many worthy men" indicates that they were indeed organized as Blackwell suggested. As Mather did not mention Phips's action in his 1691 letter, and Blackwell, who supported such action did not mention it as an example, this organized action was probably inspired by Blackwell's letter. Phips was neither a merchant nor a shopkeeper, so he could intervene only with his coins in the market for government debt. As the richest colonist, he could make a difference; his perhaps guilt-ridden intervention as the expedition's leader could have had an amplified effect because of his unique social status and wealth.

However, this only mention of Phips in the context of bills is suspicious because it appears in a posthumous biography by his spiritual mentor and self-described "dear friend." The book's goal, declared in its main title *Pietas in Patriam*, was to tell about a great patriot. The book has long been notorious for being "unreliable" at times, with many inaccuracies and exaggerations about Phips's patriotism—some of them "questionable," "difficult to believe," "ludicrous," and "unlikely," according to Phips's latest biographers, Emerson Baker and John Reid.[72] They doubt this specific story because Phips was in serious legal trouble in late December. On the 22nd and 24th, the city of Boston issued warrants and summonses against Phips and had Phips's house seized for an old commercial debt under litigation. On the 29th, Sewall and Secretary Isaac Addington visited Phips at home, reporting that Phips had been "arrested by Meneval" (that is, arrested because of a lawsuit by Acadia's plundered governor). The visitors "had very sharp discourse" about it with Phips and Mather, and the following day the council nullified Meneval's "writ." By December 31, Phips was known to be leaving on the next ship to England as the court's agent. He was there by early March.[73] With legal trouble over debts and hardly any time in Boston after the bills were issued (if at all), Mather's claim is doubtful.

Mather's claim was uncharacteristically understated and cautious: "I think, I may say, that General Phips was in some sort the leader." But Mather was recently outdone by Mark Peterson, who claims that Phips's private treasure not only helped ex post but "helped give the General Court the confidence necessary to issue paper currency."[74] There is no evidence for that, and it is highly unlikely. Much had been written about the bills of credit within a year of their issue, including court documents, the Mather and Blackwell letters, and opposition letters. None of them mentioned Phips's coins, and certainly not ex ante reliance on them. If Phips had such a critical role at such a critical moment, it would have been mentioned in real time, and in later sermons on important occasions, such as his return to Massachusetts as the new governor[75] — especially since Peterson further speculates (without evidence) that this financial contribution caused his gubernatorial appointment.[76]

Peterson's speculation is based on Mather's biased, uncorroborated claim, magnified by a risky methodology of identifying ex ante motives of participants in historical events with ex post outcomes. Peterson argues elsewhere that material gains made by Massachusetts in previous wars (wampum, land, and fur) prove that Massachusetts went to war only to obtain those material gains.[77] But clearly, wars and unprecedented financial experiments usually have unforeseen consequences. Even if Phips did convert some bills into coin, it does not imply that the court foresaw it, let alone counted on it.

There are other problems with Peterson's claim. First, Assistant Phips did not bother to show up for the December session (at least its beginning), indicating his indifference. Second, the legal proceedings against Phips took place just when the bills were approved in court. The court could not count on this debtor to save the colony from its debts. Third, Phips received only £11,000 from the shipwreck he found. It wasn't enough even to provide financial security for the lifestyle expected of a knight, and he had already spent some of it on a beach mansion in Boston.[78] In any event, the amount was far short of the colony's £40,000 debt.

To conclude, the bills of credit were designed not as Phips-backed money but as money that relied on its acceptance as tax payment—a mechanism written on the notes but ignored by Peterson.

If we take Mather's qualified claim at face value and add it to real-time evidence, it turns out that several strategies were used ex post by several influential people. Some led by example: Phips, the richest man in the colony, supposedly converted some paper money into his own coin, merchants agreed with each other to accept paper money in regular trade, with the merchant and assistant Samuel Sewall being one of them or acting independently that way. An influential minister supplied his rhetorical skills, probably not only in writing but also from the pulpit. An experienced financier contributed his knowledge and experience. Modern scholarship on the methods of how to change people's views provides a remarkably similar list to those actions taken by the Massachusetts elite in its campaign to save its money.[79]

Mather summarized:

> This method of paying the public debts, did no less than save the public from a perfect ruin. . . . The bills, which had passed about until they were again returned unto the Treasury . . . had happily and honestly, without a farthing of silver coin, discharged the debts for which they were intended.[80]

In 1697, Mather did not mention three facts that seemed important only in real time. First, he did not mention the legal promise of the bills' convertibility to coin or goods at the treasury. It was indeed a dead letter that nobody in real time bothered mentioning. Second, he did not mention the 1692 upgrade to legal tender for debts. It was indeed not very important, after the status of legal tender for taxes already did the job. (It was mentioned above mostly because it brought the bills of credit closer to our modern currency.) Third, he did not mention Canada's card money. He no longer needed it. He and Blackwell used Canada's money disingenuously in 1691 to convince people to accept paper money (of whatever type), while in 1697 Mather correctly identified the legal tender bills as a local invention. Moreover, he now preached the Massachusetts tax-based paper money to all humanity:

> In this extremity they presently found out an expedient, which may serve as an example, for any people in other parts of the world, whose distresses

may call for a sudden supply of money to carry them through any important expedition.[81]

*   *   *

Just as Mather did not mind citing the paper money experience of Catholic Canadians in 1691, he would not mind citing the inoculation experience of Muslim Turks in 1721. He would then lead the practice of inoculation in Boston, even though it was counterintuitive and came from infidels. He cared only that it worked; and this pragmatism was a defining feature of English colonists, according to the historian Daniel Boorstin, who cited this example.[82] As another example, Boorstin gives the 1701 advice of Sewall and Addington regarding the name of Connecticut's college. They explained their choice of "Collegiate School": "We on purpose, gave the academy as low a name as we could, that it might the better stand in wind and weather."[83] The "wind and weather" were political storms coming from capricious England. Replace *academy* with *paper money*, and this is a perfect description of the 1690 legal tender law. That money was called "bills" just as the college was to be called a "collegiate school."

CHAPTER FIFTEEN

Back to England's Financial Revolution, 1692–1700

Issuing so many bills of credit, made current by Act of Parliament.
 —John Blackwell, 1695

In chapter 4, we left England in 1692 with a cliffhanger, at the beginning of its Financial Revolution. That decade saw a deluge of pamphlets, laws, and new financial institutions, with the same motivation as in Massachusetts: financing the Anglo–French world war. Land banks were authorized but never got off the ground. Taxation was difficult because coins were badly worn, so one of the solutions was recoinage. John Locke and Isaac Newton participated in the policy debates, and the recoinage was performed in 1696, with much hardship.[1]

Historians of England have never given up on the claim that England invented paper money in the seventeenth century. The candidates in chapter 4 were private notes of goldsmith-bankers and public exchequer orders. We have two similar candidates in the 1690s, suffering from the usual problem of too-high denominations. Both came after Massachusetts, and at least one of them may have been inspired by Massachusetts.

Bank of England Notes

The Bank of England, founded in 1694, was not the central bank it became much later. It began as a private company, whose powers were created by Parliament as part of a new tax law to raise money for the war.

Investors committed to putting £1,200,000 in precious-metal coins in the bank; the bank lent the government some coins, but mostly lent it "bills" and "notes" convertible to coins; the government used these funds to pay its creditors; finally, proceeds of the new tax were given to the bank to pay interest to investors.

The bank never raised the full amount of coin from its investors—and that was the whole point to begin with, argues the legal historian Christine Desan.[2] Its bills and notes, backed by only a fractional reserve of coins, handled transactions of the highest value, leaving it to coins to perform the everyday functions of money. Over the centuries, this system changed to one in which the state currency lying in vaults as banks' fractional reserve is paper money, which magically backs a larger amount of balances in checking accounts that exist only in the banks' computers.

Desan claimed that the bank's 1690s notes were the first "modern money," giving a critical role to the notes' acceptance for taxes in turning them into "money." Superficially, this book seems to argue against her claim of priority. The coincidence of the 1690s, English people, and the tax-foundation theory requires a detailed comment.

At the most basic level, there is no conflict, because the word *money* has several meanings. Dictionaries define it first and foremost as physical currency, and then also as wealth in general. Economists define it differently: physical currency is the narrowest measure of money, and this is the object that this book is concerned with; a broader definition of money, known as the "money supply," includes the amount of currency held by the public rather than by banks, but also a larger component—checking accounts at banks. Why? Because we can go shopping not only with currency but also by using balances in checking accounts via checks, debit cards, and smartphone applications. This wider measure of money is the one that Desan is concerned with—the private banks' magical multiplication of the state's currency. There is no contradiction between the claims that Massachusetts invented modern currency in 1690 and that England invented the modern "money supply" in 1694.

For policy makers and most economists, the measure of money supply is more interesting than currency because it has more statistically significant correlations with macroeconomic variables, such as interest rates, inflation, output, and unemployment. The legal status of currency is far less in the news, but not because it is unimportant; legally defined currency—the object to which most financial contracts refer—is the foundation of the entire financial system (including banks). The legal status is not relevant for regular policy decisions of central banks only because they take it for granted that their legal tender currency circulates and carries on its back the rest of the "money supply." Without this currency, central banks would have nothing to play with in their daily operations, nor could they choose whether or not to inflict high inflation on their economies.

The Bank of England's pioneering role has been long known (with the exception of the 1660s Sveriges Riksbank). Desan's novel claim is that the tax-foundation mechanism—not the fractional reserve of precious-metal coins at the bank—is the main reason that the bank's notes can be called "money." Here, too, definitions matter. This book follows economists' notion that the essence of money is its general use in everyday spot transactions. The legal historian Desan, however, defines money as the object that legally discharges obligations, most notably taxes.[3] Whereas this book examines how tax acceptance can *induce* voluntary acceptance in everyday spot transactions as well, for Desan the tax acceptance itself is enough by (her) definition, and use of the object in everyday spot transactions seems to be little more than a detail.

With this definition, Desan can afford not to be worried about the £50 minimal denomination of the bank's notes[4] (an amount earned by a laborer over four years), and to claim that tallies—almost all with high, nonround denominations—were "money" in the Middle Ages, without evidence of their voluntary use in everyday transactions.[5] Economists reading Desan's useful book should be aware of these different definitions.

Caution is also warranted regarding Desan's hypothesis that English rulers understood and successfully used the tax-foundation mechanism with "tokens"—perhaps made from wood or metal—already in the *seventh* century. This assertion progresses from a hypothetical "example" of what such rulers "might" have done, through something the rulers "may have experimented with" and "speculative" "antecedents," to an unqualified statement of fact—without evidence.[6]

Exchequer Bills

The 1690s saw dozens of proposals that the government itself issue paper instruments. Historians have seen these proposals as revival of the 1660s exchequer orders and other ideas from that time (pp. 44–45), encouraged by the constitutional revolution. Several proposals wanted such paper instruments to have legal tender status for taxes alone, or for taxes and debts.[7]

It is possible that some inspiration came from Massachusetts, through various channels. First, while John Winthrop's "city upon a hill" wanted to hide its monetary invention in a bunker for political reasons, we've seen that its nemesis Edward Randolph published it in London. Second, according to the new charter's rules, the 1692 legal tender law was sent to England for approval. By 1695, the Privy Council had definitely read it.[8] Third, one of the advocates of full legal tender status was seventy-one-year-old John Blackwell. His 1695 London pamphlet advised issuing indented "bills of credit, made current by Act of Parliament." These could be used to finance war expenses, pay past debts, and maintain the money supply during the recoinage. The bills could be redeemed in coin collected in future taxes, but, argued Blackwell, it would be better to leave them circulating for good.[9] With this proposal, after half a century, we finally bid farewell to John Blackwell.

In 1696, Parliament indeed authorized the exchequer to issue "indented bills of credit" to anyone lending coin to the government. The bills were limited in quantity to the expected proceeds of a tax enacted in the same act, so that the proceeds redeem the bills. After a rough start, Parliament renamed the bills "Exchequer bills" and strengthened their status: it made them "current and pass in all payments" to the exchequer and reduced the minimal denomination from £10 to £5. Within Desan's definition of money, the former feature was enough to make them "money."[10] Within economists' definition of money, there is a problem with the latter feature (worth five months' wages). (You may recall that in Massachusetts, the minimal denomination was £0.1, and the cost of living, best approximated by wheat prices, was not different on such a scale.[11])

Anyone in Massachusetts looking at the mess of England's recoinage, the complicated Bank of England scheme, and the hesitant exchequer bills might have laughed. Massachusetts cracked the code of money, fully monetized public credit, and relegated coins to the smallest transactions. America's quiet monetary revolution was complete when England's noisy Financial Revolution barely started, and America did not need to stumble on antiquated, precious-metal leftovers. Why couldn't Old England imitate New England? This, and much more, is analyzed in the next chapter.

CHAPTER SIXTEEN

Analysis

"We see a new and happy form of human society here. . . . What created it?"
"Necessity!" said Litwak the elder. . . .
"Knowledge!" said Dr. Marcus.
  —Theodor Herzl, *Old New Land*, 1902

It is time for a general look at the story. Why and how did Massachu-setts, rather than other societies, invent modern currency? Specifi-cally, this book's subtitle refers to American Puritans. What was the significance of colonial status and heritage to the invention of modern currency? How important is the fact that the colonists were Puritans? Another issue, demonstrated by the above epigraph, is that any inven-tion is bound to create a debate on the role of "necessity" (demand) ver-sus "knowledge" (supply) in creating the invention. The two sides were mentioned in chapter 2, and now it is time to see how they played out in the context of seventeenth-century money.

Evolution through Regulation

Massachusetts started in 1630 with a bang. A deluge of alternative mon-eys and alternatives to money appeared there within the first decade. Beaver fur, various grains, and wampum became money. In law or in practice, some use was also made of cattle, land, uncoined precious metal, and bullets. Among alternatives to money, credit was promi-nent, with a quick innovation on assigning private bills and limited usage of setoff and trilateral settlements. The turn to Atlantic trade brought bad Spanish coin and flourishing of private bills, and then a mint was opened. Just before it was closed, a short-lived note-issuing land bank was born, and another such bank was almost launched after it. In six decades, Massachusetts by and large reenacted global monetary history: nonmetallic jewelry, grain, livestock, uncoined precious metal, coined precious metal, and banknotes. Then, in 1690, a paper money was invented that was legally supported only by being legal tender for all payments to the colony. It was partially legal tender for debts from the beginning, and became full legal tender in 1692.

Why this madness of reenacting global monetary history, and then topping it off with an original invention? In a word: *regulation*. The word was created in the seventeenth century, when it became very useful. Regulation was the will of the English state—Crown or Parliament—restricting the activities of individuals and organizations. Regulation, mostly concerning matters in England, is the main explanation for the odd monetary history of Massachusetts. Most of the effects were indirect and unforeseen, and can be divided into demand effects and supply effects.

Demand

What brought the necessity felt by those who were Puritans in 1630 England, and their American descendants, to use new forms of money that their relatives in England did not need? Regulation of religion led them to America. From a purely economic perspective, it led unlikely emigrants (middle-class families) to settle in an unlikely land (lacking staple goods). Their high material demands resulted in a trade deficit, which was perhaps worse than in Virginia, where poor, young single men with few material demands raised a valuable staple good. Scarcity of coin was more painful in Massachusetts—with its wage earners, artisans creating a variety of goods, and families demanding a variety of goods—than in the servant-slave economy of Virginia.

Religious regulation of Scotland then led to a constitutional struggle in England starting in 1640. The conflict stopped immigration and the flow of coin, prompting a drastic change in the Massachusetts economy and its reliance on English coin. Throughout the first two decades, another regulation was important: minting was illegal. Massachusetts's unfulfilled desire to mint is revealed by making lead bullets legal tender instead of minting lead farthings, as business owners were doing in England; by making uncoined precious metal legal tender for taxes; and by going some way toward the coinage of grain, meat, fish, and wampum.

After minting finally came to Massachusetts, it was terminated, with much delay, by regulation of the restored monarchy. There were more English regulations that impeded the flow of coin into the colonies: the Navigation Acts (by Parliament) restricted trade with foreigners for Spanish coin, and European peace treaties prohibited English pirates from stealing coin from foreign ships. Two land banks tried to replace the mint. The Fund expired in 1685, probably because of the well-founded fear for the legal status of land titles as the colony lost its charter. This was fear of land regulation in the wake of regulation of the polity itself. Then Blackwell used the new regime to promote his own land bank; but the fears proved correct once the top of the regime changed. Land regulation by the king's viceroy killed Blackwell's land bank.

Soon came the Glorious Revolution—an outcome of Parliament's regulation of religion in England. It led to an English war with Canada, and the scale of expenses in that war conclusively showed the impotence of the tax system. It was time to invent something new. But it was no time to ignore previous regulations on issuing money and on land titles, so the new money was formally only legal tender for taxes. When circumstances changed, a full legal tender status was immediately implemented.

Supply

How did the colonists get all these ideas? The supply effect started during the same Puritan exodus that was caused by regulation of religion. That emigrating population was unusually educated, experienced, and wealthy, and it designed a workable, accountable government. The elite could come up with solutions and implement them better than other colonies such as Virginia.

More religious regulation led to the Civil Wars; one effect of these wars was releasing the colonies to mint as they pleased. Only when the axe hit Charles's neck could hammers in Boston hit silver lumps and turn them into coins. The wars also advanced English monetary theory and practice with private coinage, goldsmith banking, and land banking. The private coinage of so many businesses in England probably inspired Massachusetts. Goldsmith banking popularized the idea of using standardized paper instruments in trade and the idea of banking in general.

If Massachusetts's merchants were not aware of that, the colony's agents in London certainly were.

Land banking was implemented in Massachusetts not by colonists who read English books but by new waves of Puritan refugees: Thomas Thornton after Parliament's 1662 regulation of religion (Act of Uniformity), and John Blackwell in 1685 after renewed royal persecution. Parliament's religious regulation then led to the Glorious Revolution, which gave the colony new, limited freedom to issue money.

Conclusion

The big picture is that English regulation drove much of the story.[1] Whether it was regulation in England or regulation of the colonies, affecting money directly or indirectly, from the demand side or the supply side, there is an underlying theme here: Massachusetts was challenged again and again to find new solutions to the same money problem, and new ideas kept appearing. Both phenomena were most strongly related to regulation. Of that regulation, the most direct impact was of regulation of minting, as suggested by John Hanson and elaborated by Richard Sylla; the largest, if indirect, impact was of regulation of religion in England, which was the most consequential regulation in England itself.

Legal scholars and scholars of the early modern period know that reality could play out far differently from the letter of the law. Indeed, much of the regulation I have cited was not strictly enforced; many Puritans stayed in England as Puritans, pirates violated peace treaties, and merchants violated the Navigation Acts. But the main effects of regulation mentioned here still stand: the Massachusetts Puritans, from Winthrop to Blackwell, did arrive there because of regulation of religion. The hordes of violators of that regulation who stayed in England are irrelevant to this story. Similarly, the Civil Wars and the Glorious Revolution did happen because of regulation of religion. Overall, the excessive regulation of the early modern European state was a major force in history.

Most of the regulation-related shocks came from two arrogant, stubborn men: Charles I and James II, father and son, dumb and dumber. The other James and Charles bear much of the blame, setting up their successors for failure. The hyperregulating English state of the seventeenth century aimed to create order but created disorder, which both encouraged and enabled creativity. It led some Englishmen to invent a new money by using the most fundamental law of state power—the tax law, which feeds the state. The new legal tender currency reflected the growing importance of the state and helped shape it further. The state's fiscal power was now used to support its monetary power, and the new money facilitated tax collection.

Thus a process that started in regulation in England strengthened the state—but first in America. Educated by England on the power of government regulation, Massachusetts beat its master and created a money that was entirely supported by the government rather than by the market. In one of history's finest fits of poetic justice, the American and French Revolutions would later use government-issued paper money—inspired directly or indirectly by Massachusetts—against Britain itself. Regulation is a Pandora's box. Regulator, beware.

Understanding Monetary Creativity: Other Supply-Side Factors

Innovation requires abilities and attitudes not found in every person or society. Joel Mokyr's classic book *The Lever of Riches: Technological Creativity and Economic Progress* has a key chapter following the chronology, titled "Understanding Technological Progress"; it provides a long list of factors that may explain why some societies innovate technologically more than others.[2] This section aims to do the same, mostly by applying Mokyr's list to a century of American monetary innovation.[3]

The most effective comparison is between Massachusetts on the one hand and Virginia and England on the other hand. Virginia failed again and again while Massachusetts succeeded with the mint and the bills. As Sylla argued, Massachusetts needed convenient money more than Virginia did, due to its diversified economy and its many wage workers. But Virginia did complain a lot and tried solutions. It turns out that Virginia had supply problems—of human resources, material resources, and a paralyzing constitutional structure. England had the best human and material resources, but its interest groups were too powerful. Massachusetts had great advantages over others in its mentality. I divide the relevant factors according to three stages in the creation of a new type of money: coming up with an idea, deciding to use it, and implementing it.

Ideas

Ideas can come from knowledge gained through education (including religion), or experience gained in the workplace. They can also come from other people.

INTELLECTUAL ABILITIES. From the very beginning, Massachusetts had experienced, qualified gentlemen leaders who could think of novel monetary solutions as circumstances allowed. The college and the merchants maintained that ability in the second and third generations. The college also created and maintained a tiny intellectual and scientific community that read the classics and Hobbes and looked at the stars.

Virginia started with adventurous gentlemen and relatives of nobles, but it was no country for gentle men. Diseases, wars with Indians, and the rude quality of life sent almost all of them by 1630 to either the Old World or the next world. Bernard Bailyn has shown that the new elite was composed of hardened men of humble origins whose status emanated from physical survival and great success in the brutal tobacco economy of the 1620s.[4] The monetary chaos of 1630–1645 exactly overlapped the interregnum of Virginia's gentlemen that Bailyn diagnosed— between the founding generation and the losing royalists who fled England and established a new, lasting aristocracy.

RELIGION. The "biblically hyperliterate" Puritans, as Mark Peterson calls them,[5] could find in the New Testament a surprisingly complicated, thought-provoking view on the tax-foundation theory. When Simon and Jesus were demanded to pay the temple tax, they did not sell any good or service in order to obtain a coin. Jesus supposedly made the coin come out of the blue (sea)—in the mouth of a fish. But this was the exception that proved the rule. Jesus later overthrew the tables of the money changers in the temple. Money changers were needed because of unusual circumstances: Rome's coins were not legal tender for the temple tax, according to Jewish law; only foreign coins made in Tyre were. Roman coins were legal tender for imperial taxes, and soon Jesus advised taxpayers to obey imperial tax law and give to Caesar the coins that had been issued by Caesar.[6] This incident reminds of how Hobbes emphasized the importance of the circulation of state money back into the treasury.

Among Christian denominations, Puritanism differed from Catholicism and Anglicanism in emphasizing spirit over matter, essence over
form. In an Old Testament spirit that rejected idolatry and resonated in
Jesus's life and preaching, the Puritans made a point of *not* using their
wealth to decorate churches with golden statues. They were proud of
their humble wooden churches. This was in marked contrast with the
vast Catholic use of gold in churches and cathedrals. The Puritans'
chronic de-emphasis of matter may have allowed them to see through
the precious-metal appearance of conventional money and grasp its true
meaning. Money is not about the shiny material; it's about circulation in
a barely observable, never-ending sequence of down-to-earth payments,
including to and from the treasury.

Eventually, each denomination got money related to its preferred ecclesiastical material—precious metal or wood. The American Catholic
empires of Spain and Portugal found and minted huge amounts of silver
and gold (a Brazilian gold rush began in 1693), and England remained
wedded to precious metal; but the American Puritans minted money
from paper—which had been made from wood in China (and would be
later made of wood in the rest of the world, but at that point was made
of rags). The colonists, who in 1689 told Queen Mary that their fathers
came to New England only to "use their own plainness in religion,"[7] created their own plainness in money.

EXPOSURE. An alternative to having original ideas is to take ideas from
others. As the trade hub of English America, Boston was exposed to
most types of money in the Atlantic. As the supplier of French Acadia, it
was potentially exposed to Canadian money too. Proximity to and association with New York perhaps offered another route of exposure to Canadian money and even to New Holland money. Among Bostonians, obviously the merchants were the ones most directly exposed to such ideas.
Boston's prominence attracted bank entrepreneurs—the Thorntons and
Blackwell.

The Winthrop network—in England, Boston, Connecticut, and the
Caribbean—was a specific source of information. In Boston, the banker
and paper money legislator Wait Winthrop probably knew the bank project his father, John Jr., designed, and perhaps knew about his uncle Samuel's experience with the Antiguan banks. When young Adam Winthrop
moved to England in 1670, he delivered natural curiosities from Uncle
John Jr. to the Royal Society.[8] If he planned the mercantile career he

would eventually have there, he could start nowhere better than in meeting his most connected relative: his father's cousin, his own fellow college alumnus, and treasury commissioner, Sir George Downing.[9] Adam, the future Bostonian banker, treasurer, politician, and member of the paper money committee, may have learned about exchequer orders from their creator, even before their thunderous 1672 collapse.

Decision

New ideas are nice to have, but will a legislature actually pass the laws that embody them? That is an entirely different question. The legislature needs to be (1) open-minded enough to use an idea if it is foreign; (2) willing to change the status quo; (3) unafraid; (4) unimpeded by interest groups; and (5) optimistic that the idea would work.

OPEN-MINDEDNESS. Using another's idea requires not only knowledge but also willingness. All civilizations then were bigoted toward other races, nations, or faiths. However, Mokyr notes that Europeans were unusual in that such attitudes did not in the least hamper their adoption of other nations' inventions—most notably, gunpowder and firearms. Emulation of national and religious rivals was one of the key forces of progress in the early modern period.[10] Proud John Winthrop was surely uncomfortable adopting Indian money, but the 1690 court had no problem whatsoever in taking inspiration from French Catholics in Canada, and the court's friends even quickly put it in writing. They flipped bigotry on its head: it was no crime to adopt a Catholic's invention; it was a crime *not* to adopt an invention that *even French Catholics* found useful. This was not an unusual attitude for English people—the only important invention not yet adopted by England and its colonies, for religious reasons, was the Gregorian calendar.[11] The same openness encouraged later paper money imitation among British colonies. Anglicans, Catholics, Quakers—all eventually adopted some of the paper moneys designed in Massachusetts during the period 1681–1692.

NONCONFORMISM. Inventors, says Mokyr, are "nonconformists" who "rebel in some way against the status quo."[12] The Massachusetts Puritans were literally that. In fact, they referred to themselves not as Puritans but as nonconformists, a term that included all those not conforming to Church of England rules;[13] and they were rebels when they

prepared to resist a prospective English invasion (1635), continued minting (1660–1682), and overthrew the dominion (1689). Specifically, Elisha
Hutchinson, the head of the paper money committee, was a leader of
the faction that opposed a constitutional compromise with England. His
near-duel experience was with the king's officer in Boston.

Virginia had its share of rebellious attitudes. For a while, even under a royal governor, it apparently ignored the royal prerogative; but perhaps that mint plan was aborted because of second thoughts regarding
that issue. Less dramatic was Virginia's rebellion against common law.
Virginia cared little about legal formalities, and so it preferred common
sense to common law. It wisely legislated the first general setoff rule of
any English jurisdiction. The lawyerly Massachusetts leadership probably could not even consider that option, and so private law in Massachusetts remained tied to common law.[14]

WILLINGNESS TO BEAR RISKS. Mokyr argues that invention is "always
and everywhere" a risky venture. In a technological invention, the inventor bears the risk that the investment would fail to yield sufficient profits, or would succeed too much and anger a powerful, violent opposition,
while society bears the risk that the invention would disrupt the existing
social and economic order.[15] The monetary invention of 1690 could have
resulted in inflation, mutiny, and general chaos. Perhaps it was safer to
keep the soldiers waiting for pay, as was common in that era. New Englanders would never abandon defense of their own families, right? The
1667 Chatham fiasco could not repeat in Massachusetts, hopefully. Were
the colonists mentally ready for the risk of trying something so new and
consequential as a new type of money?

Compared with fellow Europeans who stayed behind, seventeenth-
century emigrants to the New World definitely had, almost by definition, lower "risk aversion" (as economists put it). They were willing to
bear risks that others would not. Presumably, at least some of their descendants inherited that low risk aversion, through genetics and/or education. The Hutchinsons—part of what I called above a dynasty of
troublemakers—are an extreme example. Consider the following five
consecutive generations, which span the entire colonial period: Anne,
Edward, Elisha, Elisha's son Thomas Sr., and Elisha's grandson Thomas
Jr. Anne and Edward were killed in wars by Indians they trusted.
Thomas Jr., a historian, provided more information on his grandfather
and father: Elisha "seems never to have been successful in business, apt

to involve himself in debt upon plans of payment which did not succeed according to expectation." As the foremost anti–paper money activist in 1740s Massachusetts, Thomas Jr. probably hinted here at the events of 1690. Both Elisha and Thomas Sr. were damaged so badly by later business ventures that they ended their lives in somewhat embarrassing financial circumstances. The councillor Thomas Sr. "always spoke his mind without fear, either of the Governor or the people," said his son.[16] Thomas Jr. himself was Massachusetts's last civilian colonial governor. His controversial (royalist) views got him banished by the population, and he soon died in exile—much like Anne, his grandfather's grandmother. In the context of such a persistently reckless dynasty, it is not surprising to see the middle Hutchinson—Elisha—leading the colony's most risky financial experiment ever.[17]

Elisha, you may recall, was the only one we know of to almost have a duel with Edward Randolph, and this brings to mind two other duelists, Alexander Hamilton and John Law. In the following century, these two men single-handedly designed and implemented financial systems for entire nations. Both were immigrants, and both were duelists—with opposite achievements: Alexander Hamilton's financial system survived, but he did not, while John Law survived a duel, but his financial system in 1710s France did not.[18]

INTEREST GROUPS. One major obstacle for any invention is politically powerful interest groups that might lose from it, and thus may try to block it as soon as possible.[19] Interest groups were strongest in England. The Royal Mint in London repeatedly sabotaged any attempt at independent colonial coinage,[20] while the king was not excited about losing a most prestigious, symbolic part of his prerogative. The Royal Mint's coins ranged from a farthing to £5, which must be the main reason that Parliament, bank promoters throughout the century, the Bank of England, and the exchequer almost never entered that territory.[21]

In 1630s Virginia, there were conflicts of interest between king, governor, council, and assembly. Each had its own incentives with regard to coins and customs. The assembly's repeated request for silver coins to be sent from England was absurd, when the king, who called no Parliament, was desperately scrambling for coins, getting himself into serious trouble in the long run over unconstitutional taxation. The king wanted to help his crony dispose of coins, but the colonists refused to participate in an experiment that could have ended in their ruin. They did have recent experience with intrinsically useless money (from their perspective), roanoke beads; but no Indian or king could unilaterally revalue or devalue that.

With respect to customs, both king and governor personally profited from such nonparliamentary taxation, while for the population customs evasion was probably a leading if not the real reason to sabotage the clearinghouses system, which was sadly intertwined with customs collection. The constitutional structure of Virginia did not allow either side to impose its will, and so the period ended with no clearinghouses, no locally produced coins, and no imported English coins. The checks and balances of imperial rule and local rule proved a recipe for gridlock because the different parties had diametrically opposing interests.

Things were very different in Massachusetts. The court patiently waited for royalty to be abolished before opening a mint, and it was on good-enough terms with the new regime to get away with it. As there was no residing monarch or Royal Mint that really cared, it took England two decades after the Restoration to get the Boston mint shut, and it would take six more decades for Parliament to care enough in order to kill the province's paper money. A land bank was also able to arise in Massachusetts before England, although the idea came from England.

In 1690 Massachusetts, the local mint was closed (thanks to the distant Crown). Even if it were open, its owner, Samuel Sewall, was a public-spirited patriot who would not have put his own financial interests before the colony's during such a crisis.[22] He even wrote in his hand the draft of the bill of credit. Even if he wanted to object to paper money for personal gain, he would have failed. He was only one assistant in a bicameral legislature that was accountable to a large segment of the population that elected it every year. There was no treasury that could have formed an interest group, only a new treasurer who was part of the paper money committee. In any case, treasurers had long accepted mostly objects other than coin, so that was no novelty.

With the exceptions of rare English interventions, all interest groups relevant to Massachusetts lived in the colony and were united in their goal of guaranteeing the economy's survival. Therefore, local checks and balances did not paralyze the government. The 1690 bills operated entirely within the community. The soldiers were local taxpayers, as were their officers, the sellers they encountered in the marketplace, and the elected politicians. Many, perhaps most, soldiers, taxpayers, and sellers were voters. It was money of the people, by the people, for the people. It was a democratic money. It aspired to voluntary acceptance in the market. It was created by a parliament forcing its acceptance only on the state itself in taxes—taxes levied by the people for the people's defense.

Massachusetts was thus a typical frontier society, using all the knowledge of the parent society (on credit and banking) but few of its restricting institutions—and this is a recurrent theme in history.[23] Royal Virginia was not that lucky. A similar case to Massachusetts would be Scotland. Its parliament voted in 1707 for union with England. Control of Scotland was placed with the *British* Parliament, which was in London, physically and mentally. Scotland enjoyed benign neglect, and Scottish banks were free to convert Scotland to a paper money economy. Coin-backed private banknotes, especially £1 notes, served there as the main currency.[24] Some of the peripheries of Britain could do what London itself could not.

OPTIMISM. The legislature had to form expectations regarding the public's response to a new money. Would the public accept it or not? In principle, this is a separate question from that of interest groups that might block the creation of a new money in the law books. This was most pronounced in England, where there was a stark division between those who participated in the political process and those who used everyday money. The majority of English subjects were not voters and had no experience with goldsmith-bankers' banknotes and checks, and so unbacked paper money might have seemed too radical to them. A bigger problem would have been the soldiers—all of whom were fighting in Europe and most of whom were mercenaries. German soldiers in Holland could not be expected to fight for William and Mary for anything other than hard coin. They would not fight for paper money that could be used to pay taxes only in England.

In the more democratic colonies, such as Massachusetts and Virginia, the difference between legislature and population was not supposed to be significant. And yet, the Massachusetts population clearly behaved in a way not anticipated by a majority of the optimistic elected deputies and magistrates. The court apparently overestimated the colony's social cohesion, or deference to elites, or the exposure of common people to paper instruments in trade. Perhaps they underestimated the population's awareness and fear of inflation. Either way, their optimistic mistake prompted them to legislate a new money. Similarly, excessive optimism may have been responsible for numerous technological inventions.[25]

Implementation

After the legislature decides to pass a law, it needs to write it down exactly, in a way that will allow the executive to execute it properly. Implementation thus requires abilities—of both mind and hand. It may also require appropriate equipment, and enough prudence to avoid disasters.

ABILITIES. The experienced Massachusetts merchants had the proper intellectual abilities to design the details of their novel 1690 money in a workable way, just as the Bank of Amsterdam was designed by top financial experts. In contrast, Virginia's adaptation of the Bank of Amsterdam idea was instituted by amateurs. Its circumstances were too different, and therefore that bold and remarkable attempt was awkward and it failed.

Regarding technical ability, the Massachusetts mint master John Hull was a professional goldsmith, and professionals working in the ironworks could (and probably did) work in the mint. Massachusetts had printing press workers since the 1630s, and one former manager of the Boston press was an assistant in 1690. Virginia had goldsmiths at the very beginning, but they had long vanished by the 1640s as hopes of finding precious metals faded.[26] John Upton, the Virginia mint master, was typical of the new elite: a former servant and chance survivor, he was elected to the assembly and became justice of the peace and military commander of his county.[27] But there is no hint of any technical skill or managerial experience he had that was relevant for a mint.

PHYSICAL CAPITAL. Massachusetts could easily afford establishing a mint, the equipment for which—forges and iron tools—was produced in the local ironworks. By 1690, Massachusetts had printing presses in Cambridge and Boston. Virginia had ironworks, but they and their staff were destroyed in the 1622 massacre.[28] In the 1640s, metal was so scarce that inhabitants burned down abandoned houses to salvage their nails, all lead items were converted by law into bullets, and the colony could not afford to build prisons.[29] This was no place for a mint. More generally, poor Virginia became even poorer when the price of tobacco plummeted in the 1630s. Perhaps it really was too poor to afford the construction of storehouses and the boats to reach them, as the assembly argued.

PRUDENCE. One way to mitigate the risk inherent in inventions is to proceed cautiously in their implementation. The Massachusetts court made an experiment, in the spirit of the new science, with about one-sixth of the debt before it decided to print money in the amount of the entire debt. Another prudent measure—and one more fundamentally necessary—was printing no more than the amount of taxes to be collected. Both steps required a superb level of discipline, one that could be expected perhaps only of . . . Puritans. Their avoidance of gold in churches and rituals was just one component of an entire agenda of resisting nearly all human temptations with a saintly level of discipline that became legendary, and it still is their only famous enduring legacy. Checks and balances in the issuing committee were also a measure of prudence. Even with no trauma of high inflation anywhere in living memory, the Puritans knew they were playing with fire, and withstood the temptation to print quickly more than they were willing to tax. Many other governments, before and especially after, did not have that discipline, and in spite of knowing the consequences, they quickly got high on high inflation.

Innovation and Nondivision of Labor

Another factor emphasized by Mokyr—in the context of the Industrial Revolution—is communication: regular meetings and interactions between scientists, engineers, and entrepreneurs in eighteenth-century Britain brought together their different perspectives and knowledge to create the most drastic change in human history.[30] There was something equivalent in Massachusetts between court and ministers. The latter were the intellectuals and constitutional advisors, and they had the court's attention to any idea they had. Moreover, they married heavily with the secular elite, especially with merchants.[31] Cotton Mather testified on his conversations on money with his merchant father-in-law, the treasurer John Phillips.

But there was something far more effective than communication. Elisha Hutchinson, a typical legislator, hardly needed communication with others to understand the perspectives and motives of the government, soldiers, sellers, taxpayers, and tax collectors: he *was* all of these people. Consider again figure 13.3, which displays the debt problem between the government, soldiers, and seller-taxpayers. Hutchinson had long been a militia soldier and officer, and in 1690 he was the major of Boston's regiment. Most of his soldiers were presumably back from Canada, to which he might have gone too if not for his councillor position. He was one of the sellers—sometime an alcohol seller and always a merchant. He was a taxpayer, of course, but he had just been elected Boston's chief tax officer—positioned between taxpayers and the treasury. As an executive, he knew the financial situation better than most. His recent committee membership designated him a leading expert on that topic. He had all these different voices in his own head.

There's more. As a recent diplomat and lifelong land expert, he knew the significance of imperial limitations on creating official money and backing it with land. As a merchant, he knew and practiced credit, including bills, setoff, and multilateral settlements, so he could think of a solution that would leave everyone satisfied without coin. As a legislator, he knew how to write it into law. As a judge he knew how a law might be interpreted, used, or abused. Revisiting the terms from chapter 2, he was an engineer, technician, and user of money. What modern legislator—typically a former lawyer—could possibly outmatch Hutchinson in that particular situation?

Of course, Hutchinson's exact personal role is not clear. His place at the head of the committee was surely not a coincidence, but the point is that he was representative of his class. His friend Samuel Sewall, a colleague in council and the scribe of the draft bill of credit, was just as qualified. For his deficiencies in military and land, compared with Hutchinson, he compensated with a college degree, management of a printing press, and inheritance of the mint.

The amazing plethora of occupations of Hutchinson and his peers could have helped the invention of a new type of money. This claim about the benefit of *not* specializing in one job is ironic, since money as a medium of exchange exists to facilitate specialization in one job. Money overcomes the difficulties of barter and allows us to disconnect our production skills from our consumption preferences. As Adam Smith noted long ago, specialization, or division of labor, is efficient because we produce more and cheaper when we specialize.

The legal tender bill (such as a recent £20 bill portraying Adam Smith preaching the division of labor) does facilitate division of labor, but it was invented by people who at some level adhered to *non*division of labor. Division of labor restricts one's point of view and hampers one's ability to think and know outside one's area of expertise. How could the specialized pin workers on the Adam Smith bill think outside the box when they have been hammering nails all their lives? Each nail they hammer is another nail sealing the mental box, or mental coffin, around them.

Interdisciplinarity—often praised in academia—has proven useful in other inventions. Arthur Koestler has argued that the essence of original creation is the mixing of two previously unrelated elements of knowledge. For example, Darwin had his eureka moment from reading an economics book by Thomas Robert Malthus that emphasized competition between people for scarce resources; Darwin thus realized how natural selection works.[32] Two elements are more likely to have been previously unrelated if they belonged to different areas of knowledge, and were thus not known simultaneously to any specialized individual.[33] More examples are easy to find. History's most successful wrights—the Wright brothers—benefited above all from repairing bicycles for a living. They learned from the bicycle that in inherently unstable objects, movement occurs before control. The cognitive psychologist Philip Johnson-Laird stated: "In many ways, their flyer *was* a flying bicycle [his emphasis]."[34] Michael Bloomberg connected ability (supply) as an electrical engineer with demand for real-time information he encountered on Wall Street. Even this present book comes from the combined study of three disciplines—economics, law, and history.

There is no guarantee that the advantages of interdisciplinarity will outweigh its disadvantages at the political level. James Buchanan's unusually diversified background did not make him a good president. It is not clear that in the United States, former senators were better presidents than those who had specialized in the executive branch as state governors.

In conclusion, in 1690 Massachusetts, nondivision of labor probably helped the legislature (even a single legislator) understand the interests and incentives of the groups of people involved, and thus predict their behavior. My fellow economists should be more open-minded about the costs and benefits of one of our central tenets—division of labor.

Demand and Supply in a Theory of Inventions

The notion of demand for inventions and supply of inventions, used here and in chapter 2, merits generalization. The old saying that necessity is the mother of invention is still taken seriously in academic research.[35] Necessity in this context is far more than just plain demand. Demand for a better life is always there, on every aspect that will bring us closer to the Garden of Eden. But there are infinitely many problems to solve on the way there, so which one to choose?

Necessity should mean here a large, sudden, consequential negative shock to what has been taken for granted, which results in a *change* in demand. These are the phenomena that attract our attention and direct us to try and solve certain problems rather than others. Nathan Rosenberg has demonstrated these focusing devices with several examples. One theme is the adverse effects of war on supplies of raw materials: a cotton shortage in Britain during the American Civil War, and a shortage of natural rubber in the United States during World War II, prompted inventions that solved the problems; the latter case, for instance, resulted in invention of synthetic rubber. This is reminiscent of how Massachusetts had a wartime shortage of "natural" money (coin), so it invented "synthetic" money (legal tender paper money). Another pro-invention theme mentioned by Rosenberg is legal restrictions on certain activities, either by regulation (a theme analyzed above) or by others' patent rights.[36] The latter, which implies a legal monopoly, also reminds us that Massachusetts faced England's minting monopoly twice, and found new ways around it, with bullets first and legal tender bills later.

But changes in demand, or necessity, however big they are, cannot be the whole story of inventions. Mokyr emphasized *ability*, or supply. All countries fighting in World War II faced a necessity to invent jet engines and radars, not to speak of the atomic bomb, and yet each invention was made in one or two countries at most.[37] Why didn't Germany or Britain invent an atomic bomb? Because they did not have the ability to do so.

In Mokyr's analysis of overall technological creativity, there is no symmetry between supply and demand: a society is generally creative if it has the right supply—the engine of invention, if you will—while changes in demand are only the steering wheel, determining the specific areas in which inventions happen.[38] From this macro perspective, indeed, supply and demand are not of the same importance. But if we limit our attention to a *particular* (or micro) area, as I do here, then there could be some symmetry: an invention in monetary affairs could require both a general innovative capability and an increasing demand for monetary inventions (rather than an increasing demand for inventions in other areas). Given equal supply in two societies, the one with a larger increase in demand for monetary inventions is more likely to invent one; and given equal increases in demand for monetary inventions in two societies, the one with higher supply is more likely to invent one.

How did these considerations play out in the seventeenth century? There was a far higher quantity of qualified people in London than in Boston; but England's supply suffered from conservatism and special interests, and England's ruling class did not perceive a large enough demand for monetary innovation until the mid-1690s. Compared to Virginia, 1630s Massachusetts colonists probably had a higher increase in demand for monetary inventions. The middle-class colonists, used to coins in England, were probably more shocked by the absence of coin than were the poor servants of Virginia, who had little coin either before or after emigration. Massachusetts was forced to deal with drastic deterioration in its money supply a few more times: when emigration stopped, when the quality of pieces of eight and wampum deteriorated later in the decade, and when the mint was closed. With its wealth of physical resources and qualified political leaders, intellectuals, and merchants, Massachusetts definitely had higher ability than Virginia to solve its problems. Having both high increase in demand and high (though not highest) supply, Massachusetts had more successful inventions than Virginia and England.

Another comparison that needs to be made is with other New England colonies. All the New England colonies faced the same conditions that affected the demand for money and for monetary innovation. The New England weather spared these colonies from Virginia's tobacco trap. But Massachusetts was far more innovative on money, and I attribute it to its higher supply of abilities. All New England colonies had the right political institutions, but Massachusetts had many more merchants, and for financial experiments, it attracted others (the Thorntons and Blackwell).

How, then, to reconcile the critical role of ability with the old famous saying that necessity is the mother of invention? That maternity claim was contested already by Robert Boyle in 1671, in a key sentence quoted by Mokyr: scientific knowledge, with "skill and industry," he wrote, should be "the fruitful mother of diverse things useful."[39] I propose the following compromise: as Boyle argued, ability is the mother; but necessity remains relevant—it is the father. I will use Mokyr's terms to explain why, in the context of 1690: ability builds slowly over time (decades, in this book) and may lie "dormant" until an outside event (war) suddenly arrives, and this "stimulus" results in the "activation" of the ability.[40] In other words, the event impregnates the ability, similar to a sperm and an egg. I therefore suggest: *Necessity is the father of invention and ability is the mother of invention.*

This new version of the old aphorism also lends itself better than the original to cases in which inventions happen with neither demand nor a change in demand in sight. Lasers, for example, were invented long before any use for them was conceived. In such cases, ability is still the mother of invention, but it is the only parent. Such fatherless inventions can happen just as asexual reproduction happens in many species.

Lessons from Biological Evolution and Ecology

I have used the word *evolution* before in the loose sense of gradual development, but it is time to take the word seriously. Darwin used economics, and economics can use Darwin; there is a long tradition of trying to find common ground between biology and economics in the context of evolution. Proponents of such views are careful in applying principles of biological evolution to economic evolution, mainly because biological evolution is not driven by an intentional "watchmaker," whereas actual watches, all other technological goods, and many economic institutions such as money are designed by people on purpose.[41] Mokyr concluded that "evolution is bigger than either biology or economics. . . . It is a pervasive property of all systems that have a history, a budget constraint, and in which the process that generates innovation is stochastic."[42] Mokyr applied concepts from biological evolution to technological evolution and to cultural evolution. Selection occurs "at the level of a unit of knowledge or technique" in the former, and at the level of a "cultural element" (a belief, a value, or a preference) in the latter.[43]

Preliminaries

Can the same analysis be used in monetary evolution? It can be justified not only by analogy to Mokyr's work but also through analogy to language. Sociologists such as George Herbert Mead argue that money is analogous to language—money is the language of trade. It allows us to exchange goods and services with each other just as language allows us to exchange thoughts.[44] Next, consider that Darwin himself equated "the formation of different languages and of distinct species," because both "developed through a gradual process."[45] Hence, the development of different types of money could, in principle, be similar to the development of distinct species.

Does an argument for evolution contradict my earlier argument for *revolution*? Not at all, as two examples will show. First, the Industrial Revolution was part of a technological evolution. Nothing exemplifies this better than the fact that James Watt did *not* invent "the" steam engine; his main contribution was a small technical improvement to Thomas Newcomen's decades-old steam engine. And yet, this improvement made the engine cross a threshold of economic efficiency that changed the course of human history.[46] Second, we humans are a product of evolution, but we crossed a threshold of ability that has changed the face of the planet in a revolutionary way. Similarly, there was an evolutionary process of small changes in the form of money, and the 1690 step was no exception. However, it passed a threshold—between intrinsic value and law as the anchor of money—that was revolutionary in its essence and proved revolutionary in its effect on world history.

Most aspects of the current story do have striking similarities to biological evolution, with selection occurring at the level of the use of some object as money—in practice, or in law, or in a developing project. In general, Mokyr's characterization of "all evolutionary processes" as "messy and imprecise, full of false starts and dead ends,"[47] certainly fits the century-long, Atlantic-wide process described here. Copper money, seashell beads, Virginia's reforms, Massachusetts bullets, and numerous banking ventures—all failed, sooner or later.

Mokyr further says that it is "the characteristic of evolutionary systems to produce unforeseen and unintended consequences."[48] Indeed, no Massachusetts Founding Father intended or envisioned the monetary evolution that eventually replicated what happened in the rest of the world over thousands of years. The sequence of the Massachusetts monetary evolution was random, driven at every point by regulation-related shocks coming from England.

To examine this evolution in detail, I proceed as follows. First, I will review how the core principles of evolution are manifested in the story. Then I will expand on two issues that are key topics in Atlantic history research: America's relative isolation and England's external influences. The latter topic will bring us from evolution to ecology.

Core Principles of Evolution

The core Darwinian principles are variation, inheritance, and selection.[49] Variation between biological creatures is obtained by the recombination of genes in sexual reproduction and by mutations. The varied properties of perishable creatures are transmitted as information to offspring through inherited genes. Elements in the environment select those variants which are fittest in that environment by varying rates of survival and reproduction.

In this story, there was large variation in types of money, information about them was easily transmitted across the Atlantic and across time, and imperial restrictions killed off some types of money and thus indirectly selected other types.

VARIATION. Local natural resources and local human abilities created *mutations* in the ways emigrants from England replaced or supplemented their traditional use of English coins. The result was great variation in types of money and alternatives to money throughout the Atlantic World. The Massachusetts bills of credit, however, were not a mutation but a *recombination*, as they were wholly based on prior practices. The monetary laws of 1690–1692 were dissected above to their smallest components, showing for each one a precedent from earlier chapters: bill, debenture, legal tender, issue by a mixed executive committee, assignation, setoff, trilateral debt settlement, one-third abatement, indenture, and so on. The point is not the exact history of each component, but the fact that no component was new in 1690–1692. Most components had been long known even in England. The only novel thing was putting them together in a particular way, applying existing ideas in a different way and context than before. It is impossible to understand the bills of credit without awareness of the history of these many recombined components. Mark Peterson, for example, sees "on the surface, the sign of an amazing conceptual transformation" in the 1690 money. Since such an inexplicable "leap," as he put it, is an improbably large mutation, he concludes there was no mutation at all: his persistent coin-centered view has led him to speculate that the bills were designed as merely backward Phips-backed money.[50] Peterson is correct in that it was no mutation; but it was recombination, which is revealed in the credit-centered view suggested here.

INHERITANCE. Information was transmitted in several ways. Merchants and immigrants, spreading information across space, were discussed before in length. Information also easily spread across time. Everyday money, such as grain in New England, was used continuously throughout the economy, and everyone learned about it as they grew up. The legacy of failing moneys, such as bullets and wampum, could be transmitted from any parent to child, but most likely in mercantile dynasties such as the Hutchinsons and the Hull–Sewall line.[51] Information about moneys that was codified was preserved forever in colonial records, and could be preserved for decades in the brains of long-serving legislators (led by the extremely durable Simon Bradstreet), and in legislator dynasties such as the Winthrops.

SELECTION. During the period under consideration, in a faraway Dutch colony, the land-bound dodo went extinct because of land predators. It reminds us of how land-based banks failed in Massachusetts because of land predators—the later Stuarts and Andros. By eliminating land-based moneys, they selected for survival types of money *not* based on land. The Stuarts also selected types of money that looked different from coins and that were not formally legal tender for debts.

More accurately, the Stuarts and Andros can be thought of as parasites. A leading theory in biology argues that it is for defense from parasites that organisms "invented" the confusing recombination of genes through sexual reproduction. Massachusetts similarly defended itself in 1690 from the parasitic legacy of the Stuarts and Andros with a recombination of monetary features. Unlike in nature, this recombination was deliberate and carefully avoided politically destructive "genes"—coinage, formal legal tender for debts, and land backing.

Isolated America

Ever since Darwin's inspiring expedition to the Galapagos Islands, evolutionary theories have given a prominent role to isolated locations. Darwin's finches are the classic example of adaptive radiation: a species emigrates to a new area and splits, or radiates, into several varieties because of different conditions in different subareas of the new home. This often happens in archipelagos far from the mainland, such as Galapagos and Hawaii, and results in endemic species.[52] In the case of money, English people, who had all been silver-users, emigrated to a distant New World. The first English Empire, consisting of scattered colonies on both mainland and islands, can be considered an archipelago (Solzhenitsyn's generalization). There the money-using English people mutated and radiated into new, endemic varieties according to their natural habitats: tobacco users, grain users, sugar users, board users, even whalebone users on Long Island.[53]

Ernst Mayr, a leading biologist, has argued that such creation of species on islands, or in general among "peripherally isolated populations," is a major force in evolution. New species are more likely to be created in such cases than in contiguous areas. Islands easily "create" new species because mutations can survive in the small isolated population, whereas in the "very conservative" main population, a mutation is drowned by the prevalent genes and disappears. Moreover, the new species are created so quickly as to create a "genetic revolution."[54] In the history of money, a similar phenomenon happened in the western Pacific Ocean, where relatively few people on many islands created an extremely unusual variety of types of money, from whale teeth to the stone money of Yap.[55]

The quick creation of many new types of commodity money by a small number of scattered American colonists was documented above. The monetary revolution of 1690 came six decades after Massachusetts was colonized, and in terms of monetary history this is incredibly quick. It broke a two-thousand-year-old tradition of precious-metal coin use in Western civilization. More generally, it broke a longer tradition of precious metals (in whatever form) and the longest tradition of intrinsically useful commodities. The paper moneys of Canada and Massachusetts—peripheral, relatively isolated colonies in the Americas—survived for decades. They were far more durable than earlier paper moneys in "very conservative" Europe (to use Mayr's term), where mints, monarchs, or soldiers suppressed any mutation that deviated from the ancient monetary order.

Mayr thought that most major evolutionary changes have happened this way, and this could explain why one can hardly ever find a smooth transition from an ancestor to descendants in the fossil record of a given area. In a theory that has been popularized by others as punctuated equilibrium, he argues that this is due not to imperfections of the record, but to the way evolution really works: the small isolated population mutates, sometimes remigrates successfully to the ancestral homeland, and takes it over. The fossil record in the homeland shows a break only because the mutation happened elsewhere.[56]

Similarly, a Eurocentric historian will find it hard to explain the wide use of unbacked paper money during the French Revolution and Napoleonic Wars by the European experience of *peacetime* paper money, which was either convertible (Scotland) or an old failure (1660s Sweden and 1710s France). The influential mutation, one of the most important changes in the history of money, happened elsewhere—in America. Paper money spread from Massachusetts to the other British colonies and then financed the American Revolution. When Europe learned this and implemented paper money, the mutation effectively went back to the ancestral homeland and defeated the old monetary order.

England's Influences: Evolution and Ecology

The abovementioned selection made by land predators in the 1680s was performed not by local predators but by invading English predators—the Stuarts and Andros. This brings us to another major force in biological evolution: external influences, which can have both positive and negative effects. The most famous example is the asteroid that killed the large dinosaurs but enabled our few mice-size mammal ancestors to rise and evolve into thousands of larger species. Similarly, the revolutionary Massachusetts money owed its existence to external predators who killed land-backed moneys and coins.

It was not the first time that English interferences destroyed one type of Massachusetts money and helped another. The difference is that in 1690 it resulted in a genuine invention, while in earlier cases, the types of money being destroyed or helped had already existed in England, in theory or practice. This shifts the discussion from evolution (creation and extinction of species) to ecology (the population of habitats by existing species).

The term *repeated disturbance* is used in ecology for a regular phenomenon in which external forces, such as fire or flood, randomly destroy life forms in an area.[57] Similar to evolutionary theories, a calamity not only might eliminate a population but might replace it with a new population. The most useful example here is a hurricane, coming from Africa to hit the Caribbean, killing all lizards on flooded islands. Later, hurricane-driven floating debris brings new lizard populations to these islands.[58]

In the case of money, there were repeated disturbances from England's constitutional upheaval. These northern hurricanes of a sort,
coming from England to hit Massachusetts, destroyed types of money
in Massachusetts: the 1640 stoppage of emigration emptied the colony
of English coins, while the early-1680s closure of the mint damaged the
supply of local coins. England's land policy killed land banking. Decades later, legal tender paper money would also be terminated by Britain. But the constitutional hurricanes also brought by accident English
monetary ideas and political possibilities. The mint was founded after
the king was beheaded and English businesses issued their own coins,
while land banks were founded by different waves of religious refugees.

Hurricanes sometimes kill all lizards on an island, but the island is
repopulated by buried lizard eggs that survived the storm.[59] Similarly,
monetary ideas could survive even while the occasional English disturbance destroyed the money itself. The idea of increasing and supporting the circulation of an object by accepting it for taxes was perhaps buried with the mint and was surely buried with the Bank of Credit, but
hatched again in 1690.

In general, social sciences speak of "diffusion" or "transfer" of ideas,
culture, technologies, and institutions from one society to others. Legal scholarship speaks of "transplantation" of laws of one jurisdiction
in others.[60] These prolific research areas can benefit from applying concepts from ecology, as demonstrated here. Specifically, repeated disturbances from an empire's core to peripheries within and without the empire's formal borders may be detected in many cases.

CHAPTER SEVENTEEN

Conclusion

This currency, as we manage it, is a wonderful machine.
  —Benjamin Franklin, 1779

This chapter begins with a summary of the main argument, followed by relation to other research on the American colonies, a brief description of how legal tender money came to rule the world, and the new challenges to the current monetary order. The chapter ends with wider interdisciplinary perspectives.

Modern Currency

The 1690 Massachusetts money was *not* the first paper money in America. Dutch Brazil, English Antigua, and French Canada had paper money earlier. It was the first paper money in the area that became the United States, and this fact had no small impact on the spread of this invention. However, the main importance of the 1690 money is in being the first money to rely only on its legal tender status rather than commodities or compulsion in spot transactions. The New England Puritans purified money from its superfluous shiny appearance and exposed it as a circulating object under minimal auspices of the emerging fiscal-military state.

Massachusetts did it because it could and because it needed to. It *could*—that is, it had the ability to do so. It had high ability to begin with, and accumulated even more skills during six decades of intense experimentation in money, credit, and banking, much of which was England's fault. It *needed* to do it in 1690 because of very peculiar political circumstances (again, England's fault).

Massachusetts's achievement was that it understood money in the macro sense and not just the micro sense. It wasn't really important to look at every particular transaction and examine the intrinsic value that the seller got. The main point is what happens with the money. It circulates. It goes from that seller to other sellers and from all of them to the treasury. Then it goes back from the treasury to private people, who resume the circulation of money in the private economy, and so on. When money is recognized for this role, it doesn't really matter what it is made of. Numerous American politicians, even much later, have misunderstood this point, as shown by the notable legal historian J. Willard Hurst.[1]

The legal tender law which Massachusetts used in 1690–1692, and that we use today, to support our currency, is a very limited law by its nature. It only settles disputes about the medium of payment of an obligation that *already exists*. One such obligation is a contractual debt that needs to be discharged after a commodity or service had been delivered; another example is a tax. Contrary to what some people believe, legal tender laws do not force anyone to sell on the spot for legal tender currency (there is no obligation to settle yet), and they do not prohibit parties from agreeing on another medium of payment.[2] Legal scholars of money usually focus on legal tender in the context of private debts, because this is where the lawsuits are.[3] But it is the other, less litigated part of legal tender laws that matters for the very circulation of money: taxes—the lifeblood of the modern state.

My reason for focusing on legal tender money is that in the early twenty-first century, *every* normal nation or federation designates some physical objects of no intrinsic value to be legal tender for debts and taxes in the area under its jurisdiction, without any promise of backing or convertibility into any commodity. I deliberately avoided other, perhaps more popular terminology, which has no accurate legal meaning and appears in no legislation. For example, the terms *fiduciary money* and *credit money* presumably mean any intrinsically useless money. Massachusetts bills of credit are obviously included in these terms, and so is our modern currency; but Massachusetts bills had, and our modern currency have, four more properties, two negative and two positive: inconvertibility into commodities, no backing with commodities, serving as legal tender for debts, and serving as legal tender for taxes.

In the 1870s, an exact name was invented for such money: its opponents dubbed it "fiat money," to put an authoritarian label on the legal tender "greenbacks" that won the American Civil War.[4] The war veteran Berthold Fernow did not mean to compliment wampum when he called it "the first fiat money in the New World" (p. 85). The phrase *fiat money* was never a proper name because such money does *not* have the most authoritarian possible feature—that is, forced acceptance in spot transactions.[5]

Economists later loosened that strict definition, and so, for economists in the academic ivory tower, *fiat money* has come to describe any intrinsically useless, inconvertible, unbacked money—whatever other legal status it does or does not have. In mathematical models, economists have long imagined such an object with no legal status at all and typically with no government to issue it or tax it, and have called that "fiat money" too.[6] Oddly, the closest real-life assets to this theoretical construct are purely private crypto "currencies" rather than the state's fiat money (in its original meaning). The term *fiat money* was distorted to begin with when it was created for political gain, and was mutilated beyond recognition by economists. For clarity's sake, this term should be avoided.

The most accurate term is simply *legal tender*, which was widely used after the Civil War greenbacks were issued. The constitutional struggle over these bills is known to this day as the legal tender cases. The term *legal tender currency* has been used to describe types of money that were supported only by that status rather than something stronger, such as gold or criminal law. Nobody refers to a gold coin or to Kublai Khan's forced money as legal tender currency.[7] When someone says "legal tender currency," the meaning is clear enough.

Historiographical Context

One mistaken interpretation of the story could be that, as part of the grand victory of Parliament over the monarchy in the seventeenth century, Massachusetts's parliament also had a share in that it managed to put forth an independent currency instead of the monarchy's coins. Add a claim that it was inevitable, and you get the type of historiography that is most despised today: Whig history. Indeed, the original term referred to the seventeenth century, and in general it came to describe any view of inevitable progress toward a better, freer world.

This book makes no claim of either inevitability, liberation, or improvement. Regarding inevitability, the whole process was random, driven by mostly unrelated regulation in England, and the circumstances of 1690 were peculiar in the extreme. Legal tender money was invented serendipitously, while the court tried to solve a fiscal wartime problem.[8] As for liberation, while paper money did let the Massachusetts parliament escape the monarchy's coins, the true meaning of that monetary revolution actually made the monetary economy *less* free than ever. Such money would no longer depend for its value on the materials it was made of—which could be mined, grown, or produced by the private sector. Instead, it would be wholly dependent on the government and its tax powers. While in the case of Massachusetts this problem was mitigated by the fact that a representative government issued the money, most future adopters would lack that feature. Regarding improvement, no such claim can be found in the stained, mixed legacy of legal tender money (see below). Such is usually the case with great inventions. Negative consequences of legal tender money should not prevent an appreciation of the invention itself, any more than the aerial attacks on the United States in 1941 and 2001 diminish the achievements of two great Americans, the Wright brothers. The only thing celebrated in this book is the intellectual triumph of uncovering the true nature of money in the fiscal state.

The historiography of the American colonies has developed through three main stages. In the beginning, there were isolated histories of individual colonies. Charles Andrews's imperial school reminded historians that the colonies belonged to an empire, and that nothing in the colonies can be understood without reference to the mother country (and its records).[9] The Atlantic history school prevailing today generalizes Andrews; it emphasizes all the connections between the four continents that bound the Atlantic Ocean. England, the imperial core, was also influenced by the colonies. And there were connections between all colonies, and between them and Indians and Africans.[10]

The single most important theme here is that shocks from England propelled the evolution of Massachusetts money every step of the way. Andrews would have been pleased. But the detailed picture puts this book in the Atlantic school. Many other Americans contributed to monetary innovation (sometimes inadvertently), because monetary innovation, by its nature, is an open-source innovation. Indians provided wampum and beaver. The Dutch West India Company introduced wampum to Plymouth (which introduced it to Massachusetts) and exported siege paper money to Brazil. Plymouth gave Massachusetts other ideas on currency, from grain to forcing a portion of taxes to be paid in coin. The Spanish colonies provided the main coin of the era. The French in Canada monetized beaver and brought siege paper money closer to Massachusetts. Banking and clearinghouse ideas were tried or envisioned in Virginia, Barbados, Antigua, Connecticut, West New Jersey, Pennsylvania, and Plymouth.

Intellectually, the seventeenth century was the first to be centered on experiments rather than ancient writings, with an inductive search for empirical regularities in data—whether generated by designed experiments or not. Each American monetary experiment surveyed above slightly increased everyone's knowledge about the economics and politics of money. Because some inventions involved a recombination of earlier ideas, the addition of any invention could accelerate the process.[11] Did Massachusetts actually pay attention to all the Atlantic moneys? More than anyone else in society, merchants were used to looking for hard facts and accurate information from faraway lands. They looked for information relevant for their businesses—prices, quantities, and quality of their products. Their knowledge and their demand for fast and regular postal services were significant contributions even to the Scientific Revolution.[12] The types of money used in payments all over the Atlantic were surely noticed by Massachusetts merchants. In general, the constant traffic of people of different languages and religions through Atlantic trade centers made such port towns the most open-minded and intellectually dynamic places in the world.[13] Seen in this context, Massachusetts was not the only contributor to one of the first great American inventions, but only its most effective leader.

In the Atlantic context, a new puzzle is posed: the monetary Winthrops. Wherever they went, innovations in money and finance seemed to follow. Massachusetts was extremely innovative when John Winthrop Sr. roamed the Earth. John Jr. came from Connecticut to present a bank plan to the Royal Society. Samuel lived in Antigua when it invented tobacco banknotes. Their cousin George Downing invented tradable paper bonds marketed to the English public. Wait was a director in the Bank of Credit and a councillor in 1690. Adam was a Fund trustee, a Bank of Credit officer, and a member of the paper money committee. Is this a coincidence? Of all their vast surviving writing and correspondence, only John Sr.'s explanations of the 1640s depression show an understanding of monetary economics. Did the whole family have a natural talent for this? Did they talk about it but not document it? Was there an oral body of monetary knowledge that passed across generations?[14] Might a closer look at their business correspondence reveal extra sophistication not found in others' transactions? Or perhaps it is an illusion, with the Winthrops' fame, political positions, and surviving records allowing them to show up wherever monetary innovation arose.

Epilogue, 1700–2008

The Massachusetts invention did not immediately relegate gold and silver to the dust bin of global monetary history. That would take three more centuries and many upheavals.[15] Massachusetts kept printing money during wars. The committees issuing bills over the years had only one member in common—Elisha Hutchinson—until his 1717 death.[16] This is further evidence for his presumed central role in 1690. Other British colonies soon imitated Massachusetts, and some colonies founded land banks. British America became the first Western society to use, on a regular basis, paper money that was unbacked by metal.[17]

The tax-backing mechanism was sufficient to get money circulating, but it was not sufficient to prevent inflation. Colonial legislatures lost their self-discipline and issued more bills than taxes to absorb them.[18] In pioneering Massachusetts, such a change in discipline can perhaps be explained by the simultaneous decline of the disciplining Puritanism in the early eighteenth century. The increasing quantity of bills reduced their value—chronic inflation started. Parliament responded with a series of currency acts that restricted legal tender bills. Running out of monetary ideas, Americans came up with a political idea: independence.

The Age of Revolutions put paper money on the front lines. The Continental Congress financed the American Revolution with continental bills that lost almost all their value because the federal government could not effectively tax the people. But Europe noticed that Americans bought their independence with paper money. Thus the French Revolution was also financed with paper money at a critical stage, backing it with the guillotine that threatened its refusers. Just as French Canada had infected English Massachusetts by issuing paper money, so did France infect Britain: Bank of England notes finally became inconvertible legal tender with denominations as low as £1.

The following century brought a monetary consensus: when war erupts, toss gold aside and start printing as much as needed in order to win the war; after the war, get back to gold-backed banknotes to avoid inflation (silver had already lost its importance). For example, both sides of the American Civil War printed money. Nobody ever again debased their gold coins to finance wars. Similar to Massachusetts, some states printed money to solve *postwar* hardships; examples include the Republic of Texas and the Weimar Republic. In the latter, hyperinflation eroded all debts into oblivion, radically redistributing wealth in society. Within five years, German paper money lost all value. German society also lost some values.[19] The world paid the price.

Gold, however, proved to be just as bad when handled badly. Economic historians blame the ironclad commitment to gold for the Great Depression—its beginning, its deepening, and its transmission from the United States to Europe. A key step to emerging from the Depression was getting rid of gold.[20] In the United States, there was a mandatory *reverse* conversion—of citizens' gold into legal tender bills (Federal Reserve notes). Thus proclaimed an executive order of President Franklin Delano Roosevelt, a biological descendant of Elisha Hutchinson. Just like his ancestor, FDR was 6 foot 2 inches tall, and during a severe crisis he tossed metal in favor of legal tender paper money.[21]

Ironically, it was back in New England that gold made its last-ditch stand. In 1944, during an international conference held at Bretton Woods, New Hampshire, the United States agreed to be the only nation to maintain limited convertibility of its legal tender bills into gold—only when presented by foreign central banks. This anchor of the postwar international monetary system succumbed after a single generation to the widening gap between the paper printed and the available gold. In 1971, President Richard Nixon nixed that arrangement. He ordered "to suspend temporarily" the promise of convertibility.[22] The suspension remains as these lines are written, half a century later. And so a process that began in 1690 in Massachusetts—a future part of the United States—was completed in the United States after three centuries, and impacted the entire human race.

With gold gone, inflation soon rose, but in the United States it was beaten by the Federal Open Market Committee. Invented independently of the long-forgotten paper money committee of 1690 Massachusetts, the FOMC is also a politically balanced committee in charge of the quantity of money, and traditionally it has operated by trading in government bonds. This new committee evolved in the interwar period and its members represent the interests of the executive (the president's seven appointees), the legislature (the Senate confirms the president's appointees), and the private sector (five representatives of the private banks).[23]

The similarity to the 1690 mixed Massachusetts committee is striking, but it is no coincidence—the American tradition of checks and balances was already being forged in the seventeenth century, long before the US Constitution made it famous. This tradition was implemented in the FOMC in the 1930s after three earlier structures did not survive politically for more than two decades each: two overly centralized, Old World–style central banks (the first and second Bank of the United States), and an overly decentralized, privatized Federal Reserve System in its original form. In that sense, the politically balanced FOMC is a mere reinvention, a perhaps inevitable return to an old forgotten American monetary tradition, which has so far proved to be the only politically sustainable way to manage the currency. The FOMC's success in the 1980s prompted worldwide imitation, and monetary policy committees were established in the European Union, the United Kingdom, Israel, and other countries.

Crisis and the Future of Legal Tender Money

The next challenge for legal tender money was the 2008 Global Financial Crisis, which happened during the presidency of another biological descendant of Elisha Hutchinson. Ironically, the crisis was both caused and resolved by the same tool: a large increase in the quantity of money.[24] The crisis undermined popular confidence in the foundation of the monetary system—the easily manipulated, unbacked legal tender paper dollars. Alongside calls to "Occupy Wall Street" and "End the Fed," some global powers got rid of their dollar reserves and started accumulating gold like it was the Middle Ages again.

More curious alternatives to the existing monetary order soon arose. The pretentiously named crypto "currencies" and the pretentiously named "modern monetary theory" gained enthusiastic support among some crowds. Although the project that led to this book was motivated by a 1980s inflationary experience and started before the 2008 crisis, readers of the first draft asked me to comment on these new alternatives because the tax-foundation theory explains very well why they are problematic.

Crypto "Currencies"

When the first crypto "currency," Bitcoin, was launched, it declared an explicit link to the crisis.[25] But Bitcoin and its thousands of imitators did not win over the monetary systems of the world. They do not even come close, which is why calling them "currencies" is pretentious. A 2019 study found that although 2 percent of Americans reported owning crypto "currencies," almost nobody bought actual goods and services with them.[26] They are not used as general media of exchange. Such a dismal performance—during a terrible period for the prestige of state money, an incredible crypto hype, and the biggest bubble in human history (in the value of crypto assets)—testifies to one simple fact: the strength of legal tender.

The modern state is way too strong to have its currency replaced by private, intrinsically useless, inconvertible money. The key advantage of the dollar over a private crypto asset is that the former is acceptable in tax payments while the latter is not. Unlike the early modern state, the modern welfare state is so huge even in peacetime that its choice of what to accept for tax payments (and therefore in what currency it will spend) is decisively consequential for which object functions as money in the private economy. When millions of government employees and welfare recipients receive only the state's money, and many more workers and sellers need that money alone to pay taxes, state money has a gigantic advantage over any competing money.

In addition, the United States' supreme global power would allow it to prevent most financial institutions in the world from dealing with any such "currencies"—if the United States ever finds the risks of money laundering, drug dealing, and terror financing coming from such "currencies" to be unbearable. It seems that only a collapse of the entire state structure, or at least the welfare state, will give truly independent private money a chance. Crypto assets that promise convertibility into legal tender currencies, as private banknotes did in nineteenth-century United States, do have a reasonable chance to become money. The recent forced acceptance of Bitcoin in El Salvador is not likely to help it function as the global currency, given the small size of that economy.

If there was only one crypto asset such as Bitcoin was, maybe it could work. But its very nature—unbacked by any asset or law—has prompted widespread, costless imitation, leading to the failure of them all. Monetary theory predicted exactly that about such a completely "free" money already in 2005.[27] This is not to deny that many people profit from trading in crypto assets (and many others lose), but it has nothing to do with currency and monetary economics. So far the crypto phenomenon is far more similar to pyramid schemes and to the speculative purchase of modern art that is traded for millions of dollars even though few can distinguish it from a toddler's drawings of no market value.

For now, legal tender currency—whether embodied in token coin, paper, or central bank digital currency—is here to stay. This old-fashioned system will have to pick up the pieces if, unlike the modern art market, the crypto bubble bursts and brings down numerous financial institutions.

"Modern Monetary Theory"

While the crypto crowd ignores the tax-foundation theory at its peril, at the other extreme, some economists take the tax-foundation theory of money too far with "modern monetary theory" (MMT). Originally called "modern money theory," it is indeed a theory about "modern money"—the money existing since 1971.[28] The new name is pretentious because it creates the false impression that most economists working now on the theory of money subscribe to MMT.

As a theory about "modern money," MMT argues that the end of gold is a golden opportunity for government to create any amount of money it wishes in order to solve any economic problem. As the German economist Georg Friedrich Knapp put it in 1905 (and helped inspire the later hyperinflation): "Money is a creature of law."[29]

MMT is the only school in economics that champions the tax-foundation theory of money, because that is the foundation of their rewriting of macroeconomics: taxes are not needed to gather gold coins for government to spend; rather, government prints bills in the amount it wishes to spend, and collects taxes in these bills for two other reasons. First, only taxes can induce the private economy to accept such inconvertible bills from the government that wants to buy the private sector's goods and services. Second, once bills are accepted, the larger amount of money in the economy will cause inflation—unless taxes draw the excessive amount of money out of the private economy. Accordingly,

MMT wants the legislature (of taxes), rather than a central bank, to control inflation.[30]

This echoes so much of 1690s Massachusetts that perhaps MMT really stands for "Massachusetts monetary theory." Cotton Mather was apparently the first MMT publicist when he proclaimed to the world "an expedient . . . for any people . . . whose distresses may call for a sudden supply of money to carry them through any important expedition." The basics are indeed similar, but, as the economic historian Stephen Mihm has pointed out, there is a critical difference in discipline.[31] As shown above, the Massachusetts court authorized printing bills, in both December 1690 and February 1691, only at the amount of taxes enacted beforehand or simultaneously. The taxes quickly started taking the bills out of the economy, leaving no reason for prices to rise in the long run. This synchronization of tax increase and printing—in both timing and quantity—was a critical, built-in, disciplining feature of the system. Mihm may well have called it PMT—Puritan monetary theory—if only to contrast it chronologically with "modern"; but, as argued above, there could have been real causality running from Puritanism to discipline. When discipline was lost (together with the decline of Puritanism) one generation later, inflation started.

MMT is all about *denying* this discipline. According to MMT's Stephanie Kelton, experts will tell the legislature how much money should be taxed out of the economy, whenever a new plan of government expenditure is implemented, in order to prevent inflation. She hopes they will rule that new taxes are *not* needed in the same amount of the new spending. She also hopes the experts will always be correct. And she hopes politicians will listen when the experts do call for higher taxes. As Mihm notes, the latter is unlikely. History has shown time and again, all over the world, that almost all politicians, seeking reelection by a population with little understanding of economics, are tempted to implement populist measures—that is, to spend generously and not raise taxes. This is why monetary policy all over the world has been taken from the legislature and the executive and handed over to unelected central bankers. As long recognized in the judicial realm, some jobs are better performed by a different, professional, appointed branch of government.

I am in full agreement with the criticism of mainstream economists on MMT policies, such as John Cochrane's recent warning that we've already been there, in the 1970s.[32] We learned from that stagflation that in noncrisis situations, an expected, systematic, large increase in the quantity of money will bring inflation with no benefits. My only difference with mainstream economists is that they take the circulation of (inflated) money as granted and I don't. Only on this basic theoretical and historical puzzle do I find agreement with MMT. (Such is also the view of Charles Goodhart, who published an article supporting the tax-foundation theory while serving on the Bank of England's Monetary Policy Committee.[33])

MMT may have shed the Puritans' fiscal and monetary discipline, but it adopted other Puritan features. In an endnote, Kelton reserves the right to disagree with her "experts" and not tax as high as they wish, because even with an excess amount of money she thinks she can prevent inflation. Her other "options" are "wage and price controls" to prevent inflation legally and "regulations to reduce demand" of the private sector.[34] The Massachusetts court, long before 1690, had enacted such laws. It enacted maximum wages for wheelwrights and others, capped the prices of beer and other basic goods and services, and reduced demand with sumptuary laws: "superfluous and unnecessary expenses" were prevented with prohibitions on clothing items with gold, silver, and silk.[35] The latter was motivated not by Kelton's wish to "make room for government spending" but by the balance of trade. Whether Kelton imagines sumptuary laws or rationing, its combination with wage and price controls—in peacetime—and the underground economy that inevitably comes with them does not obviously constitute "the people's economy" of Kelton's subtitle.

I know that MMT economists mean well. I have met and corresponded with some of them for useful exchanges of views and facts on the theory and history of the tax-foundation mechanism, because almost no other economist cares about it. But good intentions are not enough. Knapp did not want to cause German hyperinflation, but he contributed to it. Reading Kelton's impressive checklist of all the social and climatic problems she wants to solve with easy money, the MMT (perhaps more appropriately pronounced "mammoth") spending reminded me of the time when the Israeli government was too ambitious. It expanded the welfare state, occupied half of terror-exporting Lebanon, developed a modern jet fighter, and bailed out all banks. Thus I grew up with an inflation rate of 3 percent—per *week*.

To conclude, I agree with MMT, following Aristotle, Hobbes (1651), Barbon (1690), and Knapp (1905), that modern money is a creature of law. But I do not say this in the celebratory MMT tone—"Money is a creature of law, let's party!" I say it in alarm: money is a creature of law—watch out! Specifically, be careful of MMT.

Witchcraft and Enlightenment

In the end, it is time to examine the bewitched elephant in the room—the Salem witch trials, which took place in the same 1692 summer that saw the finalizing of the form of legal tender bills. How to reconcile revolutionary monetary brilliance with the apparent stupidity of what one notable historian has called "the most infamous event in New England history"?[36] The simplest solution is that belief in witches was brought from England, like many other cultural elements such as servants and setoff. In New England, the coincidence of financial creativity and belief in witches was nothing new in 1692. As shown above, these phenomena had coexisted for six decades. The extreme stresses of war induced an unusual explosion of activity on both fronts in 1690–1692, just as they had in England during the Civil Wars.

The puzzle seems more difficult when we look at the people involved. The judges were not local rabble but councillors of the province, including William Stoughton, Samuel Sewall, Wait Winthrop, and John Richards, and others who were legislators in 1690–1692. Elisha Hutchinson was not a judge, but he was personally involved in the arrests of suspects among the elite, and reportedly advised judges in vain before the trials "to see if they could not whip the Devil out of the afflicted."[37] The key legal issue was the admissibility of "spectral evidence"—people's imagination of seeing the shape or spirit of the suspected witch tormenting them. The judges consulted the only so-called experts on spirits—the ministers, including Cotton Mather.[38] It may be disappointing that the wisest men in that society fell for the witchcraft delusion, but we should pay attention to the words "in that society." Financial geniuses are not immune to the most idiotic customs of the societies and cultures they live in. Once again, the duelists Alexander Hamilton and John Law demonstrate the point.

A bolder argument tries not only to reconcile the new money with witch trials, but to show a positive relation between the two. The literary scholar Michelle Burnham has done that through the role of Cotton

Mather in both episodes. Burnham brilliantly claims that just as paper money replaced real, physical money (silver coins), so did spectral evidence replace real, physical evidence of criminal behavior:

> Cotton Mather had just appealed for public faith in the insubstantiality of paper money in an effort to solve the colony's debt crisis. He would repeat that gesture in his qualified support for the trials and their use of insubstantial spectral evidence in an analogous effort to solve the colony's spiritual crisis.[39]

It is a similar argument to the one I made before regarding the possible relation between Puritans' religious preference—spirit over matter and essence over form—and their invention of an informal money that was not based on matter. In fact, my argument was inspired by Burnham's.

Scientific Witch Hunters

Following Burnham's focus on Mather, I suggest an additional explanation of the witch trials. This explanation is not directly related to money, but it is important here to present the mentality of the intellectual Massachusetts elite in the appropriate light—one that can easily encompass, among many things, both monetary brilliance and witchcraft accusations. This argument requires first that I make the challenge even bigger than it seems before solving it.

Cotton Mather was not only an outspoken intellectual involved in money innovation and witch trials. He was a fellow of the college, and his father was president of the college. In fact, Massachusetts was the only English colony with a college. To modern readers, this should make the witchcraft fiasco seem even more puzzling. Though usually called "the college" by contemporaries, its real name was Harvard College. I have omitted that fact until now to help those who are not colonial historians avoid the anachronistic trap of attributing to that humble college the modern prestige of Harvard University. I argue that there is no contradiction between college and the witch hunts. On the contrary, they were part of a single intellectual endeavor.

Puritan clergy were intensely interested in what they called "the invisible world."[40] Strictly speaking, the term referred to the realm of the devil, witches, and demons, but that world was populated by many other inhabitants. Mather's 1685 ordination referred not only to God and the Holy Ghost but also to "the presence of elect Angels" right there and then who witnessed the event.[41] As intellectuals and amateur astronomers, the Puritan ministers knew that the invisible world was also populated by strange *invisible forces*, which operated without visible touch: magnetism, gravity, atmospheric pressure and vacuum, and contagion in epidemics. The effects of these forces were observed but the causes were unknown. Witchcraft and astrology were considered to be of the same class as these forces: their effects presumably obvious, but the mechanisms unknown. This was the mainstream scientific view, claims Walter Woodward, John Winthrop Jr.'s latest biographer.[42]

I argue that the explanation of invisible forces operating without touch was not just an important intellectual challenge; it was the very core of the Scientific Revolution. Witchcraft accusations were a golden opportunity for the Mather scientists, at the edge of Western civilization, to understand witchcraft. In particular, the young, enthusiastic, very ambitious Cotton Mather had a great opportunity to crack a key scientific puzzle and bring glory to God, Puritanism, Massachusetts, Harvard College, and himself. As Joel Mokyr put it, "Competition for fame and reputation became a central feature of intellectual life" in the republic of letters, and reputation required "original contributions."[43] How immensely prestigious would it have been for the Mathers to explain witchcraft—the mysterious impact of one person over another without touch—and join the glorious ranks of Gilbert, Galileo, Torricelli, Pascal, von Guericke, and Newton? That would have been a scientific achievement worthy of being published by the president and a fellow of Harvard College.

Seen this way, the Mathers were mainstream scientists of their time, and this only increased—rather than reduced—their fascination with witchcraft. Like other scientists, including the contemporary Newton, one of the Mather scientists also toyed with monetary theory when his government needed his help. From their perspective, there was no contradiction.

Enlightened Witch Hunters

Salem is more infamous than far worse episodes in contemporary Europe because witch hunting is so shocking to moderns that they wrongly assume it was a medieval (i.e., European) phenomenon; as such, by definition, it should have never happened in America. The economist John Maynard Keynes, no student of the seventeenth century, was similarly baffled by Newton's research into biblical laws and prophesies and alchemy, conducted contemporaneously with his work on physics and mathematics. Keynes declared: "Newton was not the first of the age of reason. He was the last of the magicians."[44]

But Newton was comfortably both, because such was the age. James I, the antismoking demonologist, was no different. Nor was the scientist-alchemist John Winthrop Jr., whose son was a 1690s money legislator and witchcraft judge. Following up on Keynes's misplaced astonishment, I wish to end this book by exploring the possibility that 1690–1692 Massachusetts was not only the last of the witch trials but also one of the first of the age of reason.

The excessive regulation of the European state contributed not only to the creation of modern money, but also to the Enlightenment backlash. It is not clear when the Enlightenment began, but Locke and Newton of the late 1680s are often included in it. To the extent that the Enlightenment meant breaking away from the most sacred traditions—God and king—in favor of reason, we must not forget the joint embodiment of God and king on metallic state coins. English coins were stamped with *Dei Gratia* between the monarch's name and his or her title as ruler: king or queen "by the Grace of God."[45] This holy trinity of God, king, and gold was perhaps the most defining symbolic feature of the Middle Ages. By 1800, all three components were severely undermined, mostly by the American and French Revolutions.

In 1801, a German economist defined the eighteenth century not as the century of Enlightenment but as "the paper century."[46] I suggest that the Enlightenment and the rise of paper money were not parallel, unrelated phenomena. The most enlightened American, Boston-born Benjamin Franklin, was a lifelong printer, promoter, scholar, and legislator of paper moneys of various types. That was the only area in which he was active throughout his adult life. Scotland, a powerhouse of Enlightenment (especially in economic theory), was also a paper money pioneer. Its most famous economists, David Hume and Adam Smith, supported Scottish paper money. They objected to America's paper money long after it became inflated and defamed. Much earlier, another Scotsman, William Paterson, proposed to England the issue of legal tender banknotes (this proposal mutated into the Bank of England without the legal tender feature), while the Scotsman John Law made the most daring paper money experiment—in France, the epicenter of the Enlightenment.

The rational invention of 1690 Massachusetts marked the beginning of the end of gold and silver as money, shattering the ancient common-sense notion that money must be metallic. Ironically, that monetary en-lightenment was manifested in getting rid of those materials that for the most part have excelled only in reflecting light. The true light was that the General Court used reason to design a new concept of money. En-acted by an assembly, Massachusetts's legal tender money constituted lo-cal liberation from royal regulation—a major Enlightenment goal.

Another key Enlightenment feature—a belief in progress—was pres-ent as well. As Mather stated in 1697, their invention could fundamen-tally improve the public finance of any state that paid attention to the distant "city upon a hill": it "may serve as an example, for any people in other parts of the world, whose distresses may call for a sudden supply of money to carry them through any important expedition."[47]

The monetary revolution that happened in Massachusetts not only created modern currency. It should also be considered as one of the many beginnings of the intellectual movement that created the modern world.

Notes

Preface

1. The main part of chapter 1 in Goldberg (2002) was published as Goldberg (2012).

2. See Goldberg (2009); see also Goldberg (2011), Goldberg and Milchtaich (2013).

3. The historical section of chapter 1 in Goldberg (2002) was published as Goldberg (2005).

Chapter One

1. Hakluyt ([1600] 1904) XI 123.

2. California Department of Parks and Recreation (n.d.), Bancroft Library, BANC PIC 19xx.031:072–OBJ VAULT.

3. Moody and Simmons (1988) 412.

4. E.g., Board of Governors of the Federal Reserve System (n.d.), Bank of England (2020). See also Friedman and Friedman (1980) 248 and Hurst (1973) 40.

5. MAGC V 158.

6. Sylla (1982) 23–25.

7. Rosenberg (1969).

8. Mokyr (1990).

9. Steele (1986).

10. E.g., Breen (1980), Sylla (1982) 25, McCusker and Menard (1991).

11. Sewall VI 366.

12. Bailyn (1955).

Chapter Two

1. Mokyr (1990) 151–52.
2. U.S. Currency Education Program (2017).
3. Greif (1993).
4. Hanson (1979) 285.
5. Hanson (1979) 285.
6. Ellis (1934) 11, Goldberg (2012).
7. McCusker (1978) 8.
8. G. Davies (2016).
9. Pers. comm., 2008.
10. Sylla (1982) 21–22.
11. Chalmers (1893) 7–8.
12. Hanson (1979) 285–86, Sylla (1982).
13. Rosenberg (1969).
14. Mokyr (1990).
15. Mokyr (2002) ch. 2.

Chapter Three

1. Breen (1980) 70.
2. Wrightson (1982, 2011, 2017), T. Smith ([1583] 1906), Harrison ([1587] 1876), the latter two at archive.org. Biographies: EB, ODNB.
3. Redlich (1908) II 203–7, D'Ewes (1682) 396.
4. J. Bruce (1810) I 112–13.
5. Morison (1965) 18–21, Mullinger (1888) 117–18.
6. E.g., Great Britain ([1810–1828] 1963) IV-I 481, 490, 494.
7. Ruding (1840) I, *passim*.
8. T. Smith ([1583] 1906) 32, R. C. Winthrop (1864) 133, Muldrew (1998) 33–34, 84.
9. Outhwaite (1982) 23–25.
10. Ruding (1840) I, *passim*.
11. E.g., Ruding (1840) I 296–98, 302–3, 310, 339, Desan (2014) 93–94, 126, 145–46, 270.
12. Clapham (1944) I 16, Feavearyear (1963) 29, Horsefield (1960) 96 ch. 11, Desan (2014) 311–13.
13. Desan (2014) 286.
14. Oxford English Dictionary, s.v. "solider," "solidus," "sold," "sol," accessed 2022, https://www.oed.com/.
15. More ([1516] 1684) 101–4.

16. Harrison ([1587] 1876) 40–41, Great Britain ([1810–1828] 1963) IV-I 617.

17. Ruding (1840) I, 333, 335, 341, 346–47, G. Davies (2016) 213–14.

18. Schumpeter (1954) 55–56, Aristotle (1885) 16 (book I, ch. 9), Aristotle (1895) 130 (book V, ch. V).

19. Charlton (1906), Einzig (1966) 216–17, 250–51, Sargent and Velde (2002) 219–22, del Mar (1901) 182.

20. Charlton (1906) 322, Einzig (1966) 236–37.

21. Camden (1614) 198.

22. Polo (1579) 66.

23. Muldrew (1998) 315. This section is based on his ch. 4, unless otherwise noted.

24. Desan (2014) ch. 5.

25. Compare Muldrew (1998) ch. 3–4 with Richards (1929), Horsefield (1960, 1977), Desan (2014) 245n53.

26. Loyd (1916).

27. E.g., Great Britain ([1810–1828] 1963) IV–I 727, IV–II 919, 1167, 1168, 1172.

28. E.g., Thorpe (1909) I 49–57.

29. E.g., Great Britain ([1810–1828] 1963) IV–I 727.

30. Kerridge (1988) 40–42.

31. Holden (1955) ch. IV, J. S. Rogers (1995) ch. 8.

32. de Roover (1948) ch. 4, Kerridge (1988).

33. Richards (1929) 93.

34. de Roover (1948) 57. The figures here follow Neal (1990) 6, 8.

35. Muldrew (1998) ch. 5.

36. Muldrew (1998) 58.

37. Miller (1939) ch. XIII.

38. Great Britain ([1810–1828] 1963) IV–II 1028.

39. Parker (1988), Bonney (1999).

40. Van der Wee (1977) 358–75, 381.

41. Parker (1972).

42. Richards (1929) 58–59.

43. Desan (2014) ch. 4C.

44. T. Smith ([1583] 1906) 77, 96.

45. See Hanson (1979, 1980) for pioneering studies emphasizing the importance of low denominations for money, and Horsefield (1977) for a general discussion of such claims. The claim was applied to tallies by Desan (2014) ch. 4C, and is discussed on p. 37.

46. Desan (2014) 172.

Chapter Four

1. Wrightson (2011), Churchill (1966) II, III at archive.org. Biographies: ODNB.
2. Laughton (1894) II 95–97.
3. Ruding (1840) I 354–59, Desan (2014) ch. 7A.
4. G. Davies (2016) 215, Ruding (1840) I 369–71, 378, 381, 387, 389.
5. Kelly (1991) I 69.
6. Yonge (1848) 97–116.
7. Spufford (1995).
8. Richards (1929) 35–37, 93–95.
9. Gardiner (1900) IX 130–36, 157.
10. Richards (1929) 35–36, Birch (1848) II 287, CSPD-C 1640, 451, 543–44, CSPD-C 1640–1641, 524.
11. Gardiner (1900) IX 170–72, 202–3, CSPD-C 1640, 491–92, 521–22.
12. Churchill (1966) II 210.
13. Churchill (1966) II 212.
14. Tradition: CSPD-W 1689–1690, 273. Plan: Prendergast (1868) 67–69.
15. Royal Mint (n.d.).
16. Gardiner (1905) I–III, *passim*.
17. Churchill (1966) II 264.
18. BBC News Channel (2008).
19. Churchill (1966) II 307.
20. Capp (1989) 275–92, Firth (1909) II 257.
21. Nuttall (1964) 131–32.
22. Churchill (1966) II 323.
23. Gentles (1973) 633–34.
24. Churchill (1966) II 326.
25. Firth and Rait (1911) I 8, 940, 1051, II 140.
26. Gentles (1980) 573, Prendergast (1868), Gardiner (1906) 281, 300, 303, 396–98.
27. Gentles (1973, 1980).
28. Firth and Rait (1911) II 182.
29. Gentles (1973, 1980), Capp (1989) 277–81.
30. Gentles (1980) 586–87.
31. Nuttall (1964) 121–34, Firth and Rait (1911) I 940, 1127, II 997.
32. Richards (1929) 35–39.
33. Richards (1929) 233–36, Horsefield (1960) ch. 9, Wennerlind (2011) 67–75, Mokyr (2016) 194n18.
34. Boyne and Williamson (1889–1891).
35. Nuttall (1964) 134–39, Anonymous (1665).
36. Pincus (2009).

37. S. Quinn (1997), esp. p. 420, Richards (1929) ch. 2, esp. p. 51.

38. Wetterberg (2009) 25–45. Denomination: Montelius (1915). Wage: Edvinsson (2010) I 163, 176.

39. Beresford (1925) ch. 12, Chandaman (1975) 216–17, 297, Feavearyear (1963) 111. Denominations: PRO T 60/35. Wage: Clark (2021).

40. Feavearyear (1963) 113, Desan (2014) ch. 6, PRO T 60/35, E 403/2768, E 403/2801.

41. Killigrew (1690), Forde (1666) 2, 4.

42. J. D. Davies (1991) 82, Pepys (1893) VI 366–68, quotation on 366.

43. Horsefield (1960) ch. 9–10, Horsefield (1966), A. M. Davis (1901) II 26–27.

44. Churchill (1966) III 21.

45. Stevenson (1967).

46. CSPD-W 1689–90, 273, 459, CSPD-W 1690–91, 130, 242, 328, 370.

47. Churchill (1966) III 19.

48. Horsefield (1960), Dickson (1967), North and Weingast (1989).

49. Clapham (1944) I 16, Horsefield (1960) 126.

50. Webster (1974).

51. Hobbes ([1651] 1909) 193–94.

52. Barbon ([1690] 1903) 1, 16–18.

53. Merton (1970), Shapin (1996), Mokyr (2016).

54. Czartoryski (1985) 169–215, Mokyr (2016) 204, 208.

55. Rait (1900) 48–54.

56. Wennerlind (2011) ch. 1–2.

57. Demos (2008) 35–39, 44.

58. Hobbes ([1651] 1909) 17, 88, 342, Great Britain ([1810–1828] 1963) V 228.

59. Mokyr (2016) 92n39, 255n11.

60. Mokyr (2016) ch. 8.

61. Forbes (1943–1947) V 222.

62. Wennerlind (2011) ch. 2.

Part II Introduction

1. Bailyn (2012).

2. Quotation from McCusker and Menard (1991) 147–48.

Chapter Five

1. General facts for every English colony's founding and early history are in the classic Andrews (1934). Biographies: ODNB.

2. D. B. Quinn (1955, 1985) is the authoritative source.

3. D. B. Quinn (1955) 101–3.

4. D. B. Quinn (1955) 209, de Bry (1590) 23, figures VI, VII, VIII, XXI.

5. D. B. Quinn (1955) 260.

6. Mallios and Emmett (2004). Inspiration comes from Mauss ([1925] 1966) and Polanyi (1944). See also Peterson (2019) 44–45.

7. D. B. Quinn (1955) 266, 276, 282, 285, 383–84.

8. D. B. Quinn (1955) 279.

9. D. B. Quinn (1955) 281, 284.

10. D. B. Quinn (1970) 273–75.

11. Hening (1823) I 61–62, 64, 71.

12. Hening (1823) I 96–97, 109.

13. Tyler (1907) 12–14, Smith I l–li, 22, 66, 75, 78, 80, 135, Strachey (1849) 57, 67, 68, 89, 96, Percy (1922) 263.

14. Tyler (1907) 13, Smith I 19, 22, 46, 66, 75, 78, 80, 102, 118, Strachey (1849) 68, 89, 96, 109.

15. Smith I 46, II 418, 518–19 (compare Hamor ([1615] 1957) 41–42).

16. Einzig (1966) 555.

17. Hamor ([1615] 1957) 41, Smith I 74.

18. Smith I cv, cvii, cxii, cxiii, 26, 46, 75–77, 80–81, Strachey (1849) 55, 61, 103–4, 111, 114, Hamor ([1615] 1957) 41–42.

19. Smith I cviii, cx.

20. Smith I cxi, 65, II 418, Strachey (1849) 78, 113.

21. On Percy see Smith I xiii, D. B. Quinn (1970) 272.

22. Tyler (1907) 12, Smith I xliii, xlv, lxxvi, cxi, 7, 9, 29, 102–3, 148.

23. Hiring: Tyler (1907) 11–12, Smith I xliii, lxxxvi, 14, 37, 132.

24. Barter: Smith I lxxxii, lxxxv, lxxxvii, 9–10, 27, 32, 96, 101, 128, 140–41, 147, 167, 170, Percy (1922) 266. Monetary: Smith I lxxvi, 23, 100, 125, Strachey (1849) 48.

25. Smith I lxxxiii–lxxxiv, 32, 122, 125 and 168, Strachey (1849) 80.

26. Smith I xcvi, ciii, civ (thrice), cix, 9, 11, 20, 27, 39, 130 (twice), 135, 141, 146, 151 (cf. Matthew 26:15), 153, 163, Percy (1922) 262.

27. Smith I 101, 163, II 443.

28. Glass: Smith I xliii, lviii, lxiv, 6 (because early); 28, 103 (because blue). Unspecified: Smith I civ, 130, 142, 146–47. Archeology: Historic Jamestowne (n.d.c).

29. Smith I 101, 130 (twice), 133–47, Kingsbury (1906–1935) III 19.

30. Smith I 84, 170.

31. Mallios and Emmett (2004), Smith II 503, Tyler (1907) 212–13, Strachey (1849) 19, 38, 69, 103–5, 123–24, Hamor ([1615] 1957) 12–15, 42, 56–57.

32. Smith I civ, cix, Hamor ([1615] 1957) 5.

33. Kingsbury (1906–1935) I 423, III 96–98, 157, 178, 196, 300, 386, 403, 495, 672, IV 23–24, 98–99, 473.

34. Mallios and Emmett (2004), Lapham (2001) sec. 2.3.

35. Smith I 94–95, 103–4, 127–28.

36. Force (1844) III, item 2, p. 13–14.

37. Historic Jamestowne (n.d.a., n.d.b.).

38. Force (1844) III, item 2, p. 18–19, 25.

39. Smith I lxxxiii, 146–47, 149, 166, Hamor ([1615] 1957) 36.

40. Mokyr (2016) 145.

41. General information on the tobacco-based economy and society of Virginia is in Morgan (1975) and Walsh (2010), and best summarized in McCusker and Menard (1991) ch. 6.

42. Rolf (1848) 108, Virginia (1874) 77.

43. Rolf (1848) 107, Smith II 543, P. A. Bruce (1896) I 512–25.

44. Smith II 527, 535.

45. Nettels (1934) 225–26.

46. Smith I 64, McIlwaine (1915) 58, McCusker and Menard (1991) 132.

47. Sylla (1982) 25.

48. Smith II 542, Wyatt (1927a) 127, Wyatt (1927b) 246, Wyatt (1928a) 56, McIlwaine (1915) viii.

49. Kingsbury (1906–1935) III 94.

50. Kingsbury (1906–1935) III 101, 103, 104, 108, Virginia (1874) 16.

51. Smith II 538, 541, Kingsbury (1906–1935) III 78.

52. Virginia (1874) 20, 25–28, 31.

53. Smith II 594, 598.

54. Hening (1823) I 123–28, Wyatt (1927a) 125–28, Wyatt (1927b) 248–53, Wyatt (1928a) 51, 54–56, Kingsbury (1935) IV 65. Bermuda: Lefroy (1877) 279.

55. Kingsbury (1906–1935) III 78, Nettels (1934) 219–20.

56. Wyatt (1928b) 166.

57. Waters (1884) 69.

58. Hening (1823) I 143.

59. Smith II 588, 590, 599–600, Hening (1823) I 127–28.

60. J. A. Williamson (1926) 53, 55, 84–85.

61. Carr (1913) 55.

62. Prowse (1895) 95, 99n2, 100n1.

63. Lefroy (1877) 59, Lefroy (1882) 26, 37, 68, 81–82.

64. Lefroy (1877) 98.

65. Lefroy (1877) 113.

66. Smith II 653, Lefroy (1882) 76.

67. Lefroy (1877) 100–101, Crosby (1875) 17–18, Jordan (1999).

68. Lefroy (1877) 120ff.

69. Lefroy (1877) 275, 312, 342–43.

70. Smith II 670.

71. Lefroy (1877) 280, 310.

72. Lefroy (1877) 271–72, 385, 476, 482, 483 (twice).

73. Lefroy (1877) 176–77, 271–73, 487.

74. Bradford (1908) 146–47.

75. Jameson (1909) 86.

76. Bradford (1908) 158, quotation on 175.

77. Bradford (1908) 211, 228, Plymouth Records XII 7–8, 14–17, Jameson (1909) 113.

78. Bradford (1908) 228.

79. Bradford (1908) 116–17.

80. Bradford (1908) 231–32.

81. Bradford (1908) 228, 234–36.

82. Jameson (1909) 106–9.

83. Francis (1986), Jameson (1909) 71, 77, 106, 107, 130.

84. Jameson (1909) 110, Bradford (1908) 234–36.

85. Jameson (1909) 84, 130, Hastings (1901) I 62.

86. Champlain (1925–1936) V 23, 63–70, 80, 233–34, 297–98, 324, VI 27, 248–49.

87. Champlain (1925–1936) V 23, 30, 35, 48, 50, 233–34, 303, 320, 327, VI 32, 38, 68.

88. Champlain (1925–1936) VI 57, 60, 64, 75, 82, 84, 112, 147.

89. See the exhaustive list of references in Grubb (2012), n1.

90. Grubb (2012). Similarly Muldrew (1998) 91.

91. E.g., Thorpe (1909) I 69–76, III 1845.

92. Cf. Desan (2014) 162–63.

93. Grubb (2012) 3.

94. McCusker and Menard (1991) 341.

Chapter Six

1. Emerson (1976) xvii.

2. Andrews (1934) I, ch. XVII. For biographies of Warwick and others below, see ODNB or ANB.

3. MAGC I 12–14. These are the main printed records of the Massachusetts General Court.

4. ODNB: Richard Bellingham, William Pynchon, William Coddington, Theophilius Eaton, Roger Ludlow, John Humfrey.

5. Woodward (2010).

6. Breen (1980) 74.

7. Young (1846) 357n2.

8. Miller (1939) ch. XIII–XV, Breen (1980) 34–36.

9. Andrews (1934) I 447–48.

10. MAGC I 223, also 225, J. Winthrop (1908) I 315–18, Andrews (1934) I 449, Bailyn (1955) 20–21.

11. Force (1844) III, item 9.

12. Emerson (1976) 107, 225.

13. J. Winthrop (1908) I 165, 168–69, 178–80, II 23–24, 33.

14. Emerson (1976) 109.

15. Emerson (1976) 230, J. Winthrop (1908) I 293, Roden (1905) 13–17, 145–83.

16. Force (1844) III, item 9, p. 12, J. Winthrop (1908) I 266–68, 277, II 8.

17. J. Winthrop (1908) I 294, II 42, 155-6, 219, 246.

18. Emerson (1976) 228, Boston Records II 5, 10, IV 8, MAGC I 157, 181, 196, 228, J. Winthrop (1908) I 180, 219, 226, Bailyn (1955) 28–29.

19. Emerson (1976) 64, J. Winthrop (1908) I 127–28, 131, 272, Bailyn (1955) 46–47. The best summary of the New England economy remains the classic McCusker and Menard (1991) ch. 5.

20. Emerson (1976), *passim.*

21. Dunn (1984) 159–60.

22. J. Winthrop (1908) I, *passim.*

23. Peterson (2019) 39–41, citing Grafe (2003).

24. Andrews (1934) I 372–73, 377–80, 444–45, J. Winthrop (1908) I 133, 324.

25. Andrews (1934) I ch. XIX, J. Winthrop (1908) I 221, 224, 274–75, 278, 300–301, 307, Emerson (1976) 220–23.

26. Andrews (1934) I ch. XX, J. Winthrop (1908) I 124–25.

27. Miller (1939) ch. XV.

28. Later examples: J. Winthrop (1908) II 88 and 91, (Briscoe), 177.

29. McCusker (2006) 651, MAGC I 366–77.

30. R. R. Johnson (1981) 7, 10, Bailyn (1955) 159–60, Breen (1980) 44.

31. MAGC I 120, 140–41, 181, 188, 190, 213, 223, 274.

32. MAGC I 222, 279, J. Winthrop (1908) I 151, 323–24.

33. MAGC I 30, 34, 52–64.

34. Andrews (1934) I ch. XX.

35. MAGC I, *passim,* J. Winthrop (1908) I 54, 132, 149, 262–63.

36. Boston Records II, IV, *passim,* Dow (1911) I 23, J. Winthrop (1908) I 319.

37. E.g., MAGC I 138, 92, 223, 106, respectively.

38. MAGC I 124–25, similarly 188, 195, 197.

39. Emerson (1976) 116, J. Winthrop (1908) II 121, MAGC II 95. Deputies: MAGC I 120ff.

40. Towns: Breen (1980) 86.

41. MAGC I 145ff.

42. MAGC I 124ff.

43. E.g., MAGC I 92.

44. Generally, MAGC I 124ff. Treasurer: MAGC I 136, 149, 224, 237, 240, 290.

45. Peterson (2019) 84.

46. J. Winthrop (1908) I 60, 123, Emerson (1976) 203–4.

47. Bremer (2020).

48. J. Winthrop (1908) II 83.

49. MAGC I 91, 140.

50. Emerson (1976) 75n.

51. J. Winthrop (1908) I 16, 60, Emerson (1976) 55.

52. Bremer (2005) 187, J. Winthrop (1908) I 53 (twice), 54, 67, 83, 113, 115, 124, 137, 194, 279.

53. Orr (1897) 51.

Chapter Seven

1. Bolton (1919) II 459, Smith II 809, 969–71.

2. R. C. Winthrop (1864) 284–87.

3. J. Winthrop (1908) I 24, 36.

4. Boston Records II 2–52, Breen (1980) 51, 61–62.

5. MAGC I 264.

6. Breen (1980) 86.

7. MAGC I 73–77.

8. MAGC I 96, 140, 179.

9. J. Winthrop (1908) I 176, 185, 305, MAGC I 201, 252.

10. Boston Records II 33, 39, Frothingham (1846) 23.

11. MAGC I, Boston Records II, IV, VI, Suffolk Deeds I, Dow (1911) I, Dow (1916) I, Lechford (1885), Young (1846) 378–87.

12. Emerson (1976) 27, Young (1846) 351, MAGC I 65–66.

13. Emerson (1976) 49, 53, 58, 88, 116, 179.

14. J. Winthrop (1908) I 161, 272 (customs), II 6, 9–10. Cf. Emerson (1976) 107.

15. J. Winthrop (1908) I 309–10, Kupperman (1993) 313. Spanish coins: Peterson (2019) 90–91, 101–2.

16. MAGC I 83, 92, 93, 180 (explained in p. 142).

17. MAGC I 73–77, 104, 165, Boston Records II 55.

18. J. Winthrop (1908) I 237, 238, MAGC I 203, 268, Suffolk Deeds I 17, 24, 26, 37, 47, 69, Boston Records VI 2–3, Dow (1911) I 5n, 16, 17, 22, Dow (1916) I 5, 144.

19. MAGC I 92.

20. MAGC I 131, J. Winthrop (1908) I 64, 76.

21. MAGC I 140.

22. MAGC I 200.

23. MAGC I 294.

24. Nettels (1934) 209.

25. MAGC I 180.

26. J. Winthrop (1908) I 89.

27. J. Winthrop (1908) II 31, 92.

28. Bailyn (1955) 26–29.

29. Young (1846) 379, Emerson (1976) 31, J. Winthrop (1908) I 60–65, 138–40, 187, MAGC I 88, 89, 143, 179.

30. MAGC I 76, 140, 388.

31. J. Winthrop (1908) II 19.

32. Bailyn (1955) 27.

33. J. Winthrop (1908) I, *passim*, Boston Records II 5, 6, 47, IV 1–2, 38, Force (1844) III, item 9, pp. 7, 8, Emerson (1976) 108, 136, 225, Young (1846) 350.

34. MAGC I 277, Dow (1916) I 11, Boston Records IV 8, 16, 22.

35. MAGC I 74, Emerson (1976) 99, Boston Records II 55, Suffolk Deeds I 14, 15, 47, Dow (1916) 107, 144.

36. MAGC I 295, also 303.

37. Boston Records II 3, MAGC I 172.

38. MAGC I 91, 96, 97, 100, 102, 114, 120, 130, 141, 147, 149, 206, 229, 240, 261, 262, 263, 276, 278, 289, 292, 295, 398.

39. MAGC I 114, 146.

40. Dow (1911) I 15, Dow (1916) I 4–5, J. Winthrop (1908) I 322.

41. MAGC I 294, J. Winthrop (1908) I 309–10.

42. Bailey (1675), s.v. "to pay."

43. MAGC I 137, J. Winthrop (1908) I 148.

44. Ruding (1840) I 387; see also p. 39.

45. MAGC I 75, 196, II 16, 124, Dow (1916) I 30, Hening (1823) I 301, Champlain (1925–1936) V 52–53.

46. Forbes (1943–1947) III 149ff., MAGC I 84, 85.

47. MAGC I 125, Dow (1916) I 5.

48. J. Winthrop (1908) I 68, 109, 115, 129, 131, 138–40.

49. W. Wood ([1639] 1764) 72.

50. Forbes (1943–1947) III 267, 269, 286, 314, 319, MAGC I 179, Dow (1916) I 5.

51. In general: Mokyr (2016) 20–21.

52. Fernow (1892) 262–64, Peterson (2019) 53.

53. Similarly, Peterson (2019) 98.

54. Orr (1897), J. Winthrop (1908) I 186–231.

55. MAGC I 208, Peterson (2019) 52.

56. See amending and repealing legislation later than 1637: O'Callaghan (1868) 26, Plymouth Records XI 57. Few earlier laws survived from Plymouth and none from New Netherland.

57. MAGC I 211, 221, 224–25, 233–34, 242, 266, 267, 275, 286, 292, 296, 297, 299, 300.

58. Lechford (1885), Suffolk Deeds I, Dow (1911) I, Dow (1916) I, MAGC I 96, 154.

59. Bailyn (1955) ch. 2.

60. Breen (1980) ch. IV.

61. McCusker and Menard (1991) 104.

62. Lechford (1885).

63. Treasurer: MAGC I 129, 182, 204, 353. Elite: J. Winthrop (1908) I 102, 130, MAGC I 157, 165, 167, 257, 292. Constables: MAGC I 160, 179.

64. MAGC I 165, 179.

65. MAGC I 125, 141, 206.

66. MAGC I 84.

67. MAGC I 272–73.

68. MAGC I 130–32, 141, 157, 179, 182, 206, 210 (with 228), 215, 230, 243, 245 (twice), 257, 289, 292.

69. Emerson (1976), *passim*, Forbes (1943–1947), *passim*, J. Winthrop (1908) I 314, MAGC I 142.

70. MAGC I 82, 84–85, 133, 198, 218, 242, Dow (1911) I 18.

71. MAGC I 198–99 (Anderson), 92, 212 (Howe), Colonial Society of Massachusetts (1925) 17 (towns' rates).

72. MAGC I 90.

73. MAGC I 90.

74. P. R. Wood (1989).

75. MAGC I 90.

76. Dow (1916) I 144, Suffolk Deeds I 17, 47 (thrice), MAGC I 150. Wage calculated from MAGC I 109.

77. MAGC I 73, 104, 112–14, 139, 154 (twice), 292, 293, Boston Records II 38, 55.

78. MAGC I 76, 77, 109. Earlier: Wyatt (1927b) 246, Lefroy (1877) 304.

79. MAGC I 74, 158.

80. Andrews (1934) I 377–1, quotation on 380.

81. Einzig (1966) 203–6, 211–14.

82. MAGC I 73–77, 154, 294, Boston Records II 55.

83. J. Winthrop (1908) I 120, 159, 263.

84. J. Winthrop (1908) I 189, MAGC I 188.

85. MAGC I 192, 195, IV-II 133.

86. MAGC I 180, 209, 225, 232, 260, 261, 263, 294, 327, J. Winthrop (1908) I 187, II 4.

87. J. Winthrop (1908) I 186–89, 225–28, Orr (1897), *passim*.

88. MAGC I 216.

89. MAGC I 225, 240, IV-I 332, 355 (Starre), IV-II 140.

90. Grants to Patrick, Traske, Davenport, Gallop, Gibbons, and Wilson, and their aftermath: MAGC I 179, 262, 263, 289, II 241–42, IV-I 381, 402–3, 442–43,

IV-II 104, 308–9. Their service: MAGC I 193, 215, 222, J. Winthrop (1908) I 183–84, 186, Bradford (1908) 342.

91. MAGC I 188. Biographical details of these men and others in the following chapters are in Savage (1860–1862), and court membership is also in MAGC, *passim*.

92. MAGC I 195.

93. MAGC I 261, 423 (editor's interpretation).

94. MAGC I 184 (and 183).

95. MAGC I 215, 222.

96. MAGC I 200.

97. McCartney (2007) 371–73.

98. Hening (1823) I 155–70, 216.

99. Ripley (1893–1894) 110–11, P. A. Bruce (1896) II 499, Massey (1976) 18–20.

100. Hening (1823) I 220, 222.

101. McIlwaine (1915) 55.

102. CSPC 1574–1660, 238–39.

103. McIlwaine (1915) 57–65.

104. P. A. Bruce (1896) I 453.

105. CSPC 1574–1660, 99–100, 116, 117, 129, 151, 160.

106. Hening (1823) I 203–7, specifically 204.

107. Ripley (1893–1894) 145, White (1895) 7–8, P. A. Bruce (1896) I 305–7.

108. P. A. Bruce (1896) I 290–92, J. A. Williamson (1926) 99–101, Lefroy (1877) 243, 440, Bridenbaugh and Bridenbaugh (1972) 15–16, 63–65, Israel (1989) 115, de Vries (1853) 49–54.

109. Boddie (1933), Boddie (1938) I 14, 29–30, Hening (1823) I 139, 169, 187.

110. Ripley (1893–1894) 146, Massey (1976) 18.

111. Hening (1823) I 206.

112. Hening (1823) I 209–15, 221.

113. CSPC 1574–1660, 175, 184, 262.

114. McIlwaine (1915) 57–64.

115. Lapsley (1900) 278–82.

116. Browne (1904) 114.

117. J. A. Williamson (1926) 86, 92, 143.

118. CSPC 1574–1660, 123, Kupperman (1993), *passim*.

Chapter Eight

1. MAGC I, II, IV-I, *passim*.

2. MAGC IV-I 12–14.

3. MAGC I 320–25, 332, II 71, IV-I 70, 175, 315–16, 395–96.

4. J. Winthrop (1908) II 100–105.

5. J. Winthrop (1908) II, *passim*.

6. O. A. Roberts (1895) I 22, R. R. Johnson (1991) 12, MAGC IV-I 355–56.

7. J. Winthrop (1908) II 19, 31.

8. J. Winthrop (1908) II 49, 164, 218, MAGC II 58–59, 95, 259–60.

9. J. Winthrop (1908) II 118, MAGC I 320.

10. MAGC I 346, II 67, 88–89, 216–17, 231, 285, J. Winthrop (1908) II 49, 223.

11. Whitmore (1890) 35, 45.

12. MAGC II 57, 117, 197, 208, 222, IV-I 10, 335–36.

13. Andrews (1934) I 459–61.

14. Farrand (1929) xiii–xiv.

15. MAGC IV-I 152, 202.

16. MAGC II 90–96.

17. MAGC II 31, 38, 39, 46, 74, IV-I 44–45, 196, J. Winthrop (1908) II 98, 235–37.

18. ODNB.

19. J. Winthrop (1908) II 7–8, 39–40, 73–74, 94–95, 167–68.

20. J. Winthrop (1908) II 159.

21. J. Winthrop (1908) II 208, 252–53, MAGC IV-I 10, 61–63, 69.

22. J. Winthrop (1908) II 35, 70, 164, 197, 199, 206, 246, 248, 275, 322.

23. Bailyn (1955) ch. IV.

24. Peterson (2019) 75–79.

25. MAGC II 131, 168, 214 (Middlesex), 240, 253, 169, 173, IV-I 40–41, 86, 105, 145–46, 195, 198, 222, J. Winthrop (1908) II 106, 206, 248.

26. MAGC II 30, 31, 38, 41, 46, 85, 88–89, IV-I 21, 145–46, 195, J. Winthrop (1908) II 71, 74, 79, 106, 109, 116–17, 132, 133, 140, 172, 174–75, 176.

27. Morison (1965), MAGC II 167, IV-I 12–14, 100–101, 205.

28. MAGC IV-I 104, 233–34, 259, J. Winthrop (1908) II 18, Bailyn (1955) 74.

29. MAGC II 203, IV-I 321, 382, IV-II 257–60, J. Winthrop (1908) II 166, 240, Whitmore (1890) 55, Demos (2008) 104–10.

30. J. Winthrop (1908) II 6, 17, Baxter (1884) III 218.

31. MAGC I 304, 307, 326.

32. J. Winthrop (1908) II 228.

33. J. Winthrop (1908) II 19, 31, 82, 92.

34. MAGC I 332, 333 (twice), II 75, 86.

35. MAGC I 303–4, 307, 319, 326, 340, II 27, 32, 45, 51.

36. MAGC II 31, 199, 277, J. Winthrop (1908) II 80, 89.

37. J. Winthrop (1908) II 23. Again, the best summary of these developments is in McCusker and Menard (1991) ch. 5.

38. J. Winthrop (1908) II, *passim*, MAGC II 129, 218, 247–48, Gottfried (1936), Bailyn (1955) ch. IV.

39. McCusker and Menard (1991) 92.

40. Peterson (2019) 43, 98–100, 110–13, 168.

41. Nettels (1934) 223. Similarly, Desan (2014) 201.

42. J. Winthrop (1908) II 55–56, 248, MAGC II 79, 83, IV-I 189–90, 196, 282, T. Hutchinson (1795) I 164.

43. MAGC IV-I 66, 132, 227–28.

44. For a theoretical model of commodity money between three locations, see Goldberg (2007).

45. J. Winthrop (1908) II 328.

46. MAGC II 20, 29.

47. Bailyn (1955) 61–71.

48. MAGC III 92.

49. MAGC II 262.

50. MAGC IV-I 26, 63, 132, 253.

51. MAGC II 130–31, IV-I 354, 410, Bailyn (1955) 49–57, Boston Records XXXII, *passim*.

52. MAGC II 102, 184, IV-I 49, 186, 272, 283 (Hubbard and Burt petitions; on Burt, see 65), 337 (buy), 402, 420–21.

53. MAGC I 306–7, IV-I, 22, 101, 288.

54. MAGC I 302, II 27, 48.

55. MAGC I 322–23, II 261, 279, IV-I 36, Plymouth Records IX 136–37.

56. MAGC II 262.

57. Plymouth Records IX 107, X 251, MAGC II 231, 240, IV-I 313 (Woodde, p. 294), Felt (1839) 25, 37.

58. MAGC IV-I 296.

59. MAGC II 100–101, 164, IV-I 262.

60. MAGC II 130–31, 215, 246–47, 324.

61. MAGC II 104, IV-I 47.

62. Morison (1936) I 102–5. Also Bailyn (1955) 60–61.

63. MAGC II 211.

64. A. Smith ([1776] 1998) 44–45.

65. MAGC IV-I 39–40, 392.

66. MAGC IV-I 348, cf. Desan (2014) 263.

67. MAGC II 261, Weeden (1884) 28–29.

68. Hull (1857) 145, 282, Andros Tracts II 115, Peterson (2019) 102–4.

69. Crosby (1875) 30–31.

70. Andros Tracts II 115.

71. MAGC IV-I 84–85. On Hull and the mint in general: Jordan (2002).

72. Barth (2014) 495–96, 507.

73. MAGC IV-I 197.

74. MAGC IV-I 111, 182, 195, 205, 220, 296.

75. MAGC IV-I 197–98, Felt (1839) 32, 35–36.

76. E.g., J. Winthrop (1908) II 38, MAGC II 161, 185 (twice), 218, IV-I 31, 44, 46, 88–89, 183, 281–82.

77. J. Winthrop (1908) II 220–21.

78. MAGC IV-I 220, 232, 282, 314, 342, 427.

79. MAGC II 214, applied in II 266–67, IV-I 9, 20, 51, 244.

80. MAGC II 141–44.

81. MAGC I 303, II 80, 116, 278, 288, IV-I 56, 74–75, 112, 202–3, 220, 253, 277, 310.

82. MAGC II 47, 53, 77, 124, 165 (treasurer), 280, IV-I 165, 205–6, 216.

83. Dow (1916) I 34, 36, 159, 243, 268, 274, 275–76, MAGC II 27. Larger bills: Suffolk Deeds I–III, Boston Records XXXII, *passim*.

84. Single: Suffolk Deeds I 35, 64, 139–40, 190, II 180–82. Split: Suffolk Deeds II 176, III 210.

85. Farrand (1929) 4.

86. Suffolk Deeds I 24, 42, II 46, also 144.

87. Suffolk Deeds III 371.

88. MAGC IV-I 202, 337, Suffolk Deeds III 137.

89. MAGC I 314, II 54, 79, 124, IV-I 112.

90. Nettels (1934) 212.

91. Suffolk Deeds I 96, 208–9, Bailyn (1955) 67–70.

92. Hull (1857) 282, MAGC II 181, Paine (1866) 35.

93. MAGC IV-I 85–86, Felt (1839) 33.

94. General Assembly (1924a, 1924b).

95. P. A. Bruce (1896) I 307.

96. Assembly (1901) 57.

97. Assembly (1901) 54–55, Hening (1823) I 262, 267–68.

98. Hening (1823) I 281.

99. ANB.

100. Hening (1823) I 308.

101. Ripley (1893–1894) 113, Hatfield (2004).

102. Hening (1823) I 309.

103. Ripley (1893–1894) 111, similarly McCusker (1978) 205.

104. Hening (1823) I 313.

105. McCusker (1978) 205.

106. Hening (1823) I 493.

107. Hening (1823) I 296, 314, Loyd (1916) 553–55.

108. Boxer (1957).

109. Boxer (1957) 67–68, 112–13.

110. Boxer (1957) 114, 118–19, 128–29, 146, 155, 157–58, Galante (2009) 249.

111. Abreu and Lago (2001) 333, fn. 16, Galante (2009) 251.

112. Boxer (1957) 150–52.

113. Galante (2009) 251.

114. Boxer (1957) 129–30.

115. J. Winthrop (1908) II, *passim*.

116. Oppenheim (1909).

117. CO 154/1, 30.

118. Oliver (1894–1899) I xx, xxv, xxvii.

119. Oliver (1894–1899) I xxiii–xxv.

120. Oliver (1894–1899) III 252, CMHS (1882) 226, 242.

121. Oliver (1894–1899) I, xxv.

122. For more examples of forced money in history, see Goldberg (2016).

123. Whitmore (1890) 33, Farrand (1929) 1.

124. MAGC II 22, 28, 168–69, 189, 196, 209, 217–18, 260, 262, 286, IV-I 6, 22–23, 23–24, 39, 47–48, 57, 105, 119, 127, 131, 151, 182, 278, 281, 292, 327, 422, J. Winthrop (1908) II 161, 177, Farrand (1929) xiv.

125. MAGC II 215, IV-I 65, 135, 147–48, 262, 328–29, 350–51, 369.

126. J. Winthrop (1908) II 31, 88, 92 (twice), 97, also implied in MAGC I 328, II 222.

127. MAGC I 83, 93, IV-I 197–98.

128. MAGC II 222, 247, 250.

129. McCusker and Menard (1991) 95 and ch. 16.

130. Hughes (1976) 19 (quotation), 99, 133.

131. In America: Whitmore (1890) 89n45, Nettels (1934) 211n18, Peterson (2019) 52, 95, 107.

132. Bridenbaugh and Bridenbaugh (1972) 329, Harlow (1926) 124.

133. Browne (1883–1964) III 365, 383–85.

Chapter Nine

1. MAGC IV-II 165–66, 118, 211–13, Bailyn (1955) ch. V, Barth (2014) 500–507.

2. R. R. Johnson (1981) ch. I.

3. Goldberg (2009) 1097–98, Barth (2014) 506–15, and references in both. See also Toppan and Goodrick (1898–1909) III 79, 96, 132, 229, MAGC V 200, 347, CO 1/41, 29, 50–51, CO 391/2, 103, 240–41.

4. CO 1/41, 50.

5. CO 1/47, 44.

6. E.g., CO 5/940, 138–39, CO 391/2, 104.

7. R. R. Johnson (1981) ch. I.

8. R. R. Johnson (1981) ch. I.

9. R. R. Johnson (1991) ch. II–III, private correspondence with Richard R. Johnson, February 16, 2009.

10. Bailyn (1955) 144–47, 155, 157, MAGC IV-II 67, Savage (1860–1862) IV 315.

11. Suffolk Deeds, *passim*.

12. MAGC IV-II 397, 410–11.

13. MAGC IV-II 425, 436–37, V 140, 170–71, 213, 238–39.

14. MAGC V 375, IV-II 515.

15. MAGC IV-II 176, 249–51.

16. MAGC IV-II 229–31, 234, 239, 274.

17. MAGC IV-II 544.

18. MAGC V 326–27.

19. MAGC IV-II 129.

20. T. Hutchinson (1865) II 265, CO 1/41, 34, CO 1/44, 61, CO 1/46, 123, 130, CO 391/4, p. 174–75.

21. T. Hutchinson (1865) II 262–64, MAGC V 303, 312, 334–35.

22. MAGC V 423, CO 1/54, 92, T. Hutchinson (1865) II 284.

23. Batchellor (1904–1922) I 2, 7–8, Belknap (1784) ch. VIII.

24. MAGC V 470–71, 516, Perley (1912) 64–92, Drake (1856) 456–57.

25. Lewis (1974), Miller (1953) 37.

26. MAGC V 408, 467–68, 472, Sewall V 77, 82, 94, 95, 116, 132.

27. Suffolk Deeds XIV 195–202, CO 5/856, 158XXIX.

28. R. R. Johnson (1981) 38n71.

29. MAGC IV-II 5, 27, 32, 39–40, 45, 48, 88, 150, 282, 300, 346, 427, 514, 565, V 15, 83, 244, 297, 341, 351–52, 416–17, 418, 427, 467 (twice), 484.

30. Mokyr (2016) ch. 12.

31. PMHS (1878) 212–51, Morison (1965) ch. X.

32. Woodward (2010) ch. 7, MAGC IV-II 144, V 388, Morison (1965) ch. X.

33. Wampum: MAGC IV-II 4, 54, 175–76, V 319–20, 461, Plymouth Records X, *passim*. Beaver: MAGC V 273, 401, 461–62, Bailyn (1955) 56, 60, Peterson (2019) 120–21, 133–34.

34. MAGC IV-II, V, *passim*.

35. MAGC IV-II 82, 349, 353, V 23, 231, 237, 246, 263, 269, 324, 352, 412, 456.

36. MAGC IV-II 132, Kellaway (1962) 73, Felt (1839) 40–44.

37. MAGC IV-II 420–21, V 292–93, 351.

38. Trumbull (1859) III 160, 189, Staughton, Nead, and McCamant (1879) 74, 145, Browne (1883–1964) II 286–87, Leaming and Spicer (1881) 285–86, and some references in Barth (2014) 497n14.

39. Abatement: MAGC IV-II 318, 328, 568, V 16, 45, 55, 81, 121, 139, 156, 219–20, 417. Forcing: Plymouth Records III 219, MAGC V 44 (repealed 45), 156, 195, 245, 296, 307, 324, 341, 376, 398, 417, 426, 443, 454, 505.

40. MAGC V 492–93.

41. MAGC V 307, 341, 398.

42. MAGC V 444, 483–84.

43. MAC 100:239.

44. Suffolk Deeds III–XIII.

45. Barth (2014) 514, also MAGC V 347.

46. MAGC V 351, 373.

47. Nettels (1934) 87–88n93.

48. Hull (1857).

49. Trumbull (1884) 267–75, Thomas (1874) I 86.

50. A. M. Davis (1910) I 109–12, 115–16.

51. A. M. Davis (1910) I 112–15, also Bailey (1675), s.v. "Fund."

52. A. M. Davis (1910) I 112–18.

53. A. M. Davis (1904), Suffolk Deeds XII 103, 142, 150–51, 213, 255–56, 333–34. Non-Boston grantor: Leavitt (1892) 144–45. Winthrop: Sibley (1873–1899) II 247–48.

54. A. M. Davis (1910) I 109.

55. Trumbull (1884) 268–69, 270n1, 286.

56. Douglas (1892) 44, A. M. Davis (1901) II 67, 72, A. M. Davis (1904) 256, A. M. Davis (1910) I 3–7, 118–19, Nettels (1934) 252, Bailyn (1955) 184, E. A. J. Johnson (1961), *passim*, Dorfman (1966) I 93–98, Horsefield (1966) 124–25, Newell (1998) 121–26, Priest (2001) 1313, Valeri (2010a) 145, Valeri (2010b) 559, Sklansky (2017) 45–46, K. A. Moore (2019) 14.

57. Goldberg (2021).

58. A. M. Davis (1910) I 111–12.

59. He was there until 1693 (Swift [1884] 114, 116), not 1677 (as in Savage [1860–1862] IV 292).

60. A. M. Davis (1910) I 115.

61. MAGC V 421–22.

62. Press: MAGC V 323–24, Thomas (1874) I 35, 86, Trumbull (1884) 266, Sewall V 57. Henchman, Sewall, and Hull: Sewall V 17, 24, 25, 29, 32, 33 (twice), 56, Hull (1857) 254–55n3, Suffolk Deeds X 12, 30.

63. Mokyr (1990) 49.

64. Usher (1954) 240.

65. PMHS (1919) 335.

66. MAGC V 452.

67. Kellaway (1962) ch. 4, 8, Suffolk Deeds X 236–38, XII 228–29, 237–41, XIII 54–56, 66–69. Richards: Colonial Society of Massachusetts (1925) clvi, Boston Records VII 40, 46, 53, 59, 66, 74.

68. London City Guildhall, New England Company Manuscripts, 7946/18.

69. Plymouth Records X 397, 399.

70. McLellan (1903) 23–24, Plymouth Records V 191.

71. MAGC II 213, IV-I 155.

72. MAGC V 45, 49, 65, 81, 120, 173–74, 188.

73. Peterson (2019) 161, 659, Breen (1980) 87–92.

74. MAGC V 51, 65, 71–73, 78–79, 81, 90, Plymouth Records X 401.

75. MAGC V 72, Plymouth Records X 401.

76. MAGC V 180, 203–4.

77. MAGC V 71, 85, 89, 90, 95–96, 123, Plymouth Records V 182–83.

78. MAGC V 51, 90, 427, Plymouth Records X 399.

79. MAGC V 66, 82, 206, 231, 412, MAC 100:259.

80. Peterson (2019) 127–28.

81. MAGC V 114, 122, 174, 188, 206, 283, 395 and 412 (Johnson), 471, 485. Probably war-related: MAGC V 104, 120, 146.

82. MAGC V 254, 484, 490, 515, probably also 206, 278, 278–79, 430.

83. MAGC V 324.

84. A. M. Davis (1901) II 26–29, CSPC 1661–1668, #183, 194, 265–66.

85. CSPC 1661–1668, #39, 344, 696, 759, 989I, 1186, 1476, Andrews (1934) III 184.

86. PMHS (1878) 212–20, Woodward (2010) 267–69, K. A. Moore (2019) 15.

87. Gragg (1993), CMHS (1882) 60–61, 240–50.

88. CMHS (1882) 246, 252, 265, Forbes (1943) III 244, 402, IV 3, 279, 284, 440, Bartlett (1856–1865) II 48.

89. CO 154/1, 30.

90. CO 1/25, 55, CO 1/34, 18, Leeward Islands (1734) 41, 53.

91. Gragg (1993), Oliver (1894–1899) I xxxviii, III 252, CMHS (1882) 135, 150, 250–65.

92. Leaming and Spicer (1881) 444, 445, Jordan (n.d.), Orosz and Augsburger (2009).

93. Kemmerer (1956) 109n7, Prowell (1886) 454, Nelson (1899) XXI 417.

94. A. M. Davis (1910) I 191.

95. Private correspondence, February 16, 2009.

96. MAGC IV-II 125, 548, MS 288, Felt (1845) I 226–27, A. M. Davis (1910) I 199, and Mather ([1702] 1820) I 162, the latter being the presumed author of the cited text (Trumbull [1884] 279).

97. Browne (1883–1964) I 414–15, Crosby (1875) 126–27.

98. Browne (1883–1964) I 444, II 286–87, V 271, Streeter (1858) 44–45, Crosby (1875) 128–29, Nettels (1934) 206, Andros Tracts II 115–16.

Chapter Ten

1. Barnes (1923), Lewis (1967) ch. VI–X, R. R. Johnson (1981) ch. II.

2. Lewis (1974).

3. PMHS (1899) 248–49.

4. Andros Tracts I 87, 114, 125, 138–42, 165–66, II 5, 48, III 124, 194.

5. Brodhead (1871) II 289, 317–18, 467, Belknap (1784) 101–2. Complaints: Andros Tracts I–III, *passim*.

6. Barth (2014) 516–19.

7. CMHS (1886) 52, 85–86, MAC 126:214a, Boston Records VII 187, Felt (1839) 48, Toppan and Goodrick (1898–1909) IV 163, 199.

8. Batchellor (1904–1922) I 159–60, 163–64.

9. Lewis (1967) 264–67, Andros Tracts I 38–39, 48, 50, 87–101, 123–24, 142–43, 205, III 21, MAC 127:176.

10. Andros Tracts I 49–50, 93–96, 99–101, II 234–35, III 137–39 (note), 141, Sewall V 217–19, T. Hutchinson (1865) II 271–72, 294–96, MAC 128:53–55, CMHS (1861) 178.

11. Barnes (1923) 188, Andros Tracts I 88–98, Trumbull (1859) III 422–23, Toppan (1900) 491–92, Tuttle (1919), CMHS (1861) 177–78.

12. Andros Tracts I 143–44, Batchellor (1904–1922) II 154.

13. Barnes (1923) 195–98, Andros Tracts I 99–101, 141, Sewall V 206, Hall, Leder, and Kammen (1964) 56–57, Trumbull (1859) III 427–29.

14. Sewall V 219, Batchellor (1904–1922) II 226–34.

15. Burrill (1850) I 332.

16. Andros Tracts I 92–99.

17. CO 1/65, 43.

18. MAC 129, *passim*.

19. Sewall V 219–21, 237, 251, CMHS (1868) 517–20.

20. Horsefield (1966).

21. A. M. Davis (1910) I 121–46.

22. PMHS (1899) 248–49, 272, MAC 126:103–7.

23. MAC 127:66–69, 129:55, Lewis (1967) 192, A. M. Davis (1907) 354–56, K. A. Moore (2019) 15–16.

24. North, Wallis, and Weingast (2009) ch. 2.

25. Davis (1907).

26. MAC 127:66–69, 129:55–62, A. M. Davis (1910) I 153–87, A. M. Davis (1907) 346–52.

27. Andros Tracts III 84–86, MAC 129:55 (back of page). Details on causality: Goldberg (2011).

28. A. M. Davis (1910) I 124, 126, 139, 141.

29. Andros Tracts I 142–44.

30. Details and a mathematical formulation of Andros's logic: Goldberg and Milchtaich (2013).

31. McCusker and Menard (1991) 190–91, 193.

32. Budd ([1685] 1865) 10–13, Prowell (1886) 454, Nelson (1899) XXI 417, Leaming and Spicer (1881) 449.

33. Budd ([1685] 1865) 48–50, 103–5, Yarranton (1677) 10–13, 140–42.

34. K. A. Moore (2019) 22.

35. Pomfret (1951) 124–25, 127, 140.

36. Pennsylvania (1852) I 236.

37. Pennsylvania (1852) I 228–29, 312, Clarkson (1814) II 30–32, 37.

38. Pennsylvania (1852) I 236, Dorfman (1945).

39. Parkman (1874) ch. XVI, Eccles (1959) 2–3, 7, 34–37, 49, 127, 133–34, 212–13.

40. Shortt (1925) I xxxvii–xlvii, 3–53, Parkman (1874) 295.

41. Parkman (1874) 280, 300, Shortt (1925) 41, 53–63.

42. Eccles (1959) 166, 171, Shortt (1925) I 65–71.

43. Shortt (1925) I 69–73.

44. Shortt (1925) I 73–81.

45. Angell (1929) 258, Nussbaum (1957) 16.

46. Parkman (1874) 348, 373, Munro (1915) 117.

47. Usher (1954) 62–64, 76.

48. Mokyr (1990) 49.

49. Wilkinson (1895) 68–69.

50. Sargent and Velde (2002) 219n5, Serjeantson (2006) 120, Eccles ([1969] 1982).

51. Nussbaum (1957) 16–17.

52. Rabushka (2008) 358n7.

53. Galbraith (1975) 51n4.

54. E.g., Bogart and Kemmerer (1942) 148, G. Davies (2016) 486, K. A. Moore (2019).

55. Angell (1929) 257.

56. Usher (1954) 353–54, Johnson-Laird (2005) 44.

57. A. M. Davis (1910) I 24–26.

58. Morse (1935) I 16–17 ch. II, esp. p. 104.

59. PMHS (1899) 254, Andros Tracts II 216–17, MAC 126:25–26, 32–33, 329–31, 336, 128:121, 129:120–21.

60. R. R. Johnson (1991) ch. III.

61. Bosher (1995).

62. Holmes (1830), PMHS (1919) 121–32, MAC 126:363, 389, 410, 419, 127:154, 200, CMHS (1838) 182–83.

63. Andros Tracts I 202, Shortt (1898) 288, Parkman (1874) 304–12, Eccles (1959) ch. 5, p. 177.

Chapter Eleven

1. Generally, biographies of all people mentioned here are in Savage (1860–1862) for colonists, ODNB for English, and ANB for important emigrants.

2. Ereira (2004), episode 2, at 13:49–14:48.

3. G. B. Roberts (1995) 203–4.

4. ANB and ODNB (s.v. Anne Hutchinson), Bailyn (1955) 40.

5. Suffolk Deeds I 22, Lechford (1885) 69–70, 101–6, 156, 317–18, 390, MAGC I 149, Boston Records II 14–15, 19, 39.

6. MAGC I 207, 211–12, Bailyn (1955) 40.

7. Suffolk Deeds I 23, Lechford (1885) 157, 390.

8. Lechford (1885) 87, 156, Suffolk Deeds III 492, VI 1b, Bailyn (1955) 34–35.

9. MAGC I 336, 339, 340, 344.

10. Boston Records IX 12.

11. Savage (1860–1862), *passim*.

12. J. Winthrop (1908) II 138.

13. P. O. Hutchinson (1886) 465.

14. Morison (1965) ch. IV.

15. E.g., Lechford (1885) *passim*, J. Winthrop (1908) II 5, 132, 202.

16. Dunton (1867) ix–x, 65, P. O. Hutchinson (1886) 466.

17. Arnold (1894) 1–20.

18. Bartlett (1856–1865) II 29–30, 47–49, 139–40, III 143–44.

19. MAGC IV-II 303, V 515.

20. Boston Records VII 52.

21. Sanford (1928), McCusker and Menard (1991) 155.

22. MAC 39:355, 60:47, MAGC IV-II 397–400.

23. Suffolk Deeds XII 153 and V 219–20, VII 153–54.

24. MAGC IV-II 413, 582, MAC 10:221.

25. Suffolk Deeds IV 233–34, V 188–89, VII 286–88.

26. ODNB, Nuttall (1964) 128, Kellaway (1962), *passim*, Suffolk Deeds VI 1b.

27. MAGC V 25, 33, 37–38, Boston Records VII 60, 62, 86, 91, 94, Suffolk Deeds VI 342, O. A. Roberts (1895) I 214.

28. Wheeler (1827) 5–23, T. Hutchinson (1795) I 262–66.

29. PMHS (1900) 400. Similarly, Kupperman (1993) 290.

30. Rice (1908) 120 and facing page.

31. MAC 69:207b.

32. MAC 61:128, 131, Noble (1901–1928) I 61–62.

33. Suffolk Deeds X p. 33–34, MAGC V 296, Boston Records VII 154–55, R. R. Johnson (1991) 25–26, 30–32.

34. Bailyn (1955) 135–37, Noble (1901–1928) I 376, M. J. Moore (1887) 282.

35. MAC 2:193a, Bartlett (1856–1865) III 18–19.

36. Noble (1901–1928) I 44, Sewall V 13.

37. Boston Records VII 116, 123, 127, 132 (initial elections), MAGC V 279.

38. MAGC V 265, Boston Records VII 139 (explained 137 and 142).

39. MAGC V 268 and 303, 301.

40. MAGC V 339–40.

41. Toppan and Goodrick (1898–1909) III 147, 130–32.

42. Andros Tracts III 223, Toppan and Goodrick (1898–1909) III 163–64, I 171.

43. MAGC V 421–22.

44. Bailyn (1955) 177–80.

45. MAGC V 297, 341, 351–52, 416–17, 427.

46. MAGC V 275, 289, 317 (and 322–23), 418.

47. MAC, *passim*, esp. vol. 70 and 100.

48. MAGC V 374–75, 375–76, 378, 393–94.

49. MAC 39:787, CSPC 1689–1692, 803, PMHS (1919) 334–35, Bailyn (1955) 122–23, Suffolk Deeds XI 361, XII 144–45, 185–86.

50. Bartlett (1856–1865) III 140–45, Toppan and Goodrick (1898–1909) VI 148.

51. Thayer (1890) 284–86, Hough (1857) 97–98.

52. W. D. Williamson (1832) I 528, Sewall V 95, Richardson (1888) 13–14, Moody (1947) III 213–14. As money: Moody (1947), *passim*.

53. T. Hutchinson (1865) II 282, T. Hutchinson (1795) I 306.

54. MAGC V 444–45, 463–64, 467, 498–99, 501, 511, MAC 61:289, Sewall V 67–68, 77, 117–18, 124–25, 132, 137.

55. Boston Athenaeum, Mss. L350; CMHS (1843) 195–96.

56. Noble (1901–1928) I 261–62, 264, MAGC V 460, 530, Bailyn (1955) 178–79.

57. London City Guildhall, New England Company Manuscripts, 7946/18.

58. Bartlett (1856–1865) III 172–74.

59. MAGC V 516–17, Sewall V 140.

60. Bailyn (1955) 169, 174–75, 180.

61. Sewall V 143, PMHS (1899) 250, 260, 265, 280.

62. Green (1895) 64, PMHS (1899) 235, 251, Bartlett (1856–1865) III 199–203, 208–9, MAC 100:389.

63. Collections of the Maine Historical Society (1857) V 110–13, 125–30, Thayer (1890) 279–86, Toppan and Goodrick (1898–1909) IV 226–28.

64. CO 1/63, 21V, MAC 126:342a, Tuttle (1919) 294–95.

65. MAC 127:18a, CMHS (1892) 15.

66. MAC 127:66–69.

67. PMHS (1873) 109.

68. Sewall V 182, 196, CMHS (1882) 480, CMHS (1886) 68.

69. CMHS (1892) 9–17, CO 391/6, 164–65, 172–73, 177–78, 180.

70. CMHS (1868) 113–16, 699–702.

71. CMHS (1868) 675–76.

72. CMHS (1892) 17–18.

73. Bailyn (1955) 190.

74. Sewall V 91, 93, 110, 114, 121, 158, 165, 170, 184.

75. P. O. Hutchinson (1886) 467–68.

76. Sewall V 136, 156, 164, MAGC V 505, O. A. Roberts (1895) I 248, Suffolk Deeds VII 306. Captaincies: Boston Records VII, *passim*.

77. Fairbanks (1982) III 440, 460, 467–70, 472–73.

78. Miller (1953) 35, 150, Bailyn (1955) 141, 193, Sewall V 95, 102, 158.

79. Schumpeter (1954) 64.

80. See, e.g., MAGC I 175, II 23, Boston Records II 9, 108.

81. McCusker and Menard (1991) 154.

Chapter Twelve

1. Lovejoy (1987) ch. 13, MS (1988).

2. Sewall V 308–33, MS 209, 247, 300, CO 5/856, 131, 145.

3. MS 45–50, T. Hutchinson (1795) I 339, also CMHS (1889) 501–7.

4. MS 48.

5. MS 53–54, 65–66.

6. MS 71–72, 82–83, 91–92.

7. MS 86.

8. MS 108, 120, Noble (1901–1928) I 301–2.

9. MS 112, 228.

10. Sewall V 253–55.

11. MS 178, 212, 257.

12. MS 180–240.

13. MS 233, Baker and Reid (1998).

14. MS 242–43, Sewall V 322.

15. Sewall V 310–35, Church (1867) 3–4, 35, 67, 69, MAC 36:233. Absences: MS 186–227.

16. Boston Records VII 202.

17. MAGC V 298, Boston Records VII 166, 185, 195, PMHS (1899) 254, MS 54, 126–27, 141, MS 126, 141, 230, 237, Sewall V 316.

18. MS 242.

19. MS 78.

20. MS 82–83, 89–90.

21. MS 176. Justice: MS 172, 179–80, Noble (1901–1928) I 301–2. Terminology: MS 71, 88, 90, 93, 95, 197, 207, 242.

22. MS 197–201.

23. Sewall V 251–67.

24. CO 5/905, 55–56, 79, 142.

25. MS 108.

26. Barth (2014) 519–20, Andros Tracts II 115–16, 140, III 5, 16, 226, 234.

27. Andros Tracts I 137–47, MS 188.

28. Sewall V 321n, 321–22, 333.

29. MS 51, Andrews (1915) 173, Dunn (1962) 255.

30. MS 54, 65–66, 72, 82.

31. MS 172–73.

32. MS 95, 97, 102, 109, 113.

33. MS 101, 114, 126, 160, 162–63, 172.

34. MS 86, 159, 161, 163, 222–23.

35. MS 406–7.

36. MS 186.

37. MS 99, 146–48, 154, 173, 183, 210.

38. MS 100, 119, 123–26, 183, 186–87, 196, 219, 227, 230, 266, CO 5/855, 78, Sewall V 312–13.

39. MS 208–9, 234, Breen (1980) 95–96, Paige (1849) 347–51.

40. MAGC V 537–44.

41. Sewall V 333, CO 5/856, 141, MS 268–69.

42. MS 254–61, 275, CO 5/856, 145, Sewall V 332.

43. MS, *passim*.

44. Only: MS 140–41, 142, 182, 193, 225, 226, 245, 253, 254, 258–59. Dominated: MS 138, 146, 219, 226, 249, 251, 284 (twice).

45. MS 85, 122, 126–27, 138, 140–41, 192–96, 219, 225, 226, 228, 249, 251, also 218–19, 244, 245. Mercantile status: Savage (1860–1862) or Suffolk Deeds.

46. R. R. Johnson (1991) 57, MS 193, PMHS (1878) 106.

47. MS 183, 184, 194, 210, 283, Sewall V 316.

48. MS 228, 249, 251, 277–78, 284.

49. MS 60.

50. MS 95.

51. MS 96, 111, 114–16, 181, 231–32, 256, CSPC 1689 310.

52. MS 172–73, 177, 224–25, 267, 283, Sewall V 334.

53. MS 212.

54. MS 206, 217–18, 224–25, 233, 267, PMHS (1878) 104, 106, MAC 36:235–37, CO 5/856, 145.

55. MS 191, 195, 206, 232, 245, 248, R. R. Johnson (1991) 64–65, Sewall V 323, Boston Records VII 200.

56. CO 5/855, 75, 113, CO 5/856, 145, MS 248, 256, 263, 284, Mather (1697) 43.

57. Anti-Catholic: MS 261, 289. God's aid: Muldrew (1998) 144–45.

58. Boston Records VII 203.

59. MS 82, 107, 108, 143, 146.

60. MS 137, 150, 208, 218–19, Sewall V 322–23, also 311, 320n2.

61. MS 145, 151, 160, 163, 183–84.

62. MS 182, 190.

63. Massachusetts Archives, Suffolk Court Files 2613.

64. PMHS (1878) 106.

65. MS 59, 102, 171, 182n2, 239–40.

66. MS 258–59.

67. Dorfman (1966) I 105–6, Nehemiah 5, Mather (1690) 4.

68. Pennsylvania (1852) I 312–15, PMHS (1878) 107, Sewall V 323–24.

69. A. M. Davis (1910) I 204, CO 5/855, 113, MS 248.

70. MS 185.

71. MS 280, 283.

72. Cf. Desan (2014),188.

73. MS 172–73, 177, 224–25, 267, 277, 280, 283.

74. MS 103, 111, 114–15, 181.

75. MS 66, 132, 140, 143, 146, 155, 160, 177, 267, 277.

76. MS 173, 224–25, 279.

77. MS 60, 74, 127, 153, 208, 244, 255, 279, Plymouth Records VI 220.

78. MS 253–54, Sewall V 336, MAC 40:616.

79. Sewall V 316, CO 5/855, 75, 94, CMHS (1819) 239.

80. A. M. Davis (1910) I 26, Nussbaum (1957) 16.

81. T. Hutchinson (1795) I 472–73, 477, PMHS (1902) 285–90, 310–15, CMHS (1846) 101, 105–12, CO 5/856, 139, 145, also 209, CO 5/905, 268, CO 5/1306, 4. New card money: Shortt (1925) 85–87, 91–95.

82. Mather (1697) 43, MS 311.

83. CO 5/855, 122, 127, CO 5/856, 131, 138, 145.

84. Mather (1697) 43, translation in Stone (2005); CO 5/855, 127, CO 5/856, 145, CO 5/1306, 4.

85. Debenture: Massachusetts Historical Society, Samuel Sewall Papers, account book, 1688–1692. Price: MS 279. Food: Muldrew (1998) 34.

86. For similar complaints in 1688 Nevis, see Nettels (1934) 251.

87. MS 411–12, following Numbers 12:14.

88. Sewall V 336–37.

89. Sewall V 338. Biographical information: Savage (1860–1862), MS, *passim*, Boston Records II, VII, *passim*.

Summary of Part II

1. McCusker (2006) 651, 5:655, MS 80.

2. R. R. Johnson (1981), Sosin (1982) 11, Peterson (2019) 159.

Chapter Thirteen

1. MS 285, Sewall V 338.

2. MS 287–89.

3. Sewall V 339, MAC 36:260b, 36:261, MS 293.

4. Sewall VI 366.

5. K. A. Moore (2019) 13.

6. MAGC, *passim*.

7. Cf. MAC 36:164, 36:195b.

8. Mather (1697) 43.

9. MAGC IV-II 135, 329, 420.

10. Cf. Grubb (2016) 155–56.

11. MS 279; Muldrew (1998) 34.

12. Hanson (1980) 415–16.

13. Boyd and Goldenberg (2013) 78–79. I thank Sarit Moldovan for the reference.

14. Grubb (2016) 161–62.

15. CO 5/856, 131.

16. Nettels (1934) 262–63.

17. Grubb (2016) 161–62.

18. A. M. Davis (1910) I 26, Nettels (1934) 250–52, Dorfman (1966) I 106, Rabushka (2008) 360, Peterson (2019) 183.

19. MAGC V 70–71.

20. Nettels (1934) 276, Rabushka (2008) 360.

21. Barth (2014) 523.

22. Nettels (1934) 276.

23. MAGC IV-I 388–89.

24. MS 458–66.

25. MS 468–69.

26. Hall (1960) 11, Lovejoy (1987) 128.

27. Sosin (1982) 216, 221.

28. Noble (1901–1928) I 298, Boston Records VII 196, 199, 202, MS 105, 142, 254.

29. Sewall V 337.

30. Mather (1697) 43.

31. See, e.g., MS 189, 265.

32. A. M. Davis (1910) I 125.

33. Bradstreet, Phips, Dudley, Stoughton, William Hutchinson, and Peter Bulkley were wrongly identified as merchants (Bailyn [1955] 40, 163, 182, Peterson [2019] 156–59). Identification of merchants can be based on many printed sources: The biographical dictionaries Savage (1860–1862), O. A. Roberts (1895) I, and Sibley (1873–1899) I–III; the legal records Suffolk Deeds, Noble (1901–1928), Boston Records XXXII, and Lechford (1885); and diaries such as Hull (1857) and Sewall.

34. O. A. Roberts (1895) I 281.

35. Mather (1697) 43.

36. MAC 36:259b, MS 292.

37. Felt (1839) 250 noticed it but misdated it to October because December was then called the "X" month.

38. Weitzman (1998), Mokyr (2016) 41n5.

39. Nettels (1934) 275, 250.

Chapter Fourteen

1. CMHS (1886) 115.

2. CO 5/856, 131.

3. Massachusetts Historical Society, Samuel Sewall Papers, part 6.

4. CO 5/856, 136, 138, Randolph (1691) 12.

5. A. M. Davis (1910) I 201, 204; 191, 194.

6. Trumbull (1884) 279–85, A. M. Davis (1910) I 196, 206–7.

7. PMHS (1878) 106–7, Sewall V 323, CO 5/856, 148–49.

8. Mokyr (2016) 204, 208.

9. A. M. Davis (1910) I 190.

10. A. M. Davis (1910) I 189–90.

11. A. M. Davis (1910) I 191–92.

12. A. M. Davis (1910) I 191.

13. A. M. Davis (1910) I 192.

14. A. M. Davis (1910) I 190–91.

15. A. M. Davis (1910) I 191.

16. A. M. Davis (1910) I 195.

17. A. M. Davis (1910) I 194–95.

18. A. M. Davis (1910) I 205.

19. A. M. Davis (1910) I 200.

20. A. M. Davis (1910) I 202.

21. A. M. Davis (1910) I 201.

22. A. M. Davis (1910) I 197–200, 203–4.

23. A. M. Davis (1910) I 201.

24. A. M. Davis (1910) I 201–2.

25. A. M. Davis (1910) I 202.

26. A. M. Davis (1910) I 202, 205.

27. A. M. Davis (1910) I 202.

28. A. M. Davis (1910) I 204.

29. A. M. Davis (1910) I 205.

30. A. M. Davis (1910) I 204–5. For a theoretical model of how a group of traders can promote intrinsically useless money by agreeing to accept it regardless of their individual incentives, see Aiyagari and Wallace (1997), who call such a group "government."

31. The book is Reinhart and Rogoff (2009). For a related discussion of the

difference between the two courses of action, see Sargent (1982), who contrasts what economists call adaptive expectations (an unsophisticated reliance on the past and "momentum") with rational expectations in which the people can break the momentum if they "understand" the economy "approximately as well as do government policymakers" (quotations on 41–42, 90n3).

32. CO 5/856, 149.
33. Steele (1986) 274–75, 295, Sewall V 295.
34. MS 296–97.
35. E.g., MS 300.
36. MS 333.
37. A. M. Davis (1910) I 139.
38. MS 298–99, 306.
39. MS 311.
40. MS 316.
41. MS 311–12.
42. MS 334.
43. Sewall V 345, MS 354.
44. MS 329–30, 332, 333, 337, 349, 355.
45. CO 5/856, 136.
46. CO 5/856, 138.
47. Fogg (1879) 410.
48. CMHS (1886) 5, 6, 30, 64–65, 85, 119, 121.
49. Colonial Williamsburg, William Blathwayt Papers V 5, Foxcroft to Blathwayt, April 16, 1691.
50. MS 55, 73, 104, 126, 140, 244, 258–59, Randolph (1691) 3.
51. Hall (1960) 134–35.
52. CO 5/856, 139.
53. A. M. Davis (1910) I 189–208, see also Steele (1986) 104.
54. Toppan and Goodrick (1898–1909) VI 76, CMHS (1868) 100–110, Sosin (1982) 75, O. A. Roberts (1895) I 274.
55. MS 522, Andros Tracts II 262.
56. A. M. Davis (1901) I 16, PMHS (1900) 148, Chartrand (1993) I 103, 206n69, Newell (1998) 129.
57. CO 5/856, 158VII, 158X, 158XI, 158XII, 158XIV, 158XVI.
58. Fogg (1879) 410, Colonial Williamsburg, William Blathwayt Papers V 5, Foxcroft to Blathwayt, April 16, 1691, CO 5/1037, 64.
59. MS 471–72, 518, 555–56, CO 5/855, 130, CO 5/856, 158XXXI, 158XXXIV, 158XXXV, 183, 192, CO 391/7, 42, Andros II 283–84, Goodell (1869–1922) I 9–10.
60. MS 328.
61. MS 621.
62. Peterson (2019) 173.

63. Andros Tracts II 121–22.

64. Sewall V 356, Andros Tracts II 324, 326, 330.

65. Sewall V 360, Goodell (1869–1922) I 17.

66. Goodell (1869–1922) I 35–36.

67. Nussbaum (1950) 559; see also Nettels (1934) 264.

68. Compare A. M. Davis (1910) I 271, 257 with Goodell (1869–1922) I 700–701, 705–6.

69. Mather (1697) 44.

70. Mather (1697) 44–45.

71. Mather (1697) 45.

72. Baker and Reid (1998) xii–xv, 3, 9–10, 44, 58, 61, 66.

73. Baker and Reid (1998) 106–8, Sewall V 339, MS 288.

74. Peterson (2019) 185–86.

75. Cf. Baker and Reid (1998) 67.

76. Peterson (2019) 188.

77. Peterson (2019) 46–51, 122, 133.

78. Baker and Reid (1998) 50, 69, Peterson (2019) 176–78.

79. Mokyr (2016) 48–56, 133.

80. Mather (1697) 45.

81. Mather (1697) 43.

82. Boorstin (1958) 223–27.

83. Boorstin (1958) 174, Dexter (1916) 15–19.

Chapter Fifteen

1. Horsefield (1960), Kleer (2017).

2. Desan (2014) ch. 8.

3. Desan (2014) 259, following Horsefield (1977).

4. Desan (2014) 310.

5. Desan (2014) ch. 4C.

6. Desan (2014) 43, 51–52, 317.

7. Horsefield (1960) ch. 11.

8. Goodell (1869–1922) I 34, 37 in margin, shows the 1695 disapproval of other laws of that session.

9. Blackwell (1695), *passim*, quotation on 3.

10. Great Britain ([1810–1828] 1963) VII 143–44, 187–88, 236–37, 297–98, Richards (1929) 141–43, Dickson (1967) ch. 14, Horsefield (1960) 124, Desan (2014) 339–41, Graham (2019).

11. Compare MS 279 (price per bushel in taxes) with J. E. Rogers (1887) ch. VII (price per quarter or 8 bushels).

Chapter Sixteen

1. On regulation in the American colonies in general: Hughes (1976).

2. See Mokyr (1990) ch. 7.

3. It was my great fortune that Mokyr read and commented on an early version of this chapter. I exempt him from any responsibility for my remaining errors.

4. Bailyn (1959).

5. Peterson (2019) 657.

6. Matthew 17:24–27, 21:12, 22:17–21.

7. MS 201.

8. PMHS (1878) 244.

9. For the long correspondence between the Winthrops and the Downings, even after George became a royalist at the Restoration, see CMHS (1871), *passim*.

10. Mokyr (1990) 186–89, Mokyr (2016) 129, 144–46, 150, 168, 331.

11. Mokyr (2016) 239n11.

12. Mokyr (1990) 182, Mokyr (2016) 17, 19, 126–27.

13. Andros Tracts, *passim*.

14. See, e.g., Suffolk Deeds I 41.

15. Mokyr (2016) 122–23, Mokyr (1990) 153–54, 157–59.

16. P. O. Hutchinson (1886) 466–69.

17. Mihm (2019) already pointed out that relation between Anne and Elisha.

18. On Law: Murphy (1997).

19. Mokyr (1990) 178–79, Mokyr (2016) 16–17, 20, 30–31, 64–65.

20. CSPC 1661–1668, 1669–1674, 1677–1680, *passim*.

21. Chapters 4, 15, Kleer (2017) 97, 98, 143.

22. On civic-mindedness: Mokyr (2016) 13, 121. Sewall's father-in-law and mentor was a role model: Peterson (2019) ch. 2, 3.

23. Mokyr (1990) 189–90.

24. Clapham (1944) II 2.

25. Mokyr (1990) 158–59.

26. Smith I 108.

27. McCartney (2007) 708–9, General Assembly (1915) 233.

28. Kingsbury (1906–1935) II 384.

29. Hening (1823) I 291, 327, General Assembly (1915) 236–37, 243.

30. Mokyr (2002) ch. 2.

31. Bailyn (1955) 135.

32. Koestler (1964) 140, Mokyr (1990) 283.

33. See also Mokyr (1990) 281, 295, Mokyr (2002) 75–76, Mokyr (2016) 27.

34. Johnson-Laird (2005), quotation on p. 33.

35. Hanlon (2015), cf. Mokyr (1990) 151.

36. Rosenberg (1969).

37. More wartime inventions: Mokyr (1990) 183–85.

38. Mokyr (1990) 151–53.

39. Mokyr (2016) 90.

40. Mokyr (2002) 16.

41. E.g., Mokyr (1990) ch. 11, Mokyr (2006), Aldrich et al. (2008), and Hodgson and Knudsen (2008). I am grateful to zoologist Roi Dor for comments on an early version of this section and exempt him from any responsibility for my remaining errors.

42. Mokyr (2006) 1009.

43. Mokyr (1990) ch. 11, Mokyr (2006) 1009, Mokyr (2016) ch. 3.

44. Carruthers (2010) 51–53.

45. Darwin (1871) I 59, Mokyr (2016) 24n5.

46. Mokyr (1990) 84–88, 294.

47. Mokyr (2016) 20.

48. Mokyr (2016) 245.

49. Hodgson and Knudsen (2008).

50. Peterson (2019) 186, and generally ch. 2–3 there.

51. Similarly, Mokyr (1990) 277, 279.

52. EB, s.v. "adaptive radiation."

53. Whalebones: East Hampton (1887) I 347, 349, 368, 396, II 78, 233. I thank Eric Hilt for the reference.

54. Mayr (1954), quotations on p. 157, 166, 170.

55. Einzig (1966), book I, part I.

56. Mayr (1954) 175–78, Eldredge and Gould (1972).

57. Grimes (1979) 39–45.

58. Spiller, Losos, and Schoener (1998), Censky, Hodge, and Dudley (1998).

59. Schoener, Spiller, and Losos (2001).

60. In the context of money, see Sylla (1982) for diffusion and Goldberg (2016) for transplantation.

Chapter Seventeen

1. Hurst (1973).

2. Board of Governors of the Federal Reserve System (n.d.), Bank of England (2020), Friedman and Friedman (1980) 248, Hurst (1973) 40.

3. Nussbaum (1950), Mann (1982).

4. Nichol (1878) 5, Oxford English Dictionary (2022), s.v. "fiat."

5. Goldberg (2016).

6. Merriam-Webster Dictionary, s.v. "fiat money," accessed 2022, https://www.merriam-webster.com/. Early and presumably influential culprits include

Keynes (1930) I 7, Friedman (1951) 210n7, Samuelson (1958) 481 ("greenbacks" rather than "fiat"), and Clower (1967).

7. Hurst (1973), *passim*.

8. On serendipity: Mokyr (2002) 13.

9. Andrews (1934).

10. Bailyn (2005), McCusker and Menard (1991).

11. In the context of technology, see Mokyr (2016) 41n5, 55, 88, 105, Weitzman (1998).

12. Mokyr (2016) 161.

13. Mokyr (2016) 174n15.

14. In general: Mokyr (2002) 11.

15. In Goldberg (2014), I review most events up to 1850.

16. Goodell (1869–1922) I 503–4, 508, 645, 740–41; see also 666–68, 901–2, II 130.

17. Brock (1975). A new look at eighteenth-century American paper money is in many recent works by Farley Grubb, such as Grubb (2012, 2016).

18. Nettels (1934) 257–62.

19. Ferguson (1995).

20. Eichengreen (1992).

21. Executive Order 6102, April 5, 1933. Lineage: G. B. Roberts (1995) 204. Height: Kane (1993) 345.

22. Nixon (1971).

23. Meltzer (2003–2009) is the authoritative history of the Federal Reserve.

24. Taylor (2007), Weinberg (2013), Desan (2014) 5.

25. J. Davis (2011).

26. Foster, Greene and Stavins (2020), various figures.

27. Prescott and Rios-Rull (2005).

28. Wray (2012, 1998).

29. Knapp ([1905] 1924).

30. Kelton (2020).

31. Mihm (2019).

32. Cochrane (2020).

33. See Goodhart (1998).

34. Kelton (2020) ch. 1n20.

35. E.g., MAGC I 109, 126, quotation on 126.

36. Breen (1980) 104.

37. Norton (2002) 149, 190–93, T. Hutchinson (1870) 16, 32n44.

38. Miller (1953) ch. XIII.

39. Burnham (2007) 159.

40. Miller (1953) ch. XIII.

41. CMHS (1911) 99.

42. Woodward (2010) 215–16, where a similar list of mysterious phenomena is given.

43. Mokyr (2016) 155, 181.

44. Keynes (2010) 363–64.

45. Ruding (1840), *passim*.

46. McCusker (1976) 94.

47. Mather (1697) 43.

References

Abbreviations and Archives

ANB: American National Biography, https://www.anb.org/. (Requires subscription.)

Andros Tracts: Whitmore, William H., ed. *The Andros Tracts.* 3 vols. Boston: Prince Society, 1868–1874.

Bancroft Library, University of California at Berkeley.

Boston Athenaeum.

Boston Records: Whitmore, William H., William S. Appleton, and Walter K. Watkins, eds. *Reports of the Record Commissioners of the City of Boston.* 39 vols. Boston: Rockwell and Churchill, 1876–1909.

CMHS: *Collections of the Massachusetts Historical Society,* Boston, 1792–2006.

CSPC: Sainsbury, W. Noel, et al., eds. *Calendar of State Papers, Colonial Series, America and West Indies.* 41 vols. London, 1860–1994.

CSPD-C: Bruce, John, et al., eds. *Calendar of State Papers, Domestic Series, of the reign of Charles I, Preserved in the Public Record Office.* 23 vols. London: H.M.S.O., 1858–1897.

CSPD-W: Hardy, William John, and Edward Bateson, eds. *Calendar of State Papers, Domestic Series, of the reign of William and Mary, Preserved in the Public Record Office.* 11 vols. London: H.M.S.O., 1895–1937.

CO: United Kingdom, National Archives, Public Records Office, Colonial Office. Kew, Richmond, Surrey. Citations indicate division number/volume number: CO 5/855.

Colonial Williamsburg, William Blathwayt Papers.

EB: Encyclopedia Britannica Online. Accessed 2022. https://www.britannica.com/.

London City Guildhall, New England Company Manuscripts.

MAC: Massachusetts Archives Collection, Massachusetts Archives, Dorchester, Massachusetts.

MAGC: Shurtleff, Nathaniel B., ed. *Records of the Governor and Company of the Massachusetts Bay in New England.* 5 vols. Boston: W. White, 1853–1854. Citations indicate that volume IV comes in two parts: IV-I, IV-II.

Massachusetts Historical Society, Samuel Sewall Papers. Boston, Massachusetts.

MS: Moody, Robert E., and Richard C. Simmons, eds. *The Glorious Revolution in Massachusetts, Selected Documents, 1689–1692.* Boston: Colonial Society of Massachusetts, 1988.

ODNB: Oxford Dictionary of National Biography. Accessed 2022. https://www.oxforddnb.com/.

Plymouth Records: Shurtleff, Nathaniel B., and David Pulsifer, eds. *Records of the Colony of New Plymouth in New England.* 12 vols. Boston: William White, 1855–1861.

PMHS: *Proceedings of the Massachusetts Historical Society*, Boston, 1859–1997.

PRO: United Kingdom, National Archives, Public Records Office. Kew, Richmond, Surrey.

Sewall: Sewall, Samuel. *Diary of Samuel Sewall, 1674–1729.* Collections of the Massachusetts Historical Society. 5th ser., vol. V–VII. Boston: John Wilson & Son, 1878–1882.

Smith: Arber, Edward, and A. G. Bradley, eds. *Travels and Works of Captain John Smith.* 2 vols. Edinburgh: John Grant, 1910.

Suffolk Court Files, Massachusetts Archives, Dorchester, Massachusetts.

Suffolk Deeds: *Suffolk Deeds.* 14 vols. Boston: Rockwell and Churchill, 1880–1906.

Published Sources

Abreu, Marcelo de Paiva, and Luis A. Correa do Lago. "Property Rights and the Fiscal and Financial Systems in Brazil: Colonial Heritage and the Imperial Period." Chapter 10 of *Transferring Wealth and Power from the Old to the New World: Monetary and Fiscal Institutions in the 17th through the 19th Centuries*, edited by Michael D. Bordo and Roberto Cortés-Conde, 327–77. Cambridge: Cambridge University Press, 2001.

Aiyagari, S. Rao, and Neil Wallace. "Government Transaction Policy, the Medium of Exchange, and Welfare." *Journal of Economic Theory* 74, no. 1 (May 1997): 1–18.

Aldrich, Howard E., Geoffrey M. Hodgson, David L. Hull, Thorbjørn Knudsen,

Joel Mokyr, and Viktor J. Vanberg. "In Defence of Generalized Darwinism." *Journal of Evolutionary Economics* 18 (2008): 577–96.

Andrews, Charles M., ed. *Narratives of the Insurrections, 1675–1690.* New York: Charles Scribner's Sons, 1915.

———. *The Colonial Period of American History.* 4 vols. New Haven, CT: Yale University Press, 1934.

Angell, Norman. *The Story of Money.* Garden City: Garden City Publishing Company, 1929.

Anonymous. *The Case of Capt. John Blackwell, Concerning several matters objected against him.* 1665.

Aristotle. *The Politics of Aristotle.* Translated by B. Jowett. 2 vols. Oxford: Clarendon Press, 1885.

———. *The Nicomachean Ethics of Aristotle.* Translated by R. W. Browne. London: George Bell & Sons, 1895.

Arnold, James N., ed. *The Records of the Proprietors of the Narragensett, otherwise called The Fones Record.* Providence: Narragansett Historical Publishing, 1894.

Assembly (Virginia). "The Virginia Assembly of 1641. A List of Members and Some of the Acts." *Virginia Magazine of History and Biography* IX (1901): 50–59.

Bailey, N. *An Universal Etymological English Dictionary.* London: Printed for R. Ware et al., 1675.

Bailyn, Bernard. *The New England Merchants in the Seventeenth Century.* Cambridge, MA: Harvard University Press, 1955.

———. "Politics and Social Structure in Virginia." Chapter V of *Seventeenth-Century America: Essays in Colonial History,* edited by James Morton Smith, 90–115. Chapel Hill: University of North Carolina Press, 1959.

———. *Atlantic History: Concept and Contours.* Cambridge, MA: Harvard University Press, 2005.

———. *The Barbarous Years: The Conflict of Civilizations, 1600–1675.* New York: Alfred A. Knopf, 2012.

Baker, Emerson W. and John G. Reid. *The New England Knight: Sir William Phips, 1651–1695.* Toronto: University of Toronto Press, 1998.

Bank of England. "What Is Legal Tender?" 2020. Accessed 2022. https://www.bankofengland.co.uk/knowledgebank/what-is-legal-tender?msclkid=bf02b388cf7211eca8e14d60642af83e.

Barbon, Nicholas. [N. B.] *A Discourse of Trade.* Baltimore: Johns Hopkins Press, [1690] 1903.

Barnes, Viola F. *The Dominion of New England: A Study in British Colonial Policy.* New Haven, CT: Yale University Press, 1923.

Barth, Jonathan Edward. "'A peculiar stampe of our owne': The Massachusetts

Mint and the Battle over Sovereignty, 1652–1691." *New England Quarterly* 87, no. 3 (September 2014): 490–525.

Bartlett, John Russell, ed. *Records of the Colony of Rhode Island and Providence Plantations, in New England.* 10 Vols. Providence: A. Crawford Greene and Brother, 1856–1865.

Batchellor, Albert Stillman, ed. *Laws of New Hampshire.* 10 vols. Manchester: John B. Clark, 1904–1922.

Baxter, James Phinney, ed. *Documentary History of the State of Maine*, 2nd ser., vol. III. Portland: Hoyt, Fogg, and Donham, 1884.

BBC News Channel. "Prince Will Finally Pay Off Debt." June 9, 2008. http://news.bbc.co.uk/2/hi/uk_news/england/hereford/worcs/7444179.stm.

Belknap, Jeremy. *The History of New Hampshire*, vol. I. Philadelphia: Robert Aitken, 1784.

Beresford, John. *The Godfather of Downing Street: Sir George Downing, 1623–1684.* London: Richard Cobden-Sanderson, 1925.

Birch, Thomas. *The Court and Times of Charles the First.* 2 vols. London: Henry Colburn, 1848.

Blackwell, John. *An Essay Towards Carrying on the Present War against France and Other Publick Occasions.* London, 1695.

Board of Governors of the Federal Reserve System. "Is It Legal for a Business in the United States to Refuse Cash as a Form of Payment?" n.d. Accessed 2022. https://www.federalreserve.gov/faqs/currency_12772.htm.

Boddie, John Bennett. "Edward Bennett of London and Virginia." *William and Mary Quarterly*, 2nd ser., 13, no. 2 (April 1933): 117–30.

———. *Seventeenth Century Isle of Wight County, Virginia.* 2 vols. Chicago: Chicago Law Printing, 1938.

Bogart, Ernest L., and Donald L. Kemmerer. *Economic History of the American People.* New York: Longmans, Green, 1942.

Bolton, Charles Knowles. *The Founders: Portraits of Persons Born Abroad Who Came to the Colonies in North America Before the Year 1701.* 3 vols. Boston: Boston Athenaeum, 1919.

Bonney, Richard, ed. *The Rise of the Fiscal State in Europe, c. 1200–1815.* New York: Oxford University Press, 1999.

Boorstin, Daniel J. *The Americans: The Colonial Experience.* New York: Random House, 1958.

Bosher, J. F., "Huguenot Merchants and the Protestant International in the Seventeenth Century." *William and Mary Quarterly* 52, no. 1 (1995): 77–102.

Boxer, C. R. *The Dutch in Brazil, 1624–1654.* Oxford: Clarendon Press, 1957.

Boyd, Drew, and Jacob Goldenberg. *Inside the Box: Why the Best Business Solutions Are Right in Front of You.* London: Profile Books, 2013.

Boyne, William, and George C. Williamson. *Trade Tokens issued in the Seven-*

teenth Century in England, Wales, and Ireland, by Corporations, Merchants, Tradesmen, etc. 2 vols. London: Elliot Stock, 1889–1891.

Bradford, William. *Bradford's History of Plymouth's Plantation, 1606–1646.* New York: Charles Scribner's Sons, 1908.

Breen, T. H. *Puritans and Adventures: Change and Persistence in Early America.* New York: Oxford University Press, 1980.

Bremer, Francis J. *John Winthrop: America's Forgotten Founding Father.* New York: Oxford University Press, 2005.

———. *One Small Candle: The Plymouth Puritans and the Beginning of English New England.* New York: Oxford University Press, 2020.

Bridenbaugh, Carl, and Roberta Bridenbaugh. *No Peace Beyond the Line: The English in the Caribbean, 1624–1690.* New York: Oxford University Press, 1972.

Brock, Leslie V. *The Currency of the American Colonies, 1700–1764: A Study in Colonial Finance and Imperial Relations.* New York: Arno, 1975.

Brodhead, John Romeyn. *History of the State of New York.* 2 vols. New York: Harper & Brothers, 1871.

Browne, William Hand, ed. *Archives of Maryland.* 70 vols. Baltimore: Maryland Historical Society, 1883–1964.

———. *Maryland: The History of a Palatinate.* Rev. ed. Boston: Houghton, Mifflin, 1904.

Bruce, John. *Annals of the Honorable East-India Company, from their Establishment by the Charter of Queen Elizabeth, 1600, to the Union of the London and English East-India Companies, 1707–8.* 3 vols. London: Black, Parry, and Kingsbury, 1810.

Bruce, Philip Alexander. *Economic History of Virginia in the Seventeenth Century.* 2 vols. New York: Macmillan, 1896.

Budd, Thomas. *Good Order Established in Pennsylvania and New-Jersey in America.* New York: William Gowans, [1685] 1865.

Burnham, Michelle. *Folded Selves: Colonial New England Writing in the World System.* Hanover: Dartmouth College Press, 2007.

Burrill, Alexander M. *A New Law Dictionary and Glossary.* 2 vols. New York: John S. Voorhies, 1850.

California Department of Parks and Recreation. "Olompali State Historic Park." n.d. Accessed 2022. http://www.parks.ca.gov/?page_id=22728.

Camden, William. *Remaines, Concerning Britaine: But especially England, and the Inhabitants thereof.* London, 1614.

Capp, Bernard. *Cromwell's Navy: The Fleet and the English Revolution, 1648–1660.* Oxford: Clarendon Press, 1989.

Carr, Cecil T., ed. *Select Charters of Trading Companies A.D. 1530–1707.* London: Bernard Quaritch, 1913.

Carruthers, Bruce G. "The Meanings of Money: A Sociological Perspective." *Theoretical Inquiries in Law* 11, no. 1 (2010): 51–74.

Censky, Ellen J., Karim Hodge, and Judy Dudley. "Over-Water Dispersal of Lizards Due to Hurricanes." *Nature*, October 8, 1998.

Chalmers, Robert. *A History of Currency in the British Colonies.* London: Eyre and Spottiswoode, 1893.

Champlain, Samuel de. *The Works of Samuel de Champlain.* 6 vols. Toronto: Champlain Society, 1925–1936.

Chandaman, C. D. *The English Public Revenue, 1660–1688.* Oxford: Clarendon Press, 1975.

Charlton, William. "Leather Currency." *British Numismatic Journal* 3, no. 18 (1906): 311–28.

Chartrand, Rene. *Canadian Military Heritage.* 2 vols. Montreal: Art Global, 1993.

Church, Benjamin. *The History of the Eastern Expeditions of 1689, 1690, 1692, 1696, and 1704 against the Indians and French.* Boston: J. K. Wiggin and Wm. Parsons Lunt, 1867.

Churchill, Winston S. *A History of the English-Speaking Peoples.* 4 vols. New York: Dodd, Mead, 1966.

Clapham, John. *The Bank of England: A History.* 2 vols. Cambridge: Cambridge University Press, 1944.

Clark, Gregory. "What Were the British Earnings and Prices Then? (New Series)" MeasuringWorth, 2022. http://www.measuringworth.com/ukearncpi/.

Clarkson, Thomas. *Memoirs of the Private and Public Life of William Penn.* 2 vols. Philadelphia: Bradford and Inskeep, 1814.

Clower, Robert. "A Reconsideration of the Microfoundations of Monetary Theory." *Western Economic Journal* 6 (December 1967): 1–8.

Cochrane, John H. "'The Deficit Myth' Review: Years of Magical Thinking." *Wall Street Journal*, June 6, 2020.

Colonial Society of Massachusetts. *Harvard College Records: Part I.* Boston: Colonial Society of Massachusetts, 1925.

Crosby, Sylvester S. *The Early Coins of America; and the Laws governing their Issue.* Boston, 1875.

Czartoryski, Pawel, ed. *Nicholas Copernicus: Minor Works.* Translated by Edward Rosen. London: Macmillan, 1985.

Darwin, Charles. *The Descent of Man, and Selection in Relation to Sex.* 2 vols. London: John Murray, 1871.

Davies, Glynn. *A History of Money.* Cardiff: University of Wales Press, 2016.

Davies, J. D. *Gentlemen and Tarpaulins: The Officers and Men of the Restoration Navy.* Oxford: Oxford University Press, 1991.

Davis, Andrew McFarland. *Currency and Banking in the Province of the Massachusetts Bay.* 2 vols. New York: Macmillan. 1901.

———. "The Fund at Boston in New England." *Quarterly Journal of Economics* 18 (1904): 255–68.

———. "Was It Andros?" *Proceedings of the American Antiquarian Society*, n.s., 18 (1907): 346–61.

———, ed. *Colonial Currency Reprints, 1682–1751*. 4 vols. New York: B. Franklin, 1910.

Davis, Joshua. "The Crypto-Currency: Bitcoin and Its Mysterious Inventor." *New Yorker*, October 3, 2011. https://www.newyorker.com/magazine/2011/10/10/the-crypto-currency.

de Bry, Theodorus. *A Briefe and True Report of the New Found Land of Virginia*. Frankfurt: Theodorus de Bry, 1590.

del Mar, Alexander. *A History of Monetary Systems*. New York: Cambridge Encyclopedia, 1901.

Demos, John. *The Enemy Within: 2,000 Years of Witch-Hunting in the Western World*. New York: Viking, 2008.

de Roover, Raymond. *Money, Banking and Credit in Mediaeval Bruges: Italian Merchant-Bankers, Lombards and Money-Changers*. Cambridge: The Mediaeval Academy of America, 1948.

Desan, Christine. *Making Money: Coin, Currency, and the Coming of Capitalism*. Oxford: Oxford University Press, 2014.

de Vries, David Peterson. *Voyages from Holland to America, A. D. 1632 to 1644*. Translated by Henry C. Murphy. New York: 1853.

D'Ewes, Simonds. *The Journals of All the Parliaments During the Reign of Queen Elizabeth, both of the House of Lords and House of Commons*. London, 1682.

Dexter, Franklin Bowditch, ed. *Documentary History of Yale University*. New Haven, CT: Yale University Press, 1916.

Dickson, P. G. M. *The Financial Revolution in England: A Study in the Development of Public Credit, 1688–1756*. London: Macmillan, 1967.

Dorfman, Joseph. "Captain John Blackwell: A Bibliographical Note." *Pennsylvania Magazine of History and Biography* 69, no. 3 (July 1945): 233–42.

———. *The Economic Mind in American Civilization, 1606–1933*. 5 vols. New York: Augustus M. Kelley, 1966.

Douglas, Charles H. J. *The Financial History of Massachusetts*. New York: 1892.

Dow, George Francis, ed. *Records and Files of the Quarterly Courts of Essex County, Massachusetts*, vol. I. Salem: Essex Institute, 1911.

———, ed. *The Probate Records of Essex County, Massachusetts*, vol. I. Salem: Essex Institute, 1916.

Drake, Samuel G. *The History and Antiquities of Boston*. Boston: Luther Stevens, 1856.

Dunn, Richard S. *Puritans and Yankees: The Winthrop Dynasty of New England, 1630–1717*. Princeton, NJ: Princeton University Press, 1962.

——. "Servants and Slaves: The Recruitment and Employment of Labor." Chapter 6 of *Colonial British America: Essays in the New History of the Early Modern Era*, edited by Jack P. Greene and J. R. Pole, 157–94. Baltimore: Johns Hopkins University Press, 1984.

Dunton, John. *John Dunton's Letters from New-England*. Boston: T. R. Marvin & Son, 1867.

East Hampton. *Records of the Town of East-Hampton, Long Island, Suffolk Co., N.Y.* 5 vols. Sag-Harbor, NY: John H. Hunt, 1887.

Eccles, William John. *Frontenac: The Courtier Governor*. Toronto: McClelland and Stewart, 1959.

——. "Meulles, Jacques de." *Dictionary of Canadian Biography*, vol. 2. University of Toronto/Université Laval, [1969] 1982. Accessed 2022. http://www.biographi.ca/en/bio/meulles_jacques_de_2E.html.

Edvinsson, Rodney. "The Multiple Currencies of Sweden-Finland, 1534–1803." Chapter 4 of *Historical Monetary and Financial Statistics for Sweden: Exchange Rates, Prices and Wages, 1277–2008*, edited by R. Edvinsson, T. Jacobsson, and D. Waldenström. Stockholm: Ekerlids Förlag and Sveriges Riksbank, 2010.

Eichengreen, Barry J. *Golden Fetters: The Gold Standard and the Great Depression, 1919–1939*. New York: Oxford University Press, 1992.

Einzig, Paul. *Primitive Money: In its Ethnological, Historical, and Economic Aspects*. 2nd ed. Oxford: Pergamon, 1966.

Eldredge, Niles, and Stephen Jay Gould. "Punctuated Equilibria: An Alternative to Phyletic Gradualism." In *Models in Paleobiology*, edited by Thomas J. M. Schopf, 82–115. San Francisco: Freeman, Cooper, 1972.

Ellis, Howard S. *German Monetary Theory, 1905–1933*. Cambridge, MA: Harvard University Press, 1934.

Ereira, Alan. *The Kings and Queens of England*. Six episodes. UKTV History, 2004.

Fairbanks, Jonathan L. "Portrait Painting in Seventeenth-Century Boston: Its History, Methods, and Materials." In *New England Begins: The Seventeenth Century*, edited by Jonathan L. Fairbanks and Robert F. Trent, 3:413–79. Boston: Museum of Fine Arts, 1982.

Farrand, Max, ed. *The Laws and Liberties of Massachusetts*. Cambridge, MA: Harvard University Press, 1929.

Feavearyear, Albert. *The Pound Sterling: A History of English Money*. 2nd ed., revised by E. Victor Morgan. Oxford: Clarendon Press, 1963.

Felt, Joseph B. *Historical Account of Massachusetts Currency*. Boston, 1839.

——. *Annals of Salem*. 2nd ed. 2 vols. Salem: W. & S. B. Ives, 1845.

Ferguson, Niall. *Paper and Iron: Hamburg Business and German Politics in the Era of Inflation, 1897–1927*. Cambridge: Cambridge University Press, 1995.

Fernow, Berthold. "Peter Stuyvesant, The Last of the Dutch Directors, 1647–1664." Chapter VII of *The Memorial History of the City of New-York, from Its First Settlement to the Year 1892*, edited by James Grant Wilson, 1:243–306. New York: New-York History Company, 1892.

Firth, Charles Harding. *The Last Years of the Protectorate, 1656–1658*. 2 vols. London: Longmans, Green, 1909.

Firth, C. H., and R. S. Rait, eds. *Acts and Ordinances of the Interregnum, 1642–1660*. 3 vols. London: Wyman and Sons, 1911.

Fogg, John S. H. "Letters of Charles Lidget to Francis Foxcroft." *New England Historical and Genealogical Register* 33 (1879): 406–10.

Forbes, Allyn B., ed. *Winthrop Papers*. 5 vols. Boston: Massachusetts Historical Society, 1943–1947.

Force, Peter. *Tracts and Other Papers, Relating Principally to the Origin, Settlement, and Progress of the Colonies in North America, from the Discovery of the Country to the Year 1776*. 3 vols. Washington, DC, 1836–1844.

Forde, Edward. *Experimented Proposals how The King may have Money to Pay and Maintain His Fleets with Ease to His People*. London, 1666.

Foster, Kevin, Claire Greene, and Joanna Stavins. "The 2019 Survey of Consumer Payment Choice: Summary Results." Atlanta: Federal Reserve Bank of Atlanta, 2020.

Francis, Peter Jr. "The Beads That Did Not Buy Manhattan Island." *New York History* 67, no. 1 (January 1986): 4–22.

Friedman, Milton. "Commodity-Reserve Currency." *Journal of Political Economy* 59, no. 3 (June 1951): 203–32.

Friedman, Milton, and Rose Friedman. *Free to Choose: A Personal Statement*. New York: Harcourt, Brace Jovanovich, 1980.

Frothingham, Richard Jr. *The History of Charlestown, Massachusetts*. Charlestown: Charles P. Emmons, 1846.

Galante, Luís Augusto Vicente. "Uma História da Circulação Monetária no Brasil do Século XVII." PhD diss., Universidade de Brasília, 2009.

Galbraith, John Kenneth. *Money: Whence It Came, Where It Went*. Boston: Houghton Mifflin, 1975.

Gardiner, Samuel R. *History of England from the Accession of James I to the Outbreak of the Civil War, 1603–1642*. 10 vols. 2nd ed. London: Longmans, Green., 1900.

———. *History of the Great Civil War, 1642–1649*. 4 vols. 2nd ed. New York: Longmans, Green, 1905.

———. *The Constitutional Documents of the Puritan Revolution, 1625–1660*. 3rd ed. Oxford: Clarendon Press, 1906.

General Assembly (Virginia). "Acts, Orders and Resolutions of the General Assembly of Virginia at Sessions of March, 1643–1646." *Virginia Magazine of History and Biography* XXIII (3) July 1915, 225–55.

———. "Acts of the General Assembly, Jan. 6, 1639–40." *William and Mary Quarterly*, 2nd ser., 4, no. 1 (January 1924a): 16–35.

———. "Acts of General Assembly, Jan. 6, 1639–40." *William and Mary Quarterly*, 2nd ser., 4, no. 3 (July 1924b): 145–62.

Gentles, Ian. "The Sales of Crown Lands during the English Revolution." *Economic History Review* 26, no. 4 (1973): 614–35.

———. "The Sales of Bishops' Lands in the English Revolution, 1646–1660." *English Historical Review* 95, no. 376 (July 1980): 573–96.

Goldberg, Dror. "Search and Money." PhD diss., University of Rochester, 2002.

———. "Famous Myths of 'Fiat Money.'" *Journal of Money, Credit, and Banking* 37, no. 5 (October 2005): 957–67.

———. "Money with Partially Directed Search." *Journal of Monetary Economics* 54, no. 4 (May 2007): 979–93.

———. "The Massachusetts Paper Money of 1690." *Journal of Economic History* 69, no. 4 (December 2009): 1091–105.

———. "Why Was America's First Bank Aborted?" *Journal of Economic History* 71, no. 1 (March 2011): 211–22.

———. "The Tax-Foundation Theory of Fiat Money," *Economic Theory* 50, no. 2 (June 2012): 489–97.

———. "Paper Money." Chapter 26 of *The Atlantic World*, edited by D'Marris D. Coffman, Adrian Leonard, and William O'Reilly, 171–90. New York: Routledge, 2014.

———. "Forced Money: Legal Development of a Criminal Economic Rule." *Comparative Legal History* 4, no. 2 (December 2016): 162–80.

———. "The Fund in Boston, 1681–1685: Who Led It?" Working paper, 2021. http://www.drorgoldberg.com/fund.

Goldberg, Dror, and Igal Milchtaich. "Property Rights under Administrator-Dictators: The Rise and Fall of America's First Bank." *Journal of Economic History* 73, no. 4 (December 2013): 1098–124.

Goodell, Abner C., ed. *Acts and Resolves of the Province of the Massachusetts Bay.* 21 vols. Boston: Wright & Potter, 1869–1922.

Goodhart, Charles A. E. "The Two Concepts of Money: Implications for the Analysis of Optimal Currency Areas." *European Journal of Political Economy* 14, no. 3 (August 1998): 407–32.

Gottfried, Marion H. "The First Depression in Massachusetts." *New England Quarterly* 9, no. 4 (December 1936): 655–78.

Grafe, Regina. "The Globalisation of Codfish and Wool: Spanish-English-North American Triangular Trade in the Early Modern Period." Working paper 71/03, Department of Economic History, London School of Economics, 2003.

Gragg, Larry D. "A Puritan in the West Indies: The Career of Samuel Winthrop." *William and Mary Quarterly* 50, no. 1 (October 1993): 768–86.

Graham, Aaron. "Credit, Confidence and the Circulation of Exchequer Bills in the Early Financial Revolution." *Financial History Review* 26, no. 1 (2019): 63–80.

Great Britain. *The Statutes of the Realm*. 11 vols. London: Dawsons of Pall Mall, [1810–1828] 1963.

Green, Samuel A., ed. *A List of Early American Imprints*. Cambridge: John Wilson and Son, 1895.

Greif, Avner. "Contract Enforceability and Economic Institutions in Early Trade: The Maghribi Traders' Coalition." *American Economic Review* 83, no. 3 (June 1993): 525–48.

Grimes, J. P. *Plant Strategies and Vegetation Processes*. Chichester: John Wiley & Sons, 1979.

Grubb, Farley. "Chronic Specie Scarcity and Efficient Barter: The Problem of Maintaining an Outside Money Supply in British Colonial America." NBER Working Paper 18099, 2012.

———. "Is Paper Money Just Paper Money? Experimentation and Variation in the Paper Monies Issued by the American Colonies from 1690 to 1775." *Research in Economic History* 32 (2016): 147–224.

Hakluyt, Richard. *The Principal Navigations, Voyages, Traffiques and Discoveries of the English Nation*. 12 vols. Glasgow: James MacLehose and Sons (publishers to the University of Glasgow), [1600] 1904.

Hall, Michael G. *Edward Randolph and the American Colonies*. Chapel Hill: University of North Carolina Press, 1960.

Hall, Michael G., Lawrence H. Leder, Michael G. Kammen. *The Glorious Revolution in America: Documents on the Colonial Crisis of 1689*. Chapel Hill: University of North Carolina Press, 1964.

Hamor, Ralph. *A True Discourse of the Present State of Virginia. By Ralph Hamor*. Richmond: Virginia State Library, [1615] 1957.

Hanlon, W. Walker. "Necessity Is the Mother of Invention: Input Supplies and Directed Technical Change." *Econometrica* 83, no. 1 (2015): 67–100.

Hanson, John R. II. "Money in the Colonial American Economy: An Extension." *Economic Inquiry* 17, no. 2 (1979): 281–86.

———. "Small Notes in the American Colonies." *Explorations in Economic History* 17, no. 4 (1980): 411–20.

Harlow, Vincent T. *A History of Barbados, 1625–1685*. Oxford: Clarendon Press, 1926.

Harrison, William. *Elizabethan England: From "A Description of England," by William Harrison (in "Holinshed's Chronicles")*, edited by Lothrop Withington. London: Walter Scott, [1587] 1876.

Hastings, Hugh. *Ecclesiastical Records: State of New York*. 7 vols. Albany: James B. Lyon, 1901.

Hatfield, April Lee. *Atlantic Virginia: Intercolonial Relations in the Seventeenth Century*. Philadelphia: University of Pennsylvania Press, 2004.

Hening, William Waller. *Statutes at Large: Being a Collection of the Laws of Virginia from the First Session of the Legislature in the Year 1619.* 13 vols. New York: Bartow, 1823.

Historic Jamestowne. "Coin Weights." n.d.a. Accessed 2022. https://historicjamestowne.org/collections/artifacts/coin-weights/.

———. "Coins." n.d.b. Accessed 2022. https://historicjamestowne.org/collections/artifacts/coins/.

———. "Mussel Shell Beads." n.d.c. Accessed 2022. https://historicjamestowne.org/selected-artifacts/mussel-shell-beads/.

Hobbes, Thomas. *Hobbes's Leviathan.* Oxford: Clarendon Press, 1909 [1651].

Hodgson, Geoffrey M., and Thorbjørn Knudsen. "In Search of General Evolutionary Principles: Why Darwinism Is Too Important to Be Left to the Biologists." *Journal of Bioeconomics* (2008) 10:51–69.

Holden, J. Milnes. *The History of Negotiable Instruments in English Law.* London: Athelon Press, 1955.

Holmes, A. "Memoir of the French Protestants, Who Settled at Oxford, Massachusetts, A. D. 1686." *Collections of the Massachusetts Historical Society*, 3rd ser., II (1930): 1–83.

Horsefield, J. Keith. *British Monetary Experiments, 1650–1710.* Cambridge, MA: Harvard University Press, 1960.

———. "The Origin of Blackwell's Model of a Bank." *William and Mary Quarterly*, 3rd ser., 23, no. 1 (1966): 121–35.

———. "The Beginnings of Paper Money in England." *Journal of European Economic History* 6, no. 1 (Spring 1977): 117–32.

Hough, Franklin B. "Papers Relating to Pemaquid." *Collections of the Maine Historical Society* V (1857): 1–138.

Hughes, J. R. T. *Social Control in the Colonial Economy.* Charlottesville: University Press of Virginia, 1976.

Hull, John. *The Diaries of John Hull, Mint-Master and Treasurer of the Colony of Massachusetts Bay.* Boston: John Wilson and Son, 1857.

Hurst, James W. *A Legal History of Money in the United States, 1774–1970.* Lincoln: University of Nebraska Press, 1973.

Hutchinson, Peter Orlando, ed. *The Diary and Letters of His Excellency Thomas Hutchinson, Esq.*, vol. 2. London: Sampson Low, Marston, Searle & Rivington, 1886.

Hutchinson, Thomas. *The History of Massachusetts, from the First Settlement thereof in 1628, until the Year 1750*, 3rd ed. 2 vols. Boston: Manning and Loring, 1795.

———. *The Hutchinson Papers.* 2 vols. Albany: Prince Society, 1865.

———. *The Witchcraft Delusion of 1692.* Boston, 1870.

Israel, Jonathan I. *Dutch Primacy in World Trade, 1585–1740.* Oxford: Clarendon Press, 1989.

Jameson, J. Franklin, ed. *Narratives of New Netherland, 1609–1664*. New York: Charles Scribner's Sons, 1909.

Johnson, E. A. J. *American Economic Thought in the Seventeenth Century*. New York: Russell & Russell, 1961.

Johnson, Richard R. *Adjustment to Empire: The New England Colonies, 1675–1715*. New Brunswick: Rutgers University Press, 1981.

———. *John Nelson, Merchant Adventurer: A Life between Empires*. New York: Oxford University Press, 1991.

Johnson-Laird, Philip N. "Flying Bicycles: How the Wright Brothers Invented the Airplane." *Mind & Society* 4 (2005): 27–48.

Jordan, Louis. "Sommer Islands 'Hogge Money,' 1615–1616: Introduction." Last revised April 26, 1999. https://coins.nd.edu/ColCoin/ColCoinIntros/SommerIsland.intro.html.

———. *John Hull: The Mint and the Economics of Massachusetts Coinage*. Hanover, NH: University Press of New England, 2002.

———. "St. Patrick Coppers, 1674–1675 (1681): Introduction." n.d. Accessed 2022. https://coins.nd.edu/ColCoin/ColCoinIntros/StPat.intro.html.

Kane, Joseph Nathan. *Facts about the Presidents: A Compilation of Biographical and Historical Information*. 6th ed. New York: H. W. Wilson, 1993.

Kellaway, William. *The New England Company, 1649–1776*. New York: Barnes & Noble, 1962.

Kelly, Patrick Hyde. *John Locke: Locke on Money*. 2 vols. Oxford: Clarendon Press, 1991.

Kelton, Stephanie. *The Deficit Myth: Modern Monetary Theory and the Birth of the People's Economy*. New York: Public Affairs, 2020.

Kemmerer, Donald L. "A History of Paper Money in Colonial New Jersey, 1668–1775." *Proceedings of the New Jersey Historical Society*, April 1956, 107–44.

Kerridge, Eric. *Trade and Banking in Early Modern England*. Manchester: Manchester University Press, 1988.

Keynes, John Maynard. *A Treatise on Money*. 2 vols. London: Macmillan, 1930.

———. *Essays in Biography*. London: Palgrave Macmillan, 2010.

Killigrew, William. *A Proposal, shewing How this Nation may be vast gainers by all the Sums of Money, given to the Crown, without Lessening the Prerogative*. London, 1690.

Kingsbury, Susan Myra, ed. *The Records of the Virginia Company of London*. 4 vols. Washington, DC: Government Printing Office, 1906–1935.

Kleer, Richard A. *Money, Politics and Power: Banking and Public Finance in Wartime England, 1694–96*. London: Routledge, 2017.

Knapp, Georg Friedrich. *The State Theory of Money*. Translated by H. M. Lucas and J. Bonar. London: Macmillan, [1905] 1924.

Koestler, Arthur. *The Act of Creation*. London: Arkana, 1964.

Kupperman, Karen Ordahl. *Providence Island, 1630–1641: The Other Puritan Colony.* Cambridge: Cambridge University Press, 1993.

Lapham, Heather A. "More Than 'A Few Blew Beads': The Glass and Stone Beads from Jamestown Rediscovery's 1994–1997 Excavations." *Journal of the Jamestown Rediscovery Center,* vol. 1, January 2001.

Lapsley, Gaillard Thomas. *The County Palatine of Durham: A Study in Constitutional History.* New York: Longmans, Green, 1900.

Laughton, John Knox, ed. *State Papers relating to the Defeat of the Spanish Armada Anno 1588.* 2 vols. Navy Records Society, 1894.

Leaming, Aaron, and Jacob Spicer. *The Grants, Concessions, and Original Constitutions of the Province of New Jersey.* Somerville, NJ: Honeyman, 1881.

Leavitt, Emily W. "The Starkeys of New England." *New England Historical and Genealogical Register* XLVI (April 1892): 144–49.

Lechford, Thomas. *Note-Book kept by Thomas Lechford, Esq., Lawyer, in Boston, Massachusetts Bay.* Cambridge: John Wilson and Son, 1885.

Leeward Islands. *Acts of Assembly, Passed in the Charibbee Leeward Islands, from 1690, to 1730.* London: John Baskett, 1734.

Lefroy, J. H. *Memorials of the Discovery and Early Settlement of the Bermudas or Somers Islands, 1515–1685,* vol. 1. London: Longmans, Green, 1877.

———, ed. *The Historye of the Bermudaes or Summer Islands.* London: Hakluyt Society, 1882.

Lewis, Theodore Burnham Jr. "Massachusetts and the Glorious Revolution, 1660–1692." PhD diss., University of Wisconsin, 1967.

Lewis, Theodore B. "Land Speculation and the Dudley Council of 1686." *William and Mary Quarterly* 31, no. 2 (1974): 255–72.

Lovejoy, David S. *The Glorious Revolution in America,* 2nd ed. Middletown: Wesleyan University Press, 1987.

Loyd, William H. "The Development of Set-Off." *University of Pennsylvania Law Review* 64, no. 6 (April 1916): 541–69.

Mallios, Seth, and Shane Emmett. "Demand, Supply, and Elasticity in the Copper Trade at Early Jamestown." *Journal of the Jamestown Rediscovery Center* 2 (2004).

Mann, Frederick A. *The Legal Aspect of Money.* 4th ed. Oxford: Clarendon Press, 1982.

Massey, J. Earl. "Early Money Substitutes." Chapter 3 of *Studies on Money in Early America,* edited by Eric P. Newman and Richard G. Doty, 15–24. New York: American Numismatic Society, 1976.

Mather, Cotton. *The Serviceable Man. A Discourse made unto the General Court of the Massachusetts Colony, New England, At the Anniversary Election 28d. 3m. 1690.* Boston: Samuel Green, 1690.

———. *Pietas in Patriam: The Life of His Excellency Sir William Phips.* London: Samuel Bridge, 1697.

———. *Magnalia Christi Americana: Or, the Ecclesiastical History of New-England*. 2 vols. Hartford: Silas Andrus, [1702] 1820.

Mauss, Marcel. *The Gift: Forms and Functions of Exchange in Archaic Societies*. Translated by Ian Cunnison. London: Cohen & West, [1925] 1966.

Mayr, Ernst. "Change of Genetic Environment and Evolution" In *Evolution as a Process*, edited by Julian Huxley, A. C. Hardy, and E. B. Ford, 157–80. New York: Macmillan, 1954.

McCartney, Martha W. *Virginia Immigrants and Adventurers: A Biographical Dictionary, 1607–1635*. Baltimore: Genealogical Publishing, 2007.

McCusker, John J. "Colonial Paper Money." Chapter 8 of *Studies on Money in Early America*, edited by Eric P. Newman and Richard G. Doty, 94–104. New York: American Numismatic Society, 1976.

———. *Money and Exchange in Europe and America, 1600–1775: A Handbook*. Chapel Hill: University of North Carolina Press, 1978.

———. "Colonial Statistics." Vol. 5 of *Historical Statistics of the United States: Earliest Times to the Present, Millennial Edition*, edited by Susan B. Carter et al. Cambridge: Cambridge University Press, 2006.

McCusker, John J., and Russell R. Menard. *The Economy of British America, 1607–1789*, with Supplementary Bibliography. 2nd ed. Chapel Hill: University of North Carolina Press, 1991.

McIlwaine, H. R., ed. *Journals of the House of Burgesses of Virginia*, vol. 1. 1915.

McLellan, Hugh D. *History of Gorham, ME*. Katharine B. Lewis, ed. Portland: Smith & Sale, 1903.

Meltzer, Allan H. *A History of the Federal Reserve*. 2 vols. Chicago: University of Chicago Press, 2003–2009.

Merton, Robert K. *Science, Technology & Society in Seventeenth Century England*. New York: Harper & Row, 1970.

Mihm, Stephen. "American Colonists Had a Modern Monetary Theory of Their Own." Bloomberg.com, March 15, 2019.

Miller, Perry. *The New England Mind: The Seventeenth Century*. New York: Macmillan, 1939.

———. *The New England Mind: From Colony to Province*. Cambridge, MA: Harvard University Press, 1953.

Mokyr, Joel. *The Lever of Riches: Technological Creativity and Economic Progress*. Oxford: Oxford University Press, 1990.

———. *The Gifts of Athena: Historical Origins of the Knowledge Economy*. Princeton, NJ: Princeton University Press, 2002.

———. "Economics and the Biologists: A Review of Geerat J. Vermeij's 'Nature: An Economic History.'" *Journal of Economic Literature* 44, no. 4 (December 2006): 1005–13.

———. *A Culture of Growth: The Origins of the Modern Economy*. Princeton, NJ: Princeton University Press, 2016.

Montelius, Oscar. *Sedelsamlingen i Riksbankens Myntkabinett.* Stockholm: P. A. Norstedt, 1915.

Moody, Robert E. *Province and Court Records of Maine,* vol. 3. Portland: Maine Historical Society, 1947.

Moore, Katie A. "The Blood That Nourishes the Body Politic: The Origins of Paper Money in Early America." *Early American Studies* 17, no. 1 (Winter 2019): 1–36.

Moore, M. J. "Book of Eastern Claims." *Maine Historical and Genealogical Recorder* IV (1887): 278–82.

More, Thomas. *Utopia.* Translated by Gilbert Burnett. London, [1516] 1684.

Morgan, Edmund S. *American Slavery American Freedom: The Ordeal of Colonial Virginia.* New York: W. W. Norton, 1975.

Morison, Samuel Eliot. *Harvard College in the Seventeenth Century.* 2 vols. Cambridge, MA: Harvard University Press, 1936.

———. *The Intellectual Life of Colonial New England.* 3rd ed. New York: New York University Press, 1965.

Morse, William Inglis, ed. *Acadiensia Nova (1598–1779).* 2 vols. London: Bernard Quaritch, 1935.

Muldrew, Craig. *The Economy of Obligation: The Culture of Credit and Social Relations in Early Modern England.* Houndmills: Macmillan, 1998.

Mullinger, J. Bass. *A History of the University of Cambridge.* London: Longmans, Green, 1888.

Munro, William Bennett. *The Seigneurs of Old Canada.* Toronto: Glasgow, Brook, 1915.

Murphy, Antoin E. *John Law: Economic Theorist and Policy-Maker.* Oxford: Clarendon Press, 1997.

Neal, Larry. *The Rise of Financial Capitalism: International Capital Markets in the Age of Reason.* Cambridge: Cambridge University Press, 1990.

Nelson, William. *Documents Relating to the Colonial History of the State of New Jersey,* vol. 21. Paterson: Press Printing and Publishing, 1889.

Nettels, Curtis P. *The Money Supply of the American Colonies Before 1720.* Madison: University of Wisconsin Press, 1934.

Newell, Margaret Ellen. *From Dependency to Independence: Economic Revolution in Colonial New England.* Ithaca, NY: Cornell University Press, 1998.

Nichol, Thomas M., *An Argument in Favor of Honest Money, and Redeemable Currency.* Chicago: Honest Money League of the Northwest, 1878.

Nixon, Richard M. "President Nixon Address to the Nation Outlining a New Economic Policy: 'The Challenge of Peace.'" August 15, 1971. Richard Nixon Presidential Library, YouTube, https://youtu.be/0BVj2gT6CgI.

Noble, John. *Records of the Court of Assistants of the Colony of the Massachusetts Bay.* 3 vols. Boston: Rockwell and Churchill Press, 1901–28.

North, Douglass C., and Barry R. Weingast. "Constitutions and Commitment:

The Evolution of Institutions Governing Public Choice in Seventeenth-Century England." *Journal of Economic History* 49 (1989): 803–32.

North, Douglass C., John Joseph Wallis, and Barry R. Weingast. *Violence and Social Orders: A Conceptual Framework for Interpreting Recorded Human History.* Cambridge: Cambridge University Press, 2009.

Norton, Mary Beth. *In The Devil's Snare: The Salem Witchcraft Crisis of 1692.* New York: Alfred A. Knopf, 2002.

Nussbaum, Arthur. *Money in the Law: National and International.* Brooklyn: Foundation Press, 1950.

———. *A History of the Dollar.* New York: Columbia University Press, 1957.

Nuttall, W. L. F. "Governor John Blackwell: His Life in England and Ireland." *Pennsylvania Magazine of History and Biography* 88 (1964): 122–41.

O'Callaghan, E. B. *Laws and Ordinances of New Netherland, 1638–1674.* Albany: Weed, Parsons, 1868.

Oliver, Vere Langford. *The History of the Island of Antigua.* 3 vols. London: Mitchell and Hughes, 1894–1899.

Oppenheim, Samuel. *The Early History of the Jews in New York, 1654–1664: Some New Matter on the Subject.* New York: American Jewish Historical Society, 1909.

Orosz, Joel J., and Len Augsburger. "Frank Stewart on Mark Newby and the St. Patrick Coinage." *C4 Newsletter* 17, no. 3 (Fall 2009): 4–11.

Orr, Charles. *History of the Pequot War.* Cleveland, OH: Helman-Taylor, 1897.

Outhwaite, R. B. *Inflation in Tudor and Early Stuart England.* 2nd ed. London: Macmillan Press, 1982.

Paige, Lucius R. "List of Freemen." *New England Historical and Genealogical Register* III (1849): 345–52.

Paine, Nathaniel. "Report of the Council." *Proceedings of the American Antiquarian Society*, March 1866, 22–77.

Parker, Geoffrey. *The Army of Flanders and the Spanish Road, 1567–1659: The Logistics of Spanish Victory and Defeat in the Low Countries' Wars.* Cambridge: Cambridge University Press, 1972.

———. *The Military Revolution: Military Innovation and the Rise of the West, 1500–1800.* Cambridge: Cambridge University Press, 1988.

Parkman, Francis. *The Old Régime in Canada.* Boston: Little, Brown, 1874.

Pennsylvania. *Minutes of the Provincial Council of Pennsylvania.*, vol. 1. Philadelphia: Jo. Severns, 1852.

Pepys, Samuel. *The Diary of Samuel Pepys.* 10 vols. London: G. Bell and Sons, 1893.

Percy, George. "'A Trewe Relacyon': Virginia from 1609 to 1612." *Tyler's Quarterly Historical and Genealogical Magazine* 3, no. 4 (April 1922): 259–82.

Perley, Sidney. *The Indian Land Titles of Essex County, Massachusetts.* Salem: Essex Book and Print Club, 1912.

Peterson, Mark. *The City-State of Boston: The Rise and Fall of an Atlantic Power, 1630–1865*. Princeton, NJ: Princeton University Press, 2019.

Pincus, Steve. *1688: The First Modern Revolution*. New Haven, CT: Yale University Press, 2009.

Polanyi, Karl. *The Great Transformation*. New York: Farrar & Rinehart, 1944.

Polo, Marco. *The Most Noble and Famoues Travels of Marcus Paulus, one of the Nobility of the State of Venice, into the East Parts of the World*. Translated by John Frampton. London: Ralph Newberry, 1579.

Pomfret, John E. "The Proprietors of the Province of West New Jersey, 1674–1702." *Pennsylvania Magazine of History and Biography* 75, no. 2 (April 1951): 117–46.

Prendergast, John P. *The Cromwellian Settlement of Ireland*. New York: P. M. Haverty, 1868.

Prescott, Edward C., and José-Víctor Ríos-Rull. "On Equilibrium for Overlapping Generations Organizations." *International Economic Review* 46, no. 4 (November 2005): 1065–80.

Priest, Claire. "Currency Policies and Legal Development in Colonial New England." *Yale Law Journal* 110, no. 8 (2001): 1313–405.

Prowell, George R. *The History of Camden County, New Jersey*. Philadelphia: L. J. Richards, 1886.

Prowse, D. W. *A History of Newfoundland from the English, Colonial, and Foreign Records*. London: Macmillan, 1895.

Quinn, David Beers, ed. *The Roanoke Voyages: Documents to Illustrate the English Voyages to North America under the Patent Granted to Walter Raleigh in 1584*. 2 vols. London: Hakluyt Society, 1955.

——. "Thomas Hariot and the Virginia Voyages of 1602." *William and Mary Quarterly* 27, no. 2 (1970): 268–81.

——. *Set Fair for Roanoke: Voyages and Colonies, 1584–1606*. Chapel Hill: University of North Carolina Press, 1985.

Quinn, Stephen. "Goldsmith-Banking: Mutual Acceptance and Interbanker Clearing in Restoration London." *Explorations in Economic History* 34 (1997): 411–32.

Rabushka, Alvin. *Taxation in Colonial America*. Princeton, NJ: Princeton University Press, 2008.

Rait, Robert S., ed. *A Royal Rhetorician: A Treatise of Scottis Poesie, A Counterblaste to Tobacco etc. etc. by King James VI and I*. Westminster: A. Constable, 1900.

Randolph, Edward, ed. [commonly catalogued as "Savage, Thomas"]. *An Account of the Late Action of the New Englanders, Under the Command of Sir William Phips, Against the French at Canada*. London, 1691.

Redlich, Josef. *The Procedure of the House of Commons: A Study of its History and Present Form.* Translated by A. Ernest Steinthal. 2 vols. London: Archibald Constable, 1908.

Reinhart, Carmen M., and Kenneth S. Rogoff. *This Time Is Different: Eight Centuries of Financial Folly.* Princeton, NJ: Princeton University Press, 2009.

Rice, Franklin P. *Marlborough, Massachusetts, Burial Ground Inscriptions: Old Common, Spring Hill, and Brigham Cemeteries.* Worcester: Franklin P. Rice, 1908.

Richards, R. D. *The Early History of Banking in England.* London: P. S. King & Son, 1929.

Richardson, H. W., ed. *York Deeds,* vol. 3. Portland: John T. Hull and B. Thurston, 1888.

Ripley, William Zebina. "The Financial History of Virginia, 1609–1776." Chapter 1 of *Studies in History Economics and Public Law,* 4:1–170. New York: Columbia University, 1893–1894.

Roberts, Gary Boyd. *Ancestors of American Presidents.* 3rd ed. Santa Clara: C. Boyer, 1995.

Roberts, Oliver Ayer. *History of the Military Company of the Massachusetts now called the Ancient and Honorable Artillery Company of Massachusetts, 1637–1888.* 4 vols. Boston: Alfred Mudge & Son, 1895.

Roden, Robert F. *The Cambridge Press, 1638–1692.* New York: Dodd, Mead, 1905.

Rogers, James E. Thorold. *A History of Agriculture and Prices in England,* vol. 5. Oxford: Clarendon Press, 1887.

Rogers, James Steven. *The Early History of the Law of Bills and Notes: A Study of the Origins of Anglo-American Commercial Law.* Cambridge: Cambridge University Press, 1995.

Rolf, John. "Virginia in 1616." *Virginia Historical Register and Literary Advertiser* 1, no. 3 (July 1848): 101–13.

Rosenberg, Nathan. "The Direction of Technological Change: Inducement Mechanisms and Focusing Devices." *Economic Development and Cultural Change* 18, no. 1, part 1 (October 1969): 1–24.

Royal Mint. "Explore Coinage during Conflict." n.d. Accessed 2022. https://www.royalmint.com/stories/collect/explore-coinage-during-conflict/.

Ruding, Rogers. *Annals of the Coinage of Great Britain and Its Dependencies.* 2 vols. 3rd ed. London: Manning and Mason, 1840.

Samuelson, Paul A. "An Exact Consumption-Loan Model of Interest with or without the Social Contrivance of Money." *Journal of Political Economy* 66, no. 6 (December 1958): 467–82.

Sanford, Peleg. *The Letter Book of Peleg Sanford of Newport Merchant (later Governour of Rhode Island), 1666–1668.* Providence: Rhode Island Historical Society, 1928.

Sargent, Thomas J. "The Ends of Four Big Inflations." Chapter 2 of *Inflation: Causes and Effects*, edited by Robert E. Hall, 41–97. Chicago: University of Chicago Press, 1982.

Sargent, Thomas J., and François R. Velde. *The Big Problem of Small Change*. Princeton, NJ: Princeton University Press, 2002.

Savage, James. *A Genealogical Dictionary of the First Settlers of New England*. 4 vols. Boston: Little, Brown, 1860–1862.

Schoener, Thomas W., David A. Spiller, and Jonathan B. Losos. "Natural Restoration of the Species-Area Relation for a Lizard after a Hurricane." *Science* 294 (November 16, 2001): 1525–28.

Schumpeter, Joseph A. *History of Economic Analysis*. Edited by Elizabeth Boody Schumpeter. New York: Oxford University Press, 1954.

Serjeantson, R. W. "Hobbes, the Universities and the History of Philosophy." Chapter 5 of *The Philosopher in Early Modern Europe: The Nature of a Contested Identity*, edited by Conal Condren, Stephen Gaukroger, and Ian Hunter, 113–39. Cambridge: Cambridge University Press, 2006.

Shapin, Steven. *The Scientific Revolution*. Chicago: University of Chicago Press, 1996.

Shortt, Adam. "Canadian Currency and Exchange under French Rule: I. Before the Introduction of Card Money." *Journal of the Canadian Bankers' Association* 5, no. 3 (April 1898): 271–90.

——, ed. *Documents relating to Canadian Currency, Exchange and Finance during the French Period*. 2 vols. Ottawa: Canadian Archives, 1925.

Sibley, John Langdon. *Biographical Sketches of Graduates of Harvard University*. 18 vols. Cambridge: Charles William Sever, 1873–1899.

Sklansky, Jeffrey. *Sovereign of the Market: The Money Question in Early America*. Chicago: University of Chicago Press, 2017.

Smith, Adam. *An Inquiry into the Nature and Causes of the Wealth of Nations*. London: Electric Book, [1776] 1998.

Smith, Thomas. *De Republica Anglorum*. Edited by L. Alston. Cambridge: Cambridge University Press, [1583] 1906.

Sosin, J. M. *English America and the Revolution of 1688: Royal administration and the Structure of Provincial Government*. Lincoln: University of Nebraska Press, 1982.

Spiller, David A., Jonathan B. Losos, and Thomas W. Schoener. "Impact of a Catastrophic Hurricane on Island Populations." *Science* 281, no. 5377 (July 31, 1998): 695–97.

Spufford, Peter. "Access to Credit and Capital in the Commercial Centres in Europe." Chapter 10 of *A Miracle Mirrored: The Dutch Republic in European Perspective*, edited by Karel Davids and Jan Lucassen. Cambridge: Cambridge University Press, 1995.

Staughton, George, Benjamin M. Nead, and Thomas McCamant. *Charter to*

William Penn, and Laws of the Province of Pennsylvania. Harrisburg, PA: Lane S. Hart, 1879.

Steele, Ian K. *The English Atlantic, 1675–1740: An Exploration of Communication and Community.* New York: Oxford University Press, 1986.

Stevenson, D. "The Irish Emergency Coinages of James II, 1689–1691." *British Numismatic Journal* 36 (1967): 169–75.

Stone, Jon R., ed. *The Routledge Dictionary of Latin Quotations: The Illiterati's Guide to Latin Maxims, Mottoes, Proverbs and Sayings.* New York: Routledge, 2005.

Strachey, William. *The Historie of Travaile into Virginia Britannia . . . by William Strachey.* London: Hakluyt Society, 1849.

Streeter, S. F. "Sketch of the Early Currency in Maryland and Virginia." *Historical Magazine* 2, no. 2 (1858): 42–45.

Swift, Charles S. *History of Old Yarmouth.* Yarmouth Port: Charles S. Swift, 1884.

Sylla, Richard. "Monetary Innovation in America." *Journal of Economic History* 42 (1982): 21–30.

Taylor, John. "Housing and Monetary Policy." NBER Working Paper 13682. Cambridge: National Bureau of Economic Research, December 2007.

Thayer, Henry O. "The Problem of Hammond's Fort." *Collections and Proceedings of the Maine Historical Society*, 2nd ser., 1 (1890): 261–94.

Thomas, Isaiah. *The History of Printing in America.* 2nd ed. 2 vols. Albany: Joel Munsell, 1874.

Thorpe, Francis Newton, ed. *The Federal and State Constitutions, Colonial Charters, and Other Organic Laws of the States, Territories, and Colonies, Now or Heretofore Forming the United States of America.* 7 vols. Washington: Government Printing Office, 1909.

Toppan, Robert N., and Alfred T. S. Goodrick, eds. *Edward Randolph.* 7 vols. Boston: John Wilson and Son, 1898–1909.

Trumbull, J. Hammond, ed. *The Public Records of the Colony of Connecticut*, Vol. 3. Hartford, CT: Case, Lockwood, 1859.

———. "Report of the Council." *Proceedings of the American Antiquarian Society*, new series, vol. III (October 1884): 266–303.

Tuttle, Julius Herbert. "Land Warrants Issued under Andros." *Publications of the Colonial Society of Massachusetts* 21 (1919): 292–363.

Tyler, Lyon Gardiner, ed. *Narratives of Early Virginia, 1606–1625.* New York: Charles Scribner's Sons, 1907.

US Currency Education Program. "Much Ado about the Two." *Noteworthy Podcast.* September 22, 2017. https://www.uscurrency.gov/media/noteworthy -podcast/much-ado-about-two.

Usher, Abbott Payson. *A History of Mechanical Inventions.* Second edition. Cambridge, MA: Harvard University Press, 1954.

Valeri, Mark. *Heavenly Merchandize: How Religion Shaped Commerce in Early America*. Princeton, NJ: Princeton University Press, 2010a.

———. "William Petty in Boston: Political Economy, Religion, and Money in Provincial New England." *Early American Studies: An Interdisciplinary Journal* 8, no. 3 (Fall 2010b): 549–80.

van der Wee, Herman. "Monetary, Credit and Banking Systems." Chapter V of *The Cambridge Economic History of Europe: Vol. V: The Economic Organization of Early Modern Europe*, edited by E. E. Rich and C. H. Wilson. Cambridge: Cambridge University Press, 1977.

Virginia. *Colonial Records of Virginia*. Richmond: R. F. Walker, 1874.

Walsh, Lorena S. *Motives of Honor, Pleasure, and Profit: Plantation Management in the Colonial Chesapeake, 1607–1763*. Chapel Hill: University of North Carolina Press, 2010.

Waters, Henry F., ed. "Genealogical Gleanings in England." *New England Historical and Genealogical Register*, January 1884, 60–74.

Webster, Charles, ed. *The Intellectual Revolution of the Seventeenth Century*. London: Routledge & Kegan Paul, 1974.

Weeden, William B. "Indian Money as a Factor in New England Civilization." Chapter VIII–IX of *Institutions and Economics*, edited by Herbert B. Adams. Baltimore: N. Murray, 1884.

Weinberg, John. "The Great Recession and its Aftermath." Federal Reserve History, November 22, 2013. https://www.federalreservehistory.org/essays/great_recession_and_its_aftermath.

Weitzman, Martin L. "Recombinant Growth." *Quarterly Journal of Economics* 113, no. 2 (May 1998): 331–60.

Wennerlind, Carl. *Casualties of Credit: The English Financial Revolution, 1620–1720*. Cambridge, MA: Harvard University Press, 2011.

Wetterberg, Gunnar. *Money and Power: From Stockholms Banco 1656 to Sveriges Riksbank*. Stockholm: Sveriges Riksbank, 2009.

Wheeler, Thomas. "Capt. Thomas Wheeler's Narrative of an Expedition with Capt. Edward Hutchinson into the Nipmuck Country, and to Quabaog, now Brookfield, Mass. first published 1675." *Collections of the New Hampshire Historical Society* II, 1827.

White, Horace. *Money and Banking, illustrated by American History*. Boston: Ginn, 1895.

Whitmore, William H., ed. *A Biographical Sketch of the Laws of the Massachusetts Colony from 1630 to 1686*. Boston: Rockwell and Churchill, 1890.

Wilkinson, W. H. "Chinese Origin of Playing Cards." *American Anthropologist*, January 1895, 61–78.

Williamson, James A. *The Caribbee Islands under the Proprietary Patents*. London: Oxford University Press, 1926.

Williamson, William D. *The History of the State of Maine*. 2 vols. Hallowell: Glazier, Masters, 1832.

Winthrop, John. *Winthrop's Journal: "History of New England," 1630–1649*, edited by James Kendall Hosmer. 2 vols. New York: Charles Scribner's Sons, 1908.

Winthrop, Robert C. *Life and Letters of John Winthrop*, vol. 1. Boston: Ticknor and Fields, 1864.

Wood, Philip R. *English and International Set-Off*. London: Sweet & Maxwell, 1989.

Wood, William. *New England's Prospect*. 3rd edition. Boston: Thomas and John Fleet, [1639] 1764.

Woodward, Walter W. *Prospero's America: John Winthrop, Jr., Alchemy, and the Creation of New England Culture, 1606–1676*. Chapel Hill: University of North Carolina Press, 2010.

Wray, L. Randall. *Understanding Modern Money: The Key to Full Employment and Price Stability*. Northampton: Edward Elgar, 1998.

——. *Modern Money Theory: A Primer on Macroeconomics for Sovereign Monetary Systems*. New York: Palgrave Macmillan, 2012.

Wrightson, Keith. *English Society: 1580–1680*. London: Hutchinson, 1982.

——. *Early Modern England: Politics, Religion, and Society under the Tudors and Stuarts*. Yale University, 2011. https://www.youtube.com/watch?v=e3uBi2TZdUY&list=PL18B9F132DFD967A3.

——, ed. *A Social History of England, 1500–1750*. Cambridge: Cambridge University Press, 2017.

Wyatt, Francis. "Documents Sir Francis Wyatt, Governor, 1621–1626." *William and Mary Quarterly*, 2nd ser., 7, no. 2 (April 1927a): 125–31.

——. "Wyatt Manuscripts." *William and Mary Quarterly*, 2nd ser., 7, no. 4 (October 1927b): 246–54.

——. "Wyatt Manuscripts." *William and Mary Quarterly*, 2nd ser., 8, no. 1 (January 1928a): 48–57.

——. "Sir Thomas Wyatt, Governor: Documents, 1624–1626." *William and Mary Quarterly*, 2nd ser., 8, no. 3 (July 1928b): 157–67.

Yarranton, Andrew. *England's Improvement by Sea and Land*. London: R. Everingham, 1677.

Yonge, Walter. *Diary of Walter Yonge, Esq*. Edited by George Roberts. London: J. B. Nichols and Son, 1848.

Young, Alexander, ed. *Chronicles of the First Planters of the Colony of Massachusetts Bay, from 1623 to 1636*. Boston: Charles C. Little and James Brown, 1846.

Index

Rosenberg, Nathan, 7, 23, 246
Royal Society of London, 49, 120, 127, 236, 259
Russell, James, 134, 167, 195, 198
rye, as money, 82, 171

Saint Christopher, 61, 113, 128
Saint Lawrence River, 65, 137, 160
salaries, 59, 80–81, 83–84, 87, 89, 109, 121. *See also* wages
Salem, 8f, 48, 72, 73f, 267–69
Sanford, Elisha, 148
Sanford, Peleg, 145
Satan, 28, 49–50, 100. *See also* devil
Savage, Ephraim, 156–57
Savage, Perez, 218
Savage, Thomas, Jr., 170, 217–19
Savage, Thomas, Sr., 149–50, 157
Saybrook, 85
Scientific Revolution, 48–50, 120, 187, 259, 268–69
scientists, 24, 28, 43, 55–56, 111, 120, 124, 169, 174, 176, 209, 235, 243, 247, 269–70; of money, 24, 43, 48–50, 127, 209, 269–70. *See also* Royal Society of London; Scientific Revolution
Scotland, 27, 40–41, 51, 65, 75, 79, 143, 231, 241, 253, 270. *See also* James I (James VI of Scotland); Law, John; Paterson, William
sealer of weights and measures, 105–6, 114, 150, 174
seals on legal documents, 32, 71, 78, 87, 111, 119, 126, 133, 186, 198
Separatism, 28, 63–64, 69–70, 74, 94, 144
servants, 27, 30, 59, 66, 74–75, 80, 101, 143, 165, 231, 242, 247, 267
setoff, 10, 32, 34, 36, 67, 87–88, 92, 108, 111, 126, 169, 171, 230, 238, 267; and legal tender bills, 191–92, 198, 205, 210, 212, 214, 244, 250
Sewall, Samuel, 10, 124, 134, 136, 153, 155–57, 161–64, 173–74, 200, 222–23, 267; and legal tender bills, 181–82, 185, 192, 195–96, 198, 206–7, 224, 225, 240, 242, 244, 251
Sherlock, James, 132, 165
shillings, 29–30, 59–60, 64, 82–84, 86, 92, 104, 106, 110–11, 117, 129, 173; and le-

gal tender bills, 183, 185f, 186–87, 192, 203–4, 207, 213, 215–16, 218, 222
shipbuilding and shipwrights in Massachusetts, 72, 102, 123, 145, 148, 157, 199
Shrimpton, Samuel, 134, 149, 157
siege money, 31, 46, 64, 138–39, 258–59
silver, 3–5, 10, 50, 57, 79, 260–61, 266, 271; in England, 3, 29–30, 41, 48, 60, 251–52; in English colonies, 39, 46, 51, 54, 56, 63, 93, 110–11, 115, 239; in Europe, 29, 36, 50–51, 55–56, 58, 64, 213; in Latin America, 3, 10, 29, 51, 54, 58, 81, 187, 210, 236; and legal tender bills, 187, 210, 211, 213, 221, 224, 268; in Massachusetts, 84–85, 89, 107, 117, 122, 171, 232
slavery, 11, 59, 74, 91, 102, 145, 231, 258
smallpox, 4, 160, 173, 181. *See also* epidemics
Smith, Adam, 106, 244–45, 270
Smith, John, 56–57, 60, 62, 79
smuggling and customs, 81, 93–95, 105, 145, 151–53, 170, 189, 218, 239–40
Spain, 28, 29, 31, 35–36, 38–39, 41, 51, 54, 55, 58, 139, 162, 172, 187, 194, 236. *See also* Armada, Spanish; Mexico; New Holland; Peru, silver in; piece of eight
specialization, 24, 60–61, 103–4, 157–58; facilitated by money, 17, 19, 22, 130, 244; not facilitating innovation, 15, 244–45
Springfield, 8f, 98, 104. *See also* Connecticut River
Standish, Miles, 64
Stockholms Banco, 44
store of value, 16, 19
Stoughton, William, 119, 124, 131–32, 135–36, 140–41, 155, 196, 267
suffrage, 27, 75, 99, 166
sugar, 6, 11, 102f, 102, 111, 127, 145, 158; as money, 6, 103, 111, 127, 145, 159, 252
Sveriges Riksbank, 228
Sweden, 44, 51, 228, 253
Sylla, Richard E., 3, 6, 23, 59, 233, 234

Tailer, William, 149
tallies, 36f, 36–37, 191, 228
tax collectors, 5, 19, 24, 36f, 36, 61, 174, 193, 243. *See also* constables
tax-foundation mechanism and theory of money, 21, 192–93, 214, 227–28, 235, 262–66